Rescuing the Enlightenment
from the Europeans

Rescuing the Enlightenment from the Europeans

Critical Theories of Decolonization

———

NIKITA DHAWAN

DUKE UNIVERSITY PRESS *Durham and London* 2026

© 2026 DUKE UNIVERSITY PRESS
Project Editor: Livia Tenzer
Designed by Dave Rainey
Typeset in Portrait Text Regular by Westchester
Publishing Services

Cataloging-in-Publication data is available at the Library
of Congress.

ISBN: 9781478032939 (paperback)
ISBN: 9781478029458 (hardcover)
ISBN: 9781478061663 (ebook)

Cover art: Francisco de Goya, *The Sleep of Reason Produces
Monsters* (*El sueño de la razon produce monstruos*), 1799.
Etching, aquatint. Metropolitan Museum of Art,
Gift of M. Knoedler & Co., 1918.

The research project and the publication funded
by the Volkswagen Foundation.

For Nimmi and María do Mar

There is no document of civilization which is not at the same time a document of barbarism.—WALTER BENJAMIN

The Enlightenment is sick at home.—GAYATRI CHAKRAVORTY SPIVAK

We dreamed of nothing but Enlightenment.—MOSES MENDELSSOHN

Contents

Introduction

Postcolonial Dilemmas

To Renounce or Rescue the Enlightenment?

We live in a world where the rapists are in charge of the rape kit.
—GAYATRI CHAKRAVORTY SPIVAK (private conversation)

Learning from the Germans?

Germany is considered exemplary in how a country can come to terms with its historical wrongdoing. Susan Neiman (2019) famously asserted that no other land has come close to facing the crimes of its history as Germany has, and that it is a model for other nations. The United States and Great Britain, in Neiman's view, could learn from Germany in confronting their racist history of colonialism and slavery. In their effort to atone for the crimes of the Holocaust, the Germans faced the long and difficult path of coming to terms with the past (*Vergangenheitsaufarbeitung*). Progress, it is argued, is evident in educational initiatives and memory politics, as well as laws and foreign policy. While Neiman's focus is on Germany's Nazi past, the German colonial past remains a bone of contention.

In April 2020, amid the COVID-19 pandemic, a huge controversy erupted in Germany on the relationship between postcolonial and Holocaust studies. Previously, in 2012, Judith Butler, on the occasion of being awarded the Adorno Prize, was assailed for their support of the Boycott, Divestment and Sanctions (BDS) movement. This time, the philosopher Achille Mbembe, from Cameroon, the former German colony, was accused of antisemitism.[1] His comparison of Israel with the apartheid state in South Africa and his critique of Palestine's occupation as a form of settler colonialism were condemned by his detractors for questioning the Israeli state's right to exist. In the aftermath of the Mbembe controversy, a nonbinding resolution was passed by the German parliament that barred the use of federal funds for groups with ties to the BDS movement, which was declared antisemitic in its argumentation, patterns, and methods (Rosen 2019).

The imputation of so-called postcolonial antisemitism resurfaced in the context of the documenta fifteen exhibition.[2] Held quinquennially, Documenta is considered one of the art world's most important events. Documenta fifteen, which took place from June to September 2022, was curated by ruangrupa, an Indonesian art collective. Months before it opened, ruangrupa was accused of antisemitism, supporting BDS, and conducting a silent boycott of Jewish Israeli artists. Ruangrupa vehemently denied these allegations and in turn accused the German media and civil society of racism.

Four days into the show, a nearly sixty-foot-long painted banner called "People's Justice," created by the Indonesian collective Taring Padi in 2002, was removed because of inexcusable antisemitic imagery. Documenta fifteen was declared "postcolonialism's Waterloo" (Fanizadeh 2022) and triggered larger accusations of antisemitism against postcolonial studies and the global South. The respected art critic Bazon Brock (2022) had the following comment: "All these states of the 'global south' are not only religious fundamentalist in orientation, but compared to the welfare states of Western Europe, they virtually allow asocial (*asoziale*) attitudes to be taken for granted" (my translation from German). Ironically, Brock uses Nazi vocabulary to describe the postcolonial world. The inverted black triangle was an identification badge used in Nazi concentration camps to mark prisoners designated *asozial*. The Roma and Sinti people, as well as disabled people, alcoholics, homeless people, beggars, nomads, prostitutes, murderers, thieves, pacifists, and lesbians, were all tagged as *asozial*.

The metaphor of the boomerang was (once again) deployed to explain how European antisemitic imagery traveled to the global South through colonialism and returned to Documenta in the form of what the curators averred to be anti-imperial art (Moses 2022; Rothberg 2022; Weizman 2022). The entanglements and intricate complicities of colonialism, Nazism, militarism, and capitalism indicate the impossibility of unraveling antisemitism and racism, imperialism and totalitarianism. This nexus complicates straightforward understanding of power and resistance, free speech, hate speech and censorship, agency and vulnerability, perpetrators and victims.

It has been repeatedly emphasized that the blanket condemnation of the global South as antisemitic diverts attention from the serious global threat posed by right-wing antisemitism (Doughan et al. 2022a). Furthermore, efforts to decouple antisemitism, racism, and other forms of discrimination go against an intersectional approach and pit one minority against the other, in line with the divide-and-conquer strategy. This contributes to a toxic climate of censorship and mutual hostility, which makes solidarity and cooperation arduous. While the German state and civil society are condemning BDS and its supporters as antisemitic, funding is being withdrawn from events that invite Jewish and Jewish Israeli scholars who either support BDS or are critical of Israel (Weizman 2022). From the innumerable Jewish persons censured for their support of calls for a ceasefire in the 2023 Israel-Hamas war, the controversy surrounding Masha Gessen serves as a cautionary example of how efforts to combat antisemitism can inadvertently suppress critical thinking. Gessen was to receive the prestigious Hannah Arendt Prize for Political Thought, but their comparison of the Gaza strip with World War II–era ghettos drew ire in Germany. As was insightfully pointed out, even Hannah Arendt would be censored in Germany today for her political stance on Israel and her views on contemporary Zionism, rendering her ineligible for the Hannah Arendt Prize (Hill 2023). It is ironic that in Germany, the arsonists are in control of putting out the fire, to restate Gayatri Chakravorty Spivak, considering, for instance, that Documenta's cofounder Werner Haftmann was a Nazi war criminal (Weizman 2022).

Given Germany's shameful history of genocidal antisemitism, one can only commend the commitment of the German state and the civil society to be vigilant about antisemitism and to combat it. However, the strategy to "boycott the boycotters" (Cooper and Herman 2019) through a sweeping indictment of antisemitism against the postcolonial world threatens to censor postcolonial critical thought. A. Dirk Moses (2021) triggered a new *Historikerstreit* by condemning what he called "German catechism."[3] He explains that any interconnection between the Holocaust and colonialism is made impossible by this dogma, which disallows comparative approaches and engagement with colonial genocides as a relativization of the Holocaust and thus as antisemitic (Traverso 2022). In her more recent interviews and talks, Neiman has described the situation in Germany as "atonement gone haywire" (cited in Kane 2022) and "philosemitic McCarthyism" (Neiman 2023).

In the aftermath of these controversies, there have been calls in the German media and even in the German parliament (the right-wing Alternative für Deutschland [AfD] party submitted a petition) to defund postcolonial studies and make the nonbinding anti-BDS resolution legally enforceable, which would disallow state-funded institutions and events from inviting speakers who support BDS (Deutscher Bundestag 2022). Given that the majority of academic, cultural, and arts institutions not only in Germany, but also in other parts of Europe, are state-funded, the repercussions of these disputes are grave. Such controversies raise fundamental questions about the freedom of critical scholarship: the relationship between antisemitism and other forms of discrimination, between postcolonial and Jewish studies, and, finally, between Europe and the postcolonial world.

Throughout the debate, the silence of scholars of the Frankfurt School, the birthplace of Critical Theory, has been deafening. The Israeli German philosopher Omri Boehm (2015), for instance, chastised Jürgen Habermas for his reticence on Israel. In an interview in 2012, Habermas stated that, while "the present situation and the policies of the Israeli government" do require a "political kind of evaluation," this is not "the business of a private German citizen of my generation" (quoted in Limone 2012). As Boehm (2022) compellingly argues, the critical engagement with the Holocaust should contribute to global solidarity and the strengthening of universal norms of human rights and international law, instead of feeding ethnonationalistic ideologies, which exclude other forms of memorialization. Although sympathetic to Habermas's unwillingness to criticize Israel, Boehm nevertheless warns that when the master of discourse ethics and public intellectual par excellence avoids the public exercise of one's reason, he is betraying the Enlightenment critical tradition of having the courage to think for oneself. The reluctance to exercise critical judgment and deliberation in the public sphere has far-reaching consequences, presenting the ultimate test of Enlightenment thinking itself. It is not a coincidence that Habermas has been silent on colonialism and its consequences for Critical Theory. As will be discussed later, when asked about the relevance of his theory for the Third World, Habermas similarly declined to respond (Habermas, quoted in Morrow 2013, 128–29). Habermas broke his silence during the 2023 Israel-Hamas war to make a statement that the "Never again" principle entails German commitment to protecting Jewish life and

Israel's right to exist. This is in line with the Merkel doctrine that the security of Israel is German *Staatsräson* (reason of state) (Deitelhoff et al. 2023). In a sharp critique of the German discourse on protecting Jewish life, Yossi Bartal (2024), in his article "Die Wiederkehr des 'Schutzjuden'" (The Return of the "Protected Jew"), warns against the "instrumentalization of Jews" (*Funktionalisierung von Juden*). Bartal (2024) argues that historically, the policy of so-called Jewish protection as a state goal in the fight against antisemitism is part of a troubling tradition, as it paternalistically reduced Jews to passive objects, stripping them of agency. This is why the German constitution, following Enlightenment principles and the concept of equality (*Gleichberechtigung*) for all, does not elevate the rights of Jewish minorities above those of others. Rather than viewing the current German "instrumental philosemitism" (*instrumenteller Philosemitismus*), which includes the positions of Habermas and his colleagues, as a positive gesture, Bartal (2024) emphasizes that making Jews objects of protection risks the future withdrawal of that protection, as has been the case with other minorities deemed undeserving of the state's benevolence. Another astute analysis is provided by Enzo Traverso (2024), who explains that *raison d'état* (reason of state) involves invoking a "state of exception" and violating the law, for instance, in times of war for the sake of national security. He traces the historical development of the concept, which, in fact, represents a state's admission that it is undermining its own norms and values. Traverso concludes provocatively that when Germany supports Israel in the name of *Staatsräson*, it ironically and implicitly acknowledges the immorality of its own policy.

Following Russia's invasion of Ukraine, Germany moved to end its long dependence on Russian gas and sought alternative suppliers, including Qatar. If Hamas receives financial and nonmaterial support from Qatar, what does this imply if Germany buys billions of cubic meters of gas from Qatar? German Chancellor Olaf Scholz did not visit documenta fifteen amid the antisemitism controversies in June 2022, but he went to Saudi Arabia and Qatar in September 2022 to deepen the energy partnership with Saudi Arabia and Qatar. Both these countries have not recognized Israel since the latter's independence in 1948 and do not accept Israeli-issued passports. The repeated betrayal of Enlightenment norms in a country that portrays itself as a protector and promoter of universal principles of equality and freedom—by both its public intellectuals and its politicians—is one of the motivations for this book. I have chosen Germany as a starting point, as I agree with Neiman that the world can indeed learn from the Germans about the crucial importance of coming to terms with one's past. However, Germany also stands as a cautionary example of how, in its attempt to prove it has overcome genocidal antisemitism, it ironically undermines its commitment to the universal principles of the Enlightenment. Stuart Hall (1991, 16) astutely observed, "The English are racist not because they hate the Blacks but because they don't know who they are without the Blacks." Similarly, Germans cling to the figure of the antisemitic migrant and the postcolonial world to reinforce their own moral righteousness.

The Postcolonial Scare

What was previously dismissed as a provincial German controversy has, since the gruesome attacks by Hamas on October 7, 2023, and the subsequent outbreak of the Israel-Hamas war, had widespread consequences for postcolonial studies. On October 13, 2023, the right-wing activist Christopher Rufo (2023) posted the following message on X: "Conservatives need to create a strong association between Hamas, BLM [Black Lives Matter], DSA [Democratic Socialists of America], and academic 'decolonization' in the public mind. Connect the dots, then attack, delegitimize, and discredit. Make the center-left disavow them. Make them political untouchables."

One detects a certain schadenfreude in outing the postcolonial world as "closet antisemites" (Daub 2024). From prestigious film festivals such as the Berlinale (Goodman 2024b; New Arab 2024) to the glamour of the Oscars (Middle East Eye 2024), from tech giants such as Google (*Democracy Now!* 2024a) to grassroots movements such as the Abandon Biden Campaign (Abandon Biden 2024), and from Eurovision (*Democracy Now!* 2024c) to PEN America (2024), the spotlight on the idea of decolonization has never been brighter or more widespread. Regardless of the distinct historical and geographical framings of the debates, in my view, a postcolonial scare is being drummed up by the global right. There is a systematic strategy to smear postcolonial studies and other critical theories, including gender and queer studies, diversity, intersectionality, and critical race theory by demonizing them as antisemitic (Goodman 2023). For instance, despite differences among the United States, Germany, and France, in all these contexts postcolonial studies stands accused of providing the ideological foundation for legitimizing the atrocities committed in the name of decolonization. Notwithstanding geographical and historical disparities, it is, ironically, the far right that stands to benefit the most from the assaults on postcolonial critical thought. It diverts attention from their own antisemitism while simultaneously tarnishing progressive critical thought and practice. Consider the role played by pro-Trump politicians during the congressional hearings of university presidents who were grilled about antisemitism on campus (Goodman 2024a). Although most encampments and protests across the United States, as well as in countries such as France, the Netherlands, Chile, Australia, and Japan, have been peaceful, they are being characterized in the conservative media as dangerous and disorderly. Disproportionate coverage of conflictual encounters between demonstrators and the police or counterdemonstrators, along with biased media reporting, has resulted in a distorted portrayal of students' demands. Ironically, Jewish staff and student protesters were beaten by police, despite the educational institutions' claim that law enforcement was needed to protect Jewish people on campus (*Democracy Now!* 2024b).

On May 1, 2024, the US House of Representatives voted to pass the Antisemitism Awareness Act. Sponsored by a New York Republican, it requires the Department of Education to use the working definition of antisemitism put forward by the International Holocaust Remembrance Alliance (IHRA). In response, Kenneth Stern, who was involved in drafting the IHRA's definition of antisemitism, warned that "when everything is antisemitic[,] then nothing is antisemitic, and it makes it harder to fight it" (CNN 2024). Critics point out that federal law already prohibits antisemitic discrimination and harassment. The fear is that instead of mitigating antisemitism, this bill will chill free speech and bolster the backlash against critical theories.

These are but few in a series of controversies worldwide, where postcolonial scholarship is backed into a corner to defend its emancipatory credentials. In addition, the postcolonial world is once again being portrayed as purportedly barbaric and prone to violence, with the West bearing the burden of upholding norms of tolerance and equality. In my view, we need to undertake a Foucauldian "history of the present" to understand how we arrived at a point at which it is once again seen as the manifest destiny of the Europeans to fulfill what is referred to as the white man's burden and enlighten the non-Western world. This is possible only through a convenient historical amnesia about colonialism.

In view of these developments, this book aims to address the daunting challenges facing postcolonial queer feminism. Its very credibility seems to be at stake, for it is pilloried for legitimizing violent resistance. Whereas previously Mohandas Gandhi, Martin Luther King Jr., and Nelson Mandela were considered symbols of nonviolent decolonization, now writings by Frantz Fanon (Beckerman 2024) and Malcolm X—and Malcolm X's famous assertion, "By any means necessary" (quoted in *Revolution* 2024)—are produced as evidence of so-called terrorism washing (Montefiore 2023). To counter this, I outline how, to offset this divisive narrative that pits the suffering of one minority against another, we must embrace the Holocaust survivor Jean Améry's (2005 [1968], 15-16) concept of *Schicksalsverwandtschaft* (kinship of fate). This idea highlights the collective experiences of dehumanization and brutality endured by victims of both European colonialism and Nazism. Further, the goal is to challenge the delegitimization of the term *decolonization* by highlighting the diversity and complexity of its strategies and tactics.

While some might argue that the accusations against postcolonial studies are so facile, and postcolonial studies' contributions to critical thought are so obvious, that they don't warrant discussion—let alone an entire book—in my view, the severe imputations against postcolonial studies continue to proliferate. Therefore, it is imperative to set the record straight. In light of these considerations, this book has the following main concerns. First, I address the charge that postcolonial theory abets normative nihilism by being anti-Enlightenment. In my view, it is a contention whose ghosts deserve to be exorcised if we are to obtain the sort of clarity about the critical impetus of postcolonial thought. As I show, it is not postcolonial studies that violate universal Enlightenment principles of tolerance and freedom; rather, the norms themselves have been flawed since their inception. Second, I strive to trace the missed encounters between postcolonial studies and the first generation of Critical Theory, which are both charged with performative contradiction due to their respective critique of Western reason. Third, I seek to highlight the differences between postcolonial and decolonial approaches to resolve the case of what I call mistaken identity. Postcolonial studies and decolonial studies share the goal of decolonization; however, their understanding of how to achieve this sets them apart. This dispute remains at the core of the continuing theoretical slugfest about what decolonization signifies. Finally, I endeavor to examine the contribution of postcolonial studies in rethinking the nature and scope of critical thought. Despite decades of postcolonial scholarship and its laborious efforts to hold Europe accountable for its crimes against humanity, postcolonialism continues to be censured for falling into the irrationality of identity politics and perilous anti-universalism. Against these accusations, this book mounts a defense of postcolonial studies by foregrounding the coercive legacies of the Enlightenment while outlining how postcolonial studies might perform the exigent task of salvaging it. Max Horkheimer and Theodor Adorno planned to write a sequel to *Dialectic of Enlightenment* (2002 [1947]), titled "Rescuing the Enlightenment" (*Rettung der Aufklärung*) (Horkheimer 1985b [1946], 598). This recovery project was, however, not undertaken. My book is inspired by their unfulfilled efforts. Unlike the decolonial scholars' boycott of modernity and Enlightenment, I focus on the normative dilemmas that haunt postcolonial engagements with the Enlightenment. I show how critical theories of decolonization seek to contest the coercive aspects of the Enlightenment while rescuing its emancipatory norms.

Argument and Outline of the Book

Since its inception with Edward Said's *Orientalism* (1978), a recurring and grave allegation against postcolonial studies has been that it is anti-Enlightenment. From the fatwa against Salman Rushdie to Boko Haram's denunciation of Western modernity as sinful, evidence is presented of the postcolonial world's anti-Enlightenment proclivities and the dangers of postcolonial mistrust of the Enlightenment and its norms. This has serious implications, for even as colonialism is grudgingly acknowledged as indefensible, postcolonial perspectives are dismissed as uncritical and ultimately unemancipatory insofar as they fail to provide normative foundations with universal validity. While some respond to these accusations by declaring that decolonization does, indeed, necessarily entail rejecting modernity, my first objective is to outline the complex relationship between postcolonial studies and the Enlightenment. This may seem like a foregone conclusion; however, as I meticulously argue in the various chapters, this is not self-evident. Any contestation of the Enlightenment and its legacies stands accused of forfeiting emancipatory ideals of human rights, secularism, free speech, and democracy. It is my worry that the distortion of postcolonial critique as anti-Enlightenment deflects attention from the nuanced analysis of postcolonial scholars who hold the Enlightenment accountable for its failures without categorically rejecting it. Furthermore, regardless of decades of fact-checking by postcolonial feminist scholars, in which the racism and sexism of Enlightenment thinkers are exposed, we are encountering revisionist readings of scholars such as Immanuel

Kant. Champions of the Enlightenment dismiss Kantian racism, sexism, and antisemitism as banal irrational prejudice that is marginal to the emancipatory project of the Enlightenment. As I show, it is imperative to contest this whitewashing of the Enlightenment as unequivocally anti-Empire, for the stilted stereotypes about the non-European world propounded by Enlightenment thinkers still hold sway. Contrary to claims by neo-Kantians, I contend that racism, sexism, and antisemitism are not extraneous to Kantian thought but deeply entrenched in Western reason and the normative understanding of who qualifies as human and who is considered a legitimate political, ethical, and legal subject. To counter the trivialization of postcolonial critique, I devote careful attention to how these practices of dehumanization are deeply ingrained in Enlightenment norms of cosmopolitanism, tolerance, and equality. For instance, I show how Kant's idea of "unjust enemies" encompassed not only the so-called uncivilized people in the colonies but also European Jews. The Enlightenment promise to convert Jews into citizens of European nation-states was another version of Europe's civilizing mission. The alleged civic improvement of Jews was to be achieved by turning them into enlightened citizens and transforming Judaism into an apolitical religion. Drawing on such examples, the book focuses on the entanglements among different forms of discrimination and challenges the disavowal of the link among the Enlightenment, colonialism, and Nazism.

The second objective of the book is to address the unfinished conversations between postcolonial and Holocaust studies and the convergences of concerns and strategies between the first generation of Critical Theory and postcolonial studies.[4] This book, for instance, is unthinkable without Horkheimer and Adorno's masterly *Dialectic of Enlightenment*. Against the charge of so-called postcolonial antisemitism, it is my hope that, instead of being played off against each other, postcolonial and Jewish studies can mutually enrich each other. I further demonstrate how many of the accusations against Adorno, Horkheimer, Michel Foucault, and Jacques Derrida, especially by Habermas—one of the most powerful and reputable defenders of the Enlightenment—are ironically also deployed to discredit postcolonial studies. The astonishing lack of scholarship on the ambivalent affinities among the first-generation of Critical Theory, poststructuralism, and postcolonial studies motivated me to address this research gap.

The third task set in this book is to clarify the issue of mistaken identity, as postcolonial studies is often confused with the decolonial approach. As I discuss in detail, decolonial scholars categorically reject the Enlightenment and Western reason. The Latin American decolonial approach emphasizes how modernity's supposedly emancipatory claims are intertwined with the erasure of colonial genocide and the deceptive rhetoric of progress. Ironically, they, too, accuse postcolonial studies of being uncritical and unemancipatory to the extent that postcolonial critical thought draws insights from poststructuralism and Marxism. Postcolonial and decolonial approaches are often used synonymously; however, it is crucial to recognize the differences between them, particularly in their distinct understandings of decolonization and the nature of critique. Walter Mignolo (2007, 163), for instance, speaks of a "radical difference" between postcolonial and decolonial approaches. While some make tepid attempts to bridge the postcolonial-decolonial divide (Bhambra 2014), others take a more assertive stand on the dispute between the two (Colpani et al. 2022). I conduct a critical analysis of both postcolonial and decolonial arguments, positioning myself in relation to the decolonial claim that they offer a corrective to the "ideological blind spots of postcolonial theories" (Moraña et al. 2008, 5). Postcolonial studies, due to its reliance on the European critical tradition, is often accused of being compromised from its inception, with the *post* in *postcolonial* signifying its political inefficacy. In contrast, the decolonial option's raison d'être lies in positioning itself as epistemically transgressive, asserting its ability to transcend the European canon (Colpani et al. 2022, 3–4). The decolonial option stakes a claim to being more radical and activist, while postcolonialism is declared passé because of its guilt by association with so-called old white men. What is at stake in these turf battles is the ability of postcolonial theory to provide critical impetus for the task of decolonization.

Given that postcolonial studies is accused of being both anti-Enlightenment *and* Eurocentric, it may seem counterintuitive to propose critical theories *of* decolonization, as the notion of critique is deeply entrenched in the European Enlightenment tradition. Despite the burgeoning scholarship on postcolonialism, as well as new trends in normative political theory, the link and discontinuity between the two have rarely been addressed. This book brings a much needed perspective on postcolonial critical thought, which is neither simply oppositional to nor incommensurable with the Enlightenment. In rethinking the nature and scope of critical theories of decolonization, the book outlines how normative principles such as human rights, global justice, and democracy are negotiated *from* and *for* the postcolonial world. In place of offering an ideal theory of justice or democracy, this volume responds to discussions on citizenship and cosmopolitanism, social movements and alter-globalization, human rights, and sovereignty from postcolonial-queer-feminist perspectives. Taking inspiration from the European critical tradition while questioning and contesting its blank spots, the effort is to discern how critical theories of decolonization are heuristic practices rather than a set of principles. Postcolonial critical practice hones the ability to differentiate, to ask probing questions, and to judge the exclusionary and coercive impulses of the Enlightenment. However, in contrast to a "diagnostic quality of critique" (Anker and Felski 2017, 4), wherein the critic functions as a detached expert who identifies the forms of malaise afflicting society and the defects plaguing its institutions, critical theories of decolonization involve a persistent questioning of one's presumptions and biases that renders critical practice as an open-ended endeavor. An important step toward understanding the aspirations and strategies of critical theories of decolonization is to acknowledge the extent to which the addressee of postcolonial critique—namely, the Enlightenment—also inspires the task of interrogating its coercive legacies.

Accordingly, the final objective of this book is to demonstrate that desubalternizing non-Western epistemologies is unattainable without demonopolizing Europe's dominance in critical practice. This would involve rethinking the normative idea of critique as defined during the Enlightenment. Without democratizing access to intellectual labor, particularly for subaltern groups, the violence exercised in the name of emancipatory norms of the Enlightenment will endure. As the quotes by Walter Benjamin and Spivak at the beginning of this book indicate, the nonperformativity of the Enlightenment—namely, the discontinuity among the rhetoric of freedom, equality, and rights and the reality of slavery, genocide, colonialism, and Nazism—makes it incumbent on us to rescue the Enlightenment from the Europeans, who, in many ways, are its worst betrayers. In addition to the important task of investigating the omissions and gaps in European political thought, my effort is to rescue the best of the Enlightenment to realize the project of decolonization. I show that decolonizing the Enlightenment does not imply repudiating it; nor does engaging with it imply endorsing it unconditionally.

In *Provincializing Europe*, Dipesh Chakrabarty (2000, 5) argues that, almost by definition, postcolonial thinkers are obliged to engage with the principles forged during the Enlightenment, which continue to shape the theorizing of historical, social, and economic phenomena in the postcolonial world. It is not so much the European origins (*Genese*) of the ideas of human rights or democracy that compromise their validity (*Geltung*) as it is the "normative violence" (Butler 1999, xx) that is exercised on those who violate the hegemonic framings of these norms. Postcolonial, queer, and feminist theorists aim to reimagine the values of equality, freedom, and justice to create new possibilities for negotiation, appropriation, and transformation of these ideals, all while challenging their Eurocentric and androcentric biases (Dhawan et al. 2016). Though inadequate, Enlightenment norms are nonetheless indispensable in understanding the postcolonial condition (Chakrabarty 2000, 4). At the same time, the postcolonial world is not a passive recipient of these principles; it is actively involved in reconfiguring key concepts such as universality, liberty, and equality, which were and are created and re-created in the interaction between colony and metropole. The task is to thread the needle between negotiating the Enlightenment legacies of democracy, justice, and rights and avoiding the reproduction of the constitutive violence that has marked the emergence of these ideals.

The irony of Europe's self-interpellation as an alleged civilizing force is that this positive self-assessment is possible only if one incurs historical amnesia regarding the costs of this mission in the forms of fascism and colonialism. Europe has done its best not to be held accountable for its colonial past, but history has a way of catching up with its culprits. As Derrida (1998, 64), drawing on Sigmund Freud, observes, what is most interesting about repressed memories is what cannot be forgotten and obliterated in the process of *Verdrängung*, or repression. Critical theories of decolonization mark the return of the repressed.

Taking inspiration from Jewish ethics, it is my firm belief that, in the interest of repairing the world (*tikkun olam*), Europe must be held accountable for its betrayal of the Enlightenment's values of freedom, equality, democracy, justice, and emancipation. Although Europe is accused of exploiting and oppressing the rest of the world, it claims in its defense that its tradition of self-critique and self-evaluation enables Europeans to reflect on their crimes and failures and, through self-correction, emerge as more ethical and responsible. This special critical tradition is repeatedly celebrated by Europeans, in all major discourses about Europe. Europe's practice of questioning itself is considered its greatest strength and the most significant legacy of the European Enlightenment; this supposedly sets it apart from other cultures, which are deemed incapable of self-scrutiny. The imperative of relating to oneself in a critical fashion and the ensuing self-improvement in both thought and action is proclaimed to be singularly and uniquely European. But, as Adam Phillips (2015a) astutely points out, self-critique can function as an "unforbidden pleasure" because it is unimaginative and narcissistic. Europe bewitches us with its claim of being able to be self-reflective through self-reproach; I question Europe's self-interpellation as critical. In my view, European self-critique is nonperformative (Ahmed 2006). As Sara Ahmed argues, the nonperformativity of an utterance does not indicate its failure; its very success lies, rather, in not doing what it claims, even if it is read as performative—namely, as doing what it pledges. The farce of European claims of self-improvement through the practice of self-critique is that there is a negative relationship between rhetoric and reality. For all the talk about European commitments to equality and freedom, self-critical rhetoric does not deliver a postimperial politics or ethics.

However, instead of polemically dismissing European critical thought, the book attempts to conceptually reposition its role within processes of decolonization. This is by no means a straightforward task of undoing the legacies of Enlightenment and colonialism; it is a more arduous undertaking of reclaiming and reconfiguring the Enlightenment's "strange fruits."[5] Following Foucault (1984, 44), who encourages us "to refuse everything that might present itself in the form of a simplistic and authoritarian alternative: you either accept the Enlightenment and remain within the tradition of its rationalism . . . ; or else you criticize the Enlightenment and then try to escape from its principles of rationality," I strive to explore the possibility of re-enchantment with the Enlightenment while acknowledging the costs and risks involved. Thus, the question of our relationship to the Enlightenment is marked by the impossibility of categorically locating ourselves beyond it (Cascardi 1999, 5). If, as insisted, the Enlightenment *is* critique, the postcolonial challenge is to reconfigure the Enlightenment's legacies and make them work for the non-European world.

This book is not a puzzle box in which the answers click into place, providing us with a blueprint at the end for how to decolonize. Nor is it a study of any one idea, person, or approach. Rather, a number of thinkers, such as Kant, Fanon, Adorno, Foucault, Derrida, Habermas, Spivak, Butler, and Mbembe, are the main focus of my analysis as I often position myself vis-à-vis them. They present an important foil for my arguments and perspectives. I also engage with concepts such as subalternity, critique, reason, cosmopolitanism, public sphere, freedom, equality, human rights, justice, and democracy to understand how the postcolonial world negotiates the ambivalent legacies of the Enlightenment. In particular, the writings of Gayatri

Chakravorty Spivak are central to my project, as she has been a foremost proponent of the double-bind relationship between postcolonial feminism and the Enlightenment. In my view, she has tirelessly devoted sustained attention to tracing the inadequacy, but also the indispensability, of Enlightenment thought for postcolonial critique. It is my firm belief that the process of decolonization is incomplete without desubalternization.

An important clarification regarding my use of Critical Theory in the singular with a capital C and critical theories in the plural with a lowercase c (Allen 2016) is necessary. The former is marked by a well-defined geographical location—namely, Frankfurt am Main—as its birthplace. The latter is multilocational and multiperspectival, referring to interventions in cultural, social, and political theory that contest global relations of power and domination. Thus, even though the first generation of Critical Theory provides important impulses for this book, critique, in my understanding, is not reducible to the European tradition. Despite claims of universality, Critical Theory, when projected as a global perspective, remains regrettably provincial due to its narrow European focus. In contrast, the more general category of critical theories—including feminist theory, post- and decolonial theory, queer theory, and critical race theory—eschews claims of universality. These theories are aware of their historical, social, cultural, economic, and geographical situatedness. By acknowledging that differences in experiences, perspectives, and locations matter, postcolonial queer feminism illustrates how normative principles are formulated and operationalized in the non-European world. Thus, critical theories contribute significantly to addressing the gaps in Eurocentric and androcentric critical thought.

Transdisciplinary in its approach, the book is primarily theoretical while drawing on historical and contemporary examples to illustrate its arguments. In comparing and contrasting rival theories, the aim is not only to open up new perspectives in postcolonial studies, in broader scholarship on the Enlightenment, and in contemporary Critical Theory, but also to contribute to fields such as gender studies, queer studies, and critical race theory.

The book is divided into two sections. The first part encompasses three chapters that examine the normative dilemmas involved in decolonizing the Enlightenment. The focus is on the colonial and anticolonial aspects of eighteenth-century political thought, the first generation of critical theorists' critique of the Enlightenment, and the past and future relationship between Europe and the postcolonial world. The second part, also comprising three chapters, explores the political, ethical, and aesthetic legacies of the Enlightenment. It analyzes the role of critique in contemporary social movements, the relationship between resistance and nonviolence, and the importance of aesthetic education in the process of desubalternization.

Chapter 1 traces the ongoing debate between the defenders and critics of the Enlightenment and its most prominent proponent, Immanuel Kant. In recent decades, there has been a surge of revisionist scholarship (Flikschuh and Ypi 2014; Muthu 2003) that aims to correct what is perceived as a misrepresentation of the Enlightenment's epistemological investment in imperialism by recovering critical perspectives within European canonical political thought. As a counterpoint to the postcolonial critique of the Enlightenment, some argue that the Enlightenment was, in fact, anti-imperialist. Conversely, Latin American scholars such as Mignolo (1995) and Ramón Grosfoguel (2007) express disenchantment with the Enlightenment and categorically reject European modernity, questioning its emancipatory claims. They advocate a return to Indigenous cosmologies as a path to achieving decolonization. Critical scholarship—including postcolonial, queer, and gender studies—that draws on insights from Enlightenment thought is accused by decolonial scholars of reproducing Eurocentrism. In response to accusations that postcolonial studies are both anti-Enlightenment *and* Eurocentric, chapter 1 seeks to outline the middle ground taken by critical theories of decolonization and address the normative dilemmas facing the project of decolonizing the Enlightenment.

Chapter 2 is devoted to the first-generation theorists of the Frankfurt School and their critique of the Enlightenment. Their analysis of instrumental reason and its association with Nazism parallels postcolonial studies' critique of Western reason. Much like Horkheimer and Adorno's efforts in *Dialectic of Enlightenment,* postcolonial studies can be seen as an attempt to "enlighten the Enlightenment about itself" (Habermas 1982, 21). This chapter explores the relationship between the first generation of the Frankfurt School and anticolonial and postcolonial projects, as well as the unfinished conversations between postcolonial and Holocaust studies. In a counterintuitive move, the final section of the chapter employs postcolonial perspectives to defend Adorno and Horkheimer against Habermas's charges of "performative contradiction" directed at *Dialectic of Enlightenment.*

Chapter 3 examines the issue of colonial amnesia and its repercussions for postcolonial Europe. The more Europe is confronted with its violent past, the more it tends to inflict violence on those who remind it of its historical crimes. I argue that an ethical engagement with Europe's past is essential for shaping its future. Therefore, merely undoing European colonialism is insufficient to create a world free from injustice and oppression. To reimagine nondominant futures, we must rethink Europe's relationship with the postcolonial world.

Part II of the book shifts focus to the role of critique in contemporary politics, ethics, and aesthetics. In line with these goals, I explore how Enlightenment concepts such as statehood, sovereignty, and aesthetics can be reconfigured and harnessed for emancipatory politics. Chapter 4 examines whether current social movements can achieve progressive goals or whether oppositional thought might be nonperformative, thereby hindering rather than facilitating social change. Under late capitalism and neocolonialism, protest politics aim to inspire hope and optimism. However, as Adorno (1997 [1955], 35) warns, there is a danger in radical action that "calls everything into question and criticizes nothing." The chapter investigates the complex relationship among international civil society, counterpublic spheres, and postcolonial states. I outline how the will to resist and the state phobia of transnational elites ironically exacerbate rather than mitigate the disenfranchisement of subaltern collectives. Project 2025, an initiative by the Heritage Foundation, a right-wing think tank in the United States, is a troubling example of a vision aimed at dismantling certain organs of the state. Targeting policies concerning education, abortion, pornography, diversity, immigration, civil service, climate change, and taxes, its stated agenda is "to deconstruct the Administrative State" (Dans and Groves 2024, xiv). By foregrounding the importance of postcolonial sovereignty, chapter 4 argues that, for progressive and emancipatory politics, it is crucial to distinguish between criticizing the state and harboring state phobia.

Postcolonial critiques of the Enlightenment reveal how the imperative to be critical can sometimes be coercive and violent rather than emancipatory and counterhegemonic. Chapter 5 explores how, instead of fostering a nonviolent world, critical practice may perpetuate cycles of violence. It examines the works of Fanon, Arendt, Gandhi, Butler, Mbembe, and Bhimrao Ambedkar to address the enduring question of whether emancipation can be achieved through coercive means or whether violence merely perpetuates itself, with each act of violence reinforcing its own force. In addition, the chapter analyzes the ambivalent and contradictory nature of both state and anti-state violence and its relation to critical practice.

Chapter 6 explores the intersection of politics, ethics, and aesthetics within the context of decolonization. For Kant, tutelage is an inability to make use of one's own understanding without direction from another. Ironically, colonialism made it impossible for the natives to exercise intellectual labor autonomously. To move from the sublime to the obscene, Donald Trump (2016), after a decisive win in the Nevada primary, remarked, "I love the poorly educated." This chapter pays particular attention to how education can enable or hinder critical thinking. The focus is on Spivak's interpretations of Kant and Friedrich Schiller, as well as her argument that aesthetic education, which cultivates the imagination, is crucial for desubalternization and, by extension, decolonization.

The conclusion argues that critically engaging with the disenchanted present requires reimagining our understanding of change and transformation. Given the endemic problems of economic, social, and political inequality in the postcolonial world, along with the rise of authoritarian and antidemocratic forces, critical practice is closely linked to concerns of disenfranchised subjects and their struggles. The moral-political predicament of postcolonial oppositional criticism is that it must be articulated within the very grammar of Enlightenment discourses of human rights and democracy (Dhawan 2014). The postcolonial condition is plagued by unfulfilled promises and underscores the precarity of hope. While Kant's formula for Enlightenment focuses on exiting self-incurred tutelage, my reading of postcolonial studies draws on Moses Mendelssohn's insight that, for certain vulnerable groups, this tutelage is not self-incurred but systematically imposed. This makes it nearly impossible for these groups to escape it. Mendelssohn's quote at the beginning of this book echoes the postcolonial yearning for Enlightenment. However, rather than offering resolution and guarantees, critical theories of decolonization are shaped by contingencies and dilemmas, where the challenge lies in whether and how to employ the master's tools to dismantle the master's house (Lorde 2007, 110).

PART I The History of the Present

1

Who Financed the Enlightenment?

Colonialism and the Age of Reason

We must free ourselves from the intellectual blackmail of being for or against the Enlightenment.—MICHEL FOUCAULT, "What Is Enlightenment?"

In the aftermath of George Floyd's murder on May 25, 2020, and amid controversial discussions worldwide regarding pulling down monuments and statues linked to colonialism and slavery, there was also an intense debate in the German media around Immanuel Kant's legacy.[1] Kant has thus far been widely regarded as symbolic of the European Enlightenment and its norms of liberty, equality, autonomy, cosmopolitanism, and peace. While some accused Kant of being the founding father of modern racism (Zeuske 2020) and a symbol of white reason (Biskamp 2020), others defended him simply as a "man of his times" (Reemtsma 2024) and even as an embodiment of Enlightenment anticolonialism (Brumlik 2020). With the renewed global interest in the incomplete processes of decolonization, there has been a fresh focus on the interconnections among various concepts: modernity and race, capitalism and neocolonialism, cosmopolitanism and global inequality. The ambivalent relationship between colonialism and Enlightenment, too, is once again in the spotlight. In this chapter, I argue that it is important to understand the central role of Kant during the Enlightenment and his continuing influence on contemporary understandings of critical practice. Whether Michel Foucault, Judith Butler, or Gayatri Chakravorty Spivak, even the staunchest critics of Western thought orient themselves vis-à-vis Kant. Furthermore, I establish that current foreign policies of Western states, whether in the fields of development politics or military intervention, continue to draw on Kantian normative ideals of cosmopolitanism and international law. In keeping with a postcolonial history of ideas, it is imperative to address the central role of these Kantian principles in critical theories of decolonization. The option of simply circumventing Kant by canceling him as racist or sexist is unviable, as he is one of the most prominent thinkers of the Enlightenment and provides original interpretations of ideas of autonomy and critique that have been hugely influential.

As a first step toward decolonizing the Enlightenment, let us understand this contentious concept and era (Dhawan 2014). The term *Enlightenment* encompasses a wide array of concepts, practices, texts, and thinkers, such that no single definition can fully capture the extensive range of its meaning, both as a historical period and as a conceptual framework (Cascardi 1999, 21). Generalizations about the Enlightenment and its legacies oversimplify its complex critical practices, leaving the ongoing debate between its supporters and critics vibrant and controversial.

James Schmidt (1996, 2) examines how, despite differing answers to the question "What is Enlightenment?" posed against discussions of censorship, political authority, and religious faith, all respondents shared the view that it was not merely about a specific historical period.[2] Kant, whose essay became canonical, foregrounded the publicness of reason that was flourishing in the coffeehouses, salons, reading societies, and scientific academies of the time (Schmidt 1996, 5).[3] While Kant extols the capacity to reason as one of the cornerstones of the Enlightenment, which is closely linked to the autonomy of the individual, he fails to address the question: Who financed the Enlightenment?

In light of recent debates regarding the contradictory legacies of the Enlightenment, I contest, in what follows, the accusations against postcolonial studies that its criticism of the Enlightenment is misguided and even dangerous. The chapter begins with a historical analysis of the link between Enlightenment and empire and focuses on the defenders of the Enlightenment, who hope to bring to light the long-neglected anti-imperialist impulses of eighteenth-century political thought. The chapter then takes stock of the Enlightenment's simultaneously imperialist and anti-imperialist nature. I concede that postcolonial theorists indeed risk homogenizing the Enlightenment by primarily focusing on its violent legacies. However, advocates of eighteenth-century political thought, in their efforts to recuperate Enlightenment thought, do not adequately consider postcolonial-queer-feminist concerns. Instead of a presentist dismissal of the Enlightenment or simply demonstrating that many of its universal ideas are in fact merely Eurocentric, the effort in this opening chapter is to throw fresh light on the assumptions undergirding the Enlightenment. The aim is neither to denounce nor to find fault in Enlightenment thought; it is, rather, to highlight the centrality of colonialism and racism in the Age of Reason. The chapter also explores the complex dynamics among colonialism, capitalism, and cosmopolitanism. The aim is to rethink and reimagine our relationship to Enlightenment thinkers such as Kant. This is not an effort to discredit them but, rather, ultimately to be more rigorous critical thinkers than they managed to be. What better homage can a disciple offer than to surpass the master?

The Disenchantment with the Enlightenment

The impact of Enlightenment thought is profound and enduring. It extends beyond its historical and geographical origins, continuing to shape discussions on human rights, democracy, authoritarianism, migration, environmental issues, and artificial intelligence. Enlightenment ideas offer crucial intellectual, moral, and political resources for addressing these challenges. Against the backdrop of feudalism and authoritarianism, Enlightenment thinkers advocated for equality, rights, and rationality as pathways to freedom. Their ideas inspired radical movements such as the French and Haitian revolutions and influenced progressive ideologies such as liberalism and socialism. The Enlightenment fostered critical reflection on political norms, accountability, and social relations, paving the way for movements advocating suffrage, abolition, and broader civil liberties. Its legacy continues to inspire contemporary social and political activism. Kant's response to the historical question "What is Enlightenment?" filters the optimistic sentiment of modernity and goes beyond a mere periodization to capture the intellectual orientation of European thought.[4] Kant claims that reason emancipates humanity by rescuing man from nonautonomous subjectivity toward liberty and equality.

The Enlightenment aimed to achieve material, epistemic, ethical, and scientific progress through reasoned criticism of religious and political authorities. However, efforts to reform social and political structures often produced unintended and disenchanting effects.[5] Scholars in postcolonial and Holocaust studies have observed that the Enlightenment's promise of freedom through reason led paradoxically to the domination of reason itself. This period, while advancing reason and science, also ushered in terror, genocide, slavery, and totalitarianism. Colonialism and the Holocaust underscore the flaws in Enlightenment ideals, which, by dismissing non-European critical practices, claimed normative superiority. The Enlightenment's triumph of reason, advanced by a rising bourgeois class, was paradoxically coupled with the marginalization of women, nature, and non-Western peoples, viewed as "Others" to be subjugated. Postcolonial scholars highlight that Enlightenment ideals often served privileged classes and entrenched biases related to gender, class, race, and sexuality. Instead of excusing the Enlightenment's racism, sexism, and antisemitism (James and Knappik 2022) or uncritically celebrating it as the cradle of modern democracy and liberal institutions, I focus on exploring how its concepts of reason and autonomy relate to the violence they incited.

From the outset, the Enlightenment's promise of emancipation and progress was met with skepticism about reason. Thinkers such as G. W. F. Hegel, Karl Marx, and Friedrich Nietzsche debated the merits and flaws of reason, science, rights, and law. Early criticism of the Enlightenment often stemmed from its association with the French Revolution and the ensuing terror, which eventually led to authoritarianism under Napoleon.

Promises of progress depicted the so-called pre- and non-Enlightened worlds as mired in dogmatism and tyranny (Allen 2016; Cascardi 1999, 25–26). The Enlightenment, while presenting itself as a victory of reason over superstition and a step toward liberty and equality, replaced traditional religious and political authorities with new modes of social domination. Its emphasis on universal principles often disregarded other epistemologies and cosmologies, promoting an imperialist agenda that assumed all humanity aspired to these principles, regardless of race, class, or gender. Enlightenment thinkers claimed to offer objective knowledge by separating value from fact (Cascardi 1999, 90). This universalism was tied to Europe's self-definition as modern, rational, and sovereign, contrasting with a non-Western world perceived as lacking autonomy. Critics argue that the Enlightenment's drive to standardize rational utility ultimately contributed to the violence of colonialism and Nazism.

One of the staunchest contestations of the Enlightenment's emancipatory claims came from the first generation of the Frankfurt School.

In *Dialectic of Enlightenment* Horkheimer and Adorno (2002 [1947]) argue that the Enlightenment embodies Western culture's attempt at domination through instrumental rationality. (This is discussed in greater detail in chapter 2.) Another powerful critique emerges from poststructuralist thinkers, who highlight the pernicious side of the Age of Reason. Foucault (2013[1959]), for instance, challenges the self-representation of the Enlightenment as allegedly humanitarian and progressive. While Kant understands the Enlightenment as a challenge to the arbitrary use of political power, Foucault focuses on the link between rationalization and the violence of Enlightenment norms: The introduction of supposedly more humane practices and institutions, be they penal or medical, legitimized the systematic marginalization and silencing of individuals who were perceived as a threat to social norms and order. In the name of curing it, madness became mental illness and thereby effectively silenced. Modern prisons became a symbol of so-called civilized societies, with surveillance replacing torture and reform replacing physical violence as purportedly more humane. Earlier technologies were rejected not just for their cruelty, but also for their inefficiency and economic inapplicability. Teachers, psychologists, and social workers became defenders and enforcers of the norm throughout the social body. This arsenal of techniques of normalization was at the heart of a microphysics of power that emerged during the Age of Reason. Corresponding to the social institutions and practices of the classical age is what Foucault calls "the classical episteme," the distinctive way in which knowledge was ordered and determined in the eighteenth century. This confronts us with the questions: "What is this Reason that we use? . . . What are its limits, and what are the dangers?" (Foucault 2001, 358). In response to the objection that it is perilous to contest reason, Foucault (2001, 358) warns that it is equally dangerous "to say that any critical questioning of this rationality risks sending us into irrationality." He reminds us that "it was on the basis of the flamboyant rationality of social Darwinism that racism was formulated, becoming one of the most enduring and powerful ingredients in Nazism" (Foucault 2001, 358). One could add colonialism.

Influenced by the first generation of the Frankfurt School and poststructuralism, postcolonial scholars also question the Enlightenment model of emancipation. They argue that the Enlightenment's claim to have surpassed barbarism in Europe was used to legitimize its imposition on what was referred to as the uncivilized non-European world. Colonialism was framed as a way to eliminate the supposed backwardness, with European guidance purportedly ensuring social, economic, and political progress. The Enlightenment's stadial view of history defended colonialism by asserting that interaction with Europe would enable alleged primitive populations to advance to purportedly higher stages of development (McCarthy 2009). As I argue in greater detail later, Kant played a pivotal role in linking morality to reason as its highest function, such that he censured as evil any impediments to moral progress. At the same time, he argued for "necessary evil," assuming it contributed to advancing human progress. Kant's defenders emphasize that, while he condemned imperialism for being unacceptable on a moral level, given that it was seen to disseminate the gains of European civilization among what were referred to as backward societies, Kant could nevertheless view it as functionally worthwhile (Gani 2017, 443 fn. 70; McCarthy 2009, 66). Despite his differences with Kant, Hegel, in *Elements of the Philosophy of Right* (1991 [1821], 120), also argued that there is a "right of heroes" to bring the unfree native populations in Africa, Asia and the Americas into a progress of European Enlightenment.

Imperialist ideologies successfully turned their local norms and values into globally accepted paradigms. Instead of promoting freedom and equality, the Enlightenment led to legal, administrative, and economic reforms in the colonies that introduced new forms of domination, such as slavery and genocide. These processes of modernization ushered in practices of subjectification, surveillance, regulation, and disciplining of non-Europeans. Humanitarian reforms disenfranchised those they supposedly aimed to civilize. As David Scott (1999, 35) notes, colonialism had both extractive effects on the bodies of the colonized and governing effects on their conduct. A key contradiction of the Enlightenment in the colonies was its attempt to modernize presumed barbaric societies to mirror Europe, thereby threatening European uniqueness. Homi Bhabha (1994, 122) explores how, through mimicry, the native is "almost the same but not quite." Imitating the colonizers involves both mockery and assimilation.

While the focus has primarily been on temporality, it is crucial to recognize that the Enlightenment's spatial association with Europe significantly shaped its self-perception. From this perceived center, Enlightenment thinkers theorized about the presumed peripheral parts of the world, comparing European societies and cultures with those of the rest. During the colonial age of discovery, Europeans claimed to have found new worlds by encountering what they described as cannibals and savages (Hulme 1990, 20). Many Enlightenment thinkers, despite never leaving Europe or speaking non-European languages, authoritatively commented on other societies and cultures. They often collaborated with private and state bodies responsible for European colonial policies. Relying on travel literature, ethnographic sources, and literary texts, these thinkers judged the moral, political, social, and economic practices of the Americas, Asia, and Africa without direct experience (Eze 1997a).

At the core of the Enlightenment's idea of reason was the belief in mankind's progression, placing Europe at the top of a civilizational pyramid. For example, in *Leviathan*, Thomas Hobbes (1998 [1651], 85) uses events in the Americas to depict a society without order and civility: "For the savage people in many places of America, except the government of small families, the concord whereof dependeth on natural lust, have no government at all; and live at this day in that brutish manner." Hobbes proposed that the state of nature is a state of war, justifying the need for an ultimate authority, a Leviathan, to ensure peace and order. This metaphorical world map places Europe as the symbol of civilization and America as primitivism (Hulme 1990, 25). John Locke (2003a [1689], 121) famously stated, "In the beginning all the world was America." The denial of sovereignty and autonomy to non-European peoples justified their colonization under the guise of redemption, asserting that to be human, one must adopt European practices and norms.

Western Christendom debated the origins of Indigenous peoples for decades (Harvey 2012, 130). Some attributed physical and cultural differences to separate acts of creation, while others found polygenism blasphemous, as it questioned Christ's universal salvation (Harvey 2012, 130). Sixteenth-century theologians such as Francisco de Vitoria and Bartolomé de Las Casas challenged the dehumanizing view of natives as natural slaves but did not oppose imperialism itself (Anghie 2007, 27). They believed that the purportedly backward peoples could rise on the universal scale of progress with Christian help. Recognizing the humanity of the Amerindians did not prevent their subjugation. Thinkers such as Jean-Jacques Rousseau celebrated the Amerindians as "noble savages" but still viewed them as racially and morally inferior. This celebration of the "raw man" ended up animalizing the natives. The normative idea of human was defined by Eurocentric views of cognitive abilities and moral nature. Thus, even when Amerindians were formally recognized as equals, their supposedly barbaric practices such as human sacrifice and cannibalism were used to argue they had forfeited their natural rights and sovereignties. Ironically, by being acknowledged as part of humanity, they were judged by European norms, and the supposed bestowal of individual agency made the colonized responsible for their own domination (Scott 1999, 27).

The natives' inability to make rational use of land was seen as evidence of their debased condition. This agriculturalist argument justified the colonial appropriation of non-European territories and resources (Hulme 1990, 28–30). Nomadic practices of some Indigenous groups were deemed inferior to sedentary lifestyles. The existence of presumed masterless people justified enclosure and expropriation. The idle and unproductive natives were criticized for wasting the divine gift of land; this argument tied the unwillingness to labor with moral failure and an inability to plan for the future. Europeans were praised for their industriousness, cultivating land and contributing to the public good while pursuing private interests. Locke argued that the main division was between those who improve land and those who, like animals, merely gather what nature provides, with the former considered fully rational and human (Locke 2003a [1689], 116). Here, labor, foresight, and reason distinguished what were termed *savage* from civilized societies. Despite denouncing slavery, Locke was a shareholder in the Royal African Company, chartered in 1672 to monopolize the English slave trade, highlighting systemic racism in Western political thought and its connection to current narratives of extractivism and land grabbing that disenfranchise Indigenous communities.

The propertization and exploitation of land, forests, hills, and other natural resources were central to capitalist expansion. European land-use practices became standard, with common lands being enclosed into private property by colonizers, as seen in the encomienda system. The scarcity of land in Europe was resolved through the colonial theft of Indigenous territories, justified by the supposed rational use of land. This demand for land led to native resistance, which was met with retaliation and further confiscation of Indigenous land (Hulme 1990, 20). Ironically, European settlers became the legitimate inhabitants, while Indigenous people were displaced. Colonizers used the legal doctrine of *vacuum domicilium* to acquire land titles and political jurisdiction, ignoring Indigenous sovereignty.[6] Resistance to this theft led to colonial terror: not a Hobbesian war of all against all, but a war of the presumed righteous against those they saw as violating rational principles of landownership and use. The concept of a "just war" was used to legitimize imperial aggression toward natives in the name of self-defense (Anghie 2007, 24–26). Colonized societies were excluded from sovereignty by not meeting European norms, and those who held sovereignty felt entitled to dominate those who did not (Anghie 2007, 24–26). Colonialism was not just an economic and military operation but a project of subject formation on both sides of the colonial divide.

In line with Enlightenment thought, liberal notions of progress, liberty, tolerance, democracy, civil society, and the public sphere converged in the all-embracing civilization thesis. History is divided into tradition and modernity, stagnation and development, superstition and the triumph of reason. The supposed authoritarian irrationality of the East signified Oriental despotism and immoral feudalism, placing the decadent Orient at a lower evolutionary stage toward modernity. Eastern political systems were perceived as denying rationality and freedom, thus hindering the development of individuality. Colonialism's legitimization as a civilizing mission and the so-called dynamic of difference between civilized and barbaric societies allowed for the possibility of natives' becoming civilized, but only under European guidance. This infamous colonial pedagogic project aimed to help purportedly backward societies overcome their "civilizational infantilism" (Mehta 1999, 70). Refuting the doctrine of biology as destiny, imperial liberalism upheld the natives' capacity for civilization. It was argued that some societies, being at a lower evolutionary stage, needed to be educated like children to become capable of enjoying freedom. Through colonial education and modern government forms, the colonized's political incompetence could be corrected, enabling them to realize their civilizational potential. This offered natives the chance to overcome their stage of rawness, marked by instinct, and develop the capacities for reason, thereby exercising freedom and consent, which are central to political authority and autonomy. Those unable to reason could be governed without their consent (Mehta 1999, 59). While rejecting biological determinism, implicit assumptions about national character justified the exclusion of the colonized from equality and reciprocity until they were adequately civilized. This progressivist universalism legitimized European imperial rule as beneficial for presumed backward subjects, authorizing the retraction of sovereignty of many Indigenous states and increasingly interventionist policies in colonized societies' education, law, property, and religious systems (Pitts 2005, 21).

The paradox of modernity lies in the preaching of liberal values to the colonized while denying them in practice. The belief in an evolutionary difference between the metropole and the colony allowed liberal thinkers such as John Stuart Mill to advocate for freedom while endorsing enlightened, progressive imperialism. Mill (1989 [1859], 13) asserted that "despotism is a legitimate mode of government in dealing with barbarians, provided the end be their improvement." The Tunisian philosopher and historian Hichem Djait (1985, 101) rightfully accuses imperialist Europe of denying its own vision of humanity. Enlightenment ideals left behind violent and exploitative systems under the guise of modernity, progress, rationality, emancipation, rights, justice, and peace. Non-Western individuals, groups, or states had to conform to European norms to be considered civilized or risk being forcibly modernized. Meanwhile, native attempts to imitate European norms were seen as producing bad, weak, or failed copies, reinforcing the perceived superiority of the European original. In response to these colonialist moves, anticolonial nationalists pursued the selective strategy of adopting the technologies and administrative practices in the material sphere without accepting European claims of superiority in the alleged spiritual realm (Chatterjee 1993, 121). Anticolonial nationalists, while emphasizing the importance of preserving and safeguarding (often gendered) cultural identity, mimicked the Europeans in the economic and political sphere.

In response to postcolonial criticism, one of the most common tropes in defense of liberalism is to argue that these Western thinkers changed their racist and colonialist ideas in their later writings. I would counterargue that inconsistencies in the ideological positioning of liberal thinkers does not exculpate them.[7] Rather, it indicates how liberalism resists decolonization by claiming auto-correction. Alexis de Tocqueville, for instance, altered his views about what was practicable and appropriate for French Algeria as a result of his journeys while refraining from writing about India because of his inability to travel there (Pitts 2005, 6). James Mill, in contrast, boasted that his writings, which were based on his readings of English-language literature on India, were impartial and objective because he had not been distracted or contaminated through contact with the natives that plagued the perspectives of travelers and administrators (Pitts 2005, 6). Despite setbacks, Edmund Burke was unwavering in his political efforts to challenge British colonialism, especially in India. He accused British colonizers of disregarding the rule of law, which disenfranchised the Indians, as they could be fined, incarcerated, or killed without recourse to legal protection or appeal (Pitts 2005, 247). Jennifer Pitts (2005, 246) proposes that Burke was not an outlier; rather, a number of eighteenth-century thinkers were critical of cross-cultural judgments and Europe's cultural conceit. Sunil Agnani (2013) presents a contrasting portrayal of Burke as critical of the East India Company yet traditional in his views on Haiti. One wonders if Burke would have been as steadfast in his support of the oppressed Indians if there had been a violent revolution in India comparable to Haiti's. Agnani observes that the "absent Indian Jacobin" resulted in Burke portraying Indians in a sympathetic light as victims of the abuses of the East India Company. While alarmed at the events in Saint-Domingue, Burke spoke on "behalf of an oppressed people" in India. This contradiction can be understood only in terms of Burke's neglect of native resistance in India (Agnani 2013, 145).

These lessons are relevant to discussions on non-European illiberal regimes and Western liberal values and responsibility to protect. Although Tocqueville was cognizant of the violence of colonial policies, his concerns about democracy in France led him to support French colonial expansion in Algeria. Unlike Burke, Tocqueville believed that a liberal-democratic regime required exploiting non-European societies. This justified suspending human equality and self-determination abroad to ensure stability at home (Pitts 2005, 248). Tocqueville's support for imperial expansion shows how self-interest led French liberals to advocate for exclusionary and violent international politics, betraying liberal humanitarianism. The connection between imperial expansion and domestic politics reveals how democratization in the metropole was intertwined with imperial politics (Pitts 2005, 248).

The Enlightenment model of emancipation is likewise challenged by the postcolonial-queer-feminist perspective on colonial heteronormativity, which offers essential insights into the contradictions within European liberal norms. Postcolonial-queer-feminist scholars emphasize that Enlightenment-era racism and colonialism must be understood in conjunction with sexism and androcentrism. While Enlightenment principles of autonomy, equality, and universality suggest support for women's liberation, postcolonial queer feminists argue that the exclusion and silencing of non-European women were intrinsic to the Enlightenment. Proponents of Enlightenment ideals claim that extending rights and freedom to previously marginalized groups can address these issues (McCabe 2019; Mikkola 2011). Critics, however, contend that the epistemic and discursive violence embedded in Enlightenment thought cannot be easily eradicated. Feminist critics emphasize the pervasive misogyny among Enlightenment thinkers. Robin May Schott explores the decline in women's rights during the Enlightenment, particularly in France, where the uniform legal system entrenched Rousseau's notion of gender differences.[8] The Civil Code acknowledged citizens' rights but excluded women from citizenship, worsening their status relative to men (May Schott 1996, 473). The feminist Olympe de Gouges, unable to write, dictated her works to a secretary. Both France and Germany—including Königsberg University, where Kant studied—barred women from university education. Kant ridiculed women's philosophical and scientific efforts, claiming that their character was defined by natural needs rather than reason (Kant 2006 [1798], 204). Despite advocating for an "innate right to freedom" (Kant 1991c [1797], 63), Kant upheld men's "natural superiority" and deemed women "immature in civil matters" (Kant 2006 [1798], 103). This lack of civil independence relegated women to "passive citizens," contradicting Kant's view of universal freedom and equality (Kleingeld 2019, 6).

The Enlightenment's emphasis on reason excluded the feminine private sphere, associated with emotion and subjectivity, from the masculine public sphere of autonomy and objectivity (Flax 1992, 242; Outram 2019). While thinkers such as Baruch Spinoza recognized affective cognition, they did not acknowledge women's cognitive or moral equality. Thus, Enlightenment reason marginalized the feminine as the *Other*, pursuing dispassionate, objective knowledge. Kant's call for self-enlightenment ignored the social, economic, and cultural barriers faced by women, who were seen as incapable of using reason (May Schott 1996, 476–77). Kant's notion of autonomy was tailored to educated, middle-class men, excluding those deemed *nonhuman* such as women and slaves.

Western feminist writings of the time primarily addressed the exclusion of white women from political power by challenging their perceived immaturity and the analogy drawn between women and children. However, these feminists rarely contested the exclusion of colonized people, whose participation in self-governance was deemed unviable. This highlights the tenuous connections between anti-imperialist, antiracist thought and Western feminism.

The Enlightenment's pursuit of freedom ironically perpetuated new forms of domination, masked as rational progress. First-generation Critical Theory, postcolonial studies, and feminist scholarship all express skepticism about the Enlightenment's emancipatory claims.

Defending the Enlightenment. Universalism and Diversity

Colonialism is regrettably either disregarded or given negligible consideration in Enlightenment scholarship. Even critical thinkers such as Adorno, Horkheimer, and Foucault largely overlook colonialism in their contemplations on the Enlightenment. Postcolonial scholars have sought to address this lacuna by examining the Enlightenment's role in European colonialism, while prominent publications (Festa and Carey 2009; Flik-schuh and Ypi 2014; Muthu 2003) aim to correct what they perceive as a misrepresentation of the Enlightenment's involvement in imperialism. These works highlight the anticolonial tendencies of Enlightenment thinkers, countering poststructuralist and postcolonial critiques of Kant, among others. These debates are not just minor academic disagreements. They have significant implications for contemporary discussions of race and decolonization.

Supporters of the Enlightenment (Carey and Trakulhun 2009; Festa and Carey 2009; Muthu 2003) argue that knowledge of other cultures during the so-called age of discoveries enhanced awareness of cultural diversity and contributed to humanist and cosmopolitan discourses. En-counters with other peoples led to revisions of European understandings of universality and human nature (Festa and Carey 2009, 20; Muthu 2003, 266). Enlightenment thinkers such as Kant, Denis Diderot, and Johann Gottfried Herder are said to have denounced European imperial injus-tices and warned of colonialism's corrupting influence on Europe (Louden 2000, 105; Muthu 2003, 1; Wolff 2020; Wood 2008, 15). They viewed cul-tural differences as evidence of human freedom and reason, promoting a more inclusive universalism and goodwill toward non-Europeans. En-lightenment anti-imperialism emphasized cosmopolitanism, advocating the kinship of all humans and reshaping ideas of trade and travel (Muthu 2012, 218). Commerce was seen as a civilizing force that transformed feudal economies into commercial societies. Although Enlightenment thinkers were cautious about global commerce, they nevertheless defended the right to travel, exchange ideas and goods, and form partnerships. This is considered a cornerstone of their anti-imperialist stance.

In *Perpetual Peace*, Kant suggested that the violation of rights in one part of the Earth is felt by all (Kant 1991b [1795], 107–8). The flow of goods, ideas, and communication across borders made a theory of cosmopolitan justice (*ius cosmopoliticum, Weltbürgerrecht*) essential. This theory concerned not just sovereign states or commercial entities but humanity as a whole. Kant celebrated the "spirit of commerce" for fostering mutual self-interest among nations, though he balanced ideas of global society, world citizen-ship, and transcontinental trade with concerns about imperial wars and national debts (Muthu 2012, 208). He rejected the idea of a world state, envisioning global justice as a peaceful community of sovereign states. His concept of "unsocial sociability" encouraged productive resistance for self-preservation, not conquest. Close commercial ties among states would prompt conflict resolution through mediation (Muthu 2012, 222). The "power of money" lay in preventing global debt crises and financial collapse (Kant 1991b [1795], 95). Kant tempered his praise of "commercial humanity" with concerns about transnational commercial domination, acknowledging the link between imperial domination abroad and moral and political corruption within (Muthu 2012, 207). This view aligns with his rejection of violence against nonhuman animals, worrying about human "brutalization" from such acts.[9] Diderot and Adam Smith went as far as to argue that the end of global commerce's corrupting influence and international trading companies must come from outside Europe. The rise of non-European nations would lead to more equitable global economic relations through "mutual fear" rather than "mutual friendship" (Muthu 2012, 214). They saw the non-European world as humanity's hope for the future, ironically facilitated by the same global commerce and communication that produced injustice (Muthu 2012, 212).

Postcolonial studies' rebuke of cosmopolitanism stands accused of overlooking the emancipatory potential in Kant's examination of the coercive impacts of global commerce (Muthu 2012; Neiman 2021). In the next section, I address these counterarguments to the postcolonial perspective on the Enlightenment and evaluate whether postcolonial scholars misinterpret the Enlightenment or its proponents are too generous in labeling it anti-imperialist.

Imperialist Enlightenment or Enlightenment Against Imperialism?

Ironically, postcolonial scholarship is being accused of both being anti-Enlightenment *and* Eurocentric. As I discuss in greater detail in chapter 3, Latin American scholars such as Walter Mignolo (1995) and Ramón Grosfoguel (2007) denounce the Enlightenment as a harbinger of exploitation through colonialism and capitalism, advocating for a return to Indigenous cosmologies and the decolonization of postcolonial studies. Conversely, critics argue that postcolonial studies misrepresent the Enlightenment by depicting it as a unified project with singular goals instead of acknowledging its internal tensions and complexities. Scholars such as Sankar Muthu, Jennifer Pitts, Katrin Flikschuh, Lea Ypi, Lynn Festa, Daniel Carey, and Susan Neiman, alongside critics such as Mignolo and Grosfoguel, contribute to this heated discussion on the Enlightenment's ambivalent legacies.

My concern is that both defenders and critics of the Enlightenment often reduce postcolonial-queer-feminist scholarship to a simplistic dualism of pro- versus anti-Enlightenment. I examine four key issues to shed light on these allegations: (1) the critique of postcolonial scholarship as unsystematic; (2) the critique that it is anachronistic; (3) the claim that the Enlightenment in fact promotes cultural and racial diversity; and (4) the claim that it fosters religious tolerance.

The accusations that postcolonialism is "unsystematic," "ad hoc," and "haphazard" (Festa and Carey 2009, 2) ignore its eclectic nature. They draw on poststructuralism, Marxism, feminism, and psychoanalysis, which themselves are influenced by Enlightenment thought. Postcolonial studies is not only transdisciplinary but also anti-disciplinary, challenging systematic theory building. Gyan Prakash (1992, 184) responds to the idea that combining Marxist and poststructuralist insights is like riding two horses at once: "Let us hang on to two horses, inconstantly." Methodological purity excludes marginalized narratives; Prakash advocates for negotiating the fruitful tensions between theoretical approaches and encourages postcolonial critics to become "stunt riders" (Prakash 1992, 184).

The second charge against postcolonial studies is that it courts anachronism (Festa and Carey 2009, 28). Critics argue that many key categories of difference in postcolonial theory, such as gender, did not exist during the Enlightenment. However, the emergence of new concepts in gender and queer studies, such as heteronormativity, does not mean that Kant's or Herder's theories were not sexist. As Spivak (2008, 129) notes, "reproductive heteronormativity" is the oldest institution, sustaining precolonial, colonial, and postcolonial structures. Even Pauline Kleingeld (2019), a strong advocate of Kant, acknowledges that Kant contradicts his own moral principles by insisting on women's subordination and passivity.

The third accusation against postcolonialism is its disregard of the Enlightenment's acceptance of cultural diversity. The term *culture* came to replace *civilization* and *race* in colonial discourses, making it problematic to view Kant's and Herder's recognition of cultural diversity as anti-imperialist. Cultural difference and diversity, rather than merely opposing the universal, play a role in capitalist and racist colonial discourses. For example, despite recognizing cultural diversity, Kant strongly rejects race mixing and racial assimilation to avoid universal uniformity (more on this later). Even if the Enlightenment appeared diversity-friendly, it still ranked and judged non-European practices and societies as deficient while generalizing its own, particular interests to be common interests for all of humanity. The recognition of cultural diversity did not eliminate "normative violence" (Butler 1999, xx); European ideals maintained their normative power despite acknowledging diverse values. For instance, the greatest strength of the Kantian categorical imperative lies in its insistence on the fundamental equality of all moral agents; however, not everyone qualified as human. Spivak (1985, 248) rephrases the categorical imperative as "*make* the heathen into a human so that he can be treated as an end in himself." Concepts such as *morality* and *culture* are mobilized to justify the violent act of making the native into a human through the civilizing mission of colonialism (Spivak 1999, 3–4). At the same time, colonialism's economic imperative and genocidal racism are insidiously concealed. Charles Mills (2017a, 99) points out that, although the Kantian categorical imperative promotes respect for human dignity, it recognizes members of the white race as the only individuals who qualify as people.[10] So following Mills, the Kantian categorical imperative actually should read: "Act so that you treat the white race (original 'humanity'), whether in your own person or in the person of any other white individual, always at the same time as an end, never merely as a means. Members of other races can be treated as mere objects" (Mills 2017a, 99). Both Spivak and Mills analyze the normative violence of the categorical imperative. However, they both reject canceling Kant, as they are committed to salvaging Kantian ideals of universal equality and the idea of the human beings as an end in itself. They aim to purge these principles of their discriminatory proclivities.

Fourth, touted as one of the most defining aspects of their anti-imperialist positions, the claim of the religious tolerance of eighteenth-century thinkers also does not withstand scrutiny. Here it is worthwhile to focus on Kant's antisemitic fantasies (Mack 2003). This is particularly instructive in the face of accusations of postcolonial antisemitism. In *Kant's Jewish Problem*, Susan Meld Shell (2009, 332) analyzes Kant's relationship with his Jewish interlocutors, such as Marcus Herz, Moses Mendelssohn, and Lazarus Bendavid, who were pivotal in the dissemination of his thought in the 1770s. Königsberg was an important city for Jewish scholars, who regularly visited Kant, as he was never in Berlin. In the aftermath of the French Revolution, Kant's public attitude toward Judaism in his later writings became increasingly negative. While Mendelssohn, as a devout Jew, upheld the coexistence of the Jews as a minority within a larger civic community, Kant subscribed to a progressive view of history and, correspondingly, to the thesis of Christian supersession (Shell 2009, 312). Accordingly, Kant expected the enlightened Jewish vanguards, such as Herz, who was Kant's personal physician and closest intellectual correspondent when he was composing the *Critique of Pure Reason*, to become Jewish Christians. While Shell argues that Kant's stereotypes about Jewish people were not as serious as Johann David Michaelis's and Johann Gottlieb Fichte's antisemitism, Paul Rose (1992) proposes that Kant and Herder laid the intellectual foundation for "revolutionary antisemitism." Rose explains this as a secular form of hatred of the Jews, which constructed the German nation's and humanity's need for protection from both Jews and Judaism. Michael Mack (2003, 4), makes a similar argument, proposing that Kant attempts the "de-Judaization of Christianity." In the context of this secularized notion of Christianity, for Kant, the Jews "embody all that which hinders the construction of a perfect body politic in the here and now" (Mack 2003, 4). Mendelssohn's refusal to convert to Christianity was a case in point. Kant asserts that, "by the refusal to convert, Mendelssohn apparently meant to say: Christians, first get rid of the Judaism in *your own* faith, and then we will give up ours" (Kant 2001b [1798], 275). Instead of viewing antisemitism in general, and Nazi antisemitism in particular, as a reaction against the Enlightenment, as argued by Horkheimer and Adorno, Mack (2003, 1) unpacks the antisemitism of Enlightenment thought. He explains that, for Kant, "the Jews stood in opposition to reason's purity: they embodied the impurity of empirical reality" (Mack 2003, 3). While not contradicting the biblical account of creation and accepting the common origin of men, Kant viewed Jews as both corrupted and corrupting (Mack 2003, 40).

Along similar lines, J. Kameron Carter (2008, 81) outlines how, in *Anthropology from a Pragmatic Point of View*, Kant (2006 [1798]) merges the *Judenfrage* and the *Rassenfrage* to envision a modern political, racial, and theological world order in which the perfected race type—namely, the white race—prevails. In addition, Christianity is constituted as modernity's rational religion. Jews are considered by Kant as racial aliens, the internal others, who are present in the Prussian body politic and among the white nations of Europe. Kant (2006 [1798], 100) remarks, "Jews" are the "Palestinians living among us," thereby constructing a dualism between "occidental whiteness" and "oriental (Palestinian) Jewishness" (Carter 2008, 104). The so-called Oriental Jews, in Kant's view, as a "merchant people," have "earned the not unfounded reputation of being cheaters, on account of the spirit of usury" (Kant 2006 [1798], 100). Kant suggests that the "origin of [the] peculiar condition" of the Jews can be traced back to their religion and their scriptures, which enslave them to the material world (Carter 2008, 105). Instead of showing gratitude for hosting them, Jews resort to "outwitting the people under whom they find protection and even one another" (Kant 2006 [1798], 100). In contrast to more remote "alien nonwhite races," the "Jewish racial alien" lives in Europe; this made *Judentum* a source of anxiety for Kant, as the Jews could purportedly contaminate the Occidental body politic (Carter 2008, 105). Kant's concern is to reconceive civil society so as to regulate the Orient's presence within the Occident.

Unlike Fichte, who rejected giving Jews civil rights, Kant suggests that, to make themselves fit for citizenship and negotiate political modernity, Jews must follow Bendavid's example and become a "post-Jewish *Mensch*" to be part of a universal polity (Rose 2014, 41). Bendavid sees himself as acting in the Jewish interest and attempts to conceive, with Kant, a universal polity that would have a place for Jews through conversion (Rose 2014, 42). *Etwas zur Charackteristick der Juden* (On Jewish characteristics), which Bendavid authored in 1793, is considered one of the most controversial texts of *Haskalah* (the Jewish Enlightenment). In the text, Bendavid asserts that Jews could be rendered fit for citizenship in an enlightened state only through decapitation (Rose 2014, 15). To reconcile Jews with the Enlightenment's reason and citizenship, Bendavid draws on Kant's normative framework and his traditional opposition between Jews and Christians, yet he replaces this with a more secular opposition between Jews and *Bürger* (citizens), as well as the idea of Jew versus *Mensch* (human) (Rose 2014, 29–30). By linking civic with moral competence, the Kantian conception of humanity faces the difficulty of accommodating Judaism. Sven-Erik Rose (2014, 30) explains, "As a functioning ethical community that resists assimilation to the universal ethics of Kantian humanity, the Jews mark the possibility of a limit to this would-be universalist moral project." Jews frustrate the Kantian universalism, such that their assimilation into the enlightened polity and humanity is possible only through transforming the moral alterity of Jews, who must join the ranks of the "post-Jewish *Mensch*" (Rose 2014, 41). Ultimately, the Enlightenment cure for the Jewish "problem" is getting rid of the patient (Rose 2014, 42). Elad Lapidot (2020) similarly outlines how antisemitism is not about "thinking *against* Jews, but in thinking *of* Jews." Ironically, antisemitism is perpetuated by way of erasing the figure of the Jew in political and critical thought.

In response to claims that Kantian anticolonialism is rooted in his appreciation of cultural and religious diversity, I would highlight that, while Kant advocates for a pluralism of faith in the public space, he also praises

Bendavid's suggestion that Jews "adopt publicly the religion of Jesus," which would ultimately lead to "euthanasia of Judaism" (*Euthanasie des Judenthums*) (Kant 2001b [1798], 276). It is important to note that Kant is not calling for violence against the Jews but championing that, in adopting Jesus as a moral teacher, there would be only one shepherd and one flock (Carter 2008, 118). However, converting to Christianity by no means put an end to the so-called Jewish question, as the motives of the converted Jews were viewed with suspicion, and they were accused of betrayal and disloyalty to their values (Shell 2009, 333).

Aamir Mufti, too, outlines how "the Jewish question" epitomizes the conundrum of European Enlightenment. While the figure of the cultivated (*gebildet*) and assimilated German Jew seemingly exemplified the universal Enlightenment ideals of religious coexistence and tolerance, reinforcing notions of the "shared rational and moral nature of all human beings," the so-called Jewish question also posed a crisis for the secular liberal modern state (Mufti 2007, 43). Tolerance of Jewish existence and championing of Jewish emancipation in Enlightenment scholarship did not resolve the tension between the normative idea of the enlightened citizen-subject and the figure of *the Jew*, who is both cosmopolitan and citizen, "neither outsider nor one of us" (Mufti 2007, 51). The paradoxical relationship of the Jew to Enlightenment is that, to be the citizen of an enlightened state in which the majority of subjects are Christian, Jews must both affirm and negate their identity. This inflects, in Mufti's view, "the paradox of the Jewish intellectual attachment to, and critique of, the Enlightenment and its legacies" (Mufti 2007, 56).

Regrettably, Enlightenment antisemitism is mostly unaddressed in scholarship on Kant, such that Kleingeld (2011, 117) comments only in passing on Kant's antisemitism and his theory of national characteristics and points to the lack of academic literature on the topic. If one sees the Enlightenment as a "conceptual laboratory" (Rose 2014, 15) from which influential principles emerged, ideologies that endure in our times, then it is risky to underestimate or disregard the influence of Kant's antisemitism.

Finally, in my view, in highlighting the Enlightenment's alleged toleration of cultural and religious diversity, Kant's defenders fail to address how the very category of religion is a colonial construct. The universalization of the Christian understanding of religion led to the restructuring of Indigenous polytheistic belief systems into a monolithic faith (Asad 1993, 2003; van der Veer 2001). Moreover, the recognition of a religious multiplicity in no way prevented Christianity from being glorified as the highest form or essence of religion (van der Veer 2001, 49). Locke's "A Letter Concerning Toleration" (2003b [1689]), although often cited as an example of Enlightenment tolerance of religious diversity, interestingly excluded Catholics and atheists from its doctrine. In light of these considerations, Enlightenment thinkers' recognition of cultural and religious diversity as proof of their anti-imperialism obscures the ideological function of religious toleration in colonial discourses. Furthermore, Kant's support of monogenism over polygenism is consistent with his Christian faith rather than evidence of his commitment to racial equality.

Similarly, Diderot's writings warrant closer examination, as they cast significant doubts on his reputation as a defender of the oppressed and an anti-imperialist. Doris Garraway (2009, 209) explains how French philosophers such as Baron de Lahontan and Diderot used colonized figures to voice criticisms of European colonialism, covertly expressing their own grievances. Contrary to Spivak's claim that the subaltern cannot speak, French Enlightenment philosophers invoked the figure of the speaking native to criticize colonialism, Christianity, French politics, social practices, and moral order (Garraway 2009, 209).[11] Arguments that were politically and morally risky were ventriloquized through the speaking native, thereby avoiding censorship though the strategic deployment of the rhetorical device *prosopopoeia*. The European philosopher covertly communicates with the European public by speaking as a colonized native, through parodic caricatures and overdrawn imitations (Garraway 2009, 231). These fictional stagings, written at critical moments of French colonial expansion, symbolically allowed the "savage critic" to speak but did not necessarily empower them. Striking a cautionary note, Mira Kamdar (1990, 99) argues that in the staging of the native speaking subject, the Enlightenment philosopher speaks only for himself while claiming to give voice to the natives, ultimately privileging European agency. The benevolent representation of the native voice on the stage of world history ironically silences it (Kamdar 1990, 99). One could conclude that European Enlightenment philosophers' rhetorical opposition to colonialism was misleading (Garraway 2009, 210) insofar as the function of the "savage critic" was to galvanize support among the European public for a reformed "enlightened colonialism," rather than end of colonial relations. Furthermore, while drawing on the European reader's sympathy for native suffering, the voicing of resistance was not in the vernacular of the native but in the language of universal reason (Garraway 2009, 234). This Europeanization of the "savage critic," who is staged as an eloquent representative of

Enlightenment thought, ironically subverts the radicality of anticolonial opposition. Despite calls to take up arms against European despots, colonialism is ultimately redeemed as the motor of civilization in the name of commerce (Garraway 2009, 237).

Diderot's call for insurrection was a strategy to frighten the colonial rulers into enacting reforms, as well as to inspire the masses at home to rise against the moral and social order of the ancien régime (Garraway 2009, 237). Domestic class struggles and political dissent against unjust rule were projected onto the non-European world. The rhetorical defense of the colonized consolidated Enlightenment's self-conception as champions of cosmopolitan humanitarianism and universal rights (Garraway 2009, 238). Enlightenment claims about the universality of humanist values of equality, freedom, and reason were alibis for class-specific demands for political change (Garraway 2009, 238). In the name of solidarity with the oppressed natives, French Enlightenment philosophers consolidated the ethical validity of their theories of universal reason, individual freedom, and commercial exchange (Garraway 2009, 239). The trope of the "enlightened savages," the promise of reason's capacity to liberate people, and the expression of an imaginary global solidarity served to rebrand the coercive aspects of Enlightenment ideals of reason, progress, property, citizenship, and free trade (Garraway 2009, 239). A new discourse of imperialism emerged, which ironically derived its legitimacy from its supposed deployment by the natives. Thus, in response to the claim that the Enlightenment reconciled universalism with cultural diversity and religious tolerance, while being self-critical and self-corrective, I would counterargue that neglecting the imperialist nature of Kant's and Diderot's positions downplays the violence of their discourse.

Having said that, it would be remiss of me not to mention that Muthu (2003, 103) makes a compelling argument that thinkers such as Kant, Diderot, and Herder emphasized nonexploitative trade relations as a means to replace colonialism. Charitable interpretations, like Muthu's, allow for reading Enlightenment thinkers against the grain and discerning the differences among them.

The three hundredth anniversary of Kant's birth on April 22, 2024, was an event of global significance, even as it triggered debates about Kant and colonialism. Instead of simply dismissing Kant as racist or anticolonialist, I attempt in the next section to further substantiate the core argument of this book—namely, the normative dilemmas facing the postcolonial analysis of the European critical tradition. Given Kant's centrality in the

European Enlightenment, it is meaningful to engage with both his defenders and his critics. In the previous section, I focused on Kant's antisemitism and sexism to elaborate on how the champions of Enlightenment draw on its emancipatory norms to discredit postcolonial critique while dismissing the coercive aspects of the Enlightenment as inconsequential. My wager in this book is that it is impossible to rescue the emancipatory norms of the Enlightenment without addressing the systemic discriminatory aspects implicit in writings of one of the most vital protagonists of the Enlightenment—namely, Kant. To this end, I spell out my disquiet with the vindication of Kant proffered by his defenders.

Kant. The Che Guevara of European Anticolonialism?

Against accusations of racism and imperialism, Kant's defenders offer three main arguments to delink racism, colonialism, and cosmopolitanism. First, they claim that Kant's writings on race and gender are marginal to his main body of work. Second, they argue that it is anachronistic to use current standards to judge Kant's views. And third, they place focus on the alleged shift in Kant's later writings, which supposedly marked a move away from racist beliefs to a condemnation of colonialism.

Kant scholars distinguish between his serious theory and his prejudices, which they deem marginal to his political thought. In *Kant Was a Racist: Now What?* David McCabe (2019, 7) contends, "Kant's moral theory is not fatally infected by his views on race," which, in his reading, are "unambiguous in asserting equal status for all rational beings." McCabe concludes that ideas of autonomy and dignity, which can be traced back to Kant, are routinely employed to defend and protect vulnerable individuals and groups about whom Kant expressed discriminatory views. Consequently, Kant's moral theory should be disentangled from his regressive opinions. McCabe is also concerned that exposing students to Kant's racist views might discourage them from engaging with his more meaningful writings and ultimately would be detrimental to the discipline of philosophy.

In the same vein, and against the accusation that Kant was a pioneering theorist of modern scientific and biological racism, it is argued that his moral and political writings must be read separately from his texts on physical geography and anthropology. Flikschuh and Ypi (2014, 4) contend that colonialism "was marginal to Kant's body of philosophical work." In the same volume, Anthony Pagden (2014) draws attention to Kant's inconsistent use and confusion over the concept of colonialism. Meanwhile, Kleingeld (2007) and Ypi (2014) argue that when Kant abandons the idea of natural teleology, his philosophy of biology becomes independent of his moral theory, such that Kant's views mature from an incipiently colonial to an increasingly anticolonial conception. Along similar lines, Mari Mikkola (2011, 105, 107) suggests that his views on women, which are inconsistent with theories of human equality and dignity, should be "bracketed off" or "put to one side." It is further argued that when Kant uses gender-neutral terms such as *Mensch*, it indicates he also means women and thus treats them as equals. However, as Kleingeld (2019, 14) points out, unless explicitly indicated otherwise, the general term should be assumed to exclude both women and nonwhite people from Kant's reflections on ideas of autonomy and dignity, in which he primarily had white bourgeois men in mind. This alludes to the challenges of exculpating Kant's racism and sexism.

Despite differences and disagreements among Enlightenment thinkers about the origins of humans and the consequences of diversity of diet, climate, skin color, and practices, the Nigerian philosopher Emmanuel Chukwudi Eze (1997b, 5) observes that "Enlightenment philosophy was instrumental in codifying and institutionalizing both the scientific and popular European perceptions on the human race." From climate determinism to polygenism and Oriental despotism, many racial ideas and taxonomies were inventions of the presumed great minds of the Enlightenment. Considering that Kant is one of the most influential moral and political European thinkers, the centrality of racism and sexism in his thought ought not to be underestimated. Kant is undoubtedly one of the founding fathers of scientific racism and not some incidental offender (Eigen and Larrimore 2006). In *Observations on the Feeling of the Beautiful and Sublime*, Kant (2011 [1764], 61) remarked: "This scoundrel was quite black from head to foot, a clear proof that what he said was stupid." Racism here was not just based on empirical data; Kant purportedly used the evidence of Blackness to prove his scientific racism.

Kant (2007a [1775]) argues that all human beings contain *Keime* (germs, seeds), which, depending on the different physical environments across the planet to which human beings had migrated, developed in different but permanent ways to create different branches of humanity with varying cognitive and moral capacities. In his table of moral classifications, while the Americans are completely uneducable, the Africans can only supposedly be trained as slaves and servants through physical coercion and corporal punishment (Kant 2012, 320). Shifting the focus to India, Kant asserts that although the Hindus all look like philosophers, they are inca-pable of abstract thinking and hence they are unfit to be magistrates (Kant 1913, 877). In his 1782 lectures on *Physical Geography*, Kant claims that the peoples of India would be much happier under European rule (Kant 2020, 178; Kleingeld 2019, 7). In drafts of his anthropology lectures, he notes that "Americans and Negroes cannot govern themselves" (Kant 1913, 878) and they "seem to be made to serve others" (1997, 363). In his view, the arduous working conditions on the so-called Sugar Islands are conducive to them (Kant 2020, 421). Mills (2018, 13) argues that for Kant, only those capable of autonomy—namely, white men—qualify as humans in the full sense, while those ("natural slaves") who are incapable of dignity, autonomy, and self-legislation were *Untermenschen*, or sub-people. Although he had never set foot in Africa, Asia, or the Americas, Kant recycled stereotypes and prejudices about non-European peoples and cultures and offered a strong philosophical justification of the superior/inferior classification of the "races of men," even as he made proclamations of moral equality and the inviolable dignity of all humans (Eze 1997a, 115, 128–29).[12] Causally linking skin color, climate, diet, and characteristics such as morality, intelligence, and character, Kant concludes that non-European peoples are devoid of ethical principles and lack rational will (Kant 1913, 878). In his view, the only race that is capable of progress is the Europeans, such that "humanity is at its greatest perfection in the race of the whites" (Kant 1923 [1802], 316).

In addressing the dismissal of racism and colonialism as trivial in Kantian scholarship, Eze details how Kant engaged with race in both the precriti-cal and critical periods of his philosophical career (Eze 1997a, 116–19). The tendency to downplay Kant's racial theories may arise from the difficulty of reconciling his racist and imperialist views with his ostensibly more progressive ideas about cosmopolitan rights, which are crucial to con-temporary political theory. It is challenging for the Western philosophical tradition to confront the fact that even the Enlightenment's most cele-brated figures could have been deeply flawed. As Eze (1997a, 130) notes, "That which one ought to become in order to deserve human dignity sounds very much like Kant himself: 'white, European, and male.'"

Kant reinforced the idea of the intergenerational permanence of racial traits, which justified opposition to race mixing. Like Herder, who reviled miscegenation and believed it would produce a nonviable monstrosity (Kleingeld 2007, 577 fn. 12), Kant was against the alleged fusion of races that would lead to humans' becoming physically and psychologically similar. One detects a deeply racist ideology in this safeguarding of the diversity of the human species, which Muthu, meanwhile, presents as proof of Kant's anti-imperialist credentials. Regarding the groups referred to as Gypsies, Kant remarks that they come "from the scum of the earth," and despite their three hundred–year stay in Europe, their origins in the "Hindustani race" of India are evident in that they are "good-for-nothings." For Kant, the so-called Gypsies serve as proof of the constancy of races (Kant 2007b [1785], 158). In fact, Kant's contemporary Cornelius de Pauw rejected colonialism on the grounds that Europeans were so superior to the presumed savages that there was no hope for the supposed primitives ever to achieve parity with Europeans, rendering the civilizing mission a futile exercise (Harvey 2012, 202).

The intersection of modern moral and racial theory, according to Mills (1997, 70), can be traced to a common source: The racial contract underwrites the social contract. Skin color for Kant is not merely a physical characteristic; rather, the capacity to act rationally is racially determined, such that, consequently, our moral status is race-dependent, as well (Mills 1997, 53). Kant's egalitarianism in his moral and political writings only grants white men the status of personhood. Thus, there is no contradiction or tension in his hierarchy of races and his principles of universal equality. Egalitarianism becomes "equality among equals," with Black people and others being ontologically excluded from the fruits of the Enlightenment (Mills 1997, 58). Kant, in Mills's reading, does not consider Black people or women simply underdeveloped human beings; instead, for Kant, these sub-people's state is permanent, with no hope for improvement (Mills 2018, 11, fn. 4). Against the claim that Kant revised his position on race (but not gender), Mills argues that the implication of Kleingeld's periodization is that "Kant's commitment to a racial hierarchy extended over most of his professional life, covering the publication of the Groundwork and the three critiques." As Mills rightly asks, "Are we seriously to believe—especially for a philosopher so famous for the rigor and systematicity of his thought—that this invidious ranking of humanity was siloed, with no ramifications for his 'critical' theoretical claims over this period?" (Mills 2018, 11, fn. 4)

A frequently encountered defense is that Kant's sexist and racist views were typical of the eighteenth century, thus categorizing him as a man of his times. David Harvey (2012, 7), for instance, points out that it is anachronistic to denounce the racism, sexism, and Eurocentrism of Enlightenment thinkers. He further highlights that defenders of slavery and colonialism in fact mocked the naïve humanitarianism and utopian egalitarianism of Enlightenment thinkers, who claimed that Africans, Native Americans, and Pacific Islanders shared a common humanity with Europeans (Harvey 2012, 7). However, as pointed out by Kleingeld (2019, 3), Kant departed from many other commonplace opinions, so it would not be unfair to expect him to stay true to his egalitarian moral principles instead of endorsing the prevalent, concurrent sexist and racist views. Furthermore, the argument that Kant's racism is a reflection of the zeitgeist does not hold water if one considers, for instance, Kant's contemporary Anton Wilhelm Amo (ca. 1703–ca. 1759), who was the first Black academic and philosopher in Germany, tutoring in Jena and Wittenberg. In 1734, Amo defended a philosophy dissertation at the University of Halle in Saxony, written in Latin and entitled "On the Impassivity of the Human Mind" (see Amo 2020 [1734]). A dedicatory letter was appended from the rector of the University of Wittenberg, Johannes Gottfried Kraus, who praised "the natural genius" of Africa, its "appreciation for learning," and its "inestimable contribution to the knowledge of human affairs" and of "divine things" (quoted in Smith 2013). Unlike Kant, Kraus does not disqualify and devalue Amo based on his skin color, proving that Kant's racism cannot be explained merely in terms of the zeitgeist.

Against the argument that Kant was merely a product of his era, Robert Bernasconi (2003, 14) points out that Johann Friedrich Blumenbach objected to some of Kant's racial remarks against the Tahitians, but this did not lead Kant to retract them. Indeed, Kant had access to contradictory accounts about non-Europeans, but he consciously reinforced the stereotypes propagated by James Tobin, a proslavery advocate, rather than drawing on James Ramsay, a prominent opponent of slavery (Bernasconi 2003, 15; Lu-Adler 2023, 221). We must hold Kant accountable for not denouncing chattel slavery, as this was one of the most urgent issues of his day. Just as Kant was silent on many other moral issues of his times, perhaps the reluctance to acknowledge Kant's racism comes from the failures of some of his most prominent defenders in their own work—for example, Jürgen Habermas's lack of engagement with colonialism or John Rawls's disregard of racism and sexism.

Given the gap of eighty years between Kant's writings and the Berlin Conference of 1885–86, critics claim Kant's intellectual contribution to German colonialism is overestimated. In the words of Flikschuh and Ypi (2014, 3), "Even the claim that Kant's arguments would serve the interests of ruling elites would be hard to make since Prussia had no colonies of its own." This is inaccurate, as the colonial missions of Brandenburg-Prussia date back to the late seventeenth century and continued through the mid-eighteenth century, when the Brandenburg Africa Company was involved in the Atlantic slave trade and signed "treaties of protection" with local chiefs in present-day Ghana (van der Heyden 2001; von Mallinckrodt 2016). Although the German colonial period is officially viewed as having spanned from 1884 to 1918, rulers of Prussia, such as Friedrich Wilhelm, Duke of Prussia, held colonial aspirations as early as the seventeenth century, having established a foothold in western Africa, which was a hub for the transatlantic slave trade. It was not for lack of ambition that the Brandenburg-Prussian colonial attempts were unsuccessful; rather, the British, French, and other European commercial rivals thwarted their efforts.

Flikschuh and Ypi's narrow framing of colonialism ignores two important aspects. First, Orientalist scholarship produced by German Indologists (Pollock 1993) and German colonial fantasies (Zantop 1997) played an important role in influencing colonial discourses beyond Germany. In neither case did Germany have direct colonies. Yet German scholars and discourses had a profound influence on colonial politics not only in Asia and Africa, but also in the Americas. In my view, the influence of Kant's racist and imperialist writings goes beyond the limited parameters proposed by his defenders. Just as critical discourses of universal human rights, transnational justice, and global democracy function as alibis for contemporary operations of neocolonialism, Kantian cosmopolitanism sugarcoated the bitter nature of empire.

In the face of undeniable textual evidence, Kant's defenders concede that Kant initially expressed racist beliefs but contend that he revised his ideas on slavery, colonialism, and the hierarchy of races, which, they complain, is disregarded by his critics. As an example, Kleingeld (2007, 575) asserts that Kant improved his position during the 1790s and had second thoughts on race in the middle of his critical period. She admits that in his early writings, Kant endorsed proslavery views and defended racial hierarchy; however, rather than dismissing Kant as a "consistent inegalitarian," she sees him as an "inconsistent universalist" (Kleingeld 2007, 576) or, more recently, as an "inconsistent egalitarian" (Kleingeld 2019, 11). However, in my view, earlier ideas of race did not disappear but were recalibrated within discourses of cosmopolitanism, with Kant simply adapting his theory to a new phase of imperialism. As noted earlier, Kant never gave up the concept of *race* as a biological or moral category and was emphatically against race mixing as unnatural (Kant 1913, 879), claiming that "half-breeds are not much good" (Kant 1913, 598). Despite all contradictions and inconsistencies, Kant considered race an unchangeable biological fact that could not be influenced through education or other factors. Consequently, normative equality is withheld from so-called Gypsies, Orientals, Amerindians, and Black people, who receive differential treatment (Lu-Adler 2023, 5).

Furthermore, it seems to me, one should read Kant's racism together with his sexism, his misogynistic thoughts on women's incapacity to reason, and their lack of moral character (Kant 1907 [1798], 303–330). In fact, in a recent publication, even Kleingeld (2019, 3) agrees that on the issue of sexism, Kant did not have second thoughts, and the virtues Kant attributes to nonwhite peoples allude only to men and not to nonwhite women. Kant compares groups who allegedly have similar dispositions, such as "children, savages, women" (Kant 1913, 101) and "children, the common people, savages" (Kant 1913, 693). This indicates an intersectionality of racism and sexism in his writings. If Kant's racism and sexism are inextricably linked, then arguing that Kant changed his views on the intellect and character of non-Europeans but did not revise his stance on women as incapable of reason implies that he did not alter his beliefs on the superiority of white men or inferiority of nonwhite women.

Despite evidence to the contrary, Kant is defended as an egalitarian and emancipatory thinker who insisted that human beings have a moral obligation not to accept any inferior status thrust upon them (Flikschuh and Ypi 2014; Muthu 2003). Kant's cosmopolitanism and his idea of Enlightenment are considered informed by his reflections on resistance to servility. This disregards that Kant's objection to the brutality of European colonialism is offset by his firm rejection of anticolonial revolutions (Pagden 2014, 38, 40–41). Kant proclaimed that colonial conquest cannot be challenged, even if territory was acquired through force (Kant 1999 [1793], 299). He was categorically against restorative justice and the rectification of historical wrongs, arguing that invoking past grievances obstructs building trust among nations (Kant 1991b [1795], 94, 1991c [1797], 152). Kant condemned the displacement of Indigenous peoples by colonizing their land, but once this had happened, he maintained that the native inhabitants had no right to revolt against colonial misrule or to advocate for self-determination (Kant 1999 [1793], 82). Following this logic, all independence movements are illegitimate in Kant's eyes; thus, the anticolonial political actions initiated by Mohandas Gandhi or Nelson Mandela would be considered unlawful. If one were to apply his ideas to contemporary issues, Kant would have categorically rejected current demands for reparations to make amends for slavery and restitution of looted artifacts and human remains displayed in museums across Europe.

Drawing on historical and textual evidence, Inés Valdez (2019, 12) and Huaping Lu-Adler (2023, 22) conclude that, when Kant condemned colonial conflicts for the first time in 1795, he was not concerned with the plight of the colonized at the hands of European colonial powers or the racial and economic injustice inflicted on the natives. Instead, his focus was on intra-European conflicts in the colonies, clashes that threatened European stability and enduring peace. Although Kant did not object to any "healthy hostility" or conventional intra-European wars, he was particularly concerned about Britain's expansionism and its violent conflicts in the colonies with other European powers, such as France. He was concerned that this would lead to more widespread conflict on European territory (Lu-Adler 2023, 29; Valdez 2019, 48). Kant's fears seem to have come to fruition in what Hannah Arendt, Aimé Césaire, Frantz Fanon, and W. E. B. Du Bois call the "boomerang effect." Germany being stripped of its colonies after World War I by other European powers is deeply intertwined with the rise of Nazism. It is noteworthy that Kant self-censored and only indirectly addressed issues of warfare and international politics, as he wanted to avoid provoking the British (Valdez 2019, 35). Kant's anticolonialism coexisted with hierarchical views of race, meaning that his condemnation of violence against non-Europeans and the brutality of European conquest did not translate into an acceptance of the non-European societies as racially equal to European ones (Valdez 2017). Colonialism was condemned not because he recognized the humanity of non-European peoples, but because he was concerned about jeopardizing enduring peace among Europeans (Lu-Adler 2023, 40).

In response to persistent claims that Kant's later writings disavowed his early racist ideas, I argue that it is imperative to address the tensions between the rupture and reinscription of racial tropes in his early and later works. Earlier ideas about race do not disappear but are superimposed and remodeled within discourses of cosmopolitanism. In Kleingeld's (2007, 586) view, Kantian cosmopolitanism is incompatible with colonialism, as Kant grants full juridical status to nonwhite people, thus enabling them to sign binding contracts. However, those who refused to recognize the legitimacy of colonial law and revolted against it were labeled lawless and unjust enemies by Kant. While Kleingeld (2019, 8) interprets the following quote as evidence of Kant's anticolonialism and repudiation of racial hierarchy, I argue that Kant seems more concerned with the economic inefficiency of slavery than with the plight of the slaves: "The worst of this . . . is that the commercial states [viz., the European states] do not even benefit from their violence; for all their trading companies are on the verge of collapse. The Sugar Islands, that stronghold of the cruelest and most calculated slavery, do not yield any real profit" (Kant 1991b [1795], 107). One can only wonder what Kant's position might have been if slavery had been economically beneficial in the long term and had improved trade relations among European states in the colonies.

Kleingeld (2007, 591–92) proposes that Kant's change of mind may have been prompted by his general revision of his biological theory. As argued earlier, Kant never abandoned the idea of racial constancy—namely, *race* as a stable category. It is implausible that Kant suddenly overcame his biases and prejudices and achieved a state of race-neutrality or even postraciality while retaining the notion of *race* as a sui generis biological category (Lu-Adler 2023, 75, 111–12, 170). Just because most Enlightenment thinkers rejected polygenism and asserted a fundamental species equality of humankind does not imply that they abandoned their belief in the hierarchical nature of human races. Kant was evidently committed to a monogenetic Christian account of humanity's origins rather than to polygenism (Mills 2018, 7). Kant's rejection of polygenism and support of monogenism are insufficient to support his anti-imperialist credentials.

Like any thinker's, Kant's ideas changed over time, and any interpretation of his work must take this evolution into account. However, there is no textual evidence that Kant expressed remorse for his thoughts on the hierarchy of races; nor did he ever explain why he revised his earlier positions. If Kant had wanted to recant his earlier racist views, he could have distanced himself from his previous writings when they were republished in 1797 and 1799, which he did not (Bernasconi 2011, 300). Unlike many of his contemporaries, Kant did not condemn the institution of slavery or advocate abolitionism (Bernasconi 2011, 303). This undermines the link that Kant's defenders try to establish between his opposition to the slave trade and his abandonment of a racial hierarchy (Bernasconi 2011, 304). For instance, Kant explains to his students, "The Mandinka are the very most desirable among all Negroes up to the Gambia River, because they are the most hardworking ones. These are the ones that one prefers to seek for slaves, because these can tolerate labor in the greatest heat that no human being can endure" (Kant 2020, 1080). By asserting that no human (*Mensch*) can allegedly withstand the heat that the Mandinka can, Kant effectively excludes the Mandinka from the category of *human*.

How do Kant's defenders reconcile his racist remarks with his commitment to moral egalitarianism? How can they claim that Kant believed that Black people were capable of exercising autonomy, and, as human beings, are ends in themselves, while at the same time suggesting that the Mandinka, a West African ethnic group, make good slaves? How does one come to terms with Kant's support for a group that opposed abolitionism and his endorsement of slavery as late as 1788? Postcolonial thinkers reject Kant's rhetorical opposition to colonialism at face value. Europe's self-conception as a champion of cosmopolitan humanitarianism and its promise of nonexploitative commercial relations based on a plurality of human cultural values obfuscate the genocidal racist and sexist violence of colonialism. In the name of solidarity with oppressed natives, Enlightenment philosophers such as Kant secure the ethical validity of their theories of universal reason, individual freedom, and commercial exchange. These historical insights are instructive for understanding contemporary Western discourses on cosmopolitanism and humanitarianism, especially current articulations of transnational solidarity. (More on this in chapter 4.) Before moving to the conclusion, let us reexamine the claim that Kantian cosmopolitanism was an antidote to racism and colonialism, as this is central to arguments in contemporary political theory and philosophy that exonerate Enlightenment thought of malevolence.

Colonialism, Capitalism, Cosmopolitanism

The European Union (EU) is claimed to be the exemplary manifestation of Kantian cosmopolitan citizenship and the Geneva Conventions (Benhabib 2004, 31–35). Given the wide-ranging influence of the Kantian universal right to hospitality, in my view, it is worthwhile to critically engage with the blank spots in this doctrine. The differences in the treatment of Syrian and Ukrainian refugees, as well as the West's stance on the war crimes in Gaza since the start of the 2023 Israel-Hamas war, are once again proffered as evidence of betrayal of the Enlightenment. At the same time, while the postcolonial world criticizes the West for its double standards, it ironically also mobilizes Enlightenment principles of human rights and international law to demand accountability for war crimes and the plausible violation of the Genocide Conventions, as in the case of the proceedings instituted by South Africa against Israel before the International Court of Justice on December 29, 2023 (explored further in chapter 5).

In this section, I summarize in four points my objections to the claim that Kantian cosmopolitanism is anticolonial. First, I explore the link among international law, colonial violence, and global capitalism. Second, I outline how Kant's idea of "unjust enemy" violates the sovereignty of Indigenous peoples. Third, I argue that Kant's notion of "unowned objects" justifies European occupation and dispossession of the natives. And finally, given Kant's racial inegalitarianism, I examine how he does not explicitly grant cosmopolitan rights to non-Europeans.

Understanding the connection among modernity, colonialism, and capitalism helps answer the question "Who financed the Enlightenment?" (Baucom 2010; Poovey 2010). The interplay among capital, law, and colonialism justified violence against those without a state, senate, or treasury (Baucom 2010, 337). Ian Baucom argues that through Kant's cosmopolitanism, this law-money-violence nexus gains philosophical endorsement as a universal rule. As a convertible unit, money facilitates exchange across markets globally, enabling international law (Baucom 2010, 341). With money's accumulation, sovereign violence expands to protect it, leading to imperialism (Baucom 2010, 343).[13] Marx (1993 [1857–58], 524) had already diagnosed the expansionist tendency endemic to capitalism: "Capital by its nature drives beyond every spatial barrier. Thus the creation of the physical conditions of exchange—of the means of communication and transport—the annihilation of space by time—becomes an extraordinary necessity for it."

The cycle of money- and law-carried violence must inevitably target those who exist outside and beyond the civilizing legal and economic forces (Baucom 2010, 350). In *Perpetual Peace*, Kant emphasized the limits of the state's prerogative to make war against its enemies. Departing from this, in *The Metaphysics of Morals*, Kant startlingly stated that "there are no limits to the rights of a state against an unjust enemy [*ungerechten Feind*]" (Kant 1991c [1797], 155).[14] In this context, Kant explicitly mentioned pastoral and hunting peoples such as the "Hottentots" of the Cape, the "Tunguses," namely, the Tungusic-speaking indigenous nomadic peoples of Siberia and the Russian Far East, and "most native American nations" and warned that Europeans should not settle on their lands by force but should do so only by contract. He emphasized that they should not be taken advantage of because of their ignorance (an extremely paternalistic attitude, but for now let us focus on the larger problem). While Kant disapproved the act of coercing nonstate people to the civic condition (*bürgerlicher Zustand*) and statehood, he also spoke of "unjust enemies," who existed in the futile state of nature (Kant 1991c [1797], 155). Kant suggested that these presumed savages have an obligation to exit from their "wild and lawless freedom" and enter civilization (Kant 1991c [1797], 127). In the section on cosmopolitan right, Kant seemed to backtrack and limit the implications of his notion of an "unjust enemy" by arguing that instead of violence, the Europeans should enter into treaties with nonstate peoples. However, Kant's defenders, who highlight his insistence on "genuine agreement" and "informed consent," evidenced by his revised emancipatory position (Kleingeld 2014, 57), seem to disregard that Kant is faced with an impasse on how to enter into treaties without resorting to violence with those whom Europeans consider uncivilized. While Kant maintained that "lawless" people should be subordinated to law only "by treaty," their lawlessness by definition made them incapable of participating in binding contracts, and their condition of the stateless, acommercial, acontractual "war of all against all" represented a threat to the freedom of all nations (Baucom 2009, 135–36). This leads to the paradoxical and absurd situation that, while international law and cosmopolitan right should be extended only by treaty, given the impossibility of garnering the consent of the "lawless," in the interest of extending the operating spheres of global commerce, the use of violence becomes unavoidable (Kant 1991c [1797], 155). Kant's notion of an "unjust enemy" violates the sovereignty of Indigenous peoples and presents powerful counterevidence to the claim of Kantian anticolonialism.

Departing from his previous position that it was a matter of rational self-interest, Kant declared entry into civil society a duty of *Weltbürgertum*, thereby justifying juridical coercion (Shell 2009, 236). In the face of the social contract's unavoidability, Kant also authorized compelling others to enter a civil arrangement (Shell 2009, 237). As the state of nature lacks both right and justice (*status iustitiae vacuus*), the concept of *right* becomes unexecutable, even as it cannot be simply relinquished. Thus, the only available option is to establish civil society by coercion, if necessary. As Peter Niesen (2007, 92) explains, in Kant's view, "If it is right to do x, then the use of force in order to prevent the prevention of x is justified." Mutatis mutandis, to have a right implies having the capacity to put others under a legal obligation not to prevent the exercise of that right. If the law cannot be peacefully and civilly implemented, then violence is justified (Kant 1991c [1797], 55–61).

As Shell (2009, 238) explains, according to Kant, the formation of a state is a form of violence's "sublimation" (Kant 1991c [1797], 161) through which, paradoxically, violence becomes legitimate. In the face of the discontinuity between the individual and the international state of nature, Kant introduced the permissive "right of war" (*ius ad bellum*) that is justified when a state believes itself injured by another state (Kant 1991c [1797], 152). Here, the "unjust enemy" is one who "would make a peaceful condition among nations impossible, and instead eternalize a state of nature" (Kant 1991c [1797], 155). Shell (2009, 246) concludes that Kant would support regime change in purportedly failed or rogue states, whose sovereignty may be violated by so-called respectable members of the community of nations. Kant's cosmopolitan fantasy of free trade guaranteeing perpetual peace comes at the cost of reaffirming the nexus among law, violence, and money (Baucom 2009, 136). This is by no stretch of the imagination an anti-imperialist endeavor.

Another contradiction in Kant's supposed anti-imperialist cosmopolitanism is his conditional hospitality. In his discussion of *Weltbürgerrecht* (cosmopolitan ethics), Kant proposed an emerging global public sphere in which "a violation of rights in *one* part of the world is felt in *everywhere*" (Kant 1991b [1795], 108). Kant addressed the issue of the rights and duties of those who wished to cross borders and argued that all world citizens should have a right to free movement, which he grounded in the idea of a "right to the earth's surface" (Kant 1991b [1795], 106) that "the human race shares in common" (Kant 1991b [1795], 106). Cosmopolitanism was proposed as a guiding doctrine to protect people from war and to embed cosmopolitan right morally within the principle of universal hospitality, which encompassed the rights of strangers, as well as the duties and obligations of hosts. However, it was emphasized that the host can deny the guest hospitality "if this can be done without causing his death, but he must not be treated with hostility, so long as he behaves in a peaceable manner in the place he happens to be in" (Kant 1991b [1795], 106).

Kant's cosmopolitan law, it is argued, protects nonstate peoples, who did not come under the purview of international law (Niesen 2007, 94). The conflict between Indigenous populations and European explorers resulted from the claim of first occupancy/acquisition (*prima occupatio*), such that Europeans demanded that the natives recognize the European dominion over "unowned" land. Kant thwarted European justifications for colonialism, according to which a settler could lay claim to "unowned" territory by putting restrictions on both permissive law and universal hospitality. According to Kant's cosmopolitan law, there existed "no permissive law for the appropriation of unowned territory beyond the borders of one's state," thereby preventing colonial abuses (Niesen 2007, 95–96).

A counterargument against this progressive interpretation of Kantian cosmopolitan law is to consider Kant's doctrine on private law and property rights. Kant attributes to a person an innate right of freedom by virtue of which one may take into one's exclusive possession an object of one's choice. This must be reconciled with the choice of others to acquire property. Kant consequently emphasizes the universal duty of state entrance, which is the only way to adjudicate between conflicting property claims. In my view, there is an undeniable link between Kant's insistence on the coercible duty of state entrance and the justification of settler colonialism. Although in the *Doctrine of Right* Kant denounces land acquisition by Europeans in the colonies, he also emphasizes the moral necessity of state entrance, which is both unconditionally valid and coercively enforceable (Flikschuh 2017, 41). Kant does categorically reject attempts by European settlers to force nomadic peoples in the colonies into a civil condition, but this contradicts his understanding of state entrance as a universal "coercible duty." Kant warns that European settlement must be done not by force but by contractual transfer. However, to be a party to contractual transactions, nomadic people must be juridical equals, which is possible only through state entrance. Flickschuh's claim that because nomadic people do not make reciprocal property claims, they are exempt from the duty to enter the civil condition is unconvincing, because Kant approves of European settlers' entering into contractual transactions with nomadic people. This implies that the latter are in the orbit of property rights and thereby of property conflicts and the civil condition. In my reading, the moment nomadic people are granted property rights and agency to enter into contractual transfer, state entrance becomes mandatory. In contrast to Flikschuh, I would argue that it would go against the universality of Kantian thought if he were simply to exempt nomadic peoples from this moral necessity of state entrance and allow them to live in "wild and lawless freedom" (Kant 1991c [1797], 127) but nevertheless extend them property rights. The first-acquisition claims of nonsedentary pastoral peoples thereby contradict their exemption from obligation to state entrance. Property and territorial rights are nonexistent outside civil society. Subsequently, nomadic peoples cannot be a party to contractual transfer without state entrance. Kant's cosmopolitanism and his insistence on state entrance converge, insofar as they both favor European capitalism and colonialism with the idea of private property as the underlying justification. In fact, Kant repeatedly insists that those who violate their duty to leave the state of nature and enter into the civic condition "do wrong in the highest degree by willing to be and to remain in a condition that is not rightful" (Kant 1991c [1797], 122). Making exemptions and adding caveats to this universal norm would forfeit its validity and legitimacy. Thus, even though Kant seemingly censures European acquisition of land in

the colonies and seems to be circumspect about cultural differences regarding ideas of land and property in non-European societies, the universality of the duty of state entrance ultimately justifies settler colonialism
and the appropriation of "unowned" territory. The duty to enter the civic
condition is linked to Kant's view of the state as a universal moral necessity. For Kant, it is a moral duty to move from the unregulated state of nature to the state of law. Exceptions and limits to the universal idea would
disrupt the entire system of thought, making it impossible to justify transnational trade and commerce. When Kant scholars encounter an inconsistency in the Kantian system, they often suspend the universal validity of
his norms and propose exceptions. In chapter 5, I outline why the Kantian
norms of sovereignty and international law are worthy of preservation
but also require reevaluation within the postcolonial framework. An illustrative example of this is the dispute around the International Criminal
Court's jurisdiction over Gaza.

Finally, Kant's insistence on the right to temporary visitation without
the privilege of a permanent stay is seen as another progressive aspect of
cosmopolitan law. Given that the typical beneficiaries of hospitality were
European explorers, missionaries, traders, and administrators, when it
came to qualifying the right to remain temporarily or even be expelled,
it is argued, Kant was safeguarding the natives against European abuses
(Niesen 2007, 90). Niesen suggests that, unlike the common understanding of cosmopolitanism as a principle of global citizenship or protection
for the poor and needy seeking refuge, Kant's idea of the right to hospitality was an antidote to colonial expropriation.

Expanding on this interpretation of cosmopolitanism as a critique of
European colonialism, Seyla Benhabib (2004) focuses on the role of hospitality in refugee protection. Kant explicitly granted only those individuals
who were members of states cosmopolitan rights. With respect to stateless
people, Kant argued that a sovereign is entitled to withdraw all protections
and make a subject "an outlaw within his boundaries" (Kant 1991c [1797],
146). Whether such stateless people then qualify as bearers of cosmopolitan rights is open to speculation, as Kant did not directly address this
issue. Benhabib (2004, 31–35) sees Kant's provision of granting the right to
hospitality to an endangered person as a precursor to the Geneva Conventions' principle of non-refoulement. Further, it is a fundamental principle
of international law that prohibits the forcible return of refugees or asylum
seekers to a country where they are liable to be subjected to persecution
(Altman 2017, 194). In Benhabib's view, the EU, with its federalism, open

borders, and supranational rights, embodies the practical manifestation of Kantian cosmopolitan citizenship.

In the face of the plight of refugees, others denounce the EU for not being Kantian enough (Gani 2017, 428). It is emphasized that, for Kant, hospitality is not merely an expression of charity or philanthropy but a legal right of all human beings. Thus, while Kant focused on Europeans as "inhospitable (host-harming)" guests in his contemplations on international hospitality and did not focus on the abused hosts when reflecting on the ethics of hospitality, contemporary scholars primarily concentrate on the "unwanted guests," such as migrants and refugees (Gani 2017, 428). Niesen argues that while Kant's conditional hospitality attempted to protect non-European hosts against European guests, it is now misconstrued as discriminating against non-Europeans. Benhabib (2004, 37) also self-critically concedes that her arguments are somewhat anachronistic; Kant was concerned not with refugees but with the regulation of European colonizers, so his cosmopolitanism addressed "the Enlightenment preoccupation of Europeans to seek contact with other peoples and to appropriate riches of other parts of the world."

Jasmine Gani (2017, 443) argues that, with non-Europeans seen only as hosts and not as guests, Kant "fails to provide an epistemology of hospitality for the non-European visitor." Given that, according to Kant, laws can be applied only to those capable of reason—and considering that he deemed nonwhite people irrational and outside what he defined as civilized norms—he did not include them in his discussions of cosmopolitan law. Perhaps this is why the nonwhite visitor, who bears no legal or moral standing in Enlightenment epistemology, was not incorporated into this principle of universal hospitality proposed by Kant.

Ironically, the limitations on hospitality aimed at curbing European abuses in the colonies are now weaponized to deny non-Europeans the right to hospitality (Gani 2017, 444). The scrapping of the EU's Operation Mare Nostrum, a search-and-rescue effort in the Mediterranean, violates not only Kant's stipulation that no traveler whose life is endangered should be refused entry, but also the obligation of the host to at least acknowledge the traveler's claim for hospitality, even if it is eventually rejected (Gani 2017, 444). With thousands of refugees dying at Europe's doorstep, Gani (2017, 445) questions whether the EU's migration policy is "really a violation of the Kantian hospitality it claims to uphold, or is it in fact a devastatingly accurate mirroring of his cosmopolitan law and its erasure of race?"

Defenders of Kant who cite his cosmopolitanism as evidence of his anticolonial stance must address inconsistencies, especially in light of what is referred to as the Syrian refugee crisis. The plight of the refugees and the stateless have brought Enlightenment values of hospitality and cosmopolitanism, which, as noted by scholars such as Habermas (2011), are central to EU principles, into sharp focus. As the crisis worsened, Germany suspended the Dublin regulation in 2015 and opened its borders, but its touted *Willkommenskultur* (welcome culture) was short-lived. The disagreement within the EU regarding the extent of European responsibility in the face of the humanitarian crisis, the Brexit vote, the EU-Turkey deals to prevent the entry of refugees, and the demonization of refugees highlights the unfinished task of decolonizing Europe. A striking example is the exploitation of gender politics to vilify postcolonial migrants, as in the burkini ban or the call for the deportation of so-called rapefugees, an extremely racist neologism.[15] Sexual assaults by some migrants in the city of Cologne in 2015 weakened support for accepting refugees in Germany. While some feminists opposed the use of racial stereotypes (Reclaim-feminism 2016), many Germans supported deportations and "respect for women" courses for Muslim men (Emma 2015), contributing to the continuing instrumentalization of gender politics to legitimize xenophobia. Unfortunately, rising right-wing violence against migrants has not received similar scrutiny. European perceptions of Muslim immigrants as threats to cherished liberal values mobilize gendered vulnerability to justify shaming non-Western cultures as misogynistic while avoiding accounting for European bigotry. The differences in the treatment of Syrian and Ukrainian refugees, with the latter being considered more deserving because they purportedly share European values, serve as an instructive example of the fickleness of European cosmopolitan principles.

Jacques Derrida's concept of "unconditional hospitality" targets the lacuna in Kantian cosmopolitan ethics, which excludes non-Europeans from cosmopolitan law. In his deconstructive reading, Derrida traces elements of hostility intrinsic in Kantian reflections on hospitality and speaks of "hostipitality" (i.e., hostile hospitality) in reference to Kant's "conditional hospitality" (Derrida 2000, 3, 15). Given that hospitality can be denied to purported miscreants, such as the male refugees in Germany who are accused of disrespecting their hosts by attacking their women, Kant probably would have supported the deportation of these troublemakers, who were perceived as threatening order and security in Europe. In an astute analysis of Kant's inconsistent ethics, Derrida proposes that a truly cosmopolitan ethics entails absolute hospitality, which is unconditional and thus not contingent on the guest's fulfilling certain criteria or duties to receive it (Derrida 2005, 42). This restructures the relationship between the host (who may be unprepared and ill-equipped) and the guest (who may be unexpected and uninvited). Only when the host becomes the hostage of the guest are compassion and proximity possible (Derrida 2000, 9, 17–18). It is the guest who makes the host ethical, and in playing the host, one must accept the risk of hospitality by relinquishing mastery over one's house (Derrida 2000, 10–14).

The presence of postcolonial migrants has become a test for Europe's commitment to the Enlightenment principles of humanitarianism and cosmopolitanism. Contrary to the Derridean ideal, the European system of processing refugees rests on determining who is entitled to enter Fortress Europe and therefore has the right to live. The category of *deserving refugees*, who may integrate to be *good enough* citizens, raises critical questions about ethics in a postcolonial world. To counteract the pervasive disenchantment with the lofty principles of the Enlightenment necessitates rescuing norms of cosmopolitanism and humanitarianism from the cynical approach of EU migration policy. The recurring Mediterranean boat disasters are a grim reminder that not only the migrants, but also the Enlightenment's ideals, are endangered in postcolonial Europe. The inhospitable politics of EU countries epitomize not an aberration but an exemplification of coercive cosmopolitanism. Ironically, in reminding Europe of its commitment to the ideals of cosmopolitanism and humanitarianism, postcolonial refugees and migrants become enforcers of Enlightenment principles and agents of decolonizing Europe.

Mission Impossible. Decolonizing Enlightenment

As outlined in this chapter, Enlightenment thinkers did indeed occasionally reproach excesses and abuses of European colonialism, even as most of them were deeply convinced of European superiority and virtues of reason and of the industriousness and morality of white men, and consistently promoted commercial colonialism. If these do not qualify as characteristics of a racist and imperialist attitude, then, of course, it is understandable that for defenders of Enlightenment, eighteenth-century thought was egalitarian and progressive. This alludes to a fundamental disagreement concerning the understandings of racism and imperialism. As I have painstakingly demonstrated, Enlightenment thinkers were constantly adapting and re-calibrating their ideas and theories to the rapidly shifting situation in the colonies without necessarily giving up their Eurocentric and androcentric positions. For instance, certain efforts to regulate slavery by formulating slave codes—for example, by West Indian slave owners—were part of a larger effort to extend and continue the colonial project. The aim was to consider how "emancipation could sustain, and even advance, colonial enterprise" (Agnani 2013, 140).

Defenders of the Enlightenment famously allude to the antislavery movement as a prime example of its anti-imperialist impulses. Despite widespread condemnation of the brutality of slavery, which violates Enlightenment principles of autonomy, liberty, and equality, slavery for a long time was defended as a "necessary evil" (Harvey 2012, 155–56). Framed in terms of economic and climatic exigencies, slavery was, for instance, justified via the argument that white workers could not survive harsh tropical climates and excessive heat. The high death rate of Europeans justified the enslavement of Africans, who were considered immune to the colonies' harsh climate. The inhuman treatment and brutal conditions that resulted in the deaths of thousands of slaves were unsuccessful in provoking support for abolishing slavery (Harvey 2012, 165). Lofty rhetoric of how slaves could benefit from civilizing influences through contact with Europeans obscured the advantages of slavery for the European economy and standard of life. The more important plantation economies became for Europe, the more racial capitalism (Robinson 1983) influenced European politics. This was a precursor to globalization, neoliberalism, and the rise of the corporate classes.

In the aftermath of the French Revolution, while the Declaration of the Rights of Man and of the Citizen was translated into Creole and copies were available to all men older than eighteen in Saint-Domingue, it was guaranteed that France's constitution would not be applied to the colonies (Agnani 2013, 141). This safeguarded white planters' interests. After all, if the universal character of the Rights of Man were to be truly implemented, the economic interests of the planters would be jeopardized (Agnani 2013, 145). This is an excellent example of what Partha Chatterjee (2011, 250) calls the rule of colonial difference, wherein the right to declare the colonial exception is an imperial prerogative.

The abolition of slavery in British and French colonies was replaced by a ruthless system of indentured labor. While symbolically vindicating the European self-representation as "humane," the persistence of Africa's slave trade provided further justification for its colonization. Thus, even as the abolitionist movement is repeatedly cited as an example of the Enlightenment's emancipatory impulses, I would read it more as an example of how Europeans once again emerged as ethical subjects by weaponizing discourses of freedom and humanity. The call for the boycott of slave-produced goods was to exonerate Europeans, who staged themselves as enlightened consumers. These paternalistic humanitarian efforts were at the heart of the construction of what is referred to as responsible imperialism.

Accordingly, contrary to Muthu's reading, Agnani outlines how Diderot's anticolonialism was undergirded by a vision of consensual colonialism. While rejecting and censuring colonial abuses, Diderot hoped that the commingling of colonizers and colonized would consolidate the commercial bonds. The hope was for a benign empire or what Agnani, following Diderot, calls *douce colonisation* (sweet colonization), which would be more effective than a cruel and coercive form of colonialism. It was premised on the alleged uncivilized societies' acknowledging the superiority of European norms and agreeing to a mutually beneficial arrangement in which they followed the European example (Harvey 2012, 203). The argument that Enlightenment thinkers celebrated difference and diversity does not negate the fact that many of them were staunchly opposed to miscegenation, viewing it as a degeneration of the white race. Nor does it diminish their commitment to progressive universalism or Eurocentrism. Remarking on the "Bible of anticolonialism"—namely, *L'histoire des deux Indes*—Agnani unpacks the ambivalence of the Enlightenment, given that it supposedly inspired both Toussaint Louverture's anticolonialism and Napoleon's fervor for conquest (Agnani 2013, 45).

Despite textual and historical evidence of Enlightenment racism, sexism, antisemitism, and colonialism, there is a concerted effort to disregard, dismiss, and erase its pernicious elements to present a benign, contradiction-free, and sanitized theory in an attempt to redeem universal claims and obscure racist particularism (Bernasconi 2003, 15–16). The effort in this chapter has been to hold Enlightenment thinkers accountable for their discriminatory ideas without advocating for their censorship or boycott. When one is confronted with the violent and coercive history of modern European thought, it might seem logical to presume that thinkers such as Kant cannot be redeemed and one should symbolically and literally take him off of the pedestal. However, this is exactly where postcolonial intervention goes beyond naysaying, faultfinding, and a politics of blame. As I will argue in the subsequent chapters, when it comes to the Enlightenment and its legacies, postcolonial feminists speak from a site of contradiction that cannot be evaded (Spivak 1989, 208). I agree with Spivak when she argues that the feminist burden lies in the fact that it is indebted to the masterly Kantian framing of critique as opposition to dogmatism (Spivak 1989, 209). In my view, decolonization is about neither negating nor surpassing Enlightenment thought. Instead, it is an act of "critical intimacy," an acknowledgment of the double bind that postcolonial-queer-feminist approaches are circumscribed *and* enabled by the Enlightenment. The irony or the ambivalence that postcolonial feminism as critical theory faces is that we cannot not "love the structure that we criticize" (Spivak 1989, 214). Thus, even as we denounce Enlightenment thinkers such as Kant for their antisemitism, racism, and sexism, we must accept that we ironically learn from those whom we condemn. If postcolonial feminism finds in Enlightenment thinkers a fall guy, it ends up congratulating itself as a know-it-all. In contrast to this facile gesture, we must acknowledge that the unexpected lessons from our adversaries can be paradoxically empowering (Spivak 1989, 215).

This is exactly what Charles Mills does in his effort to radicalize Kant by proposing a race-sensitive categorical imperative. Despite his scathing criticism, the attempt is to redeem Kant by proposing a "black radical Kantianism." Taking the question of whether Kantianism is conducive to an antiracist retrieval as a point of departure, Mills explains that his project is located in the "Afro-modern political tradition." This is different from premodern African political thought, which is not Black, given that categories such as *Black* and *Negro* are colonial inventions. Linking Black Marxism, Black Nationalism, and Black Feminism, the endeavor is the articulation of a "black radical liberalism" (Mills 2018, 2). A feminist and socialist revisionist Kantianism draws on Kant's own proclamation of the three "rightful attributes which are inseparable from the nature of a citizen"—that is, "lawful freedom," "civil equality," and "civil independence" (Kant 1991c [1797], 125) to combat sexism and capitalism. Kantian principles and ideals of autonomy, rule of law, and cosmopolitanism are reconsidered in light of a "modernity structured by racial domination" (Mills 2018, 3). Afro-modern thought not only contests but also draws on and modifies the emancipatory principles of the Euro-modern tradition. Kant similarly provides resources for a Black radical appropriation that allows for a "*race-sensitive* re-articulation" (Mills 2018, 7). This is not merely a purging of Kantian racism, but a "genuine, race-inclusive universalism" (Mills 2018, 22). A color-blind "bogus universalism" is rejected, which simply assimilates those who were previously denied the status of personhood into the social order without regard for the history or experience of racial domination (Mills 2018, 17). In contrast, Mills's revisionist framework seeks to bring about equality rather than simply presuming it (Mills 2018, 18). "Racial vindicationism" involves Black people unlearning racial deference while white people engage in a critical rethinking of "whiteness" as Kantian exercises that would enable an "ideal of a community of reciprocally respecting persons" to emerge (Mills 2018, 18). Mills thereby shows a way forward for postcolonial critical thought to decolonize the Enlightenment.

Kant was undoubtedly a brilliant thinker, and his writings are indispensable for anyone pursuing critical thought. Postcolonial theorists, who at times homogenize the Enlightenment by primarily focusing on its violent legacies, would profit from engaging with the arguments presented by Kant's defenders and by acknowledging the ambivalent legacies of Kant's thought. At the same time, advocates of Kant who seek to recuperate his political thought would do well to heed Foucault's (1984, 42) advice of freeing oneself of being *for* or *against* the Enlightenment and, in turn, its most important proponent, Immanuel Kant.

The Nobel Prize–winning economist Ronald Coase (see Tullock 2001, 205) famously remarked that if you torture the data, they will confess to anything. I propose that if we torment Kant's writings long enough, we can find sufficient evidence to prove that he was both a racist and an antiracist. And yes, it is indeed possible to be both. We have to aspire to be better Kantians than he was. I would argue that, although Kant violates his own principles, we must outdo him to become finer Kantians. As postcolonial thinkers, we should take Kant beyond his limits by reimagining his ideas of freedom, autonomy, and equality in a nonhierarchical, nonsexist, and nonracist manner. Instead of employing the contradictions between Kant's racism and sexism and his censure of colonialism to exonerate him, we must deploy Kant's principles in critical theories of decolonization. This is not about *doctoring* Kant to make him appear less racist or sexist; rather, the discrepancy between Kant's egalitarian understanding of the innate right to freedom and the specific racist and sexist arguments should both be addressed so he is neither accused of being more inegalitarian that he was nor excused for being less egalitarian than he was (Kleingeld 2019, 18). Only then can one avoid replicating his pernicious biases while making the best out of his emancipatory insights.

Foucault's quote from "What Is Enlightenment?" encapsulates the postcolonial dilemma of how to address the violent legacies of the Enlightenment while acknowledging that it also provides us with some of our most power-ful tools (Dhawan 2014). The accusation of being anti-Enlightenment is not limited to postcolonial theory. It extends to the first generation of the Frankfurt School, who were also criticized for their efforts to reveal the pernicious legacies of the Enlightenment. Taking inspiration from Jean Améry's notion of *Schicksalsverwandtschaft* (kinship of fate), the next chap-ter is devoted to investigating the unfinished conversations between post-colonial and Holocaust studies.

2

The Self-Barbarization of Europe

Enlightenment and Nazism

The *Dialectic of Enlightenment* is a strange book.—JÜRGEN HABERMAS, "The Entwinement of Myth and Enlightenment"

On October 9, 2019, a heavily armed man tried to storm the last remaining synagogue in the eastern German city of Halle, in Saxony. The community had previously requested police protection, but this was not provided by the city. Only a wooden door kept the gunman from firing at the fifty-two Jewish worshipers attending the Yom Kippur service inside. The thwarted gunman then shot a female passerby. Subsequently, the gunman trained his weapons on Kiez-Döner, a nearby kebab takeaway, where he explicitly went in search of Muslims. Wearing combat fatigues, he filmed the shooting and broadcast it for thirty-five minutes on the internet. During the trial, the accused denied the Holocaust—a criminal offense in Germany—and propounded conspiracy theories about Jews organizing the immigration of Muslims to destroy Germany (Weizman 2022). Espousing antisemitic, racist, and misogynist ideologies, he asserted that "attacking the synagogue was not a mistake, they are my enemies" (BBC 2020).

The intersectionality of hate was also on display on January 6, 2021, in Washington, DC, during the storming of the US Capitol. Carrying

Confederate flags, symbols such as "Work Brings Freedom" and "Camp Auschwitz" shirts (Sarna 2021), the violent mob, which included neofascists and white supremacists, also occupied, vandalized, and looted House Speaker Nancy Pelosi's offices and left her messages such as "Nancy, Bigo was here you bitch" (Krook 2021).[1] Hate crimes, including antisemitic, sexist, and racist incidents in the United States, hit a four-decade high in 2019. Previously, in August 2017 in Charlottesville, Virginia, during the violent "Unite the Right" rally, white supremacists carrying Confederate flags chanted slogans such as "You will not replace us" and "Jews will not replace us." The slogans refer to what is known as the white genocide conspiracy theory, perpetuated by white supremacists. They allege that there is a deliberate plot, masterminded by Jews, to promote miscegenation, nonwhite immigration, and interracial marriage, thereby leading to the extinction of the white race. It derives from a popular conspiracy theory promoted by the French writer Renaud Camus in his book *Le grand remplacement* (*The Great Replacement* [2011]), in which he argues that the mass migration of Black and Muslim immigrants and their demographic growth have ostensibly led an invasion by alleged alien cultures, which are replacing traditional European values.

As outlined in the introduction, on the one hand, postcolonial studies and the global South are being accused of antisemitism, while European societies and states stage themselves as champions of anti-antisemitism. On the other hand, we are witnessing a rising intersectionality of hate globally, which makes it imperative to consider racism, sexism, and antisemitism together. To combat the charge of what is referred to as postcolonial antisemitism, I want to draw attention to the long tradition in anticolonial thought and postcolonial studies of trying to precisely address the entanglements of different forms of discrimination. Frantz Fanon (1986 [1952], 122) astutely diagnosed these intertwining experiences when he wrote:

> At first thought it may seem strange that the anti-Semite's outlook should be related to that of the Negrophobe. It was my philosophy professor, a native of the Antilles, who recalled the fact to me one day: "Whenever you hear anyone abuse the Jews, pay attention, because he is talking about you." And I found that he was universally right—by which I meant that I was answerable in my body and my heart for what was done to my brother. Later I realized that he meant, quite simply, an anti-Semite is inevitably anti-Negro.

Earlier, W. E. B. Du Bois narrated how his visit in 1949 to the Warsaw Ghetto, the site of the valiant revolt of Jews against Nazism, made him reassess his understanding of racism and the color line (Du Bois 1952). In the introduction to *Orientalism*, Edward Said (1978, 27–28) notes that, in writing the history of Orientalism, he was covertly also writing about Western antisemitism, with Islamophobia being a "secret sharer" of antisemitism. His focus is on the European construction of the so-called Oriental Semites, which encompasses both Arabs and Jews. Here the West has played, and continues to play, a clandestine role in maintaining the division between Jews and Arabs by focusing on the Judeo-Christian tradition. Not only does the West produce these oppositions, but maintaining these divisions is central to the reinvention of the West after 1945 (Anijdar 2002, 19).

The year 1492, in which Christopher Columbus is credited with purportedly discovering the Americas and when systematic European colonization was unleashed, was also the year in which Jews were expelled from Spain and Portugal (Goetschel and Quayson 2016, 4). The colonization of what is called the New World was partly funded by resources plundered from Jewish and Muslim communities. Accordingly, in *The Origins of Totalitarianism*, a key work for postcolonial studies, Hannah Arendt (1962 [1951]) notes the entanglements of colonialism and Nazism. She draws attention to the presence of concentration camps built in the late nineteenth century by the Spanish in Cuba during the Ten Years' War (1868–78) and by the British during the Second Boer War (1899–1902) in present-day South Africa. Colonialism's racist and genocidal ideologies and practices established a precedent for Nazism. Arendt (1962 [1951]) characterizes this as imperialism's "boomerang effect," such that dehumanizing strategies in the peripheries eventually returned to infiltrate European domestic politics. In a similar vein, in *Discourse on Colonialism* Aimé Césaire (2000 [1950], 7) describes Nazism as *un choc en retour*, which can be translated as "return shock," "backlash," and "reverse effect" (Rothberg 2009, 36). Mahmood Mamdani (2001, 12) compellingly argues that the entanglements between the Herero genocide, committed between 1904 and 1908 in the German South West Africa colony (now Namibia), and the Holocaust go beyond similar race laws, forced labor, internment, and annihilation policy. The ideological overlaps and affinities allude to the larger colonial and fascist projects of social Darwinism and biopolitics.

In the last chapter of *A Dying Colonialism* (2007 [1959]), which unfortunately has received scant attention, Fanon highlights the significant role played by Algerian Jews in the anticolonial struggle. He decries the pitting of oppressed groups against one another by encouraging rivalry over experiences of suffering. Fanon focuses on the importance of aligning efforts in struggles against dehumanizing violence. This resonates with Said's (1992, 56–58, 88) focus on the Nakba (catastrophe), which refers to the mass displacement and dispossession of Palestinians during the 1948 Arab-Israeli War, as well as his rebuke of the Arab world for its refusal to recognize Israel. Said is as critical of Zionism as he is of the refusal to engage with the Holocaust in the Arab world. One of the responses to Said's multidimensional critique was censorship, both from Zionists and Arab Nationalists, an oft-neglected detail. Said (2001, 285) makes a concerted effort to connect the Jewish tragedy with the Palestinian catastrophe, aiming to enable reconciliation and establish common ground for coexistence by outlining the affinities between these experiences of violence, without flattening the uniqueness of particular suffering and the singularity of the Holocaust. An example of this cooperation is the West-Eastern Divan Orchestra, founded by the pianist Daniel Barenboim and Said, which brings together musicians from Israel and various Arab countries to promote understanding and dialogue through music.

This resonates with similar attempts in the past to foreground the structural entanglements between the shared experiences of dehumanization faced by the Roma, Sinti, and Jews in the Nazi concentration camps. Despite centuries of residence in Germany and Europe, neither the Jews nor the Sinti and Roma were protected from genocide. It is this recognition of a "kinship of fate" that led Simone Veil, a Holocaust survivor and then the president of the European Parliament, to remark at the commemoration of the memorial at the former concentration camp Bergen-Belsen: "How could one imagine that I wouldn't come, knowing that we have suffered together, that we have mourned our dead together, those who were burned in the crematoria, knowing that the ashes of all our parents are united. . . . [W]e have not always felt enough solidarity, the solidarity of shared misfortune. Everyone knows that in the camps—and this is probably the victory of the Nazis—we lived our fate separately and often suffered separately" (Dokumentationszentrum 2010; Heuss 2017). It is noteworthy that the Memorial to the Sinti and Roma Victims of National Socialism, located in Berlin, was created by the Israeli sculptor and artist Dani Karavan.

Regrettably, the principle of "kinship of fate" was not always adhered to, as evidenced, for instance, by the plight of the Palestinians, on the one hand, and the persecution of Arab Jews, on the other. Albert Memmi (1992), for example, outlines the ordeal of Mizrahi Jews who contributed to anticolonial struggles but then faced persecution in the newly decolonized Arab states. The rise of Arab nationalism and anti-Zionism subsequent to the establishment of the State of Israel in 1948 contributed to the discrimination against Mizrahi Jews. They were subjected to violence, pogroms, and, ultimately during the Arab-Israeli wars, large-scale expulsions. Ella Shohat (1988) also writes about the experiences of discrimination faced by Mizrahi and Sephardi Jews in both the Arab world and Israel. Likewise, Lewis Gordon (2016, 105) reminds us that "the prototypical term *raza* from which the word 'race' emerged was, after all, a Medieval Spanish word to refer to breeds of dogs, horses, Jews, and Moors (Afro-Muslims)." Jews of color and Afro-Jews underscore the diversity within the Jewish community and draw attention to intersectional identities (Gordon 2016, 106). This has similarly been addressed by Beta Israel (Ethiopian Jews) and Bene Israel (Indian Jews). These hyphenated Jewish postcolonial identities provide instructive insights into the challenges of linking Jewish, Holocaust, and postcolonial studies, as well as considering antisemitism and racism together against the backdrop of historical and contemporary violence. At the same time, it is imperative that the affinities between Jewish studies and postcolonialism go beyond a reductionist approach that focuses on the shared victim status of Jewish, Black, Muslim, and other postcolonial subjects and examine the singularities of each experience while highlighting structural entanglements (Goetschel and Quayson 2016, 3).

This chapter takes up this challenge. Instead of rendering colonialism marginal to Jewish studies and the Holocaust peripheral to postcolonial studies, it walks the fine line of understanding how the Enlightenment is linked to both colonialism and Nazism (Olusoga and Erichsen 2010). In my view, memory politics and geopolitics could be transformed through a simultaneous analysis of the entangled legacies of colonialism and the Holocaust and of racism and antisemitism. However, this is not a straightforward task, as there are concerted efforts to obstruct such "multidirectional memory" politics (Rothberg 2009).

The *Vergangenheitsaufarbeitung* (coming to terms with the past) in Germany was initially spearheaded by progressive forces in civil society, with Jürgen Habermas being a key figure. The *Historikerstreit* (historians' dispute) of the 1980s and the subsequent acceptance of the singularity of the Holocaust were momentous in coming to terms with the Nazi past. Regrettably, from the very beginning colonialism was excluded and silenced in the German narrative of accountability and responsibility. Postcolonial studies' efforts to rectify this shortfall are considered an affront by some

Germans, who understand themselves as *Weltmeister der Erinnerungspolitik* (world champions of the politics of memory). Those who attempt to address instances of colonial genocide are accused of relativizing the Holocaust (Doughan et al. 2022a). Memory politics function as an excuse for intimidating the global South and racialized minorities in Germany and Europe. The viewpoint of the perpetrators is dominant. Both the German state and civil society insist that non-Jewish minorities in Germany align themselves with the German perpetrators of the Holocaust rather than with the Jewish victims (Doughan et al. 2022b). Any attempt to explore affinities between racism and antisemitism and entanglements between colonialism and the Holocaust invites censure. Jean Améry's concept of *Schicksalsverwandtschaft* would be unacceptable from this perspective.

The champions of Enlightenment contend that the supposed irrationality of racism, sexism, and antisemitism ostensibly can be overcome by Enlightenment norms of liberalism, equality, and tolerance. The Holocaust is presented as evidence of the breakdown of reason, while the defeat of Nazi Germany is proof of the victory of the Enlightenment and its values of justice, democracy, and human rights. The irrationality of the Holocaust lies in the fact that the so-called final solution went against the material interests of the German nation, yet it was carried out. The solution to Nazi totalitarianism is Enlightenment in the form of the triumph of reason over irrational, genocidal antisemitism. It should come as no surprise that the staunchest advocates of the Enlightenment, such as Habermas, Seyla Benhabib, and Susan Neiman, are all Kantians.

Adornian, poststructuralist, and postcolonial censures of the Enlightenment and, in turn, of reason are considered particularly dangerous because they allegedly risk the resurgence of irrationality. This chapter counters these claims by arguing how Enlightenment reason is not a straightforward antidote to alleged irrational racism, sexism, and antisemitism; rather, the Enlightenment rationalizes colonial and fascist violence. As I argue, the Enlightenment is not just a fail-safe solution to the historical crimes of colonialism and Nazism but, to some extent, also the origin of the problem. Sometimes the obvious must be stated again and again, for it is disavowed repeatedly.

This chapter sets up three tasks. First, it outlines the affinities between the first generation of Critical Theory and postcolonial studies in their overlapping diagnosis of the Enlightenment being at the root of the genocidal violence of colonialism and the Holocaust. It thus continues with some of the core concerns of the chapter 1 in tracing the relation between

Enlightenment and violence. This also serves the purpose of understanding the intersections among racism, antisemitism, sexism, and other forms of discrimination. Second, the chapter examines how the Habermasian dismissal of Horkheimer and Adorno's arguments, as summarized in the chapter's epigraph, is also deployed to disqualify poststructuralist and postcolonial contestations of the Enlightenment. This is particularly significant because the overlapping of concerns between the first generation of the Frankfurt School, poststructuralism, and postcolonialism remain undertheorized. I trace the missed encounters and unfinished conversations between the first generation of Critical Theory and postcolonial studies while also examining the case of mistaken identity, which confuses postcolonial and decolonial critiques of the Enlightenment. Finally, the chapter attempts to defend Adorno, Achille Mbembe, and Gayatri Chakravorty Spivak against the charges of normative nihilism and performative contradiction.

To fulfill these aims, the chapter does not follow a linear narrative; rather, there is a back and forth between understanding Horkheimer and Adorno's, Mbembe's, and Spivak's critiques of Enlightenment reason and defending them against Habermas. The two tasks are interlinked, insofar as Habermas's attacks rest on a misrepresentation of the criticism of Enlightenment reason as necessarily leading to normative nihilism. Habermas plays such a central role in this chapter because his censure of Adorno and Horkheimer was so consequential and contributed to reestablishing the prestige of Enlightenment thought while conveniently silencing its colonial and fascist tendencies. No other thinker can match Habermas's influence on reinstating the eminence of the Enlightenment while delegitimizing the criticism of it. Given that the core concern of the book is to demonstrate that a critique of the Enlightenment does not automatically entail a rejection of it, Adorno's, Horkheimer's, Mbembe's, and Spivak's writings are pivotal for my arguments. In my view, there is a stronger affinity between the first generation of the Frankfurt School and postcolonial scholars—specifically, among Adorno, Spivak, and Mbembe—than between Adorno and Habermas, Walter Mignolo and Spivak, or Ramón Grosfoguel and Mbembe. Like Horkheimer and Adorno, Spivak and Mbembe reckon that colonialism and fascism are not aberrations but, rather, are deeply rooted in Enlightenment reason. Furthermore, unlike decolonial scholars, they share the hope against hope that the Enlightenment can nevertheless be rescued (Horkheimer 1996, 873, 884).

Let us begin by first understanding Horkheimer and Adorno's groundbreaking analysis of Enlightenment instrumental reason.

Barbarous Enlightenment. The Uses
and Abuses of Reason

It is widely accepted that the publication of Isaac Newton's *Principia Mathematica* (1687), which propounded a mathematical and mechanical science of nature, ushered in the Enlightenment as both an epoch and an attitude characterized as the Age of Reason. The Enlightenment's self-understanding as the opposite of both barbarism and myth presented a simultaneous challenge to religious faith and political authority and a promise of progress, prosperity, and peace. Enlightenment reason, it was claimed in writings such as Francis Bacon's *Novum Organum* (1620) and Denis Diderot's *Encyclopédie* (1751–72), helped eliminate logical inconsistencies and distinguish value judgments from the rigorous, evidence-based scientific approach. These consistent and reliable facts were universally verifiable and thus valid across temporal and geographical differences.

However, Enlightenment reason revealed itself to be a double-edged sword: It was both boon and curse. Horkheimer and Adorno's *Dialectic of Enlightenment* presents a counternarrative of Western reason not just as historical progress but in terms of the domination of man and nature through instrumental rationality. Instead of being opposites, Enlightenment and myth are caught in a "dialectical" relation insofar as both attempt to deal with the human fear of the unknown (Horkheimer and Adorno 2002 [1947], 11). While myth identifies with and mimics that which is threatening, Enlightenment conquers anxiety by separating it stringently from the self and subjecting it to a system of identifying categories to master it. In myth, we make ourselves like the Other; in Enlightenment, we dominate that which is different in the interest of self-preservation. The triumph of reason, Horkheimer and Adorno aver, has come at the cost of widespread terror, unbridled destruction of nature, and the self-alienation of man. With its immanent tendency to absolutize itself and encompass everything within a unitary, closed system of thought, Enlightenment reason, in their view, reveals itself as potentially totalitarian (Horkheimer and Adorno 2002 [1947], 37). The Holocaust is considered tragic testimony to the insidious mix of myth (antisemitism) and Enlightenment (bureaucratically operationalized mass murder). Horkheimer and Adorno provocatively (for some) contend that the reversal of civilization into barbarism was not a random breakdown of Enlightenment principles but their systematic realization and triumph. These crimes against humanity were not some arbitrary slip into savagery but the logical outcome of dominant modern rationalism. The triumph of science and logic ironically led to the undermining of Enlightenment's emancipatory intent. The promise of control and mastery over untamed and unpredictable forces resulted in terror and inhumanity so that progressive norms brought catastrophic consequences.

The Enlightenment equation of truth with science reduces nature to a mere resource to be tamed and exploited. Immaturity is defined as an inability or lack of initiative to pursue this mastery of nature (something that the European colonizers found missing in the colonized societies): "The bourgeois, in the successive forms of the slave-owner, the free entrepreneur, and the administrator is the logical subject of Enlightenment" (Horkheimer and Adorno 2002 [1947], 65). At the same time, Enlightenment is the instrument through which the bourgeoisie came to power. In staging itself as the ultimate authority, Western reason dismisses the legitimacy of both religion and mythology as meaning-producing narratives. Instrumental reason and, by extension, capitalism flatten differences and standardize uniqueness to produce docile subjects who emerge as mere instances of a universal class, repeatable and replaceable. Ironically, the promise of equality and autonomy comes only at the cost of the exclusion of diversity and heterogeneity, with subjects being administered to the standardization and uniformity of bureaucratic processes. Capitalism and a rationalized society are threats to humankind's very survival, even as human beings are paradoxically complicit in maintaining these systems for their survival (Cook 2018, 22). Horkheimer and Adorno (2002 [1947], 234) explain that, in contrast to traditional capitalism, fascist state capitalism represents a dominance of politics over economics.

In addition to instrumental reason, Horkheimer and Adorno assail the positivist approach, which views humans and societies from an atomistic and reductive perspective. In anticipation of the *Positivismusstreit* of the 1960s, they warn of the "lapse from enlightenment into positivism" (Horkheimer and Adorno 2002 [1947], xii), which, in its focus on brute facts, delinks science from society and forecloses the theorization of emancipatory possibilities.[2] While rigorous empirical methods provide descriptive analysis, they offer no normative principles on how to enable change, thereby easily serving the interests of capitalist structures. Positivists dismiss as nonscientific any thought that goes beyond the mere observation of facts and the calculation of probabilities. All abstract thinking is disparaged as a dispensable and "old-fashioned luxury" (Horkheimer and Adorno 2002 [1947], 167), which is measured against the standard of efficiency and utility. In Horkheimer and Adorno's view, positivist anti-intellectualism is a strategy of advancing ignorance, which they link further to antisemitism. They warn that the "stupidity of cleverness" resulted in the misjudgment regarding the rise of National Socialism (Horkheimer and Adorno 2002 [1947], 173). Prognoses based on statistics and expert opinion misleadingly declared that fascism was impossible in the West.

As bourgeois philosophy, the Enlightenment promised to liberate human beings from religion and superstition; however, as "the formalization of reason is merely the intellectual expression of mechanized production," the Enlightenment became a destructive force, socially, politically, and economically (Horkheimer and Adorno 2002 [1947], 81–82). Kantian thought aspired to resolve the conflict between pure and empirical reason to attain true universality. In rendering nature and man into objects subjugated by manipulation and administration, Western reason foreclosed other ways of understanding and being in the world, making other forms of reason unimaginable and untenable. "Kant intuitively anticipated what Hollywood has consciously put into practice: images are precensored during production by the same standard of understanding which will later determine their reception by viewers" (Horkheimer and Adorno 2002 [1947], 81–82). Kant treats morals as facts, a rationalized functionality that is a matter of calculation and planning, indifferent to its ends. When no one is in doubt over their role and each agent in the system is replaceable, the resulting system becomes conducive to the emergence of totalitarian ideologies (Horkheimer and Adorno 2002 [1947], 90).

Unless the Enlightenment counters the destructive side of positivism, as well as its obsession with calculability and utility, it will forfeit its sublating character (Horkheimer and Adorno 2002 [1947], xvi). When thinking becomes merely affirmative rather than transformative, it ultimately upholds the status quo, thereby abdicating its critical and oppositional function. While sounding paradoxical, the "barbarous Enlightenment" perfectly captures the central thesis of Horkheimer and Adorno's critique: While promising unlimited advance of knowledge and the emancipation from servitude, the Enlightenment delivered "disenchantment of the world" (Horkheimer and Adorno 2002 [1947], 1) in that it "is totalitarian" (Horkheimer and Adorno 2002 [1947], 4). Friedrich Nietzsche had already alluded to the twofold character of the Enlightenment that stages itself as a harbinger of progress and emancipation but instrumentalized these norms to render the masses governable. Precisely this was weaponized by fascists. "The curse of irresistible progress is irresistible regression" (Horkheimer and Adorno 2002 [1947], 28).

Horkheimer and Adorno outline how the commodification of thought and the instrumental relation between language and mass communication functioned as key strategies for fascism. Marketing's impact on a language that is debased and devoid of meaning results in words being reduced to rote formulas, slogans, and catchwords instead of fostering critical impulses. Wireless broadcasting, like the radio, reduces its audience to a passive and anonymous mass instead of a community of active and critical listeners (Horkheimer and Adorno 2002 [1947], 129). A collectivity is formed out of not educated and critically engaged citizens but a mere mass that hears and follows a Führer (Horkheimer 1985a [1936], 30). Rather than drawing on truth claims and rational arguments, the fascist rhetoric relies for its efficacy on its "magical" ability (Schmidt 1998, 817), such that ideology critique in the Marxist vein cannot mitigate its pernicious effects. However, instead of fact checking and anti-disinformation campaigns, an educated and enlightened polity is the antidote to fascism in that it nurtures the reimagination of the relationship among citizens, as well as between humans and nature (Horkheimer 1985a [1936], 38). In contrast to universal principles, Horkheimer and Adorno propose an "unbarbaric" mode of thinking that is not rooted in foundational or absolute norms and thus is open to the unexpected, incalculable, opaque, and mysterious. The clarity and precision of thought that promises us an administered world comes at the expense of disregarding the unpredictable and the contingent. When theory loses its critical power, it ironically becomes a means to repression (Horkheimer and Adorno 2002 [1947], xv). The hope is to turn the critical force of reason onto itself, thereby revitalizing and reanimating it from its alienated mode of thinking. The effort is to urge Enlightenment thought to consider its destructive tendencies and its legacies to chart new directions and trajectories.

Insofar as all humans are viewed as susceptible to ideological manipulation, the first generation of Critical Theory is condemned for its pessimism. It is accused of rendering political change hopeless and an instrumental society inevitable (Fuchs 2016, 75). Contrary to claims that Horkheimer and Adorno endorsed an inevitability vis-à-vis the trajectory of reason, I would highlight that Horkheimer qualifies his judgment with "in civilization as we have known it so far," which promises hope for self-critical reason. In contrast to traditional theory as a cognitive activity that is directed at reproducing society in its present form or making its assimilation of nature more efficient, Horkheimer (2012 [1961], 118) foregrounds the role of education in fostering liberating reason. He and Adorno tout institutions and mechanisms that strengthen critical and reflective thought in society through antifascist education. In the aftermath of World War II, Horkheimer and Adorno also warned of the dangers of ideology's influence in everyday life—namely, that it hindered emancipation while nurturing an authoritarian personality (Fuchs 2016, 78).

For Adorno, the antidote to Nazi totalitarianism is the nurturing of a capacity for critical thought, which should not be a privilege of the elite few but a right of the masses. However, this thinking must be noncommercial, independent of corporate profit logic and the market's demands (Adorno 2003c [1973], 218–219). He opposed the idea of critical thought as a closed system of interconnected propositions supposedly based on a firm foundation with universal validity (Adorno 2005g [1969], 293). Following Karl Marx, who in *The Holy Family* (Marx and Engels 1956 [1844–45]) rejects the aim of the young Hegelians to find an Archimedean point against which existing conditions could be judged, Adorno dismisses the search for universal principles to ground critical thought and collective action. At the same time, Adorno argues against reading Marx's critique of a philosophy that merely interprets the world, rather than changing it, as a plea for the primacy of practice over theory. Rather, thinking itself must be understood as a practice that questions the status quo by critically reflecting on itself (Cook 2004, 56–57). Critical thinkers contemplate the conditions in which their knowledge emerges, as well as the power effects thereof. By facilitating critical consciousness in the oppressed and making them aware of the significance of their suffering, this form of immanent critique exposes societal contradictions, which stimulate emancipatory change. Adorno has been accused of being elitist; however, one could argue that, in a class-based racist and sexist society, critical thinking is made into a luxury in which only a privileged few can indulge. Thus, the democratization of the practice of critique requires the abolition of class-based society, which would allow a specialized division of labor to be replaced by the pluralization of human activities (Fuchs 2016, 79). To cite Marx's utopia, where "nobody has one exclusive sphere of activity but each can become accomplished in any branch he wishes, society regulates the general production and thus makes it possible for me to do one thing today and another tomorrow, to hunt in the morning, fish in the afternoon, rear cattle in the evening, criticize after dinner, just as I have a mind, without ever becoming hunter, fisherman, shepherd or critic" (Marx and Engels 1998 [1845],

53). Critical thinking can mitigate totalitarian impulses that ignore difference and otherness. It is, however, interesting to note that Adorno was skeptical of radical action as embodied in student counterculture. This point is elaborated in greater detail in chapter 4.

Let us now turn to one of the most vehement critics of *Dialectic of Enlightenment*—namely, Habermas.

The Unfinished Project of Modernity

The dark writers of the bourgeoisie—such as Machiavelli, Hobbes and Mandeville—had always appealed to Horkheimer, who was himself influenced by Schopenhauer. Clearly, from their works there still remained ties to Marx's social theory. These connections were broken by the really nihilistic dark writers of the bourgeoisie, foremost among them the Marquis de Sade and Nietzsche. It is to them that Horkheimer and Adorno turn in the *Dialectic of Enlightenment*, their blackest, most nihilistic book, in order to conceptualize the self-destructive process of Enlightenment. Although they no longer placed hope on its liberating power, inspired by Benjamin's ironic "hope of those without hope," they nonetheless refused to abandon the now paradoxical labor of analysis. We no longer share this attitude. However, under the sign of a Nietzsche restored by some post-structuralist writers such as Derrida and the recent Foucault, attitudes are being disseminated today which appear as the spitting image of those of Horkheimer and Adorno in the *Dialectic of Enlightenment*. It is the confusion of the two attitudes that I want to prevent. (Habermas 1982, 13)

The accusation against critics of the Enlightenment, such as Adorno and Michel Foucault, is that they abandon the emancipatory nature of reason and promote irrationality, thereby leading to authoritarianism and illiberalism. As one of the most renowned advocates of the Enlightenment, Habermas (1982, 14) describes the Enlightenment as a contrast to myth that counters the authority of religion and tradition with the noncoercive coercion of the better argument. Participants in rational communication processes deliberate on validity claims, whereas, in undemocratic and unemancipated societies, "cultural traditions predecide which validity claims, when, where, for what, from whom, and to whom must be accepted," without the participants themselves "having the possibility of making explicit and examining the potential grounds on which their yes/ no positions are based" (Habermas 1983, 70).

The emancipatory side of the Enlightenment is embodied in scientific knowledge, democratic institutions, and cultural modernity (Habermas 1982, 18). Sciences, it is argued, go beyond the creation of merely technologically exploitable knowledge, while institutions of constitutional democratic states embody the universalist foundations of law and morality. Finally, avant-garde art liberates society from the imperatives of purposive activity and from commonplace perspectives and practices. Habermas warns against reducing all science and technology to their positivist characteristics and bemoans that Adorno and Horkheimer deliver a totalizing critique and far-reaching rejection of the liberating force of the Enlightenment, which denies possibilities of evading instrumental reason (Habermas 1982, 22). While endorsing their critique of mass culture, even drawing on it in his reflections on the restructuring and decline of the liberal public sphere under advanced capitalism, Habermas's contemplations on an emancipated and free society take him down a different path than Adorno and Horkheimer.

The claim that reason, once instrumentalized, becomes assimilated to power and thereby forfeits its critical impulse is, for Habermas (1982, 22), a "performative contradiction." In condemning the Enlightenment, critics are accused of destroying all rational grounds for normative justification; their position is considered self-refuting, and they are unable to escape the paralyzing antinomy in which they find themselves (Schoolman 2005, 335). Accordingly, Horkheimer and Adorno's radical critique of Enlightenment is considered incongruous as they use reason to condemn reason. Contradiction, for Habermas, is a cardinal sin, which, in his eyes, invalidates Horkheimer and Adorno's claim of reason's complicity with domination. Critics of the Enlightenment are indicted for being unable to offer "any prospect for an escape from the myth of purposive rationality that has turned into objective violence" (Habermas 1987, 114). Following Habermas, Benhabib (1986, 166) accuses Horkheimer and Adorno of "relentless pessimism," arguing that one cannot rebuke the Enlightenment "by the darkness of human history at that point in time alone." It is unacceptable to contest reason without the use of reason, as reason is a presupposition for every critical intervention.

Nietzsche is considered particularly threatening by scholars such as Habermas because he declares the death not only of God but also of universal and objective truth. In Habermas's (1982, 23) view, "Nietzsche's critique consumes the critical impulse itself." As long as critique can be rationally grounded, it is fruitful; however, when the very principles of reason come under suspicion as being contaminated instruments of domination and violence, as Nietzsche avers, then Habermas fears a loss of any possibility of critical intervention founded in established norms of knowledge and morality. This robs the theorists of the critical parameters needed to distinguish among different normative claims (Hohendahl 1985, 15). Subsequently, there are no standards of judgment to differentiate between legitimate and illegitimate forms of power, and there is no possibility of transcending power.

Likewise, Foucault's critique of reason and challenge to universalist and ahistorical metanarratives (*métarécit*), such as equality, liberty, and emancipation, is also considered dubious by Habermas, whose own theory of communicative action rests on the legitimacy of a consensus arrived at through rational deliberation among free subjects (Hohendahl 1985, 17). Foucault's genealogical analysis of modern power questions not only the epistemic privilege granted to the traditional Cartesian notion of the *cogito* but also the humanist ideal of a rational and sovereign self, one who is self-reflective and self-mastering. The universal knowing and speaking subject, serving as the source of authority, morality, and power, whom Foucault targets is at the heart of Habermas's theorization of modernity, and is a hero of knowledge, progress, and liberty. Foucault considers Western reason to be only one of many rationalities, such that it can be contested without lapsing into irrationality. Habermas (1983, 249), in contrast, is committed to a universal structure of rationalization. His teleological account of history and his claim that social and political practices are framed by universal norms that can be rationally justified and are ahistorical is contested by Foucault's genealogical questioning of progressive narratives of history (Hohendahl 1985, 18; see also Allen 2016).

While Habermas touts reason as empowering, in that it enables subjects to develop the capability of rationally examining, autonomously choosing, and universally justifying their preferences, Foucault (1984, 45) outlines how Western reason coerces and disciplines. For Foucault, it is imperative to experimentally transgress the limits set on us by norms, including the Western understanding of reason that we have inherited from the European Enlightenment, so that we may understand how we are subjectified and subjugated. This opens up the possibility for us to be otherwise, transforming prevailing power relations in the process (Love 1989, 275). Contra Habermas's misrepresentation of Foucault as anti-Enlightenment,

I would like to draw attention to Foucault's (1984, 45) understanding of the Enlightenment as a critical attitude that questions "what we are saying, thinking, and doing through a historical ontology of ourselves." In my view, whereas Foucault falls short of adequately outlining the normative grounds on which resistance to coercive practices, including those of Western reason, may be justified, Habermas fails to address how reason constrains subjects and believes that reason can be freed from power. It is noteworthy that both Foucault and Habermas draw on Kant's understanding of the Enlightenment as a critical exercise that questions what can be known, what must be done, and what may be hoped.

Prior to Foucault, Adorno had already insightfully and compellingly argued that, to become more enlightened, we must reflect critically on the Enlightenment's legacy. This involves rethinking the complex relation among critique, emancipation, and coercion. *Dialectic of Enlightenment* cautions us to rethink our approach to Western reason and its coercive and violent proclivities and legacies, which might end up destroying humanity (Cook 2018, 94). Enlightened reason was supposed to emancipate humanity; however, the "wholly enlightened earth is radiant with triumphant calamity" (Horkheimer and Adorno 2002 [1947], 1). At the same time, to rectify the situation, the critical tools of the Enlightenment become indispensable, creating a paradoxical situation to negotiate. Nevertheless, there is hope that a robust critique of Western reason could "prepare a positive concept of enlightenment" (Horkheimer and Adorno 2002 [1947], xviii). Thus, instead of abandoning the Enlightenment, the demand is that it scrutinize itself. Horkheimer and Adorno (2002 [1947], xvi–xvii, 172) cite Friedrich Hölderlin's (1968, 463) insight that "where danger threatens, that which saves from it also grows" and claim that "Enlightenment itself, having mastered itself, and assumed its own power, could break through the limits of enlightenment." In the next section, I proffer arguments for how Adorno and Horkheimer propose to redeem the Enlightenment.

Rescuing the Enlightenment. Dominating Versus Liberating Reason

It is noteworthy that *Dialectic of Enlightenment*, subtitled "Philosophical Fragments" in German, with its aphorisms, appendixes, and excursuses, displays a certain convergence of form and content (Rocco 1994, 85). In keeping with Horkheimer and Adorno's rejection of the positivistic virtues of order and unity, the textual fragments frustrate the expectation of coherence and systematicity, offering instead plurality and partiality. Ackbar Abbas (2012, 9–10) points out: "What is striking about Adorno's texts, besides the density of the argumentation, are those lapidary aphorisms that leap off the page. Each aphorism is a kind of thought-object that turns thought against itself. . . . Each aphorism is the result not of an epiphany, a sudden understanding of the whole picture, but the result of a *negative epiphany*, an understanding about the impossibility of total understanding." What Habermas and other critics condemn as "performative contradiction" can be read as a concerted textual and theoretical effort to undermine epistemic totality and certainty (Rocco 1994, 86). One must bear in mind that *Dialectic of Enlightenment* is in fact an incomplete and open-ended work. Despite proclaiming that "the rescue of the Enlightenment is our concern" (Horkheimer 1985b [1946], 598), the planned sequel, which promised to elaborate a positive program by which the Enlightenment might be salvaged, never materialized. The hope was that the foundation for a critique of instrumental reason might be found within the very structure of language itself, in which other subjects were treated not as means but always as ends (Schmidt 1998, 823). Freeing reason from instrumentality by eschewing formalism would enable critical interventions.

Confronted with the question of how thinking in its critical mode can be recuperated from its coercive, repressive, and dominating impulses, Adorno explains that critical thinking aims at revealing neither the errors nor the inaccuracies of dominant thought. Rather, it outlines the antinomies that inflect them without guarantees of overcoming, reconciling, or sublating them. The simultaneous impossibility and necessity of negotiating the aporias without resolving them is the promise of the utopian moment in critical thinking, the not yet. Utopia entails rejecting the closed thought, which claims that the object can be "captured" (Rose 1976, 84). Nietzsche's warning against the dangers of accepting concepts as invariants is indeed an important inspiration for Adorno (2004 [1966], 192), who outlines how concepts conceal their origins and operate as "terminological masks." A critical approach traces how categories emerge historically and materially and unearths their antinomies and contradictions, thereby guarding against their self-concealment (Rose 1976, 82). The process of critical thinking becomes an end in itself rather than merely being a vehicle of radical politics (Rose 1976, 85).

Accordingly, even though Horkheimer and Adorno condemn Enlightenment norms of justice, democracy, or freedom as ideological, they resist offering positive alternatives, lest these too become reified. According to Benhabib (1986, 222), Horkheimer and Adorno fail to offer a satisfactory response to the question: "What is the normative standpoint of critical theory?" Their suggestion that art may offer an alternative to Enlightenment domination is rejected on the grounds that aesthetic reason is nonconceptual and even irrational (Schoolman 2005, 358). While Benhabib (1986) rejects the epistemic and normative purchase of the aesthetic experience, Adorno focuses on how autonomous art undermines attempts to extract truth claims from aesthetic experience, thereby becoming a politically privileged site for social critique. Autonomous art unwittingly reveals the historical premises, which would otherwise be taken for granted, and through divulging the inconsistencies in discourses, truth emerges unintentionally, like Freudian slips of the tongue (Buck-Morss 1977, 96). Aesthetic reason is a form of thinking that disrupts identitarian logic; it is an effort to think the unthought without teleological purpose toward the not yet (Schoolman 2005, 359). It carries no promise of certainty, predictability, or calculability, and it is not threatened by contingency, uncertainty, or interminability. In direct contrast to the undifferentiated and all-encompassing approach of instrumental reason, aesthetic reason aspires to represent that which it excludes (Schoolman 2005, 359). By compelling the subject to reason aesthetically, mimesis broadens and diversifies reason, opening it up and rendering it receptive to previously foreclosed possibilities and potentialities. Through aesthetic reasoning, the limits of instrumental reason are understood and its dominant mode is undermined; this broadens the Enlightenment and inclines it toward a higher order of reflection that is not just purposive (Schoolman 2005, 360). Aesthetic Enlightenment serves as an antidote to instrumental and purposive rationality and is considered redemptive.

Kant argues that the nonconceptual nature of aesthetic judgments, which differs from theoretical and practical discourse, implies that although aesthetic critique is universally valid, it cannot be cognitively demonstrated and goes beyond reasoned critique. Instead of a radical segregation of epistemic, ethical, and aesthetic modes, in aesthetic criticism all three are inextricably intertwined. Along similar lines, in Adorno's view, genuine critique in the form of a "negative dialectic" is a critique of identity thinking, which assumes mastery over existence through cognition. Identity thinking consolidates the status quo insofar as it accepts the way things are or seem as a factual given that is permanent and unchangeable, thereby dismissing possibilities of transformation. The domination of identity thinking is rooted in the negation of alterity and difference, such that the other must be either assimilated or eliminated. Horkheimer and Adorno trace the long historical trajectory of identity thinking, of which capitalism and fascism are more recent manifestations. Adorno's (2004 [1966], 13, 197) non-identity thinking circumvents domination by contesting the subsumption of particulars under universals, thereby revealing unintentional truths. Drawing on Ernst Bloch and Walter Benjamin, Adorno argues that the uniqueness of concrete particulars and their resistance to systematization, categorization, and normalization presents the utopian traces of non-identity (Buck-Morss 1977, 89–90). In contrast to reason, which is purposive, aesthetic mimesis for Adorno is a form of judgment that cognizes without concepts. This holds the promise of nondominating aesthetic practices that supersede reasoned critique.

In chapter 6 I return to the role of aesthetic Enlightenment in the processes of decolonization, but for now, let us turn our attention to the unfinished conversations between the first generation of Critical Theory and postcolonial thought. In response to the charge of normative nihilism, Adorno, Horkheimer, Spivak, and Mbembe outline how critical practices do not inevitably have to be grounded in instrumental reason. The convergences of concerns and strategies between the two, unfortunately, have been insufficiently examined. I began this chapter by summarizing how postcolonial studies has engaged with the entanglements of colonialism and Nazism and of racism and antisemitism. I now engage with the missed encounters between postcolonial studies and the first generation of Critical Theory.

Ambivalent Affinities, Unfinished Conversations, and Mistaken Identity

When Horkheimer and Adorno were writing *Dialectic of Enlightenment*, much of the world was under European colonial rule.[3] Given their engagement with Marx and Marxism, it is regrettable that they do not address either the transnationalization of capitalism through European colonialism or the violence of slavery and colonial genocides. Despite their concerns regarding the consequences of fascism and the ills of capitalism in the West, they disregarded the deep link among colonialism, capitalism, and neocolonialism.

The historian Enzo Traverso (2016, 166) traces the "missed dialogue" between Adorno and C.L. R. James, who met on a number of occasions in the 1940s through their common friend Herbert Marcuse. Both Marxists, they were of course aware of each other's work, but, unfortunately, the exchange between the two intellectual giants failed or was impossible. While Adorno would not have understood the cultural concerns of an internationally recognized specialist of cricket such as James, James, in turn, would have rejected Adorno's assessment of jazz. Neither mentioned the other in their influential writings, and Traverso bemoans the "wasted opportunity" (Traverso 2016, 167), seeing this as a loss not only for the two intellectuals and for Marxism, but also for critical scholarship at large. Traverso wonders whether the encounter failed because, despite their critical impulses, the scholars of the Frankfurt School were trapped within a Eurocentric Marxist framing. They were thus unable to appreciate the importance of Black and non-European Marxism, which contributes to a fundamental recalibration of class analysis by shifting the focus to the non-Western world and its experiences.

Despite claims of aesthetics as a counterpoint to instrumental reason, Adorno's remarks on jazz are an instructive example of incomprehension of the critical nature of non-Eurocentric aesthetic practices. Admirers of jazz highlight how Adorno disregards the sociohistorical context from which many of the creative impulses of *Black music* emerged and in which they flourished. Adorno stands accused of ignorance and snobbery in his dismissal of jazz as nondialectical and repetitive. In his view, jazz has a monotonous tone and beat and is thus easy to commodify, massify, and instrumentalize for capitalist and totalitarian purposes. Adorno (1989–90 [1936], 67–68) declared jazz to be socially non-emancipatory and even approved of the Nazis' regulation of jazz (Gilroy 2000, 295). The historian Eric Hobsbawm (1993, 300) rebuked Adorno's writings on jazz as containing "some of the stupidest pages ever written." His defenders see Adorno as a cultural critic who contests the onslaught of mass cultural kitsch, as well as identity thinking, so that his dismissal of jazz has less to do with Eurocentric music tastes or elitist aesthetic standards than with his political convictions.

If one were to compare Adorno's reflections on jazz with Angela Davis's (1999) or Stuart Hall's (2000) analysis of the role of jazz in *Black culture and politics*, as well as everyday life, Adorno's Eurocentric bias in both aesthetic and political matters is disappointing insofar as he misrecognizes the significance of jazz in Black liberatory struggles. As Hall (2018, 130) explains, in jazz, "One could hear a whole historical experience of oppression and suffering being resumed and coming through into sound." In contrast to Western classical music, which primarily appeals to middle-class audiences, jazz is popular across class lines and was crucial for the evolution of Black political consciousness. This building of collectivity is assailed as identitarian insofar as, in Adorno's view, jazz as a work of art belongs to a specific social setting and is therefore not fully autonomous (Okiji 2018). Only when the work of art goes beyond the function of documenting the ideas, experiences, and situation of a particular class would Adorno (2002 [1970], 116, 217, 319) consider it worthy. He argues that the truth value of authentic works of art transcends the historical moments from which those works emerge, even as they are grounded in them. According to him, only supposedly authentic works of art can offer aesthetic opposition to instrumental reason and the culture industry. Jazz, for him, does not qualify as an antidote to the coercive force of capitalism and totalitarianism. Regrettably, only by disregarding the rich tradition of improvisation in jazz music can Adorno uphold these claims. Adorno also disregards the "shared cosmopolitanism" of Jewish and Black jazz players (Gilroy 2000, 294). The Jewish saxophonist Stan Getz famously stated: "Every time I try to play Black, it comes out sounding Jewish" (cited in Hersch 2013, 259). This is an instructive example of the failures of the first generation of Critical Theory in thinking beyond its limits, which Adorno ironically advocates.

Another notable coincidence happened in 1950, when both Adorno's *The Authoritarian Personality* and Aimé Césaire's *Discourse on Colonialism* were published (Bardawil 2018, 777). Césaire (2000 [1950], 36) argues, "Colonization works to decivilize the colonizer, to brutalize him," and the barbarism that was born in the colonies "boomerangs" in the form of fascism in Europe. Fadi Bardawil (2018, 780) argues that, while Adorno's regression narrative anchors the emergence of antisemitic Nazism within standardized capitalism, ultimately eroding democratic traits, Césaire's explanatory account links the colonizer's subjectivity to the material practices of colonial domination. In dehumanizing the natives, Europeans decivilize themselves (Bardawil 2018, 780). The violence exerted elsewhere turns inward.

A "counterfactual intellectual history" of the missed opportunity is also traced by Said, who focuses on the affinities between Adorno and James as two examples of exiled intellectuals who shared a similar approach to history and society (Traverso 2016, 167). Both of them, Said (1994, 63) explained, were "contrapuntal" thinkers who rejected conformism and escaped canonical views. Despite important differences, both elaborated a similar diagnostic of Western civilization, depicting it as a process of self-destruction. Perhaps one point of agreement between James and Adorno would have been that it is indeed worthwhile to preserve the emancipatory potential of the Enlightenment. The non-encounter between James and Adorno could be considered a lost opportunity for both Critical Theory and postcolonial studies.[4] An inspiring counterexample is how Fanon's writings on colonial violence, torture, and trauma influenced Améry's understanding of his own experience with fascist violence in the Nazi camps (Fareld 2021, 58). The notion of *Schicksalsverwandtschaft* (kinship of fate) bears witness to the shared pain of the victims of colonialism and Nazism (Améry 2005 [1968], 15–16). Améry's (1980 [1966], 68) loss of trust in the world (*Weltvertrauen*) resonates with the postcolonial disenchantment with the Enlightenment and resentment toward Europe.

While the ambivalent affinities between the first generation of Critical Theory and postcolonial studies are unmistakable in their shared criticism of the Enlightenment, post–Adornian Frankfurt School theorists have largely disregarded colonialism and its consequences. In this context, the writings of Amy Allen (2016) and Charles Mills (2017b), both of whom concentrate on contemporary Frankfurt School critical theorists, are particularly valuable for understanding the postcolonial disenchantment with post–Adornian Critical Theory. Allen (2016) bemoans that, despite their commitment to freedom and emancipation, post–Adornian Frankfurt School theorists have failed to engage with struggles for decolonization. She cites Said (1993, 278), who laments: "Frankfurt School critical theory . . . is stunningly silent on racist theory, anti-imperialist resistance, and oppositional practice in the empire." In addition, Allen (2016, 73, 83) assails Habermas for presuming that Euro-American participants in dialogue are "developmentally superior to members of traditional or 'nonmodern' cultures," and Axel Honneth for viewing Western societies as more evolved. As an illustration for the realization of freedom in European modernity, Honneth offers the example of cultural and legal recognition of homosexual relationships and the expansion of marriage rights to homosexuals as the culmination of a "progressive democratization" (Allen 2016, 98). This implies that societies that do not permit gay marriage purportedly need to catch up with European modernity. What Honneth conveniently overlooks is that in most of the postcolonial world, homosexuality was criminalized and pathologized during European colonial rule, and in countries such as Uganda and India, colonial sodomy laws (section 377) continue to be promoted by European and US American Evangelicals (Dhawan 2013a; Rao 2020).

Along similar lines, Mills indicts Habermas and Honneth for claiming that European Enlightenment is an advance over so-called premodern, nonmodern, or traditional forms of life. For Habermas (1983, 44), "Our occidental understanding of the world" is not merely one among many possible traditions of reasoning, but the only universally valid one. The language of progress and development feeds into narratives of European superiority vis-à-vis the supposed backwardness of the non-European world. Mills (2021, 17–18) reads this as a reinforcement of the "philosophical color line."[5] Recoding the metaphors that associate Enlightenment with whiteness, Mills (2021, 26) argues that Blackness does the illuminating, such that "black light" dispels the darkness of "Euro-cognition." The supposedly oxymoronic concept of *Black Enlightenment* suggests not just philosophy by Black scholars, but philosophy that emerges from "the distinctive experience of racial subordination in modernity" (Mills 2021, 25). Mills (2021, 26) hopes that *Black Enlightenment* may be more genuinely universal than the "bogus" universality of "White Enlightenment."

However, the questioning of the ideas of rationalism, secularism, and humanism in the European Enlightenment is, in turn, accused of normative nihilism and cultural relativism. It is argued that, to be truly emancipatory, critical principles must be underpinned by normative foundationalism. By emphasizing the contingency of norms such as human rights, secularism, and democracy, postcolonial studies is disqualified as uncritical and as abandoning progressive ideals. In the face of the universalism-versus-difference conundrum, postcolonial scholars negotiate the double bind by upholding normative commitments without recourse to foundationalist premises. Contingent normativity is considered more conducive to the postcolonial condition—one marked by ambivalence, difference, and diversity. Instead of claiming that norms must be undergirded with universal principles, the complexities of normative commitments are outlined. Accordingly, conceptions of justice, human rights, and democracy must be reimagined in light of the experiences of colonialism. Insofar as normative theorists reinforce the superiority of European norms, the supposed universal principles reveal themselves to be provincial (Chakrabarty 2000). The antidote to Eurocentrism and imperialism is certainly not nativism but, rather, a pluralization and diversification of normative legitimacy and its narratives. It is an acknowledgment that differences in experiences, perspectives, and location make a difference in how normative principles are formulated and operationalized. Eurocentric norms, furthermore, are not always sufficient to understand the postcolonial world and its practices. I delve into this further in chapter 5, where I explore the distinction between the genocidal and the missing state.

Kantian scholars such as Neiman (2021) and Omri Boehm (2024), who are also committed to the principle of universalism, warn that the postcolonial focus on differences ontologizes and reifies alterity, thereby feeding "tribalism." Zionism and postcolonialism, according to Boehm, are two sides of the same coin, as both reject universal norms as inherently coercive and, in the face of their respective experiences, are disillusioned with the Enlightenment. Although sympathetic to their well-founded distrust of Enlightenment promises of equality and humanism, Boehm (2024) assails both Zionism and postcolonialism as identity politics. They may seem oppositional, but in his view they actually reinforce each other. His solution to circumvent the violent outcome of the so-called identity politics of Zionism and postcolonialism is to insist on the principle of universalism.

In response to Boehm's dismissal of postcolonial studies as identity politics, I want to draw on Arendt (1994, 12), who astutely remarked: "If one is attacked as a Jew, one must defend oneself as a Jew. Not as a German, not as a world-citizen, not as an upholder of the Rights of Man." Jewish resistance to genocidal antisemitism, according to Arendt, has to be articulated in the very vocabulary of debasement and not simply in terms of the assimilationist liberal idea of human, which supposedly overrides parochial group identities. Agency is embodied and entrenched in particular experiences and cannot be simply disembedded and exercised in generic terms of rights of man. Emancipation of the Jews by the Allied forces was insufficient, Arendt (1978 [1943], 121) explained, because "from the disgrace of being a Jew there is but one escape—to fight for the honor of the Jewish people as a whole." It is all the more ironic that she was accused of having "no love of the Jewish people" (Aharony 2019). Emphasizing the "givenness" of being Jewish, which for Arendt was not a matter of choice, did not detract from her commitment to the idea of world citizenship and her focus on the human condition at large.

Similarly, Albert Einstein, who renounced his German citizenship at sixteen, choosing statelessness over military service, not only fought against antisemitism but was also a staunch critic of American racism. He famously remarked: "Being a Jew myself, perhaps I can understand and empathize with how black people feel as victims of discrimination" (quoted in Francis 2017). Einstein was a firm supporter of the Civil Rights Movement, signed anti-lynching petitions, and volunteered to testify as a character witness in the trial of the writer and philosopher W. E. B. Du Bois, who was indicted by the Federal Bureau of Investigation as a foreign agent in 1951. I evoke Arendt and Einstein to illustrate once again the fraught relation between particular identities and universal norms.

Boehm does not explicitly mention any postcolonial scholar by name, so it is unclear whom he has in mind when he dismisses postcolonial studies as identity politics. It is, however, evident that Boehm disregards that critique of the Enlightenment is not automatically anti-Enlightenment; nor is the unpacking of the inconsistencies and contradictions of universal norms inevitably a negation of these norms. For instance, postcolonial studies is unthinkable without Marxism, yet postcolonialism also takes to task the Marxist universalist understanding of capitalism, labor, and worker. Boehm seems to overlook that postcolonial thought places itself squarely within the Enlightenment tradition when it criticizes the Enlightenment, not to delegitimize it, but to rouse Europe from its self-deception and to enlighten it about its violent legacies to eventually rescue it.

In addition to the unfinished conversations between postcolonial and Holocaust studies, I want to draw attention to the issue of mistaken identity, where postcolonial studies is often confused with the decolonial approach. Whereas postcolonial studies emphasizes the Enlightenment's contradictory consequences for the postcolonial context, the decolonial approach unequivocally repudiates the Enlightenment and its enduring legacies. Grosfoguel (2007, 212) rebuffs efforts to recalibrate Western theories and concepts to explain non-European societies and practices and chastises Habermas for his "Eurocentric fundamentalism." Grosfoguel (2011, 29) claims that subaltern identities serve as an epistemic alterity that offers a "radical critique of Eurocentric paradigms and ways of thinking." Meanwhile, the decolonial scholar Nelson Maldonado-Torres (2004, 40–41) targets Horkheimer and Adorno and argues that the critique of instrumental reason does not suffice to address the question of coloniality. The Peruvian sociologist Aníbal Quijano (2007, 177), in turn, remarks that "the pretension that the specific cosmic vision of a particular ethnie should be taken as universal rationality" makes epistemological decolonization imperative.

Decolonization movements, in Mignolo's (2011, 64 fn. 8) view, failed partly because they could not fracture the frame of the modern episteme. For instance, the idea of the state within a global capitalist and imperialist political economy persisted and was appropriated by native elites in Asia and Africa, as it had previously been in the Americas, with Haiti being an instructive case in point (more on this in chapter 4). In Mignolo's view, decolonial states regrettably capitulated to the liberal game and remained within the logic of modernity. Drawing on Quijano's notion of *desprenderse* (delinking), Mignolo (2011, 45) elaborates decolonial options of "epistemic disobedience" that precede civil disobedience and open up alternatives to the logic of coloniality/modernity. Following the Zapatistas, he contends that "decolonial pluri-versality" challenges "imperial uni-versality" and opens a world that would fit many worlds. It also promises "another world [is] possible" that is not liberal, Christian, or Marxist or a mix of the three (Mignolo 2011, 50–51). According to Mignolo, decolonial thinking serves as a counterpoint to the framework of modernity/coloniality by opening "a space for the unthinkable in the imperial genealogy of modernity" and by giving voice to that which has been silenced by imperial epistemology (Mignolo 2011, 47–48). The focus is shifted toward alternative cosmologies, testimonies, and archives. By disengaging from European modernity, the emphasis is placed on local histories, with the aim to decolonize the imagination and facilitate the reclamation of non-European sources of knowledge. To this end, Andean Indigenous communalism is seen to offer a counterpoint to Western capitalism. According to decolonial theorists, Indigenous traditions provide a critical vantage point and normative resources outside the circuits of Western modernity (Ingram 2018, 505–6). Thus, in their view, the failings of Western thought, including Frankfurt Critical Theory, can be rectified by re-turning to non-Western perspectives decoupled from capitalism and modernity. However, Mignolo (2007, 155) concedes that decolonial thinking is "a particular kind of critical theory," which is "not the norm or the master paradigm against which all other projects should be compared, measured, evaluated and judged." One can hardly find fault with Mignolo's emphasis on recognizing and valuing non-Western perspectives, which hitherto have been suppressed by colonialism. Instead of fostering mutual respect, Indigenous epistemologies were silenced. The decolonial efforts to rectify these historical wrongs are certainly a commendable step in the right direction. However, my objection lies in the constructed rivalry between the perceived radical nature of the decolonial approach and the supposed timidity of postcolonial studies.

Insofar as postcolonial studies is inspired by Western theories, decolonial scholars rebuke it for disregarding precolonial and antimodern epistemes. Postcolonial theory is accused of ignoring Indigenous epistemologies, which are posited as existing beyond the modernity/coloniality complex. Mignolo asserts that poststructuralism and postcolonialism both are Eurocentric and must be decolonized, as their critique of modernity "cannot be valid for . . . those who are not white or Christian" (Mignolo

2002, 85–86). Indigenous understandings of fundamental concepts such as time, space, land, nature, universe, humanity, and animals offer a counterpoint to Western approaches that tend to instrumentalize and rationalize these ideas. In addition, it is argued that Indigenous spirituality counters Western secularism (Mignolo 2007, 163).

In light of these accusations, in the next section I defend postcolonial studies against charges of being anti-Enlightenment, "nativist," and "tribalist" (Neiman, Boehm), as well as against accusations of Eurocentrism (Grosfoguel, Mignolo). I unpack the affinities between postcolonial scholars and the first generation of Critical Theory, with particular focus on Spivak, Emmanuel Eze, and Mbembe, to explain the overlaps with Horkheimer and Adorno's critique of Western reason. In defense of postcolonial studies, I argue that, unlike for decolonial thinkers, the relationship of postcolonial thought to the Enlightenment is not one of "alienation but of agonizing proximity" (Varadharajan 1995, xxviii), such that the effort is to resist the destructive elements while embracing the enabling ones. This chapter began with delving into Habermas's attack on *Dialectic of Enlightenment* for being a "black," "dark," and "nihilistic" book. In what follows, I draw on the work of postcolonial scholars to defend Horkheimer and Adorno against Habermas's accusations. Like Adorno, Mbembe contests the emancipatory promise of the Enlightenment, highlighting the racist and colonialist dimensions of instrumental reason.

Critique of Black Reason

Does reason have a color? Does color influence the nature of reason (Eze 1997a)? Enlightenment thinkers such as Kant would answer both of these questions with a resounding no, for in their understanding, reason is objective and universal and thus purportedly color-blind. Yet Kant proclaims that women, Black people, Indigenous peoples, so-called gypsies, and other non-European subjects lack reason and morality, which is possessed solely by white bourgeois male subjects. This indicates the "racial unconscious" (Eze 2001, x) of Western thought and the place of race within the Enlightenment, which determined who was (in)capable of reason.

Given that non-Europeans were denied rationality, the effort of anticolonial thought—for instance, Négritude—was to understand themselves beyond Western definitions of Blackness. The aim of thinkers such as Léopold Sédar Senghor, the Senegalese poet, philosopher, and statesman who became

the first president of independent Senegal and a leading figure in the Négritude movement, was to reinstate the humanity of Black people by making
a claim to an African form of reason that was in direct contrast to exclusionary and dehumanizing Western reason. However, despite Négritude's
and Africana philosophy's efforts to nullify the "core racial assumptions"
of Western thought, according to Eze (2001, xvi), they were unsuccessful in
developing a postracial account of reason. In his view, "Négritude ... failed
the interests of modern African philosophy when it opposed a supposedly
European technical 'eye-reason' (instrumental rationality) to an African
'feeling-reason' ('participant' rationality)" (Eze 2001, 148–49). Eze not only
rejects the essentialization of coercive and violent Western versus humane
and benign African reason but also draws on Horkheimer and Adorno to
critique Senghor's claims of all-encompassing African "feeling-reason."
Notwithstanding his critique, Eze (2001, 118) acknowledges that Négritude
offered a momentous "embodied and institutionalized critique of colonial
Reason [and] a philosophical affirmation of Africanity."

In the face of European Enlightenment's racialization of reason and
the lack of non-racialized versions of reason in anticolonial thought, Eze
(2008, xiv) proposes exploring other accounts of reason, which emerge
from the "conceptual everyday" and the "conceptual vernacular." Akin to
Horkheimer and Adorno (2002 [1947], 67), who observe that the "Enlightenment expels difference from theory," Eze (2008, 8) raises the question: "How
do you articulate diverse historical forms of rationality?" Situating himself
within "an Afro-modern postcolonial vernacular tradition of thought,"
Eze (2008, 3, 12) claims that reason is inherently heterogeneous and plural;
it is produced through and because of difference. He proposes, "*Anaghi
akwu ofu ébé ènéné manwu*: Rationality, like a work of art, is best appreciated
from multiple points of view" (Eze 2008, xiii).

Habermas believes that only actors who fulfill formal criteria, such
as speaking the language of modernity and adhering to communication
standards that represent values of secularism and reason, are legitimate
interlocutors in deliberation and are capable of learning political-moral
lessons that emerge as history progresses. In contrast, Eze focuses on those
who are placed on the purportedly wrong side of modernity. Like Adorno,
Eze suggests that differences in languages and experiences imply that reason is neither singular nor universal. Given that language is thoroughly
historical, thinking, too, is tied to particular historical conditions, such
that there are multiple languages of reason (Eze 2008, 9). Eze (2008, 246)

offers the comfort of "ordinary reason" with his "vernacular theory of rationality" being "admittedly burdened, imperfect, but serviceable."

Rejecting the opposition between "European rationalism, materialism, and individualism" and "African intuitive reason, empathy, and spiritual values," Eze (2001, 151) reminds us that what Senghor attributed to white culture was seen by Marx and Max Weber as characteristics of capitalism. And the qualities Senghor assigned to *African* or *Black cultures* were for Marx precapitalist and preindustrial. Weber bemoaned the overrationalization and overmechanization of Europe as ushering in a cultural and spiritual "disenchantment." Eze strives for a postracial future of humanity in which categories such as Black and white become "signposts from the past" and no one "must automatically bear the privileges or costs of a racial tag" (Eze 2001, 180, 223). Eze plays a prominent role in my arguments because, unlike those who take the decolonial approach, he neither romanticizes non-European epistemic, ethical, and aesthetic practices nor offers fanciful solutions for complex normative dilemmas. Rather, akin to Horkheimer and Adorno, Eze (2001, x) understands postracial philosophy as an effort to follow uncharted paths in the hope that we may think again critically.

Like Eze, Mbembe (2017, 17) relates reason to differences in experiences of colonialism, slavery, and apartheid and outlines how reason is linked to different temporalities and geographies. While the Age of Reason is extolled by European philosophers for its emancipatory and progressive norms, it also marked the peak of the transatlantic slave trade (Mbembe 2017, 67). Colonial brutality and violence were justified as an allegedly humanitarian enterprise in the name of a rational cause of civilizing so-called primitive societies. Victor Hugo declared: "Whites made Blacks into men; . . . Europe will make Africa into a world" (quoted in Mbembe 2017, 76). However, the slave revolts in Saint-Domingue put an end to sympathy and solidarity extended by the "Friends of the Blacks" (Mbembe 2017, 74–75). When Western reason's power was threatened, its limits and fragility were swiftly unmasked.

Mbembe (2017, 36) delves into the unconscious of Western reason to locate how the Black man, whose stolen labor and dehumanization fertilizes and haunts European modernity, is witness to a "mutilated humanity." With the rise of the colonial plantation economy, a new form of governmental reason emerged that considered the world an unlimited market. The Black body became an object to be possessed as property, merchandise to be employed and exchanged toward the accumulation of wealth globally (Mbembe 2017, 79). Revolutions in Europe, fought in the name of liberty and equality, did not automatically overcome slavery or racial segregation. Ironically, while the French and American revolutions were celebrated as symbols of Enlightenment ideals of freedom and emancipation, in the aftermath of slave revolts, Black individuals were systematically stripped of their rights and dignity, ranging from lifetime slavery to civic destitution. In response to the question, "Can Blacks govern themselves?" the Enlightenment thinkers expressed their doubts regarding Black people's aptitude for self-rule. The alleged lack of reason and ability to exercise autonomy disqualified Blacks as "human apart" (Mbembe 2017, 85–86).

The fiction of Blackness continues to endure, despite the formal end of colonialism and apartheid. New imperial practices and the dual violence of race and capital are universalizing the *Black condition*, or what Mbembe calls the "Becoming Black of the world" (Mbembe 2017, 6). The contradiction that marks the relationship between race and democracy is that the formal equality and emancipation of former slaves has not ushered in a postracial world (Mbembe 2017, 83–84). From migration to biometrics, from tourism to citizenship, racial tropes are mobilized to manage populations and justify violence against certain bodies marked as threatening (Mbembe 2017, 21).

As an antidote to the Western perception of Blackness as a symbol of abjection and degradation, Mbembe (2017, 28) foregrounds the Black consciousness of itself. The fight is against the adjective *inferior* being attached to the nouns *Black* and *Africa*. Taking away Europe's monopoly on the future, the formerly colonized go beyond the task of mere survival to "construct himself [sic] as a subject capable of projecting himself [sic] into the future" (Mbembe 2017, 154). Ironically, it was the native's lack of foresight and inability to envision and plan for the future that justified colonialism as *mission civilisatrice*. Négritude and Pan-Africanism aimed to reconfigure the noun *Nègre*, making it into a "miraculous weapon" of self-determination that underwrote calls for reparations, restitution, and justice (Mbembe 2017, 43). These critical narratives, emerging from a polyglot internationalism, shape the Black imaginary as an expression of self-determination. In a dialectic move, Mbembe gives us insight into the emergence of Black self-reconstruction, where Black subjects overcome their experience of a "castrated humanity" (Mbembe 2017, 26).

Drawing on a comprehensive, albeit exclusively male, lineage of Black radical thought, Mbembe outlines how the term *Black* came to be resignified in terms of radical reversal (Mbembe 2017, 40). The attempt is not to overcome the interpellated colonial identity and escape into the universality of the category *human*. It is worth remembering the African American lesbian feminist Pat Parker's poem "For the White Person Who Wants to Know How to Be My Friend," which begins this way:

> The first thing you do is to forget that I'm black.
> Second, you must never forget that I'm black. (Parker 2000, 73)

This insightfully captures the ambivalence at the heart of wounded identities, which are at once a site of vulnerability and a source of agency and empowerment. This resonates with Améry's (1980 [1966], 82) predicament "on the necessity and impossibility of being a Jew." Césaire, by contrast, proclaims, "Black I am and Black I will stay" (quoted in Mbembe 2017, 159).

Mbembe, like Eze, is cognizant of the dangers of ontologizing Blackness and takes seriously Fanon's warnings to Négritude and Pan-Africanism about the pitfalls of valorizing Blackness. He draws on the insights of the Cameroonian philosopher Fabien Eboussi Boulaga and warns that claiming Black difference does not automatically lead to self-determination. Instead of overcoming racial stereotypes, one can end up reenforcing the logic of race in both affirming and denying identities. To usher in a world without race would involve a critical memory politics, as well as a radical rupture in the unconscious investment of Black subjects in the colonial project. It is not enough to simply cease being a slave; one must also avoid becoming a master.

To survive under slavery, Black subjects developed strategies of resilience that shaped Black consciousness. Even as this is a source of strength, it must also, in Mbembe's view, be transcended—not through a repudiation of Blackness by "conversion to Christianity, the introduction of market economy . . . , and the adoption of rational, enlightened forms of government," but through a return of humanity to racialized subjects (Mbembe 2017, 87–88, 182). In a dialectical move, Mbembe focuses on the singularity of Black experience to contest colonial stereotypes while hinting toward a future that is free of the "burden of race," erasing the distinction between *Black* and *white*, resulting in a "world that everyone has the right to inherit" (Mbembe 2017, 167). In focusing on Blackness not in terms of biological destiny but as a consciousness of *Black experiences* in all their diversity and heterogeneity, Mbembe (2017, 177) aspires to a "world-beyond-race." Instead of the particularism of identities associated with *Blackness* and *Africa*, the impossible but necessary project of redeeming a universal critical humanism (Mbembe 2008) would entail once racialized subjects becoming "human amongst other humans" (Mbembe 2017, 167).

Despite being "exploitable objects," Mbembe highlights how, historically, the positions of Black people—for instance, on plantations—were unstable and reversible, such that they embodied the ambivalence of power, with former slaves themselves becoming slave owners and hunters of fugitive slaves (Mbembe 2017, 18). Here, his analysis departs from the scholars of the decolonial option, who disregard the ambivalent nature of Black agency and thereby romanticize the so-called abject subject. Mbembe suggests that instead of forming an attachment to the signifier *Black*, one must approach it with a certain caution and with the aim of deontologizing it (Mbembe 2017, 173). He laments that the "concept of Africa invoked in most discourses on 'decolonization' is deployed as if there were unanimity within Africa itself about what is 'African' and what is not. Most of the time, African is equated with the 'indigenous'/'ethnic'/'native,' as if there were no other grounds for an African identity than the 'indigenous' and the 'ethnic'" (Mbembe 2021, 78). He bemoans the lack of critical engagement with Indigenous epistemologies, which are at times paternalistically valorized. In an indirect criticism of Mignolo's "epistemic delinking," Mbembe (2021, 89) warns: "If 'decolonial acts' are to be anything more than mere acts of disconnection or separation," then "they must work through connectivity and elasticity, continuous stretching, and even distortion." Given our planetary entanglements, decolonization, for Mbembe (2017, 1), opens up possibilities but also presents dangers for critical thought.

To conclude this section, I turn to the Habermasian accusation that critique of (Western) reason renders emancipatory politics untenable. According to Rolf Tiedemann, Habermas's influential essay "The Entwinement of Myth and Enlightenment: Re-reading Dialectic of Enlightenment," which appeared in *New German Critique* in 1982, not only served the purpose of discrediting Adorno (Tiedemann, quoted in Rocco 1994, 93), but also functioned as a foil for his attack on the French postmodernists.[6] Habermas called Foucault and Derrida "Young Conservatives" and accused them of being anti-Enlightenment and anti-normative. Unsurprisingly, Habermas attacked both Adorno and Derrida on similar grounds.

It is noteworthy that Habermas was not alone in diagnosing overlaps in the first generation of Critical Theory and poststructuralism. In fact, Foucault (1996b, 353) expresses his remorse over the belatedness of his encounter with the writings of Adorno: "If I had known the Frankfurt School at the right time, I would have been spared a lot of work. Some nonsense,

I wouldn't have expressed and taken many detours as I sought not to let myself be led astray when the Frankfurt School had already opened the ways." In response to Habermas's censure, Foucault (1984, 43) objects to the intellectual tug-of-war of having to choose between being "for" or "against" the Enlightenment, such that "all criticism of reason and every critical test of the history of rationality" is given the choice of either recognizing reason or being cast into irrationalism (Foucault 1996b, 353).

Habermas's choice of words in his condemnation of Horkheimer and Adorno is telling. He laments that under the influence of "dark" authors, Horkheimer and Adorno destroy the foundations of reason (Habermas 1982, 21–22) by writing the "blackest, most nihilistic book" (Habermas 1982, 13). As previously discussed, for Habermas the Enlightenment is characterized by modern science and technology, positive law, secular ethics, and autonomous art. These presumed positive and illuminating forces of history, in his reading, have been misrepresented by wayward thinkers such as Nietzsche, whose counter-Enlightenment positions are dangerous for the future of humankind. Along similar lines, in condemning both society and rationality as repressive, Horkheimer and Adorno are accused of pulling the rug out from beneath their own feet, thereby depriving themselves of the intellectual and normative grounds for emancipatory thought (Habermas 1982, 23). If reason were so corrupted by purposiveness, Habermas argues, there would be no possibility of rescuing the Enlightenment, which would render the entire project of Critical Theory untenable. Habermas (1982, 23) remarks: "It is still difficult to understand a certain carelessness in their treatment of, to put it quite blatantly, the achievements of Western rationalism. How can the two advocates of the Enlightenment (which they always claimed to be and still are) so underestimate the rational content of cultural modernity that they observe in its elements only the amalgamation of reason and domination, of power and validity?"

Instead of an excess of reason, Habermas diagnoses a deficiency of rationality as obstructing the project of modernity. To fulfill the unfinished project of modernity, the realization and institutionalization of the process of rationalization are imperative. Habermas seeks to reground normative critique in communicative action to salvage the emancipatory potential of the Enlightenment. He assumes that as equal rational beings, we are all entitled to the same rights and duties; it is not the differences but, rather, our commonalities as speaking and acting agents that form the basis of justifying shared ideals that govern interpersonal relations through the institutionalization of norms.

However, the triumph of reason can be celebrated only by disregarding issues of race, class, gender, sexuality, religion, and colonialism. In Habermas's scheme of things, differences do not make a difference. In his understanding of a future as the fulfillment of what is already latent in the present, there is a substantive inevitability and irrevocability (Benhabib 1986, 276). Furthermore, as Benhabib points out, for Habermas, the norms of modernity are neither historical nor contingent but universally binding. For him, all that is nonuniversalizable and culturally specific falls outside the bounds of truth and morality.

When asked whether his theory was relevant for the Third World, Habermas responded: "I am tempted to say 'no.' . . . I am aware of the fact that this is a Eurocentrically limited view. I would rather pass the question" (quoted in Morrow 2013, 128–29). Morrow admits that Habermas could be accused of omission but pleads that Habermas is not paternalistic in offering lessons to the non-European world. It is further argued that Habermas's notion of modernity as an "unfinished project" can encompass multiple modernities and diverse forms of life, indicating that he recognizes the ambivalent nature of human rights and is open to being enlightened by non-European cultures (Morrow 2013, 129–30). Along similar lines, James Ingram (2018, 502) argues that, while Habermas upholds the universal validity of modern, rational norms, he concedes that they must be culturally and politically contextualized and are provisional regarding their moral content.

However, as Allen (2016) compellingly demonstrates, in the name of immanent critique, which understands knowledge and validity to emerge from historical processes, the post–Adornian Frankfurt School theorists reinstate the preeminence of European norms. Habermas elevates the West as the standard for other societies and cultures. Despite claims to universality, his insights are deeply parochial, reflecting a specifically Eurocentric history and experience. The narrative of modernizing Eurocentric progressivism is furthermore decoupled from the history of colonialism. So, for instance, when Habermas draws on Kant to analyze the emergence of bourgeois public spheres as the site of deliberative democracy and gives the example of coffeehouses where the public use of reason flourished, I would ask of Habermas: Where did the coffee come from? Where did the sugar in the coffee come from? Or the tobacco the bourgeois men smoked? Who financed the Enlightenment? As Fanon (1963 [1961], 102) remarks: "Europe is literally the creation of the third world."

In my view, Habermas's (1982, 13 and passim) choice of words when condemning *Dialectic of Enlightenment* as a "strange book," "dark," "black," and "nihilistic" is indicative of his race politics. One can deduce that his accusations against Horkheimer and Adorno would also be levied against postcolonial critique of Western reason, for ultimately, in Habermas's (1983, 249) view, multiple rationalities must be subsumed under the universal structure of rationalization. His teleological account of history and his claim that social and political practices are framed by universal norms that are ahistorical leave no room for the singularity of Black experiences. Akin to Kant, reason is color-blind for Habermas; accordingly, he would reject the Black critique of Western reason for underplaying the accomplishments of modernity with the primary focus on colonialism, apartheid, and slavery. In Habermas's view, Mbembe's *Critique of Black Reason* would be as "dangerous" a book as *Dialectic of Enlightenment* because of their shared criticism of Western reason and the Enlightenment, which leads to normative nihilism.

In the face of Habermas's claim that a rational critique of reason leads to aporia, one could argue with Kant and Adorno that the self-reflective nature of reason makes it possible for reason to scrutinize itself. This is exactly what Mbembe undertakes in his critique of Black reason. He deploys reason to rebuke reason and does so only to redeem it. Adding *Black* before *reason* exposes the contingency of both terms. It is instructive to recall Fanon's reflections on the impossible relation between Black and reason. Fanon observes that Western ideas of reason are not only the outcome of racial inequality but are produced for the purposes of legitimating it. Reason is not merely tainted by barbarism but is the handmaiden of domination: "I had rationalized the world, and the world had rejected me on the basis of color prejudice. Since no agreement was possible on the level of reason, I threw myself back toward unreason. . . . I am made of the irrational; I wade in the irrational. Up to the neck in the irrational" (Fanon 1986 [1952], 123).

Habermas (1987, 116) questions the normative grounds of critiques of modernity. Deborah Cook (2018, 87) compellingly argues that the basis for Adorno's critique lies in "determinate negation" (Adorno 2008 [1965], 28)—namely, in the negation of the negative social conditions in which we live. For Adorno (2005d [1969], 151), "the false" alludes to what is right and better because it points dialectically to its own reversal. For instance, our understanding of freedom derives from the negation of unfree conditions. Instead of failing to provide ideals, Adorno takes the nonideal conditions as the point of departure and inverts them to arrive at ideal ones (Pritchard 2002, 293). Adorno's immanent critique goes against David Hume's law, which rejects moving from descriptive statements to prescriptive ones.

By resisting what is, those who experience unfreedom, injustice, and oppression give insight into how things should (not) be. Adorno believes that, to strive for an improved life, the critical dissection of damaged life is imperative: "We may not know what people are and what the correct arrangement of human affairs should be, but we do know what they should not be and what arrangement of human affairs is false. Only in this particular and concrete knowledge is the other positive one open to us" (Adorno 2003a [1953], 456). Against Habermas's harsh condemnation of Adorno's lack of a normative framework to ground his critique, Cook (2018, 88–89) argues that Adorno's "negative prescription" gleans guidance from a critique of damaged life. This is undertaken without offering a secure standpoint or moral certainty for critique, which is bound to frustrate those in search of normative foundations. The search for a better life arises from pain, outrage, and suffering (Adorno 2004 [1966], 202, 365) rather than from robust universal normative principles, on which Habermas insists (Cook 2018, 89). Thus, instead of providing categorical moral grounding for emancipatory action, the focus is on injustice and violence to show that people resist when conditions become intolerable, and not because of a textbook understanding of right and wrong. Adorno thus eliminates the need to dictate to people what they should do, because, like Marx, he does not wish "to prefigure the future, but . . . to find the new world only through criticism of the old" (Marx 1978a [1843], 13).

Like Adorno, Mbembe chastises Western reason by drawing on the experiences of its victims, who have been dehumanized and disenfranchised by its principles. The Habermasian demand that criticism of slavery and genocide must be substantiated with normative foundations seems cynical and disingenuous in light of European colonial atrocities and crimes against humanity. Thus, instead of a politics of recognition in which the presumed master acknowledges the rights of the so-called slave as those of a legitimate political and ethical subject based on shared normative principles, Adorno and Mbembe offer a more complex framing of power relations. As Adorno explains, "To assure the black that he is exactly like the white man, while he obviously is not, is secretly to wrong him still further. He is benevolently humiliated by the application of a standard by which, under the pressure of the system, he must necessarily be found wanting, and to satisfy which would in any case be a doubtful achievement" (Adorno 2005a [1951], 103).

In the Hegelian master-slave dialectic, the subject (the master) reinstates its identity at the expense of the object (the slave). In contrast, the

Adornian dynamic between subject and object is marked by dialectical negation, which is characterized by the recalcitrance of the object rather than dialectical reciprocity (Varadharajan 1995, xxii). Mbembe rehearses Adorno's position in arguing that the Black consciousness of Blackness in refusing the reality of the white consciousness of Blackness offers the promise of a different future. By eluding the instrumental rationality of the knowing subject, the object disrupts its epistemological desires (Varadharajan 1995, xxiii). Adorno's advice on how to negotiate the reduction to friend-foe relation is "not to choose between black and white but to abjure such prescribed choices" (Adorno 2005a [1951], 132). Adorno would reject fetishizing concepts such as *Black* and *Africa*, which homogenize particulars into universals, thereby disregarding their singularity.

To conclude: A Black critique of Western reason offers hope for redeeming the Enlightenment from its pernicious legacies. In a dialectical move, Mbembe (2017, 36–37) reveals how the very experience of dehumanization "produced by the dual violence of race and capital" also carries with it the possibility of "radical insurgency." Adorno, who is often accused of despair, is surprisingly hopeful when he remarks: "What can oppose the decline of the West is not a resurrected culture but the utopia that is silently contained in the image of its decline" (Adorno 1997 [1955], 72). Mbembe takes this Adornian insight to heart.

Western reason and Enlightenment are defended by Habermas, who proposes discursive rationality as a counterpoint to the coercive nature of instrumental reason. He thereby offers an emancipatory and progressive aspect of Enlightenment reason. In the concluding section, I draw on Spivak's postcolonial feminist critique to problematize the Enlightenment valorization of the resistant speaking subject. This is a core concern of the book as it links decolonization with desubalternization. Let us turn to Spivak for some answers.

Redemptive Critique and Reenchantment of the Enlightenment

Dialectic of Enlightenment, as Schmidt points out, "ends with an image of awakening from a dream, of a coming to a possession of one's powers." Interestingly, one of the eighteenth-century meanings of the word *Aufklären* signifies a return to consciousness after a period of illness or sleep (Schmidt 1998, 835). Horkheimer and Adorno believed that the Enlightenment could be reset from its destructive path toward nondominant futures (Schmidt 1998, 835). The key questions are, of course: How can the Enlightenment be rescued? And who will rescue it?

Articulations of resistant agency and fleeting moments of escape from the totality of power in *Dialectic of Enlightenment* are interestingly linked to the figure of woman (Hewitt 1992, 147). While Horkheimer and Adorno examine the exclusion of woman and nature as an inherent feature of the Enlightenment, they also highlight the redemptive force of the feminine in overcoming totalitarian systems of power (Hewitt 1992, 156). Such elisions make patriarchy, fascism, and capitalism vulnerable to resistance and subversion. However, the valorization of women as liberators of humanity as such essentializes and homogenizes the feminine, even if in positive terms. This feminist counternarrative, seen as a model of liberation and a form of reenchantment with the world, overlooks the complexity and diversity inherent in the category of woman.

The potential for redemptive critique is anchored in marginalized subjectivities, who embody radical alterity, offering alternative modes of thinking and being. This begs the question of whether resistant subjectivities bear within themselves the trace of that which is nonidentical to rationalized capital, or whether locating critical potential in these subjectivities risks a romantic vision of politics (Marasco 2006, 100). The messianic powers assigned to these subjectivities to redeem utopian futures disavow how the desires, imaginaries, and practices of these marginalized subjects and collectivities are themselves, to a certain extent, the effects of bourgeois rationality (Marasco 2006, 106). These subjectivities emerge and bear traces of the memories and practices of the violence done to them. Resistant agencies are not impervious to dominant forms of rationality and power, even as they are presented as a radical alterity and excess thereof. Thus, these resistant subject positions emerge as a historical product of the dominant rationality, even as they embody the aporias and vulnerabilities of that order and, thus, a promise of subverting and overcoming it (Marasco 2006, 107). In "The Communist Manifesto," Marx (1978b [1843], 483) wrote: "What the bourgeoisie therefore produces, above all, are its own grave-diggers. Its fall and the victory of the proletariat are equally inevitable." By creating a vast underprivileged working class, the bourgeoisie produced its own antagonists, as this oppressed class is bound to organize itself and overthrow the bourgeoisie in a revolutionary way.

Unlike Marx's gravediggers, Spivak warns against celebrating subalterns as revolutionary agents of history and repositories of a utopian imaginary.

(Chapter 4 focuses in detail on the relationship of critique, resistance, and subalternity.) Instead, Spivak views subalternity as an effect of hegemony, as well as its limit—that which escapes incorporation into totalized rationality. Resistant subjects can frustrate and destabilize rationality's impulse for total domination; however, this is only part of their agency. Spivak argues that the impulse to reify the agency of subaltern subjects must be eschewed. This raises challenging questions for postcolonial-queer-feminist resistance, particularly regarding how a critique of colonial and patriarchal violence can genuinely lead to emancipation. The portrayal of resistant subject positions often reveals a nostalgic longing for imagined innocent pasts and an infatuation with untainted agency, overlooking their entanglement with the historical legacies of the Enlightenment. It is essential to complicate the relationship between otherness and revolution, recognizing that there is no outside from which to redeem or renounce the Enlightenment. All strategies, tactics, imaginaries, desires, practices, and epistemologies employed for emancipatory purposes are inherently intertwined with the Enlightenment project, which cannot be entirely repudiated. The decolonial aspiration to access untouched pasts and pure knowledge, free from historical complicity, is untenable. This approach disregards the complexities and dangers of categorically rejecting the Enlightenment.

At the same time, drawing on the insights from the chapter's epigraph, engaging with the Enlightenment does not imply an uncritical acceptance of its legacies. Dipesh Chakrabarty (2000) challenges Eurocentric assumptions by recontextualizing Europe as merely a province rather than as a universal entity or dominant center within historical narratives (Vázquez-Arroyo 2008, 459). While affirming that concepts such as citizenship, the state, civil society, humanism, and the public sphere are intrinsic to political modernity, Chakrabarty observes that these ideas are ineluctable and yet insufficient. The postcolonial world must navigate this dual legacy: "Modern social critiques of caste, oppressions of women, lack of rights for labor and subaltern classes in India, and so on and, in fact, the very critique of colonialism itself are unthinkable except as a legacy, partially, of how Enlightenment Europe was appropriated in the subcontinent" (Chakrabarty 2000, 6). Along similar lines, instead of a deferential and abject acceptance of the fruits of the Enlightenment, Spivak focuses on the inadequacy and indispensability of the critical legacies of the Enlightenment and recommends an "affirmative sabotage" of the master's tools. (This is discussed in greater detail in chapter 4). As Fanon (2007 [1959], 90) already remarks in A Dying Colonialism: "Expressing oneself in

French, understanding French, was no longer tantamount to treason or to an impoverishing identification with the occupier. Used by the *Voice of the Combatants*, conveying in a positive way the message of the Revolution, the French language also becomes an instrument of liberation."

Contrary to both a Habermasian view of modernity as an unfinished project and the decolonial rejection of the Enlightenment, I propose an understanding of modernity in terms of its ambivalence. Decolonial scholars perceive modernity not as an ideal to emulate but as a problem to be addressed by eliminating European epistemic, sociocultural, and political practices from the global South. However, I remain skeptical of the decolonial approach's nostalgia for an idealized past and the notion that adopting non-European Indigenous perspectives alone can lead to a decolonization of the mind. Instead, I suggest a reorientation in the geography of reason, advocating for an attitudinal shift toward modern concepts such as citizenship and political agency.

Postcolonial-queer-feminist theory thus remains "ambivalently critical" (Marasco 2006, 110), as the norms of equality and freedom that frame its emancipatory aspirations are indebted to the European Enlightenment. Critique entails a historically inflected practice that is contingent on, contextualized within, and complicit in the conditions from which it emerges, even as it aspires to transform them. Understanding the subaltern as a negation of the hegemonic does not imply that the subaltern can be considered separately from it. Herein lies the fragility and the conundrum of postcolonial-queer-feminist critical practice: It is both framed and constrained by the historical conditions from which it emerges, without the security of stable foundations or the promise of radical overcomings. Postcolonial-queer-feminist critical practice eschews eschatology in favor of holding on to the tension and discontinuity between knowing and hoping, between actuality and potentiality (Marasco 2006, 112).

This begs the question of the most efficient formula for decolonization: Is it a move beyond the canon by drawing on nonwhite, non-European, non-heterosexist perspectives? Or does this end up essentializing and romanticizing the Other? Is a poststructuralist "decolonization from within" sufficient to purge the Eurocentrism of Enlightenment thought? Or do Marxism and poststructuralism need to be decolonized, as well?

Honneth (2009, 41–42) claims that the "critical project will have no future" unless it offers a rational concept of "emancipatory interest" that can relate to itself reflexively. Yet what are the lures and limits of critique in its redemptive mode? Frankfurt School Critical Theory prides itself on taking seriously the social conditions that facilitate the emergence of critical practice, yet it has ignored colonialism and its consequences. Equating world history with the Enlightenment disregards other forms of reason and perspectives on temporality and spatiality. However, is a postcolonial provincialization of Europe sufficient to decolonize the globe? As Talal Asad (2009b, 138–39) notes, "In the process of thinking, one should be open to ending up in unanticipated places—whether these produce satisfaction or desire, discomfort or horror." In addition to contesting androcentric and Eurocentric positions, critical theories of decolonization must unsettle and disorient their own assumptions. While decolonial approaches seek modes of thinking untainted by Enlightenment rationality, I do not subscribe to the recovery of pure forms of thought, which supposedly existed prior to or beyond the Enlightenment. In my view, the disenchantment with the Enlightenment cannot be reversed merely by repudiating it. Here we must heed Hegel's (1977 [1807], 331) warning that every struggle against the Enlightenment only exacerbates the problem.

Allen (2016, 33) suggests that a corrective to Eurocentrism involves adopting a "stance of modesty or humility, rather than one of superiority toward our own moral certainties." Being cognizant of one's biases "facilitates a willingness to have one's own commitments destabilized in the encounter with other forms of life" (Allen 2016, 76). Moreover, such humility will "suspend the assumption that my form of life is superior to those of the cultural Others with whom I am in dialogue" (Allen 2016, 76). Although compelling, this attitude of epistemic modesty assumes that we have our prejudices and stereotypes under control and that we can unlearn and rearrange them at will. This perspective disregards the role of the pre- and unconscious in our intellectual, ethical, and materialist formations. If one does not assume an epistemologically transparent knowing subject, capable of directly and deliberately altering their intellectual formations, then decolonization, as an "uncoercive rearrangement of desires" (Spivak 2003a, 615), reveals itself as a complex and potentially impossible project of unlearning racism, heterosexism, and imperialism. In this context, the relationship between the hegemonic and subaltern groups must be reconfigured.

Subalternity is produced when the disenfranchised are exiled from critical thinking by denying them access to the "master's tools." Once hegemonic norms are internalized, subalterns, constituted as docile workers and obedient citizens, effectively become "the principle of their own subjection" (Foucault 1995, 203). In contrast, the elite perceive themselves as vanguards and messiahs, thereby monopolizing agency. To guard against a purely rationalist, cognitivist, or voluntarist conception of critique, one must remain vigilant about the role of ideology in the constitution of the subject. Concurrently, we must resist efforts to reduce critical practice to political psychology, as this risks diminishing decolonization from a matter of economic and political justice into one of collective therapy. Instead of explaining racism, fascism, and heterosexism as symptoms of personality disorder or behavioral problems, the focus should be on subject constitution on both sides of the colonial divide. This overlaps with the concerns of Adorno, who, to understand fascism, examines "the personality forces that favor its acceptance" to diagnose the sources of antidemocratic thought and action among individuals (Adorno et al. 1950, 1). While Adorno focused on antisemitism and critical race scholars such as Mbembe engage with racism, Spivak analyzes how gender and class intersect to produce both imperial *and* subaltern subjects. She traces the precolonial processes of subalternization, which were bolstered during colonialism and did not end with the achievement of formal independence. Like Adorno, Spivak emphasizes the significance of education in nurturing democratic impulses and mitigating societal subjugation.

While Kant explains immaturity as a result of laziness or cowardice, Adorno argues that a lack of maturity is not always self-incurred but is systematically produced and willed (Cook 2018, 84). Adjusting to the status quo to survive entails self-abnegation and obedience, which impede personal and collective maturity. As long as we submit to authority figures and demagogic leaders, the possibility of totalitarianism persists (Cook 2018, 82). When individuals are able "to resist established opinions and . . . existing institutions, to resist everything that is merely posited, that justifies itself with its existence" (Adorno 2005f [1969], 281–82), they achieve a state of being able to think for themselves.

Likewise, subalternization is produced by cultural and educational institutions that foster a docile acceptance of authority instead of facilitating critical intelligence. Instead of coding resistance in terms of street protests or political action, Adorno and Spivak understand it as the capacity to think critically. Spivak would agree with Adorno that if subalterns were cognizant of "what the world has done to them," they would be "different from what they are and could not be turned into whatever it is that the course of the world has made of them" (Adorno 2006 [1964–65], 73). To resist the status quo, subalterns must first understand themselves as a power effect of these very social, political, and economic conditions. Only then can they become more than the submissive subjects of capitalism and neocolonialism. This perspective is markedly different from those of Foucault, Deleuze, and Butler, who assume the resistant agency of the masses. (This is discussed in greater detail in chapter 4).

Following Adorno, Spivak is also interested in the fate of our desires and imaginaries as shaped by late capitalism (Cook 2018, 14). Historically, power inflects the body to obey, thereby constituting subalterns as politically acquiescent citizens and economically useful subjects. Instead of focusing on universal rational speaking subjects, Spivak examines how subalterns are formed under specific historical conditions and how they understand and recognize themselves through a stereotype of themselves. She is suspicious of anthropological universals, as they ignore what is historically distinct—namely, the singularity of subalternization.

Before concluding this chapter, I present my understanding of the postcolonial feminist arguments advanced by Spivak and draw on them to defend Adorno against Habermas's charges of performative contradiction. In the hope of salvaging the critical energies of the Enlightenment tradition (Jay 2016, 114), Habermas seeks "the replacement of the critique of pure reason by the critique of linguistic reason" (Schnädelbach 1995, 270) that emerges as a harbinger of emancipation, progress, freedom, and equality. He highlights the emancipatory possibilities of discursive rationality, which he views as noncoercive. His understanding of the unfinished project of modernity involves an ongoing process of deliberation about everyday issues, which, by definition, is open-ended. Since rationality is never fully attainable, it is proposed as a regulative ideal (Jay 2016, 137).

Habermas shifts the focus from subjectivity to intersubjectivity, proposing communicative rationality as an antidote to instrumental rationality, grounded in principles of freedom and equality. However, his vision of deliberative democracy, where differing claims are rationally and consensually resolved through the force of the better argument without coercion or constraint, entails a Eurocentric and androcentric normative bias that produces consensus through exclusion. Habermas disregards racist, sexist, and heterosexist violence that affects intersubjective relations and distorts deliberation. A scholar focusing on the lifeworld—ordinary social situations in which humans interact and in which language and culture play crucial roles—fails to address the economic, cultural, political, and social legacies of colonialism. It should come as no surprise that the history of modernity is presented in a progressive mode, with Europe and Europeans as role models, without sparing any thought to the global violence committed by Europe to promote and protect norms of modernity. Habermas's focus on intersubjective communication as the panacea for the problems that afflict modernity knowingly disregards the issue of subject constitution and the roles of race, class, gender, religion, and nationality. His assertion that the presumed better argument would prevail in interactions between properly communicating individuals (Habermas 1990, 89, 198) fails to consider the role of power and violence in determining who has the authority to adjudicate these deliberations.

According to Habermas, rational individuals are naturally inclined toward a democratic community, assuming a speaking subject who is self-aware and open in communication. This perspective ignores how speech acts and subjects that do not align with androcentric and Eurocentric norms are often silenced or excluded. The emphasis on communicative rationality and transparency disregards the complexity and diversity of discursive practices and their contexts. As Foucault argued, the pressure to conform to normative ideals is particularly insidious when promoted in the name of freedom and equality.

Habermas (1982, 23) finds it "difficult to understand a certain carelessness in [Horkheimer and Adorno's] treatment of, to put it quite blatantly, the achievements of Western rationalism." In my view, Horkheimer and Adorno make a compelling case in linking the Enlightenment to the Holocaust, leaving one to wonder how Habermas can still boast of the purported achievements of Western rationalism. Adorno (1993) often described his Critical Theory as "messages in a bottle," suggesting it was untimely and lacked an audience or addressee. After reading Habermas's critique of *Dialectic of Enlightenment*, it seems evident that he was not receptive to Adorno's messages. Furthermore, his neglect of postcolonial studies exemplifies the short-sightedness of post–Adornian Frankfurt School theorists. In his celebration of Western modernity, Habermas displays a "careless" (to use his own term) disregard for colonial history. As one of the most revered contemporary thinkers and a major proponent of ethical discourse, Habermas—who has championed the role of the public intellectual and cited Heinrich Heine as a role model, offering his opinions on major controversies in German public life such as the *Historikerstreit* in 1986 and the Israel-Hamas war in 2023— has been shockingly and disappointingly silent on Germany's colonial legacy. One might sympathize with Philippe Lacoue-Labarthe's chastisement of Jean-François Lyotard for engaging in a debate with Habermas, stating: "Why take seriously a kind of dinosaur from the *Aufklärung*? And why go after him?" (Lacoue-Labarthe, quoted in Ronell 1994, 262).

Nancy Fraser, drawing on Spivak's understanding of subalternity, contests the Eurocentric and androcentric bias in Habermas's idea of the public sphere, where rational subjects deliberate over common interests. Fraser (1997, 123) introduces the concept of transnational subaltern counterpublics, described as "parallel discursive arenas where members of subordinated social groups invent and circulate counter-discourses to formulate oppositional interpretations of their identities, interests, and needs." She critiques the Habermasian public sphere for allowing bourgeois European men to position themselves as the "universal class," thereby justifying their fitness to govern (Fraser 1992, 114). Transnational subaltern counterpublics challenge this by creating competing publics, enabling disenfranchised groups to develop and share counterhegemonic discourses and identities. Fraser argues that these counterpublics empower marginalized groups by providing a platform for their voices in political discourse; facilitating discussions on redistribution, recognition, and representation; and challenging dominant forms of rule across economic, cultural, and sociopolitical arenas, thereby showcasing their emancipatory potential.

Spivak (2008, 3, 154) elucidates that subalternity emerges when subjects are barred from accessing the public sphere, which itself is a legacy of European colonialism. Against the Habermasian claim that "the non-coercive coercion of the better argument" prevails in public spheres (Habermas 1982, 14), Spivak would argue that, first, if one takes the issue of ideological subject constitution seriously, then not everyone is "trained for intellectual performance" (more on this in chapter 4), which prevents them from being equal partners in the process of deliberation and contestation. The consensus that is produced through the process of deliberation does not account for differential distributions of power, agency, and vulnerability within society. Second, even when subalterns speak, they are not heard, which problematizes Fraser's promise of subaltern counterpublics as emancipatory. It is not merely a matter of making the public sphere more inclusive; rather, the formation of public spheres is constitutively exclusive. Thus, the term *subaltern counterpublics* is a *contradictio in adiecto*. In place of a presumed expressive subject of modernity, Spivak's "Can the Subaltern Speak?" is a rhetorical question, as the impossibility of subaltern speech acts is inherent in the notion of subalternity.

Habermas's discourse ethics, as a framework for emancipation, offers everyone the opportunity to participate equally in exercising the use of reason publicly. Silence proves menacing for Habermas (2002, 67), who avers that "the person who is addressed and remains silent, clothes himself or herself in an aura of indeterminate significance and imposes silence. For this, Heidegger is one example among many. Because of this authoritarian character, Sartre has rightly called silence 'reactionary.'" In arguing that the subaltern cannot speak, Spivak is challenging Habermas's claim that speech is a sign of political agency and available to all rational subjects, a norm deeply rooted in Enlightenment thought. The impossibility of subaltern speech is not incidental but constitutive of their subject formation. Spivak problematizes the redemptive effort to narrate history from the standpoint of its victims, as if the recovery of subaltern perspectives is a straightforward exercise of reinstating them as speaking subjects. Instead of celebrating subaltern agency, Spivak (1991, 172) outlines how the native becomes "the unemphatic agent of withholding," thereby frustrating imperialist designs of integrating the other into the self.

In chapter 4, I offer an extended discussion of the novel *Foe*. For now, I limit myself to a brief insight into the conundrum of subaltern silence. In his retelling of Daniel Defoe's *Robinson Crusoe*, J. M. Coetzee focuses on Friday, Crusoe's mute Black servant, who evades the control of reason and serves as a counterexample to the Western understanding of an enlightened, speaking subject. If the modern project presumes a knowable and logocentric universe, then the unspeakable and the unrepresentable pose a challenge for its efforts at mastery (Spivak 1991). The mute subjectivity of the subaltern is perceived as an offense against Enlightenment rationality. Here Spivak aligns closely with Adorno's position on how capitalism and the culture industry (with Spivak additionally considering the roles of colonialism and feudalism) create compliant subjects, even as she does not valorize subaltern agency in terms of the speaking and thus resisting subject.

Spivak's postcolonial dilemmas are akin to Adorno's reflections, which suggest that, despite the most rigorous intellectual efforts, something always eludes and cannot be fully captured by the identifying processes of thought. While Habermas diagnoses the contradictions in Adorno's arguments as flaws and failures that must be addressed or resolved, for Adorno, an aporia is to be pursued dialectically. Following the ancient Greek idea of aporia as a non-path, Adorno emphasizes that one must examine the difficulty of the situation instead of pursuing quick resolutions (Morris 1996, 749). As Abbas (2012, 11) astutely states: "In Adorno we find, then, not so much a critique of the impossible and the false, but critique itself as what an impossible or false situation elicits." Performative contradiction is nearly a philosophical sin for Habermas and other critics, as it entails absurdity, illogicality, and incongruity.[7] However, if the very aim of the argument is to reveal that logic, consistency, and coherence are norms whose content is nondemocratically determined, then violating these norms is a success and not a failure of the critical thought project. Since thought is bound by the identity principle, Adorno suggests that critical thought must oppose identity thinking. By undoing instrumental reason, critique creates the possibility for the unthought to emerge. It refuses to "annex otherness" (Hewitt 1995, 86), allowing it to remain as the unknown other, beyond our hegemonic concepts. Adorno's critique of modernity and Enlightenment rationality calls for a shift in cognition away from coherence and mastery toward a form of critical thinking that is fragmentary, unsettling, and open-ended. The recalcitrant object can open up space for thought to imagine what it cannot yet anticipate. *Negative Dialectics* begins with the remark, "Philosophy, which once seemed obsolete, lives on because the moment to realize it was missed" (Adorno 2004 [1966], xi). Adorno thereby alludes to the promise of failure, suggesting that what is yet to be realized is bursting with the critical potential of what is to come.

This approach challenges the liberal-humanist view of speech as a means to achieve freedom and rationality, rooted in Aristotle's idea of humans as political and speaking beings and foundational to Habermas's discourse ethics. Instead of considering free speech as a tool for emancipation, it highlights the interplay of language, power, and violence. The idea that speech inherently produces rational freedom is contrasted with the notion that language itself can exercise violence. Furthermore, listening plays a crucial role, as hegemonic norms dictate what is considered intelligible and legible, thereby silencing those who are unable or unwilling to conform to the normative order. For example, it is essential to examine not only how a Third World woman might become an agent of decolonization but also how the category itself is shaped and limited by the discursive structures through which liberation is sought.

The postcolonial feminist Rey Chow (1993, 36–37) notes that when speech acts are embedded in systems of domination, efforts to amplify silenced voices risk failing to capture their myriad experiences. Echoing Spivak, the Black feminist Abena Busia (1989–90, 84) shifts the focus from whether the subaltern can speak to the issue that subalterns' words are often not understood or heard. This suggests that, rather than emphasizing the silencing of voices, it is more important to focus on the dominant's inability to listen and their selective hearing. Similarly, Spivak (1990, 158) argues that the essential question is not "Who should speak?" but "Who will listen?"

Commenting on Ludwig Wittgenstein's suggestion to pass over in silence what cannot be spoken, Adorno (2008 [1965], 74) maintains that critical thought represents the contradictory dialectical effort "to say what cannot be said." Spivak similarly argues that postcolonial feminist politics and ethics constitute an exercise in listening to the unheard and the silent. Simultaneously, given that all speech is embedded within power and violence, silence can function as a strategy of critique rather than merely as a passive act of submission or unvoicing. It can challenge the monologue of dominant discourses, thereby creating conditions for the invisible and the unsaid to emerge. This approach shifts the focus from the traditional logocentric strategies of emancipation to the possibilities of subversion through listening, which transform the power dynamic between the active speaker and the passive listener. Spivak, like Adorno, is aware of the risk that every attempt to articulate the unsaid carries the danger of imposing the logic of speech on it. Thus, against Habermas's speaking subject, the emphasis is on a postcolonial feminist ethics of listening.

The effort in this chapter was to address the ambivalent affinities between the first generation of Critical Theory and postcolonial queer feminism. It was inspired by Améry's belief in *Schicksalsverwandtschaft* between victims of entangled forms of historical violence and their shared but vexed relation to the legacies of the European Enlightenment. In the final chapter of part I, I focus on what might be called the mission impossible of decolonizing Europe. On January 12, 2023, Germany issued a statement that, under Article 63 of the International Court of Justice (ICJ) Statute, it would intervene as a third party on Israel's behalf in South Africa's legal case before the ICJ in The Hague, accusing Israel of genocide. The day also marked the 120th anniversary of the Herero-Nama genocide, which is considered the first instance of genocide of the twentieth century. In a press release, Namibia's President Hage Geingob chastised the Germans, remarking that Germany had demonstrated its inability to draw lessons from its horrific history. The anger, shared by several independent human rights experts, was directed at the dismissive tone in which Germany censured South Africa. Irrespective of the outcome of the case before the ICJ, what dismayed the postcolonial world was Europe's inconsistency and selectivity in its commitment to norms of international law, democracy, and human rights. This example is another proof of Europe's betrayal of the Enlightenment.

3

Europe: What Can It Teach Us?

To acknowledge our debt to the ideas of the Enlightenment is not to thank colonialism for bringing them to us. —DIPESH CHAKRABARTY AND AMITAV GHOSH, "A Correspondence on Provincializing Europe"

Given that the majority of the formerly colonized world has achieved formal independence, and with the rise of the intergovernmental organization known as BRICS (consisting of Brazil, Russia, India, China, South Africa, Egypt, Ethiopia, Indonesia, Iran and the United Arab Emirates), one may wonder why the issue of decolonization is still relevant. I would offer a twofold response to this question: The growing economic power of postcolonial countries such as India, which at times mimic major imperial powers, has not benefited the majority of their citizens, let alone the broader postcolonial world. Despite declarations of South-South cooperation, decades of formal independence have not undone global inequality. This indicates a failure of decolonization, with the elites in the global South replacing the former colonial masters. Second, the enduring global hegemony of the West, whether economic or political, necessitates the decolonization of global power relations. As argued in the previous chapters, colonialism was not just about economic exploitation and military occupation. It was also about the production of imperial and subaltern subjects. Unlike decolonial scholars such as Walter Mignolo (2009,

10), who celebrate the rise of China and India, I believe that decolonization without desubalternization is incomplete.

In what follows, I outline how the global redistribution of wealth must be accompanied by a reconfiguration of the relationships between Europe and the postcolonial world, as well as between the elites and the subalterns, in both the global North and the global South. I begin with the birthplace of the Enlightenment—namely, Europe—to demonstrate how it continues to thwart the project of decolonization by evading its historical responsibility.[1] Subsequently, I outline in greater detail the differences between decolonial and postcolonial understandings of decolonization. Thereafter, I engage with the objections of a group of Marxist scholars who accuse postcolonial studies of being anti-universal and consequently anti-Enlightenment, arguing that this hinders the process of decolonization. This debate is crucial for my argument, because Marxism is a critical legacy of the Enlightenment, even as it contests the Enlightenment notion of the free market. Its considerable influence on anticolonial and postcolonial thought is accompanied by a postcolonial critique of the Eurocentrism inherent in Marxism. In the context of the transnationalization of capitalism through colonialism, Marxism views decolonization as a global struggle against the universal phenomenon of class oppression. At the same time, postcolonial theory rethinks Marxism by foregrounding racial regimes of exploitation associated with slavery and imperial capitalism (Robinson 1983). The complex relationship between Marxism and postcolonial theory is an edifying example of the challenges of decolonization. Finally, I elaborate on how, in my view, the desubalternization of non-European epistemologies and the dehegemonization of the Enlightenment are inextricably linked. This chapter attempts to clarify the task and scope of critique in a world burdened by the legacies of colonialism and totalitarianism.

Another Europe Is (Im)possible

It is my firm belief that, to address the challenges of decolonization, we must reimagine our relationship with the Enlightenment and its legacies. As I have shown in the previous two chapters, postcolonial scholars have been accused of being both anti-Enlightenment *and* Eurocentric. While European thinkers such as Jürgen Habermas tout the accomplishments of European modernity, decolonial scholars such as Walter Mignolo and Ramón Grosfoguel propose a (re)turn to Indigenous epistemologies and cosmologies as a form of "epistemic delinking" to "decolonize the mind." They accuse postcolonial scholars of an overreliance on European critical traditions. Interestingly, Third World Marxists also assail postcolonial scholars for being anti-Enlightenment. What follows is an effort to understand the challenges of dehegemonizing and decolonizing the Enlightenment while desubalternizing non-European epistemologies.

In his lecture "Philosophy and the Crisis of European Humanity," delivered in Vienna in 1935, Edmund Husserl identified a profound crisis in Europe, with Nazism as merely a symptom. He suggested that only a complete reconfiguration of Europe could address this peril (Gasché 2009, 2). Husserl (1970 [1935], 273) described Europe not as a mere geographical, historical, cultural, political, or economic entity, but as a vision driven by a commitment to reshape humanity through universal reason. This project aimed to define human relations broadly rather than through specific linguistic or ethnic identities (Husserl 1970 [1935], 6). In the lecture, Husserl acknowledges that other cultures also offer world-encompassing ideas and grand narratives. However, he argues that these non-European perspectives lack universal validity, as they are tied to parochial traditions (Husserl 1970 [1935], 283). In contrast, Europe's quest for universal humanity and scientific knowledge is seen as transcending particularities, thereby legitimizing the global validity of European norms and values. Husserl (1970 [1935], 16) contends that Europe's self-awareness is historically unique and that Europe has a responsibility for the "Europeanization of all other civilizations." He views European thinkers as "functionaries of mankind" who safeguard "the telos which was inborn in European humanity" (Husserl 1970 [1935], 15–17).

Interestingly, the term *Europe* was coined by the Greeks, who did not consider themselves European, even though Greece is often regarded as the cradle of European culture (Gasché 2009, 9–10). The name signifies the onset of darkness after sunset, referring to the land of the evening (*Abendland*), in contrast to the Orient (*Morgenland*), where the sun rises. It is ironic that Europe is named with a term of non-European origin, reflecting a history in which Europe defines itself from an external perspective.

Husserl is not alone in viewing Europe as uniquely positioned to pursue a universal vision of humanity. Despite its history of exploitation and oppression, Europe is often praised for its tradition of self-critique and self-correction, which is seen as a strength stemming from the European Enlightenment. This practice of self-examination is considered Europe's greatest asset and is highlighted in European discourses as setting it apart from other cultures, which are perceived as lacking similar critical reflection.

Habermas, as discussed earlier, warns that reducing the European Enlightenment to a simplistic, instrumental form of reason ignores its liberating and critical aspects. He celebrates Enlightenment ideals of freedom, equality, and justice as enabling progress. The self-reflective capacity of the Enlightenment outweighs its destructive tendencies, so despite past missteps, Habermas argues, the final balance tilts in favor of the European Enlightenment (Habermas 1982, 17–18). A Eurocentric view often suggests that the issue lies not with the Enlightenment itself, but with the incomplete project of modernity, which has yet to be fully realized. Habermas's concept of Eurocentric time implies that Europeans are in a more advanced stage of modernity compared with others, who are considered less rational and stuck in the past (Habermas 1987, 4–6).

Questioning the progressivist Enlightenment narrative that positions Europe as the source and standard of critical thought, Dipesh Chakrabarty (2002, xix–xx) insightfully asks: "Can the designation of something or some group as non- or premodern ever be anything but a gesture of power?" Postcolonial perspectives challenge nostalgic narratives of an idealized past and the assumptions that current political and economic structures are inevitable outcomes of history's progressive arc. The paradox of Europe's self-perception as an allegedly emancipatory force lies in the historical erasure of the costs of its mission—slavery, exploitation, plunder, and genocide in the colonies through military, material, and epistemic violence.

Despite these shameful legacies, postcolonial critiques of Europe and efforts to "provincialize Europe" are often met with suspicion. Husserl (1970 [1935], 16) accused those who censure universal discourses as Eurocentric of "lazy reason" (*faulen Vernunft*). Similarly, postcolonial scholars who highlight Europe's historical crimes are often accused of essentializing Europe as a homogeneous entity of domination and oversimplifying its complex history (Neiman 2021). Critics argue that by questioning the emancipatory nature of Enlightenment norms such as justice, human rights, and equality, postcolonial studies promotes cultural relativism and even "tribalism" (Neiman 2021).

In my view, labeling postcolonial critique Europhobic is a misguided attempt to divert attention from the astute insights offered by postcolonial queer feminism. Europe's self-congratulatory narratives often ignore the coercive contexts that enabled Europeans to position themselves as ethical saviors of so-called backward peoples, promoting freedom, rights, and justice. Until Europe and Europeans acknowledge and learn from their historical mistakes and wrongdoings, they are likely to repeat them.

In *The Other Heading: Reflections on Today's Europe*, Jacques Derrida (1992, 24) notes that Europe has long viewed itself as the "cultural capital" of the world, leading the way for "world civilization or human culture in general." This self-assigned role as a "norm-producer," both legally and culturally, suggests that what benefits Europe is also conducive to the rest of the world. Europeans see themselves as having a mission to spread freedom, rights, and justice globally, a mindset that echoes the idea of the "white man's burden" (Kipling 1899). This belief legitimizes European intervention as a liberating force, with any resistance framed as barbaric opposition to freedom and democracy. Such a viewpoint justifies the suppression of dissent, racial discrimination, cultural subordination, and economic exploitation of non-Europeans, all under the guise of promoting progress and development and protecting equality, freedom, and liberty. According to this reasoning, moral and rational native peoples invariably welcome Western intervention.

European claims to global leadership in justice and human rights rely on asserting moral and military superiority, which underpin Western foreign policy legitimacy and set standards for global governance and the international rule-based order. Western nations monopolize the normative power to define what is fair and legal, while others are reduced to merely being norm consumers. For instance, the norm of "responsibility to protect" has been used to entrench Euro-American dominance. Regrettably, the formal transfer of power from colonial rulers to native elites has not led to the decolonization of either the global South or the global North. The fundamental impediment to decolonizing Europe is its inability to approach the non-European world in a non-Orientalist and nonhierarchical manner.

Europe faces a crucial choice: continue its legacy of claiming moral, economic, and military superiority over the non-European world or evolve into a more responsible entity that respects difference and alterity. An ethical relationship with Europe's past is indispensable for the future of Europe, the Europe that is to come. Today, Europe remains stuck between the past and the future, with democratizing efforts often overshadowed by nationalism, racism, and xenophobia. As both a remainder and a reminder of colonialism, the discrimination experienced by, for instance, postcolonial migrants and refugees poses a challenge to Enlightenment ideas of world citizenship.

The experiment with a transformed Europe involves embracing what Derrida calls "autoimmunity," which refers to self-deconstruction through radical self-contamination. Autoimmunity represents a dual nature: both a strength and a vulnerability, where an entity simultaneously protects and endangers itself (Derrida 2005, 39–40). It is thus both self-destroying and self-protecting, poison and counterpoison (Derrida 2005, 123). For example, during the so-called Syrian refugee crisis of 2015, some European Union (EU) countries reinstated border controls, compromising one of the founding principles of the EU, purportedly to secure Europe. By restricting mobility and the right to asylum, Europe turns against itself and adopts traits of its supposed enemies to protect itself. This paradox of safeguarding through self-destruction tests Europe's commitment to its Enlightenment ideals of humanitarianism and cosmopolitanism. Derrida reminds Europeans that, for hospitality to be unconditional, it must be extended without imposing any stipulations on the guest. This also implies a reconsideration of the host's understanding of home.

Inspired by Sigmund Freud, Homi Bhabha (1994, 10) explores the concept of the uncanny (*unheimlich*), referring to that which should remain hidden but unexpectedly emerges, within the context of postcolonial migration. Bhabha connects the way postcolonial migrants in Europe force Europeans to confront their colonial past with the provocative reminder, "We are here, because you were there." Migrants possess an unsettling ability to belong anywhere, thereby disrupting conventional notions of *home* and *belonging*. As Brexit illustrates, the presence of migrants can transform a familiar sense of home (*heimlich*) into something profoundly alien (*unheimlich*), causing disorientation and fear of losing sovereignty. For some Europeans, the presence of postcolonial migrants evokes an uncanny sense of estrangement.

This disorientation also provides Europe with an opportunity to reassess its views on citizenship and belonging. How can Europeans balance the preservation of European identity with the embrace of difference while challenging their understanding of superiority? Such responsibility involves navigating the conflicting imperatives of preserving and transforming Europe. The challenge is how Europeans might approach this normative dilemma, in which hospitality "makes me the hostage of the other" (Derrida 2005, 42–84). The non-European Other reveals Europe's limits, thereby pushing Europe to reimagine itself by engaging with the "im-possible" (Derrida 2005, 84). The geographical, economic, and political entity with the boundaries that we know as Europe is a result of the complex colonial production of space, which is projected backward in time. Instead of the geography-as-destiny argument, which views Europe as an identifiable region assigned a superior position in a Eurocentric world history, the challenge is to understand Europe in terms of its plurality—not as a fixed point of departure, but as a horizon of arrival. Therein lies both the promise and the challenge of a postimperial Europe yet to come. Europeans would do well to heed the apocryphal suggestion attributed to Mohandas K. Gandhi. When asked by a journalist, "What do you think of Western civilization?" Gandhi (1967) reportedly responded, "I think it would be a good idea."

Beyond De-Westernization. Epistemic
Delinking and Decoloniality

The decolonial option focuses on Indigenous epistemologies, cosmologies, ethics, and aesthetics to advance decolonization. It critiques the prefix *post-* in postcolonialism for implying colonialism's end and rejects First World paradigms as inadequate for understanding the so-called peripheral contexts. Mignolo (2013, 144) asserts that postcolonialism arose in Euro-America and the English-speaking world, not the Third World. Postcolonial scholars are censured for their overreliance on the Western canon and for their neglect of non-English colonial experiences, such as those in Latin America. Besides lacking "economic and materialist approaches" (Moraña et al. 2008, 15), postcolonial studies, with its "Indocentrism," is accused of "regionalist aristocratism" (Sarlo, quoted in Natali 2012, 310). The differential quality and specificity of Latin American colonial history and the dissimilarity among Spanish, Portuguese, and British colonialism are emphasized (Moraña et al. 2008, 6). According to Mignolo (1993), while postmodernism is an "internal" critique of modernity, postcolonialism is its Asian and African variant. In contrast to these, post-Occidentalism represents a Latin American critique. Both Marxism and postmodernism are dismissed as Eurocentric criticisms of capitalism and modernity. Conversely, decolonial thinking entails "delinking" from both coloniality/modernity and postcolonial studies (Mignolo 2011, 52). The birth of European modernity is traced back to the colonization of the Americas as the oldest colonial system. Spanish colonialism and not the Enlightenment, as assumed by postcolonial scholars, is viewed to have "instituted modernity," legitimizing European domination as emancipatory (Mignolo 2009, 8). Despite differences in British, Spanish, and French colonial rules, they are all glued together by what Aníbal Quijano (2007) calls the "colonial matrix of power" (*patrón de poder colonial*), which also links "the conquest of America to the war in Iraq" (Mignolo 2005, 397).

This contests Eurocentric presumptions of the critical thinker as a detached observer, a presumed neutral seeker of truth and objectivity. By decentering and decolonizing Western epistemology, Mignolo (2009, 5) focuses on the Third World as a site of enunciation that shifts "the geography of reasoning." He argues that, caught in Western epistemics and hermeneutical vocabulary, subjects from former colonies with secondary education fall prey to a colonization of the mind (Mignolo 2014, 202). Instead of imitation and integration, the decolonial method, according to him (Mignolo 2014, 201), seeks to depart from Western philosophical, scientific, religious, and aesthetic concepts, going beyond a mere "de-westernization" (Mahbubani 2001). By emphasizing the "relative subalternity" (Mignolo 2009, 7) of Creoles and vernacular elites, and through the restitution of Indigenous knowledge from Latin America, one can effectively confront the "coloniality of power" (Quijano 2000). Unlike the Christian, colonial, developmental, or other modernizing missions, as well as systems of ideas such as liberalism, Marxism, or Islamism, which all play out in the context of the state, decoloniality, according to Mignolo (2013, 131–32), emerges from the local histories, bodily experiences, and epistemic and interpretive frameworks of the Third World. Decoloniality at work is evidenced in how Indigenous understandings and narratives about nature contest the European notion of land as property and resource advanced by Christian missionaries, merchants, plantation owners, civilizers, and developers (Mignolo 2014, 199).

At the same time, Mignolo warns against the impulse to regionalize decolonial epistemes and reduce native subjects to mere tokens of their presumed cultures. A person from Latin America is often stereotyped as embodying and representing supposed Latin American cultural values. However, this does not apply to Western societies and subjects, who are under no obligation to function as authentic representatives of their colonialist cultures. The dilemma for non-Western subjects is that, to qualify as rational, autonomous subjects, they are expected to internalize and mimic European norms and values. This echoes Frantz Fanon's (1986 [1952], 18) insightful remark that the colonized "will come closer to being a real human being—in direct ratio to his mastery of the French language."

A call for the decolonization of postcolonial studies is also made by Grosfoguel (2011), who claims that postcolonialism reinforces the model of area studies despite efforts to chart alternative epistemologies. Postcolonial studies allegedly reduces the global South to providing raw data that is assimilated into theory in the global North. Postcolonial scholars, according to Grosfoguel (2011, 2), produce knowledge "about the subaltern rather than studies with and from a subaltern perspective." Decolonial critique, in contrast, pluralizes and diversifies our understanding of epistemologies and cosmologies by giving voice to hitherto silenced racial/ethnic and feminist perspectives from the global South. Drawing on Enrique Dussel's idea of a geopolitics of knowledge and following Fanon and Gloria Anzaldúa, Grosfoguel advocates for a body politics of knowledge that contests the Western nonsituated universal epistemology that erases the location and site from which knowledge is produced. He draws a link between the Cartesian *cogito ergo sum* (I think, therefore I am) and *ego conquistus* (I conquer, therefore I am). Differentiating between a poststructuralist/postmodern "Eurocentric critique of Eurocentrism" and a decolonial critique that radically contests Eurocentrism from subalternized perspectives, Grosfoguel (2011) rebukes postcolonial scholars for their excessive dependence on European thought, which deradicalizes the project of critique.

Although compelling in its arguments, one of the biggest pitfalls of the decolonial option, in my reading, is the idealization and sentimentalization of non-European subjectivities, epistemologies, and societies. In my view, any discussion of colonial forms of economic, political, social, and epistemic violence must also address the coercive and insidious aspects of native power relations. The romanticization of non-European societies and communities often involves relativizing precolonial forms of violence related to sexuality, labor, language, religion, caste, age, or gender. Grosfoguel (2011) does this in his remarks about rural communities and agrarian production, particularly when he celebrates the presumed wise elders in these communities, thereby downplaying the violence they might exert. As a counterexample, consider northern India's *Khap Panchayats* (traditional precolonial tribal and village administrations). Members of *Khaps* are typically elderly men with considerable power, and they often make authoritative decisions on social issues that affect women. They are infamous for their violent enforcement of caste norms, which has led the Supreme Court of India to deem them illegal. This form of traditional community organization is not only undemocratic but also unconstitutional. It highlights a significant counterpoint to the decolonial option of returning to Indigenous traditions as a means of decolonization. In contrast to their insistence that colonialism alone initiated the processes of dehumanization—described as "the massive transformation of human life into disposable material (that for the first time began to occur in the history of the 'human race' in the sixteenth century)" (Mignolo 2011, 61)—postcolonial, queer, and feminist scholars also emphasize the existence of native and precolonial forms of caste, class, race, and gender-based domination and exploitation. Consider the remarkable case of a group of children who survived a plane crash in the Amazon rainforest in Colombia on May 1, 2023. Over the course of forty days, they relied on Indigenous knowledge passed down by their grandmother to navigate and endure the harsh conditions of the forest. The ancestral wisdom allowed the children to find food, water, and shelter, ultimately ensuring their survival (Youkee 2023). After this inspiring story, it was sobering to learn that the mother, who had experienced domestic violence, perished in the crash (Associated Press 2023). The contribution of postcolonial queer feminism lies in its ability to emphasize the enabling aspects of Indigenous epistemologies without losing sight of the violence within Indigenous communities.

By foregrounding race as the central organizing principle of colonialism (Grosfoguel 2011), other categories, such as gender, sexuality, class, religion, and caste, are relegated to a secondary position. This approach, among other issues, contradicts the principles of intersectionality. Despite claims of adhering to a nonreductionist perspective, Grosfoguel (2011, 10) observes that "the global gender hierarchy is also affected by race: contrary to pre-European patriarchies where all women were inferior to all men, in the new colonial power matrix some women (of European origin) have a higher status and access to resources than some men (of non-European origin)." It is noteworthy that, legally, Black men in the United States were granted voting rights before white women. While Jim Crow laws and voter suppression of Black citizens must be considered when examining the intersectional impact of race and gender on social and political relations, prioritizing race over gender—as Grosfoguel does—can harm both antiracist and antisexist struggles, as argued by Black feminists.

Postcolonial studies is also accused of perpetuating the Eurocentric myth that colonialism has ended (Grosfoguel 2011). Contrary to the supposed focus of postcolonial studies on the historical condition of colonialism, Grosfoguel (2011) argues that the term *coloniality* captures the ongoing continuity of colonial forms of oppression and exploitation within the current global system. This insinuation perpetuates the common misconception that the prefix *post-* in *post*colonialism signifies an end to colonialism, thus relegating it to the past. In contrast, as postcolonial scholars have repeatedly emphasized, the *post-* refers to a complex temporality that encompasses the ongoing sociopolitical, economic, and cultural consequences of colonialism. Similarly, Mignolo (2009, 8) argues that the Third World challenges the epistemic privilege of the First World by shifting from passive consumption of Western knowledge to the active production of its own epistemologies. He further asserts that "there is a good chance that Maoris would know what is good or bad for them better than an expert from Harvard or a white anthropologist from New Zealand" (Mignolo 2009, 14–15).

Drawing on Indigenous traditions, decolonial scholars such as Mignolo and Grosfoguel—who are mostly not Indigenous themselves and are typically based at prestigious universities in the United States—claim to offer a more rigorous approach to decolonization. Raymond Morrow (2013, 127), however, highlights inconsistencies within the decolonial approach. For example, he notes that since most Black and Indigenous people in Latin America practice Christianity, they would, according to the logic of Mignolo and Grosfoguel, be deemed guilty of a "colonial mentality." Morrow draws on Victor Li to argue that decolonial scholars employ radical alterity to advance their antimodern stance. Li suggests that "the primitive is valorized *in order to save us*, its radical heterogeneity *all too predictably serving our desire for a way out of modern civilization*" (quoted in Morrow 2013, 127). The decolonial gesture of supposedly allowing Indigenous voices to be heard is misleading, as it does not facilitate desubalternization. This approach overlooks one of Gayatri Chakravorty Spivak's key arguments in her analysis of Foucault and Deleuze: that subalternity is a condition of lacking identity, and thus decolonization is not merely a simple process of reinstating subaltern voices (as discussed in greater detail in chapter 4).

Another issue with postcolonial studies, according to Grosfoguel (2011, 11), is that it treats "the capitalist world-system as being constituted primarily by culture, while political-economy places the primary determination on economic relations." The "coloniality of power" approach, in contrast, views the choice between culture and the economy as "a false dilemma, a chicken-egg dilemma that obscures the complexity of the capitalist world-system" (Grosfoguel 2011, 11). In Grosfoguel's view, world systems theorists such as Immanuel Wallerstein do not sufficiently address the cultural aspect, while postcolonial theorists fail to engage with political-economic processes. Part of the problem, as diagnosed by Grosfoguel, lies in disciplinary limitations, with the former predominantly comprising social scientists and the latter comprising mostly humanities scholars. Grosfoguel (2011) suggests that only the decolonial approach is capable of overcoming the twin dangers of economic reductionism and culturalism. It is instructive to recall Stuart Hall's (1996) critique of Aijaz Ahmad's (1992) juxtaposition of "Third World Marxism" and "First World Poststructuralism," which is relevant to this dispute. Hall cautions against reducing domination to an either-or framework of economic versus sociopolitical-cultural forms. For Hall, following Fanon, decolonization must be multidimensional, addressing both material and nonmaterial struggles. Hall points out that postcolonial studies aims to integrate the radical critical insights of Marxism and poststructuralism without prioritizing one over the other.

The claim that postcolonial studies emerges in the First World while decolonial options originate in the Third World homogenizes both spaces, thereby ignoring the plurality and heterogeneity of power relations in each. For instance, just because microcredits were pioneered in Bangladesh as an antidote to global poverty does not make them any less exploitative or problematic. It is disingenuous and naïve to claim that all that is proffered from a disadvantaged location by historically discriminated subjects is automatically benign. Kwesi Wiredu's "'Africa, know thyself,'" quoted approvingly by Mignolo (2009, 10), takes on an ominous tone, given the rise of pernicious nationalism in the Third World. I strongly concur with Wole Soyinka (2007) that decolonization involves opposing the "oppressive boot and the irrelevance of the colour of the foot that wears it." Celebrating non-Western forms of Chinese or Asian capitalism, along with non-Western subjectivities, economics, and politics, as inherently subversive and progressive is, in my view, at best naïve and at worst dangerous (Mignolo 2009, 14). Although he insists that he is not advocating a return to precolonial temporality, Mignolo (2009, 10) nonetheless romanticizes antimodernity politics as emancipatory: "China and India, today, are not 'going back in time.' Neither are they waiting for orders from the IMF [International Monetary Fund] or the White House or the European Union to know what they have to do to be 'properly modern' so as not to fail or miss the train of 'modernity.'"

Mignolo claims that knowledges produced in Indigenous languages enable the decentering and multiplying of epistemic practices. Contrary to Mignolo, I would argue that the vernacular is not necessarily a site of subversion or "disobedience." It is noteworthy that most decolonial thinkers neither speak nor understand Indigenous languages such as Aymara or Quechua. Furthermore, our access to these languages is mediated through colonialism. Thus, for example, in 1612 the Jesuit priest Ludovico Bertonio published the seminal *Vocabulario de la lengua Aymara*, a dictionary of the Aymara language that continues to be used by students today. Bertonio imposed the rules of Latin and Romance languages on this Indigenous language, thereby transforming its grammar and vocabulary (*Encyclopedia* 2024). This demonstrates that there is no uncontaminated access to precolonial language worlds.

Mignolo (2014, 198–99) rejects the concept of *representation* as Eurocentric, contrasting it with the concept of *enunciation*. He distinguishes enunciation from mere representation as the continuous reinvention of the world through speech. This represents one of the key differences between Mignolo and a postcolonial feminist such as Spivak, who in "Can the Subaltern Speak?" situates the politics of representation—both *Vertretung* and *Darstellung*—at the core of the decolonization project (discussed in greater detail in chapter 4). Spivak urges us to avoid subscribing to the notion of *purity* in languages, epistemologies, or cosmologies. According to her view, no narratives are entirely *untouched* by modernity or Enlightenment influences.

Mignolo (2005, 390) suggests disengagement and dis-identification as decolonial strategies and emphasizes the singularity of the political agency of the *damnés*, which he regards as a "racial category." Despite decades of Black feminist scholarship, activism, and the purported hype of intersectionality, both Mignolo and Grosfoguel exhibit a blatant disregard for intersectional feminism. Mignolo (2011, 63) claims: "The common element between Waman Puma, Cugoano, Gandhi, and Fanon is the wound inflicted by the colonial difference (e.g., the colonial wound)."[2] All the non-Western male thinkers named by Mignolo are literate, elite natives who, despite their vulnerability as colonized subjects, were still privileged compared with their fellow subaltern citizens. Mignolo faults the South Asian Subaltern Studies collective for their reliance on Karl Marx, Antonio Gramsci, Michel Foucault, and Jacques Derrida, accusing them of Eurocentrism, but he disregards their critique of anticolonial nationalism embodied in the figure of Gandhi (discussed in greater detail in chapter 5).

Like Mignolo and Grosfoguel, Fernando Coronil (2008, 414) emphasizes the distinctiveness of Latin America's historical experiences. Coronil (2008, 413) draws on the parable of "the seven blind men and the elephant" to argue against the privileging of African and Asian postcolonial perspectives while marginalizing Latin American viewpoints. Bemoaning the lack of reference to Latin America in postcolonial studies, Coronil (2008, 413–14) remarks:

As a reflection on the relationship between postcolonial and Latin American studies, the parable appears as a literal story, the absence of indigenous elephants in the Americas justifying the identification of postcolonial studies with scholarship on Africa and Asia. If we take the parable literally, since the only elephants that exist in the Americas are imported ones, artificially confined in zoos or circuses so as to protect them from an inhospitable terrain, we may have the desire to see only those rare creatures who have managed to mimic their Asian or African counterparts—our Latin American "elephants."

At the same time, Coronil cautions against glorifying "Latin American exceptionalism" or rejecting the relevance and significance of postcolonial studies and South Asian subaltern studies for Latin America. He warns against viewing "Latin America as a self-fashioned and bounded region" and romanticizing "its autochthonous intellectual productions," which purportedly need protection from postcolonial studies as an import (Coronil 2008, 414). In his view, the "inclusion of Latin America in the field of postcolonial studies expands its geographical scope and also its temporal depth. A wider focus, spanning from Asia and Africa to the Americas, yields a deeper view" (Coronil 2008, 415). While Asian perspectives attempt to "provincialize" European thought (Chakrabarty 2000), Latin American perspectives aspire to "globalize the periphery" (Coronil 2008, 414).

Spivak's (1993a, 57) claim that "Latin America has *not* participated in decolonization" illustrates the uneasy relationship between postcolonial studies and Latin America. It is notable that Spivak was questioning the claim that Latin American magical realism functions as a paradigm for Third World literature. Drawing on the insights of the renowned Latin American anthropologist Jorge Klor de Alva can help decipher what Spivak means by the miscarriage of decolonization in Latin America.

Klor de Alva (1995, 256) explains that, in the aftermath of the arrival of the Europeans in the Americas, "diseases and genes" led to the decimation of the majority of the original inhabitants in many areas. Meanwhile, "the population of non-Indians increased and they became socially and economically more powerful." Consequently, in his view, "It is misguided to present the preindependence, non-Indian sectors as colonized; it is inconsistent to explain the wars of independence as anticolonial struggles and it is misleading to characterize the Americas, following the civil wars of separation, as composed of postcolonial states" (Klor de Alva 1995, 247). Like Spivak, Klor de Alva (1995, 270) concludes that "neither postcolonialism nor decolonization can be said to have ever taken place in the Americas as it did in South Asia, Africa, or any other part of the Old World, where after liberation the ideal of a precolonial past could at least inspire a newly freed people who ethnically did not identify themselves with their former colonizers." He explains that, in the Americas, "the mestizo, mulatto, and especially criollo sectors" freed themselves from imperial Spain and established sovereignty. However, this did not automatically translate into decolonizing initiatives for the Indigenous peoples.

Marcos Natali explains that both Spivak and Klor de Alva question the appropriateness of the term *decolonization* when it merely describes the transfer of power from European colonizers to native elites. As Natali (2012, 314) astutely points out, independence movements had as "protagonists largely descendants of the Iberian colonizers," rather than the Indigenous peoples, who did not inherit political power. This resonates with the conditions of subalternity outlined by the South Asian historians. And though "Mexico is not another version of India" (Klor de Alva 1995, 247), the failure of decolonization in both contexts points to both divergences and similarities. While decolonial scholars do not tire of pointing out the differences among Latin America, Africa, and Asia, it is important to note that countries such as Cuba and Argentina (Mignolo's birthplace) differ significantly from Guatemala, Bolivia, and Peru, where the majority of the population is Indigenous (Natali 2012, 316).

This begs the question of how terms such as colonialism, postcolonialism, and decolonization should be represented to address both the singularities and affinities in diverse spatial and temporal contexts. And despite the claims of decolonial intellectuals to give voice to subaltern perspectives, are these voices not once again silenced in the name of valorizing indigeneity? Spivak (1993a, 57) remarks that "the radicals of the industrial nations want to be the Third World." While Indigenous communities have not undergone decolonization, native elites often equate national independence with decolonization. Echoing Spivak, Natali (2012, 325) avers that "an indigenous locus of enunciation has been practically inexistent in the Latin American public debate and in the collective imaginary."

While both postcolonial and decolonial approaches criticize the European Enlightenment for its coercive and violent aspects, we face a significant conundrum. On one hand, decolonial scholars argue that postcolonial theory's engagement with the Enlightenment represents "epistemological servitude," or an effort toward "hallucinatory whitening" (Fanon 1986 [1952], 100)—an attempt to mainstream previously marginalized approaches to gain legitimacy within Western academia. On the other hand, decolonial thinkers stand accused of being anti-Western and of romanticizing and "museumizing" Indigenous epistemologies as supposedly uncorrupted insights awaiting recovery by the morally conscientious radical thinker. In my view, it is imperative to sidestep the false choice between Eurocentrism and Europhobia. The antidote to Eurocentrism and imperialism does not lie in nativism or in the categorical negation of Enlightenment normative theorizing. Rather, it involves acknowledging that differences in experience, perspective, and location make a difference.

While decolonial scholars reject both Marxism and postcolonialism for their Eurocentrism, let us now turn our attention to the Marxist critique of postcolonial theory and the postcolonial critique of Marxism. This section is crucial to my argument because the decolonial option claims that postcolonial studies must be decolonized due to its overreliance on Western Marxism. At the same time, some Marxists, particularly from the global South (Ahmad 1992; Chibber 2013), assail postcolonial scholars for being anti-Enlightenment. In what follows, I outline the knotty relationship between postcolonialism and Marxism, which makes for or against positionings pointless.

De-Universalizing Europe. What Difference Does Difference Make?

Marx is all right, but we need to complete Marx. —AIMÉ CÉSAIRE, *Discourse on Colonialism*

Marxism is often regarded as a radical extension of Enlightenment thought, with Marx's analysis of capitalist economic relations being one of the most incisive and seminal forms of critical theory. Despite Marxism's European origins, its broad influence—from Cuba to Vietnam and from China to South Africa—demonstrates its global impact. Yet even among its supporters, Marxism faces criticism. In his masterly treatise *Black Marxism: The Making of the Black Radical Tradition* (1983), Cedric Robinson argues that in foregrounding European models of history, Marxist analyses obscure the agency and unique experiences of Black individuals both in the West and in the postcolonial world. This resonates with a postcolonial critique of Marx's materialist conception of historical progress. Marx's model of history bears similarities to developmental thinking and results in a Eurocentric portrayal of the mode of production. It views the Asiatic mode of production as less advanced compared with the industrial capitalist economies of nineteenth-century Western Europe (Morton 2007, 74). Marx's analyses of British colonialism in India exemplify his Eurocentric perspective on world history: "England, it is true, in causing a social revolution in Hindostan, was actuated only by the vilest interests, and was stupid in her manner of enforcing them. But that is not the question. The question is, can mankind fulfil its destiny without a fundamental revolution in the social state of Asia? If not, whatever may have been the crimes of England she was the unconscious tool of history in bringing about that revolution" (Marx 1978c [1853], 658). While Marx laments the decline of family-based communities and local industries in rural Indian villages, he also asserts that these idealized village communities underpin Oriental despotism (Morton 2007, 74). Thus, Edward Said (1978, 153–54) rightly criticizes Marx for perpetuating the stereotype of Asia as inherently backward and condemns his "Romantic Orientalist vision."

Unlike Immanuel Kant or G. W. F. Hegel, Marx did not regard non-Europeans as lacking historical agency. Instead, he controversially argued that colonialism was a "necessary evil" that would aid in transitioning feudal societies to capitalist economies by changing both the mode of production and the ownership of the means of production. Marx was notably perceptive in highlighting the essential connection between colonialism and capitalism: "The discovery of gold and silver in America, the extirpation, enslavement and entombment in mines of the aboriginal population, the beginning of the conquest and plunder of India, the conversion of Africa into a preserve for the commercial hunting of black-skins, are all things which characterize the dawn of the era of capitalism production. These idyllic proceedings are the chief moments of primitive accumulation" (Marx 1990 [1867], 915).

Challenging Marx's view that so-called advanced modes of production merely replace supposedly primitive ones, postcolonial Marxist scholars, including those from the South Asian Subaltern Studies group (hereafter, Subalternists), argue that the Asiatic mode of production does not fully vanish in the era of global capitalism. They question Eurocentric historical narratives that assert universality and regard subaltern labor as inherently primitive (Chakrabarty 2000, 93). By examining the diverse histories of subaltern labor, Subalternists disrupt the view that precapitalism is merely a lower stage in the linear progression of global capitalist accumulation (Morton 2007, 94). Western Marxists and global justice activists are urged to consider heterogeneous registers of subaltern labor, including the reproductive work of subaltern women in the global South. This would expand and diversify the limited conception of productive labor put forth by Marx's labor theory of value (Dhawan and Castro Varela 2024).

The industrial production and labor conditions of nineteenth-century Western Europe that Marx analyzed have increasingly been replaced by a flexible, casual, and nonunionized workforce in the global South (Morton 2007, 73; Spivak 1999, 91). To highlight the ongoing significance of the Asiatic mode of production in today's global economy, Spivak reevaluates Marx's labor theory of value through the lens of the geographical dynamics of the gendered and racialized international division of labor. Indeed, Spivak (1999, 167) commends Marx for foreseeing the growing significance of women's labor in modern industry and underscores the new forms of superexploitation faced by nonunionized, subcontracted, and precarious female workers in today's global capitalism.

Marx argued that capitalism would inevitably collapse and be replaced by socialism, as it harbors the seeds of its own demise. In contrast, Spivak (1999, 430) views socialism as an ongoing and enduring ethical and political endeavor to undo capitalism. While Spivak advocates for labor movements and the redistribution of wealth to promote economic justice, she questions the feasibility of a programmatic socialist alternative to capitalism (Morton 2007, 89). She reconceptualizes socialism as a *différance* of capitalism, rather than as a direct opposition to it or as a means of its overcoming or sublation. This approach shifts from an evolutionary linear narrative to a more indeterminate understanding of postcapitalist futures.

Let us now consider the Marxist response to postcolonial critique. A common and enduring criticism of postcolonial theory is that, by challenging universal concepts such as progress and development as Eurocentric and insufficient for grasping the practices and experiences of non-European societies, postcolonial studies ontologizes the difference between the West and the East. If, as proponents of universalist theories argue, humans truly have common basic needs and interests that transcend cultural and economic differences, then the postcolonial endeavor to "provincialize Europe" (Chakrabarty 2000) and highlight the specific histories of diverse contexts becomes problematic. In addition, any criticism of the

Enlightenment and its violent legacies is often perceived as abandoning emancipatory politics while simultaneously legitimizing the exoticization of the East as fundamentally different.

Opposing the view that the non-European world merely imitates Europe, postcolonial scholars examine the emergence of diverse cultural, political, and economic practices globally to understand the varied manifestations of modernity. They argue that the non-Western world does not simply mimic European models, suggesting that, while Western theories on capitalism and modernity are relevant, they are also inadequate for analyzing postcolonial contexts (Chakrabarty 2000). Despite their Marxist influences, many postcolonial scholars contest the universalist assumptions of historical materialism, which posited that colonial capitalism would uniformly spread from Europe to other parts of the world. This Eurocentric perspective, which projects Enlightenment and Marxist categories globally, often overlooks the realities of the postcolonial world. By emphasizing the uniqueness of non-European societies, postcolonial theorists face criticism for undermining the universal validity of norms such as modernity and secularism, which are assumed to be shared by all humans regardless of cultural, racial, gender, or religious differences.

The Marxist sociologist Vivek Chibber's critique of postcolonialism as anti-Enlightenment repeats this gesture. He contends that Chakrabarty rejects a "universal history of capital" by claiming that power relations in postcolonial contexts diverge from those of European modernization (Chibber 2013, 103–9). Chakrabarty's focus on distinct political domains, especially among India's subaltern classes, contrasts with normative models of European capitalism and political systems. Chibber (2013, 130–31) counters that capitalism's universalization does not necessitate the homogenization of social diversity or cultural and religious differences but can accommodate and sustain them. He argues that although subjects in resisting capitalism draw on local cultures and practices, this does not negate the existence of common basic needs—such as food and shelter—that motivate all people universally (Chibber 2013, 199–200). By highlighting differences in collective action between Indian and Western peasants, Subalternists are accused of endorsing the same cultural essentialism they criticize in colonial discourses (Chibber 2013, 179, 192, 208). Chibber believes that a universal theory of human agency, as proposed by Enlightenment and Marxism, supports democratic politics while avoiding Orientalism, and that viewing Indigenous communities as driven by unique cultural differences rather than common needs undermines universal human interests.

In his rejoinder, Bruce Robbins (2014) argues that Chibber's Marxist reproach of postcolonialism neglects economic diversity and fails to adequately address the various forms of capitalism. Partha Chatterjee (2013, 74–75) responds by arguing that Western capitalist modernity did not achieve universality, as it failed to fundamentally transform preexisting modes of production in the non-European world. The issue addressed by subaltern studies is not the psychological or cultural difference between the so-called West and the East, as Chibber suggests, but the contrast between the dissolution of peasant classes in capitalist Europe and their continued existence under capitalism in the non-European world. Chatterjee explains that, despite apparent similarities, subaltern studies extends beyond the Marxist project. Unlike the disappearance of the peasantry in Europe during the rise of capitalism, the transformation of agrarian societies in the non-European world followed a different trajectory (Chatterjee 2013, 74–75). Capitalism did not universalize in contexts such as India because, instead of abolishing semifeudal labor practices, the colonial state harnessed them. This led to the development of capitalist formations that were distinct from those based on free wage labor. Challenging Chibber, Chatterjee argues that accurately understanding European history alone is not enough to address issues in the non-Western world (Chatterjee 2013, 75). In addition, Chatterjee warns that by asserting that political action is rooted in a universal human nature, Chibber uncritically adopts the principles of contractarian liberal political thought (Chatterjee 2013, 74).

Chibber (2013, 197), following universalists such as Martha Nussbaum, argues that human aspirations are not culturally constituted; rather, common interests and basic needs, such as physical well-being, are fundamental characteristics of human nature. This universalizing gesture overlooks postcolonial feminist critiques, which highlight that such views disregard the diverse historical configurations of family, community, society, and state that frame vulnerability and agency differently in the postcolonial world. Furthermore, Chibber's assertion that subalterns—who, he believes, share a common political consciousness—will inevitably seek "liberal democracy" to enhance their well-being (Chibber 2013, 179) ignores the question of ideology, as well as the discontinuity between interests and desires. This is a key issue addressed by Spivak in "Can the Subaltern Speak?" (This is discussed in greater detail in chapter 4.)

Hall (1996) argues that postcolonial studies turn to poststructuralist concepts of difference and contingency as a response to the limitations of traditional Marxist theories, which tend to concentrate predominantly on political economy. This is a point conveniently overlooked by Marxists such as Chibber. If, as Chibber claims, the logic of capital is truly universal and its expansion in postfeudal and postcolonial societies generates a "universal history of class struggle," then how can we account for the numerous varieties of capitalism, each with distinct contexts and historical experiences of political economy? Furthermore, it is essential to consider how the same commodities are manufactured and consumed under varying conditions while simultaneously competing in both local and global markets.

As Spivak (2014, 188) notes, from Gramsci's reflections on the *Risorgimento* to W. E. B. Du Bois's analyses of the Pan-African movement, the concept of subaltern social groups was not meant to depict an international proletariat. Instead, it referred to segments of society that the universal logic of capital could not fully incorporate. Class distinctions intersect with factors such as race, religion, gender, and history, producing a variety of capitalist systems. Chibber's notion of resistance that is supposedly race-free and gender-free fails to account for the connections between the internationalism of the labor movement and colonialism (Spivak 2014, 188). In contrast to a universalist and idealistic leftist narrative, Spivak, drawing on Gramsci, argues that subaltern social groups are inherently fragmented and cannot achieve unity until they become a state (Spivak 2014, 193). By idealizing the subaltern classes and incorporating them into a universal proletarian class, Marxists such as Chibber effectively merge them into "the same history as Europe" (Spivak 2014, 197). Such approaches result in a Western-centric Marxism—what Spivak refers to as "Little Britain Marxism"—which marginalizes alternative interpretations of Marx's theories (Spivak 2014, 197). Ultimately, the broader issue is not simply a matter of choosing between "Marxism or Enlightenment versus postcolonialism." Rather, it concerns how to apply the concepts developed by Marx, Kant, or Hegel to contexts that these thinkers neither encountered nor anticipated. This involves engaging with Marxist or Enlightenment theories in ways that account for geopolitical and historical differences (Dhawan and Castro Varela 2024).

In contrast to the decolonial option, which denounces the Enlightenment and advocates a (re)turn to non-European epistemologies, and the (orthodox) Marxist approach, which rejects a focus on differences as anti-universalist, the next section outlines the link between desubalternizing non-Western epistemologies and dehegemonizing Eurocentric theories.

Can Non-Europeans Philosophize?

An unequivocal response to the question "Can non-Europeans philosophize?" would be to highlight African, Asian, and Latin American epistemologies and ethical principles as evidence of paradigms distinct from the European tradition. However, in my view, merely acknowledging the existence of non-European epistemologies is not sufficient to decolonize the mind (Dhawan 2017). Regrettably, the normative idea of critique, as defined during the European Enlightenment, continues to devalue non-European viewpoints as deficient. Accordingly, I firmly believe that desubalternizing non-Western perspectives involves addressing the uneven distribution of intellectual labor globally by rethinking the relationship between postcolonialism and the Enlightenment. I use Spivak's ideas of transnational literacy and planetary ethics to support this argument (Dhawan 2017).

In his essay "Can Non-Europeans Think?" Hamid Dabashi (2013) questions why European epistemologies are classified as philosophy while African, Asian, and Latin American perspectives are often categorized as ethnophilosophy. Dabashi (2013) argues that European thought asserts itself as the "measure and yardstick of globality" by obscuring its provincial origins, with philosophers such as Kant considering themselves as pioneers of universal reason and ethics. This self-perception reflects European self-centrism and ignorance, dismissing other ways of being in the world and disregarding alternative critical approaches.

If Europe imposed its norms and values through colonialism, decolonization must involve undoing Europe's claim to universality. The dilemma for postcolonial theorists is how to "provincialize Europe" (Chakrabarty 2000) when academic fields such as philosophy, history, and sociology are dominated by European perspectives. This makes the goal of deuniversalizing Europe essential yet seemingly unattainable. Another crucial question is who will undertake this task: Who has the authority and resources to challenge European intellectual dominance? Furthermore, given that academic disciplines are both Eurocentric and androcentric, how does postcolonial-queer-feminist scholarship work to desubalternize non-Western critical thought?

Dabashi (2013) asserts that, with a more equitable and democratic platform, contemporary non-European thinkers, poets, artists, and public intellectuals are challenging Eurocentric epistemic dominance, resulting in the rise of perspectives that are rooted in their local contexts yet have global implications. While this is compelling, Dabashi's optimism about non-European perspectives' displacing European philosophical hegemony does not necessarily lead to a global reconfiguration of power relations. For example, precolonial Indian philosophical traditions excluded women and those referred to as untouchables from intellectual work, labeling them *jñānaśūnya*, or devoid of intellect (Dhawan 2007; Sharma 2021, 53). Simply incorporating marginalized non-Western thought into the canon will not undo the normative violence of European philosophy; desubalternizing non-European epistemologies is akin to untying a Gordian knot: intricate and requiring transformative action.

One key insight from postcolonial theory is that there are no presumably authentic non-Western perspectives that can be easily recovered through decolonization by merely undoing Western influence (Dhawan 2014). Ignoring this reduces postcolonial theorists to mere native informants, relegating their roles to information retrieval and data extraction for the Western academy. Colonialism's normative violence effectively devalued non-European epistemologies, replacing native philosophies and languages with colonial education—a colonization of the mind. Natives were considered unreliable sources of their own cultural knowledge, leading Europeans to assume the task of translating these perspectives back to the colonized societies (Niranjana 1992, 2). This Orientalist endeavor of translating native theories into European languages was crucial for governing through knowledge (Niranjana 1992, 16). The process laid the groundwork for area studies, which classify Latin America, Asia, and Africa as distinct regions within a Eurocentric world history. These categories are integral to fields such as history, international relations, anthropology, philosophy, and literary studies. Colonies served as essential sites for producing Western knowledge, while the postcolony continues to grapple with the ambivalent legacies of Enlightenment thought.

Instead of defining what is classified as distinctly Indian or African philosophy by highlighting unique aspects of these epistemologies that set them apart from Western thought, it is imperative to rethink the nature of critical practice in these regions. Richard King (2000, 1) argues that there is no unified so-called Indian philosophy as a singular way of thinking endorsed by all in India. This reveals the myth of cultural homogeneity that distorts both Western and Indian self-perceptions. In addition, categories such as Latin American, Asian, or African fail to capture their inherent diversity and are themselves colonial legacies. The Western concept of philosophy has historically been exclusionary, shaped by hierarchies of class, religion, and gender. Early Western Orientalists, for example, often equated Indian culture with the elitist thought of the Vedic male Brahmins, overlooking *nāstika* (heterodox) critical perspectives such as Buddhism and Jainism (Dhawan 2007; King 2000, 7).

Recognizing the contributions of Latin American and African philosophy is a step in the right direction. However, this can also marginalize these philosophies by emphasizing their cultural specificity in contrast to the universal claims of European philosophy. Efforts to establish the presumed respectability of non-European thought (King 2000, 28) often result in attempting to straitjacket Asian or African philosophies into European paradigms of critical thought. Despite the presence of diverse epistemologies, European thinkers remain disappointingly Eurocentric, failing to genuinely engage with non-Western perspectives. Thus, the major challenge for postimperial critical theory is to foster a respectful engagement not only with non-Western thought but also with what is excluded even *from*, and *by*, the margins (Dhawan 2017).

Economic globalization has significantly challenged Eurocentric worldviews, including colonialism and Orientalism, leading non-Western perspectives to interrupt the monological privilege of Western discourse. This has prompted European thought to undergo self-questioning and decentralization. That said, simply incorporating non-Western epistemologies into Western frameworks and using them as counterimages of the West will not decolonize philosophy. The impulse to preserve theoretical rigor often stems from Western philosophy's inability to shed its colonial and Eurocentric biases. To deconstruct the binary between Eastern and Western thought, it is essential to analyze genealogically how terms such as Asian and African are effects of colonial power. By the same logic, we must investigate how European becomes an elastic universal concept that subsumes other perspectives, turning every will to difference into an economy of sameness. The fault lines of European critical thought emerge in its very conception, as it frequently remains trapped within the epistemological frameworks established by colonial and patriarchal discourses. There is a pressing need to explore how postcolonial queer feminism can expand the boundaries of critical theory by challenging the unquestioned authority of Eurocentric and androcentric normative frameworks and reconfiguring dominant concepts such as epistemology, ethics, and aesthetics. In addition to including previously marginalized perspectives, they confront Western thought's colonial epistemological burden and push it to reflect on its own coercive historical trajectory.

Postcolonial-queer-feminist theory questions the self-referentiality of Western critical thought, whose "conceptual arsenal" is insufficient to interpret the world (Bardawil 2018, 774). It would enrich the Western world to rediscover "one's own critical commitments in a foreign idiom"; this estrangement could broaden the horizons of European critical thought (Bardawil 2018, 774). It would be intellectually humbling for Europe to see itself as the postcolonial world sees it (Ramgotra and Choat 2023). As Theodor Adorno (2005a [1951], 39) astutely observes, "It is part of morality not to be at home in one's home." At the same time, rejecting European Enlightenment will not accomplish decolonization; rather, a conceptual repositioning of Europe is necessary (Agnani 2013, xvii). The rise of Chinese or Indian capitalism, as touted by Mignolo, will not usher in postimperial futures. Instead, to realize the processes of decolonization and desubalternization, following Spivak, I would urge for transnational literacy and planetary ethics.

Epistemic Change. Transnational Literacy and Planetary Ethics

The global exchange of ideas, theories, images, and norms presents the challenge of reconciling different epistemic approaches. When concepts are translated from one language to another, does this result in a reconfiguration of power relations? Are these discursive exchanges and encounters seamless? (Liu 1995, xv, 21). Can we establish reliable comparative categories that apply across different historical contexts? (Liu 1995, xv). For instance, when we ask, "What is the word for critique in Mandarin or Swahili?" the absence of a direct equivalent in the vernacular language is often interpreted as a presumed lack, or the local term is compared with its Western counterparts. The interaction between Eastern and Western languages has wide-ranging implications, indicating that crossing language boundaries involves more than just linguistic concerns (Liu 1995, 6). Given that language politics is central to colonialism, decolonization must address the difficulties of translingual practices. Can the power dynamics between East and West be redefined when non-Western concepts are translated into European languages, and vice versa? I would argue that non-European languages do not automatically undermine Eurocentrism, so the vernacular is not a guaranteed means of decolonization. Transnational literacy involves more than merely comparing ethical concepts such as *Ubuntu, pachamama*, or *dhamma* in native languages, as these concepts also carry their own ideological baggage related to gender, religion, sexuality, race, and class.[3] Therefore, terms in Bantu, Quechua, or Pali are not inherently counterhegemonic.

To envision postimperial politics, we must resist idealizing the local, national, or global. Under capitalist globalization, "monocultures of the mind" (Shiva 1993) arise from a standardized education that centers on mastering the lingua franca of finance capital (Spivak 2004, 539). Desubalternization, however, involves more than technological literacy and rights training. Contesting the understanding of knowledge in terms of positivist approaches of computing and digital competence, Spivak focuses on the enigmatic and elusive nature of planetarity. To foster an ethical relationship with the planet, we must embrace "transnational literacy" (Spivak 2008, 30), a practice of learning to read and decipher the world responsibly. This approach links literature, culture, and economics, reshaping our understanding of the world and our role within it (Spivak 1999, xii). It inspires us to become familiar with the unfamiliar while also inviting us to defamiliarize the familiar, thereby reorienting our normative commitments and enriching global academic and policy discourses. Unlike theorists of global ethics, who in the name of doing good offer one-size-fits-all solutions, decentered practices of "transnational literacy" and "planetary ethics" involve intervening in the universal deployment of epistemology and ethics as alibis for imperialism. Acknowledging the limits of our epistemic practices opens the door to rethinking our approach to ethics across borders. Crossing of epistemic borders allows for diverse forms of meaning making to overlap and enrich one another by cultivating ethical reciprocity between the hegemon and the subaltern. In contrast, transnational illiteracy arises when one disregards how neocolonialism obstructs subalterns from accessing epistemic agency and exercising intellectual labor. To combat this, synergies between different epistemic and linguistic communities must foster multidirectional exchange while resisting the commodification of alterity and exoticization of the margins.

Planētes, the ancient Greek term for wanderers, inspires a planetary approach to ethics that encourages the dissemination of diverse epistemologies and ethical principles. This framework prompts a reexamination of dominant paradigms that are predicated on "extractive learning" for mass consumption. In contrast to ethical approaches that espouse the values of inclusion and diversity while paradoxically perpetuating moral imperialism through paternalistic attitudes toward cultures deemed foreign, planetary ethics eschews the harvesting of data from these cultures for the exclusive benefit of Western consumption. To mitigate the marginalization of subaltern histories and experiences, planetary ethics seeks singular forms of encounters between the dispensers and receivers of solidarity, aiming to facilitate a less disparate relationship. These are not merely idealized empowerment strategies; rather, they are political efforts conscious of the risks of reproducing subalternity (Spivak 1999, 429).

Spivakian planetary beings, unlike Kantian cosmopolitan world citizens, do not operate from a morally superior stance (Spivak 2003b, 72). Rather than being courageous agents of Enlightenment reason who dare to know, they exercise ethical responsibility by caring to know the other. This involves commitment to subversive listening that makes subaltern speech both audible and intelligible. Decolonization cannot succeed if it is confined to reactive humanitarianism or sporadic human-rights interventions without ensuring subaltern access to intellectual labor. Most critical approaches suggest that improving material conditions leads to desubalternization. However, economic and political empowerment alone is insufficient without continuous pedagogical efforts that sustain lasting epistemic change (Spivak 2004, 560). This approach addresses the ideological subject constitution of the oppressed, which persuades them into their accepting subjugation as inevitable. Subalterns need access to Enlightenment tools to unlearn the obedience inherited from feudalism and colonialism (Spivak 2008, 55) (more on this in chapter 4). Developing critical intelligence and intellectual labor is more crucial than merely providing immediate material comfort (Spivak 2004, 557). Simultaneously, metropolitan elites must unlearn their imperialist mindset and the belief in their manifest destiny to solve global problems.

Offering a more responsible framework for understanding the world and our collective role within it, planetary ethics envisions us as guardians rather than occupiers of planetarity (Spivak 2003b, 72). This shift involves moving from "rights-based cultures" to "responsibility-based cultures," where we are responsible *to* the other rather than *for* the other (Spivak 2004, 541). Planetary ethics goes beyond simply distributing aid to the needy. It involves engaging with the desires and imaginations of both the hegemon and the subaltern. Moreover, it requires transnational elites to critically examine their own complicity and the historical processes that have established them as dispensers of justice and rights. This involves embracing self-doubt as a crucial aspect of ethical practice and moving away from global solutions to local issues. Rather than endorsing normative foundationalism, critical theories and decolonization practices prioritize the contextualized deployment of norms. The justification of human rights and justice is situated within specific sociohistorical contexts rather than being conceived as transcendent principles. This safeguards that normativity emerges through localized negotiations instead of being imposed from above. To reconfigure both European and non-European critical thought and their relationship, it is imperative to revise our unexamined premises and conclusions regarding the notions of critical and theory.

As outlined in the first three chapters, the effort in part I was to examine the ambivalent legacies of the Enlightenment and Western reason, as well as to respond to the accusations against postcolonial critiques of modernity and European critical thought. In part II, the chapters turn to contemporary events, addressing the politics, ethics, and aesthetics of decolonization.

Where Does the Future Come From?

4

The Nonperformativity of Critique

Protest Politics, State Phobia, and the Erotics of Resistance

In the greater part of the Third World, the problem is that the declared rupture of "decolonization" boringly repeats the rhythms of colonization.—GAYATRI CHAKRAVORTY SPIVAK, *Outside in the Teaching Machine*

This chapter focuses on the shift from the anticolonial struggle for independence, sovereignty, and self-determination to contemporary understandings of decolonization in terms of anti-statism. A litmus test for a radical intellectual is being anti-state. To bring an end to neocolonial power, decolonization in contemporary postcolonial debates is increasingly being coded in terms of abolitionism—namely, a world without states. This would entail replacing the bureaucratic-military state machine with decentralized democratic stateless societies (Davis et al. 2019). The project of antislavery and anticarcerality is augmented with calls for the defunding and dismantling of the racialist capitalist state and its policing functionaries (Gilmore 2022). It is argued that, to ensure decolonization is not merely a "metaphor" (Tuck and Yang 2012), it is imperative to dismantle the state monopoly on violence by abolishing the state itself. The hope is that the withering of the state will usher in the disintegration of the capitalist economy, the end of exploitation of the working class, and the disappearance of racist and heterosexist society. The failure of liberal reforms has triggered current social movements and brought the protesters into focus as agents of decolonization. No one committed to the project of decolonization can disagree with any of these critical interventions, and yet, as I argue in this chapter, one must distinguish between criticizing the state and state phobia. Drawing on theoretical insights and historical examples, I suggest that instead of anti-statism, decolonization must be coded in terms of reimagining the relationship between the state and the subalterns. I outline the nonperformativity of critique of protest movements and advocate that we understand the state, one of the most important legacies of the Enlightenment, as *pharmakon*—namely, as both poison and medicine. From Haiti to India and South Africa, the end of colonial rule ushered in the establishment of postcolonial states with progressive constitutions. The territorial integrity and sovereignty of these postcolonial states was imagined in the grammar of the Enlightenment, even as they were translated and tailored to the aspirations of the newly decolonized societies. These historical examples offer instructive lessons for thinking decolonization today. Ultimately, this chapter is about the critical function of the state, as well as of nonstate actors, and their respective roles in decolonization.

Civil Disobedience. Then and Now

Much ink has been spilled on the role of critique and political action in achieving social change, with scholars and activists addressing in differing ways the legality, legitimacy, and efficacy of resistance. While some dismiss civil disobedience as seditious and immoral and fear that it may result in anarchy, others advocate it as an essential aspect of political participation and the democratic process. Whether in the form of the suffragette movement and anticolonial struggles or the antiapartheid movement and civil rights protests, it has been the vision and courage of dissidents that continually inspires subsequent generations. The term *civil disobedience* encompasses a wide variety of practices, including riots, sit-ins, protests, demonstrations, hunger strikes, picketing, and boycotts, among other noncompliant activities. The goals vary from educating the majority about a particular problem through public action to bringing about concrete and enduring social and political transformation. The tactics range from accepting prescribed punishment for violating the law to overthrowing rulers and installing a new regime. The justification for civil disobedience is derived from the following postulate: When the rule of law perpetuates violence instead of eradicating it, the state forfeits its legitimacy. When peaceful protest is not effective, then resorting to violence, it is argued, becomes imperative in the face of state violence; nonviolence, otherwise, becomes a smokescreen, ultimately protecting the repressive state apparatus. As Martin Luther King Jr. (1968) famously remarked, "Riot is the language of the unheard." Earlier, Frantz Fanon, in his text *Concerning Violence*, outlined how, if humanity hoped to break out of the impasse to usher in noncoercive relations, cycles of violence were paradoxically unavoidable. This was less a justification *for* violence than an effort to understand how violence both emerges and is deployed to put a definitive end to it. In this regard, the conundrum of reconciling means and ends remains a challenge. (More on this in chapter 5.)

A range of recent protests globally reveal the ambivalence of civil disobedience's critical function. When protests are peaceful and orderly, they are often employed as an alibi in the West to shame non-Western powers such as China, Russia, North Korea, and Iran as rogue and to demonstrate how the "carnival of democracy" is supposed to function. The West enlists these social movements to (re)validate its superior status as tolerant and open, thereby embarrassing non-Western states for their "democracy deficit." However, when protests turn violent, Western states often criminalize and delegitimize the critique by branding the protestors "tourists of violence" (*Gewalttouristen*).[1]

This highlights the tenuous back and forth between critical theory and collective action. Some propose that by altering consciousness, critical thought transforms social reality, while others insist that critical theory must remain disengaged from the exigencies of everyday struggles; otherwise, it becomes pedantic and prescriptive. The effort in this section is to historically trace different approaches to the relationship between critical thought and political action to understand the limits and lures of the politics of resistance.

One of the most important contributions of the Enlightenment is the impetus to reimagine the politics of the governed—namely, the association between citizens and the state. Michel Foucault (2010, 33) explains the Enlightenment as a reconfiguration of the asymmetrical dynamic between the state and its institutions and individuals: "What *Aufklärung* has to do, and is in the process of doing, is precisely to redistribute the relationships between government of self and government of others." Enlightenment thinkers argue that it is the citizens' duty to obey the state, for, to protect its citizens and enforce laws, at times coercively, governments must be unopposable. The legal maxim *Rex non potest peccare* (The king can do no wrong) encapsulates the doctrine of sovereign immunity. In exchange for obedience, the sovereign's monopoly on violence enables it to regulate conflicts between subjects, thereby guaranteeing rights and order. The purpose of the social contract is thus to bring an end to warfare and insecurity. This would be impossible if the private use of violence remained legitimate in the face of unequal distribution of might within the population.

However, distinguishing between the illegality of an armed rebellion and legitimately exercising the right to resist, thinkers of the Enlightenment concede the importance of speaking out against unjust and oppressive practices and legislation that go against the general will of the people.[2] While rebellion threatens the constitution and foundations of political sovereignty, mute subordination and docile complacency jeopardize active citizenship, open society, and vibrant democratic rule. The Enlightenment slogan of *Sapere aude* (dare to know) is a call to have courage to use one's reflexive judgment. Even as the law assures individuals equal freedom while necessitating a degree of obedience in return, the autonomy of the free rational being remains paramount (Reiss 1956, 180–81). In this view, the right to revolution conflicts with the imperative to obey the law and the indispensability of the constitution, which leads Immanuel Kant (1991c [1797], 131) to proclaim that people must endure "even . . . an unbearable abuse of supreme authority." By this logic, the legitimacy of the actual state cannot be judged according to the normative idea of the ideal state that governs in compliance with the general will of the people. Society's crude imperfections do not automatically warrant defiance of the sovereign (Cummiskey 2008, 232).

Kant (1991c [1797], 131) follows Thomas Hobbes's objection to a revolt against the Leviathan's authority and rejects the right of citizens to resist unjust rule, as doing so would endanger peace and order. Revolt against the state entails the paradox that the permission to resist must come from the very authority against which resistance is exercised; this ultimately leads to an untenable situation. Furthermore, it would call on the coercive powers of the state to protect the citizens' right to resist the powers of the state, rendering the juridical state inoperative (Williams 1983, 200). Kant heeds Hobbes's warning that disobeying the laws of the sovereign would undermine public rights, jeopardizing the very possibility of legitimacy itself. Rather than transitioning to a more just state, the overthrow of a coercive regime can result in lawlessness and a return to the state of nature. Just as a law that permits lawlessness would be contradictory, following Hobbes, a bad government is considered better than no government at all. Although Hobbes's position resonates with those of many Enlightenment thinkers, some nevertheless concede that civil disobedience is a legitimate and rational breach of the law, for it is imperative to publicize unjust and violent political rule.

Despite controversial differences and inconsistencies in their positions, post-Hobbesian philosophers such as John Locke, Jean-Jacques Rousseau, and Kant all acknowledged the possibility and permissibility of criticizing tyrannical rule as a moral duty and obligation of enlightened citizens. Furthermore, it was argued that it is the state's duty to protect the inalienable right of its citizens to what Kant terms *publicity*. The right to political criticism is not just a principal right; it is a condition of all rights and thus a fundamental duty, for, in Kant's view, public debate in the form of political speech is indispensable for society's moral progress. By respecting and responding to public criticism, the sovereign can make revolution unnecessary, all while fostering citizens' critical capabilities to guard against a paternalistic obedience of laws.

In "An Answer to the Question: 'What is Enlightenment?'" Kant (1991a [1784], 55) remarks: "The public use of man's reason must always be free, and it alone can bring about enlightenment among men." The employment of one's critical faculties is not a mere entitlement but an obligation of each individual; complementarily, the state is responsible for providing citizens the conditions for self-reflection and critical expression. Kant (1999 [1793], 302) explains that the "freedom of the pen" is "the sole palladium" of the rights of the people, without which people would have no way to make any claims to rights at all. Thus, for him, citizens have a duty to enter civil society, where the capacity for critical deliberation is fostered. In fact, he even justifies coercion when necessary to establish civil society. Kant (1999 [1793], 291) warns against paternalistic governments that treat their citizens like children, promising them happiness instead of nurturing the active exercise of reason. Kant (1991c [1797], 176), however, adds a caveat: "Obey the authority who has power over you (in whatever does not conflict with inner morality)." This hints at conscientious refusal and permissible civil disobedience, albeit more in the spirit of Mohandas Gandhi's nonviolent resistance than violent revolution (Cummiskey 2008, 232).[3]

At the heart of this debate is the difficult question of legitimate civil disobedience and choice between civil and coercive means to resist. Despite his unconditional rejection of rebellions in general, particularly violent ones, Kant, for instance, appraised the French Revolution as evidence of the moral progress of mankind (Axinn 1971, 424). It earned him the nickname "the old Jacobin" (Beck 1971, 411). However, he also strongly condemned the reign of terror, favoring reform and gradual political emancipation as more desirable means of achieving political change— that is, through the gradual enlightenment of the people. Kantian scholars controversially debate his surprising enthusiasm for the American and French Revolutions to this day (Reiss 1956, 179).[4] Concurring with Heinrich Heine, Karl Marx (1975 [1842], 203) called Kant's philosophy "the German theory of the French revolution." Kant might principally reject the right to resistance, but he would not claim that resistance in and of itself is not right (Nicholson 1976, 220). As Kant (2001a [1793], 134 fn.) puts it, "When human beings command something that is evil in itself (directly opposed to the ethical law), we may not, and ought not, obey them." The choice seems to be between resisting the sovereign to prevent injustice, on the one hand, and obeying the sovereign to make justice possible, on the other (Nicholson 1976, 222).

Kant's reflections on the right to resist is also influenced by his position on property rights and civil society (Cummiskey 2008, 220). As discussed in chapter 1, property rights include a person's legitimate authority over external things (Kant 1991c [1797], 68–69). Laying claim to a previously unowned object by virtue of first possession precludes others from using these things. This diminishes their freedom, without their being able to consent (Cummiskey 2008, 223–24). Given that unilateral coercion cannot provide a legitimate basis for the enforcement of rights, Kant (1991c [1797], 77) explains that "only in a civil condition can something external be mine or yours." One of the crucial functions of a shared civil society is to regulate the legitimate use of coercion in accordance with the general will of the people. Inversely, general will is based on a common interest in having public laws to enforce property claims (Cummiskey 2008, 226). The right to property is rendered possible in a civil society, wherein the reciprocal duty to respect each other's legitimate claims is enforced. In the state of nature, all property claims are temporary; conflicting claims cannot be legitimately adjudicated and thus do not qualify as lawful property rights (Kant 1991c [1797], 77). Thus, private ownership and the compulsion to participate in civil society are closely interlinked. Objects would be rendered unusable without private ownership, and those who refuse to enter civil society are seen as a threat to those who do (Cummiskey 2008, 224).

Furthermore, the duty to enter into a civil society is inextricably linked to a prohibition of rebellion; rather than the matter of particular unjust rulers, opposition to revolution is rejected because it harms the rule of law itself (Cummiskey 2008, 235). In our everyday understanding, critical thought is assumed to facilitate democracy and justice, and Kant is one of the foremost scholars mobilized to support this claim. It is thus worthwhile to focus on the inextricable link between private property and capitalism, as I undertake in chapter 1, and to understand the link between civil society and the rejection of revolution in Kant's philosophy, which are extremely instructive in analyzing the function of critical thought in enabling and hindering transformation, especially in the context of decolonization. As I demonstrate, civil society is the site not just of emancipatory politics but also of the building of hegemony.

General will, according to Rousseau (2012 [1762]), mirrors the unified and common interest of the body politic, which rises above individual and conflicting private interests. Kant's understanding of civil society draws on Rousseau's notion of the general will, and insofar as it is a shared civil society, by virtue of being inclusive, it can facilitate the resolution of possible conflicts among citizens. Kant obliges subjects, such as women and slaves, both of whom he regards as a type of property, to obey the very laws that sometimes oppress them. This denies them the right to revolution to bring about a change in their circumstances. While Kant is inconsistent about the actions of those he considers citizens, his position on other subjects is unambivalent. Kant thus seems to foreground unconditional political obedience and law-abidingness over civil disobedience. Plato's *Crito* (2008; written ca. 390 BCE) is an excellent example of the appropriate Kantian response to injustice: Although Socrates stands accused of being a lawbreaker (on charges of corrupting the youth and atheism), he refuses to break the law (by escaping from prison) even in the face of death. In response to the argument that only wrong judgment and not the entire law should be opposed, Socrates argues that in choosing to live in Athens he consents to the laws of Athens and so he prefers execution, although unjust, to living in a disordered anarchic state.

In contrast, Henry David Thoreau, who coined the term *civil disobedience* in his 1849 essay, outlined the urgency of certain forms of criticism, even if it resulted in being branded an enemy of the state. Thoreau (1992 [1849], 238) spoke from personal experience; his refusal to pay a tax imposed by the federal government, which was engaged in a war with Mexico and propagating slavery at the time, resulted in his imprisonment. He also helped escaped former slaves avoid recapture, which violated the Fugitive Slave Act of 1850. This act required northern US states to return fugitive slaves to the southern states. Thoreau emphasized the duty of civil disobedience, which included abolishing a government if it abused or disregarded the principles and goals for which it was instituted in the first place. Thoreau's violation of the law on war tax was not an attempt to draw public attention to unjust implementation. He did not seem to attempt to set an example. Rather, given that his refusal to pay the war tax and his aiding of people escaping slavery came to light only years later, his acts seem to have been more a case of conscientious objection than promoting civic education. In his view, immoral laws lose legitimacy, such that their violation is not justiciable.

While Thoreau refused to pay war taxes and thereby aspired to enact a peaceful revolution by withdrawing from funding violence, Kant, despite his commitment to peace, insisted that it was the duty of citizens to pay war taxes, even if the state waged an illegal war (Kant 1999 [1793], 308).

Perhaps Vladimir Lenin had Kant in mind when he famously lamented that a revolution in Germany was unlikely, as the Germans were so law-abiding that they would first line up in an orderly queue to purchase platform tickets before protesting at the railway station (Minnerup 2003, 103). In contrast, for Marx (1978b [1848], 500), communist goals "can be attained only by the forcible overthrow of all existing social conditions," with revolution being the only means to change for the proletariat, who "have nothing to lose but their chains." Marx highlights the power of collective political action by organized citizens such as the workers. This was considered threatening by thinkers such as John Stuart Mill (1977 [1835], 51), who remarked: "The capacity of cooperation for a common purpose, heretofore a monopolized instrument of power in the hands of the higher classes, is now a most formidable one in those of the lowest." Instead of undergirding political action with rational deliberation, Marx draws a link between revolution and collective fervor. According to him, no agent can operationalize political emancipation "without awakening a moment of enthusiasm in itself and in the masses" (Marx 1992b [1843–44], 254). This goes against the Kantian and Habermasian model of rational deliberation and anticipates queer feminist affect theory and politics.

However, the workers' resistance can end up being merely reactionary *ressentiment* without facilitating revolutionary consciousness (Caygill 2013, 45). Although the material conditions determine the scope of resistance and the worker's subjectivity, Lenin (1987 [1929], 76) claims that class consciousness will not just emerge automatically from economic struggles. Without supplemental, external intervention and the influence of vanguards, who nurture the consciousness, organized resistance will remain reactive and not be able to metamorphose into something new (Caygill 2013, 46). In place of a break with prior history, Lenin fears "the inverted inscription of that history in the resistance itself. The struggle for more wages accepts the wage form, the struggle for better working conditions accepts the discipline of factory production—resistance, in short, tends towards reform rather than revolution" (quoted in Caygill 2013, 46). In contrast, Rosa Luxemburg inverts Lenin to argue that consciousness follows the movement of a resistance instead of determining it. Further, Luxemburg focuses on minor, albeit persistent, acts and moments of resistance rather than a single glorified event. These instances of resistance nevertheless leave traces, which modify future struggles. Thus, Luxemburg maps not only conscious but also unintentional and spontaneous undercurrents of political action. Lenin, of course, in contrast, was interested in transforming spontaneous local struggles into organized global revolution (Caygill 2013, 104).

While Lenin and Luxemburg reflect on the conditions conducive for the possibility of resistance, Sigmund Freud outlines how resistance can be complicit with repression instead of being a force of emancipation (Caygill 2013, 141). In Freud's (1981a [1925], 159–60) view, the patient cultivates an attachment to illness, thereby ironically resisting recovery. Subsequently, if the analyst exposes the patient's repressions, the patient is more likely to reject the analyst's interpretations thereof. Freud (1981b [1926], 224) proposes that the analyst has to persuade the analysand to overcome opposition to stir the desire to be healed instead of being invested in their ailment. Here, a history of repression must be interrupted to facilitate broader recovery. The stronger the patient's resistance, the more the analyst must undermine the patient's capacity to oppose. This would open up more affirmative desires for the future. Thus, resistance can feed repression as much as it can enable liberation. Howard Caygill (2013, 55) compellingly contends that if fascism and Nazism are acts of resistance to the perceived menaces of modernity and communism, then resistance to these resistances cannot be achieved through confrontation. Rather, following psychoanalysis, only through the constitution of an affirmative resistant subjectivity can there be healing and repairing.

Theodor Adorno proposed another contentious perspective on the dynamic between resistance and repression, famously dismissing protests and demonstrations as mere "actionism," which he diagnosed as a symptom of despair. Against the "noisy optimism of immediate action" (Adorno 2010, 235), which, in Adorno's view, is predestined to fail, he foregrounds autonomous critique that defies the distraction and fleeting satisfaction provided by immediate action. Instead of exclusively focusing on specific local experience, Adorno recommends an analysis of "societal totality," without offering recipes for successful resistant political action.

In the oft-cited interview in the German magazine *Der Spiegel*, Adorno emphasizes that the impact of his ideas does not directly translate into political action; rather, the focus is on changing minds. He remarks: "Even though I had established a theoretical model, I could not have foreseen that people would try to implement it with Molotov cocktails" (Adorno 2010, 233). Adorno (2010, 236) strongly rejects any use of violence, for in his view, the "only meaningfully transformative praxis that I could imagine would be a non-violent one." When accused of "ivory tower scholarship," Adorno (2010, 233-34) clarifies that he is unafraid of the term *ivory tower* but is concerned about theory being subjected to a "practical precensorship." In his view, the predominance of practice goes hand in glove with an antipathy and hostility toward theory. This violates the dialectical approach propounded by Marx, in which theory and practice are equally necessary and mutually dependent forms of human activity.

Contrary to Jürgen Habermas's discourse ethics, Adorno highlights that, in activist contexts, political discussions often devolved into narcissistic games. Instead of equal participation and respectful listening to ensure fair decision making, ideological clashes occurred, with particular interests presented as universal ones by participants (Cook 2004, 55). Dissident positions were "hardly perceived, and then only so that formulaic clichés can be served up in retort" (Adorno 2005d [1969], 269). Utopian critical thought, in his view, creates room for ideas that resist being assimilated into prevailing identitarian and universal categories.

Adorno's position is condemned as elitist for decoupling theory from practice. In response, he defends himself by rejecting the romantic celebration of revolutionary action for being self-indulgent and warns of the dangers of the pressure to act in the face of the exigency of the here and now. For this, Adorno was attacked by students and activists, particularly those aligned with the Extra-Parliamentary Opposition, who had once seen him as their ally. In the summer of 1969, during the student occupation of the Institute for Social Research, Adorno, jointly with Habermas, made the decision to call the police; the students considered this an unforgivable act from a theorist of antifascism (Richter 2010, 228-29). His lectures were repeatedly disrupted. On another occasion, three female students showered him with flower petals and bared their breasts, which was later called the infamous "breast action" (*Busenattentat*). Adorno left the lecture hall, and leaflets titled "Adorno as an Institution Is Dead" were distributed all over the campus (Richter 2010, 230). The activist and politician Daniel Cohn-Bendit called Adorno a "reactionary pig" who deserved to be castrated (quoted in Scheible 1989, 144).

Unlike Adorno, Herbert Marcuse, who actively participated in the civil rights movement and antiwar protests in the United States, held a very optimistic view regarding the potential of student activism to bring about the "internal collapse of the system of domination" (Adorno and Marcuse 1999 [1969], 133). This strained his relationship with Adorno, whom he criticized in a letter for involving the police:

> To put it brutally: if the alternative is the police or left-wing students, then I am with the students. . . . And I would even take on board a disruption of "business as usual," if the conflict is serious enough for that. You know me well enough to know that I reject the unmediated translation of theory into praxis just as emphatically as you do. But I do believe that there are situations, moments, in which theory is pushed on further by praxis—situations and moments in which theory that is kept separate from praxis becomes untrue to itself. (Adorno and Marcuse 1999 [1969], 125)

In response, Adorno expressed his disappointment with Marcuse's endorsement of the "student stunts" and voiced his concerns about potential funding cuts to the institute due to the student protests (Adorno and Marcuse 1999 [1969], 127). He also opposed the students' demonization of the police, who, Adorno noted, treated him better than the students did. While reassuring Marcuse that "I am the last to underestimate the merits of the student movement: it has interrupted the smooth transition to the totally administered world," he also rejected what he saw as "barren and brutal practicism," asserting that it had nothing to do with theory (Adorno and Marcuse 1999 [1969], 127, 136).

I speculate that if both were to offer commentary on the 2024 pro-Palestinian protests on university campuses, Adorno might adversely comment on encampments and slogans by what he might describe as "calculating regressives" with "left-fascist" tendencies, who, he believed, confused "regression with revolution" (Adorno and Marcuse 1999 [1969], 128, 131). He would almost certainly caution that "a movement, due to its inherent contradictions, can transform itself into its opposite" (Adorno and Marcuse 1999 [1969], 128). Contrarily, Marcuse would have argued that "it is irresponsible to sit at one's writing desk advocating activities to people who are fully prepared to let their heads be bashed in for the cause" (Adorno and Marcuse 1999 [1969], 129). Marcuse presciently explains that "the rulers have a more accurate assessment of the meaning of the student opposition than it has itself: in the United States repression is most urgently organized against schools and universities—when co-optation does not help, the police do" (Adorno and Marcuse 1999 [1969], 133).

Political action is frequently coded as opposition to the state and its institutions, as well as to the capitalist markets. Another ubiquitous adage is that suffering spurs dissent to no longer tolerate injustice and violence. In contrast to Kant's claim that action is motivated by reason, poststructuralists locate the impulse to resist in unconscious, involuntary, and unintentional sources. Interestingly, while Foucault famously claimed that "where there is power, there is resistance," Adorno observed that resistance is infrequent and mostly inefficacious (Cook 2018, 63). Instead of political activism, Adorno (Adorno 2004 [1966], 245) advocates for critical thought to guard against the danger that struggles "turn out for the worse even if meant for the best." Complicating the relationship between theory and practice, Adorno (2008 [1965], 58) turns Marx's dictum around to argue that "one reason why the world was not changed was probably the fact that it was too little interpreted."

Surprisingly, like Adorno, Foucault (1990, 122) does not categorically endorse revolution, for, in his words, "To engage in politics—aside from just party politics—is to try to know with the greatest possible honesty, whether the revolution is desirable." Questioning the self-evident and the obvious, Foucauldian critique consists in estranging individuals from "the assumptions, . . . familiar notions, [and] unexamined ways of thinking" (Foucault 2000, 456). Rejecting reform through minor changes, Foucault advocates persistent destablizations of power through a critical relationship with the self (*rapport à soi*) (Cook 2018, 66, 69). Resistance is not emancipation from power; it is, rather, counter-conduct to the conducts of power. It is noteworthy that Achille Mbembe (2015) echoes Adorno and Foucault in his warning: "In these times of urgency, when weak and lazy minds would like us to oppose 'thought' to 'direct action,' and . . . precisely because of this propensity for 'thoughtless action,' . . . hard questions have to be asked."

In light of these theoretical contemplations, let us turn to an instructive historical example of the Haitian Revolution to understand the complexities and contradictions of resistance practices in processes of decolonization. In his powerful book *Conscripts of Modernity*, David Scott (2004, 135) traces how anticolonial utopias turned into postcolonial nightmares. Unlike romance, which is oriented toward resolution and guarantees, Scott draws the crucial link between tragedy and critique: Tragedies are marked by moral conflicts, contingencies, vulnerabilities, and the reversibility of all aspirations and accomplishments. Distracting us from a progressive dialectical resolution, tragedies do not offer consolations. The postcolonial condition, haunted by unfulfilled promises, is neither the extension of the Enlightenment project nor its rejection. The Enlightenment is the "permanent legacy" that sets the "conditions" of future postcolonial possibility and "which therefore demands constant renegotiation and readjustment" (Scott 2004, 20–21). The Haitian Revolution is not merely the successful realization of progressive Enlightenment norms; it is also marked by the trials and tribulations of anticolonial liberation.

Decolonization as Tragedy

With its sugar and coffee plantations playing a major part in the world economy, Saint-Domingue was considered the world's richest colony in the late eighteenth century. This led to a vicious rivalry among Spain, France, and Britain (Agnani 2013, 141). Saint-Domingue was a deeply contradictory site, where "the plantations were amazingly modern capitalist enterprises that did business with places like Amsterdam (for their banking), Africa (to obtain their workers), Newfoundland (to obtain cod), and Mexico (for the silver specie)," even as slaves were treated inhumanely (Girard 2017). Philippe Girard (2017) observes that the "supply chain for a loaf of sugar wasn't that different from that of an iPhone today!" This "world-system of slave-based agricultural capitalism" (Nesbitt 2008, 4) was contested by the Haitian Revolution. Described as the only successful slave revolt in history, which resulted in Haitian independence in 1804 and the establishment of the first postcolonial state apparatus, it has been an inspiration for subsequent anticolonial struggles and a beacon for postcolonial critique. In light of a Eurocentric understanding of agency and resistance, the late Haitian scholar Michel-Rolph Trouillot (1995, 73) remarked insightfully: "The Haitian Revolution thus entered history with the peculiar characteristic of being unthinkable even as it happened." Nick Nesbitt (2008, 7) observes that the Haitian Revolution was "a creative process of subjectification, of the invention of new, unheralded, and scandalously inadmissible subjects of enlightenment." Human autonomy was considered not a given, as presumed by Western liberal theory, but an aspiration to be realized in a free and equal society (Nesbitt 2008, 20). Considering the precarity of slaves' lives, "sheer survival and existence represented in itself a form of resistance" (Forsdick and Høgsbjerg 2017, 8).

The key figure of the revolution, Toussaint Louverture ("the opening") has been idealized as "black Spartacus" (Hazareesingh 2020) for avenging the crime of slavery. In being simultaneously committed to "the republican principles of liberty and equality" and "one-man rule" (Girard 2016, 209), Louverture himself in some ways embodied the contradictions of the Enlightenment. On the one hand, he is celebrated as an iconic Black revolutionary, an emancipator and a nationalist; on the other hand, it has been pointed out that Louverture was a slave owner and one of the wealthiest planters, whose main aspiration was to earn respect and be accepted into white French society. Despite copious and highly mythologized accounts of his life, including claims by his son that he descended from the royal dynasty of the Allada from Benin, surprisingly little is known about Louverture's early years (Forsdick and Høgsbjerg 2017, 19). Born into slavery around 1743, Louverture was freed in his thirties at a time when slave mortality was tragically high. As a devout Catholic, Louverture distanced himself from early rebellions that drew inspiration from Vodou (later, in 1800, he attempted to end the influence of Vodou) (Forsdick and Høgsbjerg 2017, 92). In the 1780s, the Saint-Domingue planters were anxious in the face of growing calls for abolition. Drawing inspiration from the American Revolution, they realized that they could claim political autonomy from France while continuing with the profitable institution of slavery. However, this "revolution from above" failed (Forsdick and Høgsbjerg 2017, 27). Although Louverture was not part of the insurgency's early leadership, by October 1791 he had joined the rebels and eventually became military leader of the Black slave army (Forsdick and Høgsbjerg 2017, 40, 47). While *The Declaration of the Rights of Man and the Citizen* in 1789 mentioned neither enslaved people nor women, with news of the French Revolution reaching Saint-Domingue, the colony was ripe for ending the "aristocracy of the skin" (Forsdick and Høgsbjerg 2017, 28).

C. L. R. James points to how the French Revolution propelled Louverture and the slaves to aspire to Enlightenment ideals of liberty, equality, and fraternity. Louverture astutely grasped that the revolutionary slogans of liberty and equality were "great weapons in an age of slaves" and "used them with a fencer's finesse and skill" (James 2001 [1938], 120). Invoking a universal and unqualified human right to freedom, Louverture victoriously led the revolution under the banner of "liberty or death" (James 2001 [1938], 9, 51). He did not merely parrot or hybridize the Enlightenment; he offered an inspiring anticolonial interpretation of the norms of liberty and equality: "Let us go forth to plant the tree of liberty, breaking the chains of our brothers still held captive under the shameful yoke of slavery. Let us bring them under the compass of our rights, the imprescriptible and inalienable rights of free men. [Let us overcome] the barriers that separate nations, and unite the human species into a single brotherhood" (Louverture 2008 [1797], 28).

The Saint-Domingue revolutionaries spoke the Enlightenment language of rights and emancipation even as they radicalized and singularized the Enlightenment by articulating particular and local experiences of slavery and dehumanization, reconfiguring Eurocentric framings of reason (Nesbitt 2008, 29, 54). The slave revolution revealed the inability and unwillingness of Europeans to truly comprehend the universal nature of rights and emancipation. Criticizing Habermas, Nesbitt (2008, 70) understands Saint-Domingue in terms of an inclusive and enlarged transnational subaltern public sphere; he presents a romantic representation of the resistant, anticolonial subject. In contrast, I argue that Louverture not only embodies the universal ideals of the Enlightenment but also its inconsistencies and ambivalences.

Even as the plantation system was being abolished, Louverture, ironically, became the wealthiest planter; he implemented a forced (albeit paid) labor regime to restart the plantation economy. It is noteworthy that female workers were the majority in the forced labor system. The assembly convened by Louverture to draft a new constitution for Saint-Domingue was composed exclusively of white people and free so-called *colored* people such as Julien Raimond, without a single former enslaved African aside from Louverture (Forsdick and Høgsbjerg 2017, 94). According to the new constitution, Louverture became governor for life without restraints on his power. While it was the first constitution ever to assert the universal right to freedom from enslavement, it also reinforced the obligatory nature of work on the plantations in Article 14. With Louverture's totalitarian-style regime, statements such as these raised suspicion of his being "The Black Robespierre" (Forsdick and Høgsbjerg 2017, 99): "You are free; what more can you want? What will the French people who are ready to arrive here say when they learn that, having been given this gift, you have been so ungrateful as to dip your hands in the blood of their children?" (Louverture, quoted in Forsdick and Høgsbjerg 2017, 90). Louverture's unpopular rural code of laws and militarization of plantation labor was resisted by landless Black workers (Forsdick and Høgsbjerg 2017, 93). Article 6 reinforced the earlier ban on Vodou and upheld Catholicism as the only permissible publicly professable faith. In a regressive move away from more gender equality, divorce was rejected (Forsdick and Høgsbjerg 2017, 95). In claiming that the constitution was met enthusiastically by the masses, he overlooked the frustration and anger of Black laborers and officers (Dubois 2004, 249–50). To his credit, collaborating with white plantation owners in Haiti as well as Europeans abroad, Louverture managed to revive the economy (Dubois 2004, 249–50). Nesbitt (2008, 5) contends that this resulted in slave labor being dismantled once and for all, the failings notwithstanding.

Regrettably, European writings on the Haitian Revolution mainly highlighted racialized violence rather than the Haitians' emancipatory aspirations of universal liberty. Thomas Jefferson dismissed Louverture as a "cannibal," while for Edmund Burke, the slave insurgents were a "race of fierce barbarians" (quoted in Forsdick and Høgsbjerg 2017, 75). It is no wonder that in much of the Western world, the Haitian Revolution evoked associations not with liberation from slavery but with the massacre of whites by "murderous" blacks. The white Europeans' lack of immunity against yellow fever impeded Napoleon Bonaparte's counterrevolutionary efforts to restore slavery and regain colonial control over Saint-Domingue. James warns that the French deployed this argument as an excuse to justify severe losses on the side of the French army and to downplay the accomplishments of the slave revolution. Haiti became proof of the ultimate illustration of "black savagery" owing to its revolutionary violence (Garraway 2017, 293).

By contrast, Pompée Valentin Vastey, who is said to have fought in Louverture's army, described the Haitian Revolution as the rightful reclamation of human and political rights not only of the formerly enslaved peoples, but also of their proper place in civilization. Vastey maintains that Haiti is the agent of divine retribution, and its revolution was an act of sacred violence against the forces of slavery (Garraway 2017, 293). In his view, European colonialism had derailed the progress of universal civilization and perverted the sacred path of history. The implication was that only by recognizing Haiti and truly upholding the Enlightenment principles could Europe redeem itself morally and spiritually (Garraway 2017, 291).

Despite controversial differences in their assessments, most scholars agree that Louverture embodied the contradictions and ambivalences of the

Enlightenment. Sudhir Hazareesingh (2020) credits Louverture with establishing a "creole republicanism" that drew on Enlightenment philosophy, Caribbean mysticism, and African political traditions, all while combining European and African military techniques to inspire the desire for freedom among the enslaved. Louverture may have succeeded in emancipating the slaves and reviving the economy, but he ultimately failed to set up a free, democratic society. As James (2001 [1938], 144, 231–33) observed, Louverture's failure is comparable to that of Robespierre. His is a cautionary tale for the postcolonial world. Given the high mortality of slaves, Girard (2016, 5) contends, Louverture was a "social climber and self-made man," and his freedom from bondage was accomplished through ingratiation, while his subsequent victories were achieved through a combination of political savvy and military tactics, making him "history's most famous slave." Louverture's complex volte-face in 1794 as he defected from the Spanish to join the French is often cited as an illustration of both his pragmatism and his canniness. Another example from his tumultuous life is that, just as Louverture had a hand in murdering his Black allies, he was betrayed by those closest to him. Until the end, his ambivalent relationship to the Enlightenment is evident: Even in his autobiography, written while he was imprisoned at Joux, Louverture presents the drafting of the 1801 constitution as an act of loyalty, not hostility toward France. Tragically, this all failed to move Bonaparte, who ensured that Louverture died a painful death.

While Louverture believed in the possibility of cooperation among the different ethnic groups, Jean-Jacques Dessalines, who took over the fight against Bonaparte's counterrevolutionary forces and became the first leader of independent Haiti, was solely focused on defeating the French and eradicating white colonizers' control from Saint-Domingue. Once victory was achieved, Article 14 of the 1805 constitution of the independent state of Haiti declared that to be Haitian was to be Black (Forsdick and Høgsbjerg 2017, 126).

Another astute account of the complexities of the relationship between the Enlightenment and the Haitian Revolution is offered by the American historian Jeremy Popkin, who focuses on the figure of Julien Raimond. A wealthy free man of color, Raimond was child of an interracial marriage and a prominent figure in the Haitian Revolution. Like Louverture, Raimond is full of contradictions. As a major slaveholder Raimond was not keen on abolishing slavery; his endeavor, rather, was to get the French government to reform racially discriminatory laws against free people of color in Saint-Domingue. Raimond urged the abolition of distinctions between whites and free nonwhites, advocating for the formation of a single, united class of free people capable of maintaining their dominance over the slaves who outnumbered them (Popkin 2017, 274).

In Popkin's reading, ideological battles between so-called mulatto elites and Black enslaved people were less about race than about Enlightenment virtues, which the former claimed that the latter must acquire before becoming free. Unlike the abolitionists, Raimond was not focused on the slaves' suffering. He insisted instead that the slaves must presumably earn their freedom by proving that they were fit to govern themselves. He demanded that the slaves acquire rational individualism; respect property rights; nurture morals and social virtues, as well as the habit of work; and, above all, become good consumers (Popkin 2017, 276). Raimond proposed that slaves buy their freedom so that the masters were compensated for their losses. Haiti ended up paying France ninety million francs as restitution for the supposed loss of property—namely, enslaved people and the land. It took until 1947 for Haiti to fully settle what came to be known as the independence debt.

When news of the slave revolts arrived in France, the president of the Assemblée Générale de Saint-Domingue, P. de Cadusch, wrote a letter to the *Moniteur*, the main newspaper during the French Revolution, blaming Enlightenment thought for the rebellion. He asserted, "Our slaves are armed to destroy us, and philosophy, which appeared made to console men, brings us only despair" (quoted in Nesbitt 2008, 143). What made the Haitian Revolution so threatening to the Europeans was not just that it put an end to the profitable system of colonial slavery and directly contested European racism in the name of Enlightenment values of freedom and equality but also that, in establishing a sovereign independent state, the colonized asserted their ability and capacity to govern themselves without direction from the European masters (Nesbitt 2008, 131). In *Anthropology from a Pragmatic Point of View*, Kant (2006 [1798], 124) contends that "the most important revolution from within the human being is 'his exit from his self-incurred immaturity.'" The Black slaves in Saint-Domingue embodied this Enlightenment principle insofar as they refused to be treated as property of white masters. Kant would not consider the Black slaves in Saint-Domingue subjects of the Enlightenment, although they ironically expose the parochialism and inaccuracy of Kantian claims regarding the inferiority of non-Europeans (Nesbitt 2008, 111).

G. W. F. Hegel's position on the Haitian Revolution is also a matter of dispute. In her influential work *Hegel, Haiti, and Universal History*, Susan

Buck-Morss (2009) claims that Hegel's analysis of the *Herr-Knecht* (master-slave) dialectic represents the events in Saint-Domingue without explicitly mentioning them. In her reading, Hegel upholds the justification of the right of slaves to revolt. In contrast, Nesbitt (2008, 115), following Jean Hyppolite, observes that instead of leading to revolt, the master-slave dialectic creates the social relations of slavery. The life-and-death-struggle is antecedent to slavery and not a response to it. The lord-bondsman relationship emerges from the bondman's failed struggle, which leads to the establishment of slavery. In Hyppolite's reading of Hegel, through the slaves' coming-to-self-consciousness of their autonomy, the state of servitude can be overcome (Nesbitt 2008, 116). This occurs when the slave acquires "a mind of his own" (Hegel 1977 [1807], 119), which, in Hegel's view, the slave achieves through his labor and through the realization that he has the capacity to freely transform the world. The masters, on the other hand, dependent as they are on the slaves for their status as master, are unfree (Nesbitt 2008, 120). Thus, Hegel avers that the slave achieves freedom not through local revolt, but through the institution of the state. As Hegel (1991 [1821], 88) puts it: "The Idea of freedom is truly present only as the state." The constitutions of 1801 and 1804, the abolition of slavery, the declaration of independence, and the establishment of the state of Haiti confirm Hegel's claim that freedom cannot be truly achieved by being bestowed by the benevolent from above. Rather, it must be embodied and institutionalized in the state, as in the case of the state of Haiti (Nesbitt 2008, 123). Interestingly, even as the Haitian constitutions of 1801 and 1804 were inspired by the French constitutions of 1791 and 1793 (Fischer 2004, 264), whereas the French and American constitutions failed to abolish slavery, the Haitian constitutions attempted to set up a postracial society. The ambivalences and contradictions of the Haitian constitutions bear witness to the conundrums of the processes of decolonization at large and the question of abolition. Haiti is exemplary of how the (im)possibility of freedom, equality, and justice can be sustained in a newly decolonized state even as the larger geopolitical and economic context was dominated by pernicious European colonial ideology and corresponding economic structures. Unfortunately, Haiti could not immunize itself from the racial capitalism of the global context at large.

After decades of neglect, there is a growing interest in the Haitian Revolution among Western scholars. The transformation of slaves into citizens offers a fascinating narrative of emancipation, thereby providing justification for the universality of norms of freedom, equality, and sovereignty. Scott (2004, 2) devotes his attention to the heroic but tragically flawed figure of

Louverture and notes that the painful lesson of the Haitian Revolution is that escape from bondage does not guarantee freedom. The Haitian Revolution is not just a tale of triumph of universal human rights. It is also the tale of a tragic failure of Black self-determination. Against romantic readings of the slave revolts, Scott (2014, 35) asks: "What is the conceptual conundrum or the ideological problem-space in relation to which Haiti is made to appear today as the visible sign of a predicament, a resolution, a truth? . . . What, in short, is the question to which Haiti is offered as an exemplary answer?"

Needless to say, Scott's analysis is significantly different from cynical accounts such as Hesketh Pritchard's travel memoir *Where Black Rules White*, published in 1900. Pritchard traveled to Haiti in 1899 to investigate the Black Republic. In his final chapter, he asks: "Can the Negro Rule Himself?" For Pritchard, Haiti provided the conclusive answer to this query. He observes: "[The] negro has had his chance, a fair field and no favour. He has had the most fertile and beautiful of the Caribbees for his own; he has had the advantage of excellent French laws; he inherited a made country, with Cap Haytien for its Paris. . . . At the end of a hundred years of trial, how does the black man govern himself? What progress has he made? Absolutely none" (quoted in Scott 2014, 45).

Haiti allegedly provided proof of the incapacity of Black sovereignty and necessity of European patronage. Scott (2014, 46) explains how, in response to such disparagement, a "vindicationist counterdiscourse" emerged, glorifying Haiti as a leading force in Black liberation and sovereignty. James, for instance, in Scott's reading, depicts the self-emancipation of the slaves as an instance of universal history in which "the main protagonist, Louverture, as a world historical figure, fails even as he succeeds" (Scott 2014, 48). Similarly, Sunil Agnani (2013, 133) insightfully observes that the greatest slave revolution in history is plagued "by the weight of liberators turned tyrants (Toussaint to Christophe)." While the abolishing of slavery in 1804 under the banner of freedom and equality was one the greatest achievements of anticolonial Enlightenment, from 1834 on, the system of indentured labor from India (coolies) and China effectively replaced slavery. This new regime of superexploitative debt bondage recruited bonded laborers to work on sugar, cotton, and tea plantations, as well as on rail-construction projects in the colonies. Tragically, following Gayatri Chakravorty Spivak, such historical events are marked by "repetition-in-rupture," making decolonization a never-ending, ongoing process (Spivak 1999, 102).

In light of these historical considerations, let us now turn to current events and discussions about political action and its relation to critical thought. Two of the most exciting contemplations on the question of critique and resistance have come from Spivak and Judith Butler and their respective focus on subalternity and precarity. Drawing on these two ideas, I outline my concerns about the nonperformativity of critique and the risks of state phobia in ongoing processes of decolonization.

The Will to Resist. Critique and Protest

Protest movements around the world seek to drive radical political change, holding states and international institutions accountable by exposing their abuses of power. The global rise of street politics has reshaped how agency and resistance are performed (Butler and Athanasiou 2013). The occupation and reclaiming of public spaces signify a shift in the political landscape, moving beyond traditional centers of power to the streets. By introducing new actors into the political arena, these "subaltern counterpublics" (Fraser 1997, 82) ignite debates on redistribution, recognition, and representation. Unlike Habermas's (1992) model of rational deliberation, subaltern counterpublics function as affective spaces where public anger, outrage, and frustration redefine the relationship between the state and civil society. The emergence of countermovements against neoliberalism and neocolonialism highlights the complex, intersecting dynamics of power. In reclaiming democracy from capitalist and corporate influence, these movements reveal the subversive and disruptive potential of dispossessed bodies (Butler and Athanasiou 2013, 140). Although these movements vary in their goals and strategies, they share a horizontal structure and the use of social media. Their street-level direct action unites diverse groups, fostering spontaneous solidarity. As these crowds assemble to contest political and economic dispossession, their physical presence and collective action are seen as expressions of the people's will and tangible demonstration of popular sovereignty (Butler and Athanasiou 2013, 150).

The effectiveness of clicktivism, manifested in so-called TikTok revolutions and Insta insurgencies, in fundamentally transforming social, political, and economic relations within the context of postcolonial late capitalism remains an open question. In my view, these protest movements are inherently ambivalent. On one hand, they rely on the ideas and imagination needed to envision an alternative political order. In this way, they effectively challenge the TINA (There Is No Alternative) principle.

On the other hand, it appears that the aspirations driving current protests, both consciously and unconsciously, may perpetuate the subalternization of marginalized subjects and collectives who already have a tenuous relationship with the state and the international civil society and counterpublic spheres. The idealistic fervor of these movements tends to overshadow the exploitative and exclusionary conditions that enable the agency of resisters. For example, when an anticapitalist protester engages in hashtag activism using a device produced under exploitative conditions in the global South, the fantasy of subverting capitalism turns into a surreal instance of class-privileged *jouissance*. This erotics of resistance underscores the new international division of labor, which perpetuates the divide between those who resist and those who cannot. To Foucault's (1990, 122) claim, "Where there is power, there is resistance," I would counter, "Where there is resistance, there is also power."

Let us now focus on Butler's analysis of public assemblies as arenas for critique and resistance against precarity and state violence. Next, I compare the concepts of *precarity* and *subalternity*. This comparison is crucial for my argument, as it demonstrates how precarious subjects, according to Butler, primarily target the state in their critique and seek to eliminate state violence. In contrast, Spivak's view of subaltern subjects highlights their exclusion from civil society and public spheres, leaving them unprotected and overlooked by the state.

It is important to consider the limitations of framing critique and resistance solely in terms of anti-statism. To address this, I draw on Antonio Gramsci's insights on civil society as a site of hegemony and Foucault's analysis of state phobia as a neoliberal strategy of governmentality to outline the nonperformativity of critique. While my perspective diverges from Butler's, I engage with their work, as well as with the contributions of Hannah Arendt and Adorno, to refine my position. I remain indebted to Butler's insights, which serve as a foil for my analysis.

The State as *Monstre Froid*

Friedrich Nietzsche's (2006 [1883–85], 34) portrayal of the state as *monstre froid*—the coldest of all cold monsters—has profoundly shaped contemporary critiques of the state, influencing thinkers from Louis Althusser, with his concept of the repressive state apparatus, to Mbembe, with his notion of necropolitics. The state's judicial mechanisms, which ostensibly are designed to protect and provide justice for its citizens, are increasingly seen as instruments of oppression, often targeting the very people they are meant to serve. Concepts such as precarity, bare life, disposable lives, and outcasts have been mobilized to capture the experiences of marginalized political subjectivities. Despite their differing frameworks, these concepts share a focus on the conditions of disenfranchisement and dispossession. They expose how the governmentality driven by efficiency, profitability, accumulation, and optimization renders large swaths of the population expendable and disposable, perpetuating cycles of exploitation and militarization.

Butler also tends to focus primarily on the penal and coercive functions of the state, which is accused of abdicating its responsibility vis-à-vis its precarious citizens. The focus is on the coercive and disciplinary proclivities of the state, which has triggered protest movements globally. Resistance is explained in terms of the public assembly of precarious bodies struggling for livable lives. Mass demonstrations, for Butler (2015, 26), are a collective critique of the socially and economically induced precarity that renders populations disposable. Public protests, in the aftermath of the murders of George Floyd and Mahsa Amini, have become symbols of global resistance.[5] In confronting state brutality, protesting bodies demonstrate both their precarity and their right to persist in the face of efforts to eradicate them. As beacons of political action, public assemblies, especially nonviolent ones, threaten the state with delegitimization (Butler 2015, 83). In Butler's view, a permanent principle of revolution resides within democratic orders.

Against an increasingly individualized sense of anxiety, public assemblies embody collective vulnerability, even as they provide an alternative to neoliberalism's isolationist tactics (Butler 2015, 6). Shared precarity functions as a galvanizing condition for embodied action and enables coalitional framework across differences. It is not out of love for humanity or peace that we cohabit, but because we have no other choice (Butler 2015, 122). While a politics of alliance presupposes an ethics of cohabitation, we should also be vigilant regarding divisive politics, wherein the allocation of rights to one group is weaponized to disenfranchise basic entitlements to another (Butler 2015, 70). A good example of this is the demonization in Europe and the United States of migrants and refugees, who are pitted against the white working-class citizens. Butler acknowledges that bodies on the street can equally campaign for right-wing causes. Not all forms of assembly struggle for justice, equality, and democracy and are emancipatory (Butler 2015, 124).

In contrast to Arendt (1998 [1958]), who distinguishes the private sphere as a space of dependence and inaction from the public sphere of independent action, Butler (2015, 129) emphasizes interdependence in the realm of the public. Performative action, in this view, happens not alone but only "between bodies," those that are dependent on and vulnerable to other bodies. However, interdependence is not a harmonious coexistence; rather, there is an unchosen dimension to our solidarity with others (Butler 2015, 152). At the same time, notwithstanding claims of the universal right to appear, differentiated forms of power regulate who can and cannot participate (Butler 2015, 50).[6] The public sphere, in which the speech act qualifies as the paradigmatic political action separated from the private sphere, historically excluded populations such as women and slaves. The feminized and racialized body was restricted to the private sphere, with the public sphere enabling the political subjectivity of the speaking male white citizen (Butler 2015, 45).

In *On Revolution*, Arendt (2006 [1963], 113–14) refers to the poor, who are driven to the streets by something "irresistible." For Arendt, the poor act from want, hunger, and need; they seek liberation from life's necessities by means of violence. Necessity thereby invades the political realm (Butler 2015, 46). Liberation for the poor, in this view, is not *toward* freedom but *from* the necessities of life. However, the elite strive toward freedom in the abstract, such that the poor seem to act from the body, while the elite act from the mind. Contesting this mind-body dualism and the traditional focus on anchoring politics in rational deliberative processes, Butler's (2015, 179) queer feminist approach foregrounds embodiment as central to politics and critique. They claim "everyone is precarious"; this follows from our interdependence and vulnerability (Butler 2015, 118). Street politics often involves bodily exposure to possible harm, such that vulnerability is mobilized as a deliberate and active form of political resistance (Butler 2015, 126). SlutWalk protests (Wikipedia 2024b), for example, are an effort to "claim the streets as a site that should be free of harassment and rape" (Butler 2015, 138).

Instead of trying to integrate the previously marginalized into the public sphere, the attempt is to expose the contradictions in the constitution of the sphere itself. Rather than being pregiven, demonstrations dispute and fight over the very public character of the space, even as the crowd produces the public by repurposing the material environment (Butler 2015, 71). Given the state of infrastructure in the global South, one cannot always take for granted the street or public square as a site for political action. In keeping with market logic, the privatization of public spaces is an assault on freedom of assembly (Butler 2015, 174). When infrastructural conditions for politics are unavailable, assemblies are rendered impossible (Butler 2015, 126–27).

Criticizing Giorgio Agamben's understanding of "bare life" for presuming that disenfranchised subjects have no agency and are precluded from the sphere of action (Butler 2015, 79), Butler suggests demonstrations are an embodied and plural performativity in the name of *we the people*, even as they are necessarily partial and never all-inclusive (Butler 2015, 8). The term *the people* does not represent a preexisting group of people. Rather, the collectivity is always a work in progress; its inadequacy and self-division are part of its enacted meaning and promise (Butler 2015, 169). Without a pre-established collective subject, there is, nevertheless, collective acting, such that an assembly of bodies performs the *we* (Butler 2015, 59).

Interestingly, both Adorno and Foucault warn against the use of the *we*. Adorno (2005b [1962], 4) cautions: "Talk of a 'we' one identifies with already implies complicity with what is wrong." He suggests that, even as individuals free themselves from "the particularity of obdurate particular interest," they must also free themselves from "the no less obdurate particular interest of the totality" (Adorno 2006 [1964–65], 45). Along similar lines, Foucault points out that Richard Rorty derides him for failing to "appeal to any 'we.'" In response, Foucault (1997, 114) explains that "the problem is, precisely, to decide if it is actually suitable to place oneself within a 'we' in order to assert the principles one recognizes and the values one accepts; or if it is not, rather, necessary to make the future formation of a 'we' possible by elaborating the question."

Butler (2015, 216) faults Adorno for ruling out the idea of popular resistance, of forms of dissidence that emerge when bodies come together on the street to articulate their opposition to contemporary regimes of power. Adorno is pilloried for reducing the practice of critique to "no-saying" on the part of the self that would otherwise want to go along with (*mitzuspielen*) the status quo. At the same time, self-critique, for Adorno, is an internal check against complicity (Butler 2015, 217). Butler asks whether the mere disavowal of being implicated makes us innocent. Is a morally pure critic the model of resistance? Rejecting the limits Adorno puts to the idea of opposition and against the dismissal of protest politics as ineffectual in the long term, Butler links the temporary nature of popular assemblies to their critical function, with such gatherings serving as democracy's incipient or "fugitive moments" (Butler 2015, 7, 20).

Every assembly risks forfeiting the right to gather and is haunted by the threat of violence and incarceration. Police actions expose state-sponsored coercion, while opposition to state violence, even peaceful protests, is often delegitimized as "unrest" and "riots" (Butler 2015, 26). Butler sees the prison as the limit case of the public sphere, with the state determining who may be incarcerated or even killed, sometimes simply for congregating (Butler 2015, 173). The persecutions of protestors in not only Iran and Russia but also the United States and Germany are chilling examples of this. Unlike Butler, for whom incarceration is the state's tactic of waging war on precarious subjects by barring access to public space, Spivak understands exclusion not just in terms of confinement through criminalization. Rather, the ideological subject constitution of the subaltern entails being cut off from accessing the enabling functions of both state and civil society. The lack of access to intellectual labor of the subalterns ensures that their bodies are simply trained to serve the hegemons. The threat is not just from the state, but also from fellow citizens.

While Butler associates the state with violence, brutality, and terror, civil society becomes the realm of nonviolent practice, striving to constitute a different world. Drawing on Gandhi, Butler suggests that resistant bodies cultivate collective action into a nonviolent practice, which goes beyond heroic individualism (Butler 2015, 192). Nonviolent strategies such as boycotts and strikes are not war by other means; instead, they are ethical alternatives to more outright conflict (Butler 2015, 192) (more on violence and nonviolence in chapter 5).

Butler's (2015, 187) claim that assemblies can succeed only if they subscribe to principles of nonviolence surprisingly converges with Kant's position—namely, that the deployment of violence delegitimizes critique. Spivak, however, highlights how subaltern insurgencies have been repeatedly discredited throughout history as violent and dangerous. Drawing on the case of Bhubaneshwari Bhaduri, who was instructed to assassinate a colonial officer but could not carry out the assignment and instead, ashamed at disappointing her comrades, killed herself, Spivak (1994a) demonstrates how the subaltern is nonviolent not because of ethico-political principles but because of the inability to exercise violence, except on itself. It should come as no surprise that subalternity and suicide often emerge as illustrations in Spivak's writings.

Precarity Versus Subalternity

While concepts such as disposable lives and precarity evoke vivid images of vulnerability and are often mobilized by anticapitalist protesters, I argue that many of these approaches tend to reproduce Eurocentric perspectives. For instance, critical engagements with precarity are largely tied to the decline of the European welfare state, a perspective that conveniently overlooks the fact that such fiscal insecurity has long been the norm in the non-Western world. The majority of the population in the global South has never had access to formal labor markets, health insurance, or unemployment benefits and has lived for decades with the distress and anxiety that come from casualized employment systems.

The irony here is that the site of exploitation has expanded. What was inflicted upon the non-Western world through structural adjustment programs is now being implemented in the global North. There is an inherent Eurocentric bias in the term *precarization*, which primarily refers to the transition from protections, such as unemployment benefits, to the instability of a casualized and flexible labor market. Since the welfare state never fully developed in newly decolonized nations—or was dismantled early in the postcolonial state-building process by international financial organizations—the concept of precarization is largely irrelevant to the majority of workers in the postcolonial world.

Another concern I have is that the enthusiasm for hashtag activism and fantasies of hyperagency often overestimate the impact and reach of these political initiatives. This tendency reflects a self-centeredness among resistant subjects in the global North, who frequently overlook the exclusions they create and the inequalities their politics perpetuates. Social media is a prime example of this dynamic, where the focus on visibility and engagement can obscure the broader and more complex realities of global inequality. Butler (2015, 153), for instance, argues that "social networking produces links of solidarity that can be quite impressive and effective in the virtual domain." (Social) media is touted as "countersurveillance" of military and police action (Butler 2015, 94).

Facebook, for instance, conceded that it was culpable in not doing enough to prevent the incitement of violence and hate speech on its platform against the Rohingya Muslim minority in Myanmar. A class-action complaint was lodged in December 2021 with the Northern District Court of California in San Francisco, which stated that, "for better market penetration," Facebook's algorithms "amplified hate speech against the Rohingya people; it failed to invest in local moderators and fact checkers; it failed to take down specific posts inciting violence against Rohingya people; and it did not shut down specific accounts or delete groups and pages that were encouraging ethnic violence" (Milmo 2021). The proliferation of hate speech on Twitter, even before the takeover by Elon Musk, flies in the face of the promise of digital counterpublics.

The manufacturing of electronic devices has been outsourced to the global South, where they are produced under highly exploitative conditions. Thus, the notion that we can tweet our way out of capitalism rings hollow. In *Anti-Oedipus: Capitalism and Schizophrenia*, Gilles Deleuze and Félix Guattari (2003, 293) elaborate the erotics of capitalism: "the way a bureaucrat fondles his records, a judge administers justice, a businessman causes money to circulate; the way the bourgeoisie fucks the proletariat; and so on. . . . Flags, nations, armies, banks get a lot of people aroused." The allure of radical change through hashtag activism excites many young, urban, and class-privileged people. The performative nature of such resistance, often experienced as a form of *jouissance*, leads them to believe that it is their mission to save the world and show solidarity with the marginalized. This perception conveniently masks their own complicity in the very systems they challenge. In addition, the normative concepts of civil society and counterpublics are often limited to a small elite who meet specific criteria for citizenship, leaving disenfranchised groups with only uneven access to organized political spaces. Consequently, even within resistance movements, exclusions arise, complicating any straightforward understanding of power, agency, and vulnerability.

In Butler's (2015, 119) view, "everyone is precarious," but I would counterargue that not everyone is subaltern. This has important repercussions for our understanding of critique and resistance. Subalternity is not just about being excluded from organized struggles; the ideological subject constitution of subalterns implies that they cannot imagine themselves belonging to the abstract idea of *the people*. Subalternity is the condition of not being able to make one's interests count, for subalterns' speech acts have no addressee; neither civil society nor the state listens to them. At this point, it is worthwhile to engage with the Gramscian notion of subalternity, which is a key concept in postcolonial contemplations on processes of disenfranchisement and agency. Despite decades of important scholarship, the term *subaltern* remains misunderstood and misused, as it is deployed interchangeably with *the poor, the migrant, queer, Black*, or BIPOC (Black, Indigenous, People of Color). For this reason, I devote considerable effort to clarifying my understanding of the concept and its centrality for my arguments.

Considered one of the most influential political thinkers, Gramsci was a founding member and onetime leader of the Communist Party of Italy. He was incarcerated by Benito Mussolini's fascist regime. During his imprisonment, in his minuscule prison cell, Gramsci wrote 2,848 pages that were published as thirty-six prison notebooks. Gramsci rejects the inevitability thesis—namely, that the crisis of capitalism will automatically lead to socialism. His political aspiration is not only for more wages and shorter working hours but for a fundamental rearrangement of social relations. Instead of focusing on the revolutionary function of economic crisis, which would simply result in replacing one order with another, Gramsci's interest lay in reconfiguring the relation between freedom and coercion, with a particular focus on those citizens who were subject to the latter without access to the former. He analyses how state and civil society work together to produce subalternity by tracing the easy coalition between socialist workers and capitalist managers at the expense of rural peasants. He outlines how the lack of an alliance between urban proletarians and rural farmers made it possible for Italian fascism to flourish. In a surprising move, Gramsci shifts the focus away from revolutionary struggles to arguing that only the state can enable desubalternization.

In the prison notebooks (*Quaderni del carcere*, 1929–35), Gramsci (2011a) speaks of *classi subalterne, classi subordinate,* and *classi strumentali* to describe nonhegemonic collectivities. Particularly in the twenty-fifth prison notebook, *On the Margins of History: History of Subaltern Groups,* Gramsci contends that subalternity is a result not only of economic exploitation but also of social, political, and cultural domination. He foregrounds the suffering and marginalization of rural peasants, moving away from the traditional Marxist emphasis on the exploitation of industrial workers. Marx claims that rebellions are most likely to happen in developed economies that turn labor into capital and laborers into proletarians, where industrial progress and the concomitantly high levels of exploitation of the working class create conducive structural conditions for a successful revolution (Marx 1990 [1867], 929). At the same time, if workers gain from robust economic growth, they are unlikely to jeopardize the benefits in their lives by risking a failed revolt. Marx further warns that class cohesion is threatened by conflicts—for instance, those between Black and white workers—that impede solidarity. Lacking revolutionary class consciousness, organization, and leadership, rural peasants were not regarded as agents of change in Marx's analysis of class conflict. When rural revolts did happen, they were, according to Marx, often organized by urban revolutionaries or leftist political parties, thereby confirming his claim of lack of agency among the peasantry.

Eric Hobsbawm (1969, 1971 [1959]) similarly dismisses mass rural and agrarian struggles as purportedly antimodern or emotional forms of social protests. Their allegedly primitive mindset lacks the intellectual framework to understand the changes caused by capitalism and to develop an adequate response to it. In contrast to urban social movements, such as the labor movement, Hobsbawm argues, social banditry and millenarianism are spasmodic and temporary and thus cannot produce long-lasting political transformations. Ultimately for him, robust ideology and systematic organization distinguish between sporadic struggles and systemic movements: "Demonstrations, whose original purpose in labor movements was utilitarian—to demonstrate the massed strength of the workers to their adversaries, and to encourage their supporters by demonstrating it, became ceremonies of solidarity whose value, for many participants, lies as much in the experience of 'one-ness' as in any practical object they may seek to achieve. A set of ritual furnishings may arise: banners, flags, massed singing and so on" (Hobsbawm 1971 [1959], 150).

In contrast, Gramsci provides a nuanced analysis of power and resistance to the multiple and complex dynamics of marginalization and disenfranchisement experienced by subaltern classes, which extend beyond mere economic factors. While hegemonic groups consolidate their power in and through the state, subalterns are able to access neither the state nor civil society even as they are excluded from building alliances with other marginalized groups, such as workers. Gramsci observes that, in military terminology, *subaltern* refers to someone who follows orders and remains obedient. Oppositional political practices of subalterns are dismissed as unsystematic and ineffective in challenging hegemonic groups. They exist outside organized struggles, and this exclusion renders them unable to represent themselves or assert their interests without institutional recognition. Gramsci, rather than celebrating or glorifying subaltern agency, views desubalternization as the process of dismantling the conditions that subordinate the subaltern to hegemonic groups. He underscores the importance of developing a consciousness of one's agency, arguing that desubalternization is possible only when there is a sense of self-worth. Subalterns are not merely those who have yet to gain power; rather, they are stripped of the means to exert power. Subalternity is defined by the absence of unity and solidarity. It is the inability to make one's resistance count. Spivak harks back to this powerful insight and applies it to the postcolonial feminist condition.

While Butler positively focuses on the critical function of collective political action based on the principle of solidarity and shared vulnerability, for Spivak the process of desubalternization is persistently hindered by the vanguardism of international civil society, which is marked by the discontinuity between those who resist and those who cannot. In Butler's

(2015, 156) view, when the idea of abstract rights is vocally claimed by precarious individuals, the very idea is transformed, and this gives way to a plurality of embodied actors who enact their claims in the name of *the people*. This seems to suggest that the subaltern can speak, and we just need to listen better to go beyond normative framings of the political that tend to overlook the political agency of the dispossessed. Furthermore, the claim is that, notwithstanding structural and material constraints, vulnerable groups are capable of collectively exercising critique.

In my view, this disregards Spivak's powerful critique of Foucault and Deleuze in "Can the Subaltern Speak?" Spivak accuses them of romanticizing political action and resistance and disregarding the ideological subject constitution of subalterns, such that subalterns neither consent nor dissent, as they do not understand themselves to be bearers of rights. Rather, their subjectivity is constituted in terms of being obedient, à la Gramsci. I briefly summarize Spivak's critique before outlining how Butler seems to repeat Foucault's and Deleuze's oversight.

In a conversation titled "Intellectuals and Power," Foucault (1977, 207) argues that the masses are not caught in ideology and are capable of expressing themselves, which makes the role of intellectuals redundant in political processes. According to Spivak, Foucault is guilty of abdicating responsibility for representation with his postrepresentationalist vocabulary, which conceals an essentialist agenda (Dhawan 2023). In contrast, Spivak considers representation crucial for the process of decolonization. Invoking Marx, she discerns two meanings of the word *representation*—namely, *Vertretung* (speaking for) and *Darstellung* (speaking about) (Spivak 1994a, 71). While Foucault and Deleuze suggest that only speaking about is sufficient, Spivak asserts that *Darstellung* is untenable without *Vertretung*. Despite the interconnectivity of the two concepts, Spivak maintains that they should not be subsumed under a single, overarching notion (Spivak 1994a, 72). In defining disempowered groups as coherent political subjects, the aesthetic portrait, which symbolically represents them, is often regarded as a direct expression of their political desires and interests. Spivak asserts that this model of political representation, when applied to the Third World, accentuates the disparity between aesthetic and political representation.

Among the key issues for critical theory in general, and for postcolonial queer feminism in particular, are the challenging questions: Why do subjects acquiesce to their own subordination? How are we constituted to desire against our self-interest? It is worthwhile to turn to Deleuze and Guattari, who, invoking Baruch Spinoza and quoting Wilhelm Reich, ask:

Why do men fight *for* their servitude as stubbornly as though it was their salvation? . . . The astonishing thing is not that some people steal or that others occasionally go out on strike, but rather that all those who are starving do not steal as a regular practice, and all those who are exploited are not continually on strike. . . . No, the masses were not dupes; at a certain point, under a certain set of circumstances, they *wanted* fascism and it is *this* perversion of the desire of the masses that needs to be accounted for. (Deleuze and Guattari 2003, 29)

If, as postcolonial scholarship suggests, colonialism extends beyond the mere annexation and occupation of territories and the exploitation of labor and resources to include the colonization of the mind, then decolonization cannot be achieved solely through the transfer of power from European colonizers to native populations. Given the enduring social injustice and economic exploitation in the postcolonial world, Spivak contends that genuine decolonization necessitates an intervention in the construction of both imperial and subaltern identities. Consequently, political and economic reforms must be supplemented by an epistemic change to dismantle the legacies of colonialism (Spivak 2012a).

While Butler focuses on how vulnerability is unevenly distributed and how, despite this differential precarity and uneven access to the right to assembly, different forms of political action are integral to struggles for justice, Spivak resists extoling subaltern agency. She emphasizes the ideological formation of subaltern subjects, who internalize their subjugation as both inevitable and fated. The subalterns lack a conception of themselves as bearers of political rights, thereby accepting their economic and social marginalization as what Gramsci terms *common sense*. According to Spivak, overcoming subalternity necessitates more than mere economic and political empowerment. It requires a pedagogical intervention to dismantle the conditions of subalternity. This approach surpasses the Subalternists' attempts to recover and restore subaltern agency (Dhawan 2023).

Whereas Marx dismissed subaltern groups for being unorganized and not offering a systematic and effective counterpoint to the bourgeoisie, seeing instead mainly urban proletarians as agents of revolution, Gramsci focused on rural subalterns who had been dismissed as prepolitical by both Marxists and Leninists. Gramsci famously repudiated the conviction that the "dictatorship of the proletarian" (Gramsci 2011b, 11; Q 6 §12; Marx 1983 [1852], 58) is sufficient to overcome domination. *Subaltern* is a relational term for Gramsci, whose counterpoint is the hegemon—namely, groups that realize their historical unity in the state, composed of sections from political and civil society. It is important to bear in mind Gramsci's understanding of state as consensus, produced in civil society and armored by coercion. This implies that civil society is not located outside the state and in opposition to it but, rather, is a significant site, where the state exerts its influence through persuasion rather than explicit violence. In contrast to the hegemonic groups whose interests are unified in the state, the interests of subaltern groups are fragmented, and they are unable to access the state. In Gramsci's view, an alliance between urban industrial proletarians and rural subalterns can engender a critical counterhegemonic political bloc.

The Subalternists, inspired by Gramsci and Foucault, sought to "listen to the small voice of history" (Guha 2010, 11). They elucidate how subaltern insurgencies were systematically dismissed as disorganized, sanguinary, and devoid of legitimate leadership, thereby relegated to the realm of criminality. Consequently, postcolonial nation building evolved into an elite-driven endeavor, wherein colonial interests were supplanted by those of the native privileged class. By recuperating the voice, the will, and thereby the agency of subaltern groups, the Subalternists seek to advance the process of decolonization *and* desubalternization. Taking the example of postcolonial India, they elaborate on how people who fought against feudalism and colonialism were deprived of participation in nation building, which is once again exclusionary and elitist.

Spivak supports this endeavor but cautions against the dangers of glorifying subaltern agency and constructing a subversive, resistant subaltern subject as a counterpoint to hegemonic historiography. She explains that attributing the so-called will to resist to subalterns would be an example of metalepsis, where the effect is mistaken for the cause (Spivak 2006, 280–81). Subalternity is not an identity but a power effect arising from being excluded from access to hegemony. In their quest to reclaim subaltern agency, historians frequently attribute a presumed authentic and heroic political will and consciousness to these groups (Spivak 2006, 349–50). In the process, the subaltern is constructed as a sovereign subject retrospectively romanticized as an agent of resistance with clear intentions, desires, and knowledge about what is in its self-interest.

This implies that desubalternization is impossible without addressing the discontinuity between desire and interest—namely, how subjects are constituted to desire that which is against their self-interest. Foucault's and Deleuze's argument rests on the coherence between desire and interest and disavows the role of the intellectual in obstructing, as well as facilitating, desubalternization. In contesting the claim that the masses know the script of their subjugation and can overcome it, Spivak, in fact, reminds us of the most important lesson that Foucault has taught us: that our interests and desires are not always known to ourselves. In contrast to ostensibly expressive subjects who know and speak for themselves and thus do not require representation, Spivak explains that the question "Can the Subaltern Speak?" is rhetorical. This is true because the very notion of subalternity implies the inherent impossibility of subalterns being heard. Thus, the intellectual plays the mediating role of representing subalternity, which she describes as an "inaccessible blankness" (Spivak 1994a, 89), impossible but necessary.

In contending that assemblies are sites where precarious/vulnerable/marginalized/silenced individuals and collectivities can become visible/audible/intelligible, Butler, like Foucault, seems to suggest that they have the possibility to speak for themselves. This supposes a transparent and straightforward act of self-representation and assumes that vulnerable subjects are aware of the ways in which they are exploited and silenced, such that public assemblies enable them to voice their disenfranchisement and contest state coercion. Butler, following Foucault and Deleuze, disregards the importance of ideology critique. As Spivak (1999, 244) cautions, the moment we make room for subalterns' speech and claim to have heard them is precisely when they are silenced. It is a gesture of effacement in disclosure. Against the glorification of the militant female subject, transnational elites must be cognizant of our complicity in making subaltern speech impossible. Spivak (1985, 245) avers that "if we are driven by a nostalgia for lost origins, we run the risk of effacing the 'native' and stepping forth as 'the real Caliban.'" This is an indirect critique of the decolonial call for a return to Indigenous epistemologies (Spivak 2008, 273 fn. 25).

While some dispossessed individuals are indeed heard by gaining the attention of hegemonic groups, subalternity in some ways marks the limits of legibility and intelligibility. Let us briefly explore this point by returning to Spivak's reading of J. M. Coetzee's novel Foe (mentioned in chapter 2). In Robinson Crusoe, Robinson carries out the civilizing mission of the European imperialist by teaching Friday, the native, to speak English. Similarly, in Foe, the female narrator of the novel, the Englishwoman Susan Barton, attempts to give Friday a voice (Spivak 1991, 169). The violence of a colonial education, which was effaced in Robinson Crusoe, is foregrounded in Foe, and it is revealed that Friday had his tongue removed by slave traders. Spivak underlines the fact that one of the words that Barton teaches

Friday is *Africa*, in an attempt to give Friday the language to assert national independence and challenge the colonial narrative. For Spivak, the word *Africa* is a catachresis or an improper word, because it was historically imposed on a continent by a European colonial power (Spivak 1991, 170). After several unsuccessful attempts, Barton concludes frustratedly: "How can Friday know what freedom means when he barely knows his own name?" (Spivak 1991, 171).

The failure of Barton's writing lesson is instructive for readers of postcolonial texts. Rather than a passive victim of colonial history, Friday is an "agent of withholding in the text" who refuses to bring forth an authentic native voice (Spivak 1991, 172). There is no rhetorical space available to Friday in Barton's benevolent anticolonial narrative. His refusal to speak could thus be seen to push back against the agendas of nationalism and identity, which Barton employs in an attempt to emancipate Friday and restore his voice. Spivak proposes that Friday's agency lies in his refusal to be represented, in his silence.

Those on the privileged side of transnationality should certainly pay attention to subaltern silence. With it, one must also accept that something necessarily escapes our best efforts to hearken. This realization represents a significant contribution from Spivak, who complicates the political aims of subaltern studies by introducing deconstructive and poststructuralist critiques into the Marxist paradigm. Spivak reveals the limitations of a simplistic revolutionary agenda by highlighting the constraints and complexities inherent in the quest to recover subaltern agency.

An even bigger challenge than a lack of access to the public sphere is a will to obedience that is ingrained in the gendered subaltern, who internalizes her condition of disenfranchisement as simply normal. Robbed of the privilege to imagine oneself in the abstract as part of the nation-state, the subaltern is completely unprepared for the public sphere. The biggest task of decolonization is thus to bring subalternity into crisis. However, this cannot be accomplished merely by making the subaltern economically independent or politically empowered: Formalized democratic rights do not automatically enfranchise economically impoverished citizens, even as economic empowerment does not translate into desubalternization.

The Aristotelian ideology that not all individuals possess the requisite practical wisdom or ethical virtue to be integrated into the governing class continues to underpin governmental practices in numerous postcolonial societies. Given this framework, the question arises: How can the subaltern subject be reconstituted as a citizen? Instead of adopting the free market's definition of democracy as job creation for unskilled labor, Spivak (2009a, 36), following Gramsci, suggests that subalterns become citizens not merely by being able to vote or earn a living but by having the capacity to govern. When redress is impossible without remote mediation, desubalternization is obstructed. Thus, there is an urgent need to draw the line between exercising one's own agency and creating the conditions necessary for subalterns to exercise agency.

Supporting struggles aimed at establishing more enduring conditions of livability in the face of systematically induced precarity and racial destitution (Butler 2015, 183) is undeniably urgent. However, undoing subalternity is more complex than merely facilitating access to basic necessities. While poverty alleviation is certainly necessary, it does not inherently ensure desubalternization (Spivak 2008, 24–25). Redistribution of income and wealth cannot resolve entrenched power imbalances. Habitual deference to class hierarchies can be unlearned only when subalterns are integrated into the "circuit of citizenship" (Davis et al. 2019, 71). One must resist the temptation to romanticize the piety of those who suffer. Spivak explains that subalternity represents a position devoid of identity, meaning that the poor—poor women or poor brown women—are not automatically subalterns. Against the positivist quest to depict and recuperate the subaltern as a coherent political agent, Spivak counterintuitively warns that, despite the allure of the "theoretical fiction," the subaltern can be represented only through the intervention of the elite (Morton 2003, 54, 2007, 101–5). One must guard against ontologizing the category *subaltern* in response to the query *Who is a subaltern?* Something always escapes the best efforts to represent subalternity, such that it presents a limit case for our knowledge production. Spivak's approach defies the expectations for clear political blueprints.

Subaltern Counterpublics. A Paradox?

If, as Spivak explains, subalternity arises when individuals are excluded from the public sphere, then the notion of transnational subaltern counterpublics is inherently contradictory. The lack of access to both national and international civil society, as well as the state, suggests that subalterns are effectively deprived of citizenship rights (Spivak 2011). Subaltern groups are relegated from postcolonial nation building even as they are subjected to the forces of neocolonial globalization. Because the norms of recognition are not in their favor, the political claims of subaltern groups appear both unintelligible and illegible. Inversely, this means that when a previously disenfranchised individual or community gains recognition as a legitimate political subject, subalternity is brought into crisis.

Against the claim that our shared vulnerability brings us together, I would counterargue that deep asymmetries of power and wealth cannot be corrected simply by copresence in cyberspace for a common cause or facing police violence together in the street. While we might be facing the same storm, we are not all in the same boat, and that makes all the difference. Civil society and social movements are marked by hierarchies and exclusions that are disturbingly overlooked in celebratory discourses concerning their opposition to the state. The fabricated fiction that all bodies are equal in the street or in digital counterpublics disregards that there is still a crucial difference between being an unemployed youth in Spain and a farmer in India who loses his land because he has been forced to buy genetically modified Monsanto Bt cotton. The former contest their precarization in the streets of Madrid as part of the *indignados*, the 2011 anti-austerity movement, while the latter may be one of the nameless thousands who have committed suicide since the introduction of genetically modified seeds in 1996 in India—not as an act of resistance but because of their inability to make their interests count and make the postcolonial state respond to their subalternization.

Caught in a double bind, international civil society actors must acknowledge that we inhabit intimately the very structures that we seek to critique. The voice of *the people* as an articulation of the will of *the people* reveals itself as a phantasma, such that protest movements can ironically subalternize the masses at the very moment that they ostensibly allow them to speak. Our complicity in the continued reproduction of subalternity confounds notions of alliances along the lines of class, race, and gender while raising troubling questions regarding the challenges of postimperial politics in the era of neoliberal globalization. Elite transnational actors must resist the inclination to become self-appointed moral vanguards tasked with solving global issues. It is imperative to reconsider and reimagine our approach to politics by examining how, despite the earnest efforts of international civil society actors and institutions, subaltern groups continue to be seen as mere recipients of benevolence rather than being recognized as active agents of transformation.

Furthermore, the staging of the state as an agent of terror and civil society as an agent of salvation can have vicious neocolonial and imperialistic consequences, particularly for subaltern groups, who are disproportional targets of civil society paternalism and state violence (Spivak 2009b). Transnational counterpublics tend to empower privileged civil society actors, whose will to do good is marked by feudality and enabled by a neoliberal framing. It is thus imperative to ask whether enthusiastic discourses of resistance are empowering for disenfranchised communities or whether they simply reinforce relations of dominance between those who act and those on whose behalf these colorful and lively uprisings and revolts are being staged.

Tools for political resistance and global protest are not always accessible to the underclass in the global South. In the absence of an intermediary capable of bridging the gap between subaltern groups and transnational power structures, the struggle for the subaltern must still be waged within the confines of the state (Spivak 2012a). Decolonization's biggest task is to bring subalternity into crisis, which goes beyond organizing material goods for the suffering classes. Simply having rights is not enough if there is no training in the practice or exercise of freedom. Agency and political power remain but empty promises for subaltern groups, who do not have access to even basic benefits of citizenship, despite being de jure citizens (Morton 2007, 105).

The process of desubalternization is unbearably slow, while the fantasies of revolutions via Twitter and Instagram move at the speed of thought. (For Marx, as Spivak reminds us, it is capital that moves at this speed [Gedankenschnelle]). Desubalternization is not just about teaching subalterns how to resist through political indoctrination or consciousness-raising. The class-privileged must unlearn the impulse to monopolize agency in the name of saving the world, while subalterns must be enabled to unlearn the "class-habit of obedience" (Spivak 2008, 55). This would necessitate the shift from street politics as the site of desubalternization to other arenas of intervention, such as the postcolonial state, for instance, which is like *pharmakon*—both harmful poison and beneficial medicine. In contrast to the state-phobic rhetoric of protest movements, I exhort that the relationship between the postcolonial state and the subaltern must be reconfigured, thereby transmuting poison into counterpoison.

In light of these considerations, it is a challenge to reimagine the dynamics between critique and resistance while keeping an eye on the question of subalternity. Subaltern groups in the postcolonial world persistently face exclusion from intellectual labor, relegated instead to serving the ruling class through physical labor. To reverse this process, the subaltern must be inserted into hegemony, not through empowerment training, but by "activating" habits of democracy (Spivak 2008, 49). An immense effort is required to convince subalterns that everyone has the same inalienable rights.

Access to global telecommunications and the right to bear microcredit are equated with subaltern political empowerment as such, as free-market globalizers suggest that these changes will establish a level playing field (Spivak 2012a, 100). The conflation of citizens and consumers makes choices in the market continuous with the will of the people in a neoliberal democracy. The challenge is: How can the subaltern subject be transformed into a citizen? Assurances of universal human rights and market-based justice offered by development politics fall short of addressing the underlying issues. The expansion of electronic access does not automatically translate into "epistemic change" (Spivak 2008, 50). To prevent disenfranchised citizens from becoming reliant on patronizing forms of aid, Spivak advocates for an "uncoercive rearrangement of desires" in both the global North and the global South (Spivak 2008, 31) that extends beyond mere poverty alleviation.

A case in point is the transnational feminist movement, which claims to enhance the participation of disenfranchised women in global politics through advocacy within international civil society networks. However, subaltern women often remain outside the scope of organized movements representing Third World women's resistance. Despite the integration of local struggles into global gender politics, the dominance of elite feminist agendas has become more entrenched. Since the United Nations (UN) Cairo Conference (1994) and Beijing Conference (1995), there has been a notable rise in what can be termed *imperial feminism*. Thus, decolonizing feminism would involve "feminists with a transnational consciousness" acknowledging their own "agency in complicity" (Spivak 1999, 399).

Postcolonial states continue to be crucial intermediaries between the imperatives of global capital and disenfranchised groups. Instead of viewing the state solely through the lens of its repressive functions, which typically necessitates a pro or con stance regarding the nation-state, it is essential to envision an alternative conception of the state that would facilitate the processes of desubalternization. By falsely dichotomizing the ills of state planning against the virtues of the free market, advocates of neoliberal political economy partly fuel attacks on the state. This obscures the fact that the state is an essential precondition for neoliberalism. By "altering the redistributive priorities of the state" (Spivak 2009b, 89) and empowering subaltern groups to assert their claims within the formal framework of rights and citizenship, state phobia can be mitigated, fostering a "democracy from below."

With exclusive focus on how to combat state power, which is coded in repressive terms, most advocates of abolitionism fail to consider the toxic politics of certain sections of civil society. Pegida, for instance, is a right-wing movement that often holds assemblies in German cities to protest against the German state's granting of asylum to refugees. Here, the violence and coercion comes from the public assembly, not from the state. To give a further example, during the COVID-19 pandemic, so-called freedom demonstrations and anti-restriction protests were a regular occurrence in big cities such as Berlin and were organized mainly by the German right wing across the country. Under the slogan "We Are the People," anti-vaxxers, science deniers, antifeminists, hooligans, neo-Nazis, Holocaust deniers, evangelicals, and esotericists scapegoated Jews and immigrant communities for the spread of the virus in Germany while accusing the state of curtailing freedoms and mobility. Groups such as Querdenken and Widerstand [Resistance] 2020, among others, claim to be protecting the basic democratic rights of citizens from the German state. This illustrates the ambivalences of performances of *das Volk*. The United Kingdom riots of 2024 provide yet another example. After a mass stabbing in Southport, disinformation and inflammatory messages were posted on social media speculating that the attacker was a Muslim asylum seeker. This triggered anti-immigration protests involving far-right activists, white supremacists, and fascist groups, who attacked police officers and set fire to police stations and vehicles. In response, the state and police implemented measures to protect antiracist rallies, as well as homes and businesses owned by immigrants and hotels housing asylum seekers (BBC 2024).

While the state and its institutions are undoubtedly responsible for inducing precarity, one should not lose sight of the role of privileged civil society actors who directly profit from state phobia. The violence exerted by nonstate actors against one another must not be neglected. Butler (2015, 58), for instance, gives the example of the Occupy Wall Street demonstrations as an open space where "no one is ever asked to produce an identity card before gaining access to such a demonstration." While Butler repeatedly focuses on the conditions defining the possibility of appearance, they do not address that the appearance of some is subject to the not being able to appear of others. They highlight intersubjective dependence and vulnerability but disregard what I refer to as parasitic agency. Two concrete examples point to the multidirectionality of violence and exclusion:

first, the sexual assaults that occurred at Tahrir Square in Cairo during the Egyptian revolution of 2011 (Kingsley 2013); and second, while men could continue demonstrating against the government's austerity measures in 2011 at Syntagma Square in Athens, women went home to do the housework and care work. Just as in the case of the Athenian *polis*, where the *demos* was constituted by the adult men of Athenian descent, whose participation in the public assemblies was parasitic to the slave economy and labor of women, who were not considered part of the *demos*, civil society in postcolonial late capitalism is marked by "class apartheid" (Spivak 2008, 32). While Butler focuses on the agency of the protesters and their right to resist and challenge the state, Spivak engages with the inability of subalterns to make themselves heard. The subalterns do, of course, speak, but they are not listened to by either civil society actors or state authorities. For Spivak, the addressee of subaltern speech is the state. Once the state recognizes the subaltern as a legitimate political subject—that is, one who can make claims on the state—a first step toward desubalternization will have been taken.

In response to the question: "Does freedom of assembly depend upon being protected *by* government or does it depend upon a protection *from* government?" (Butler 2015, 158), I would argue that, paradoxically, it is incumbent on one organ of the state to protect the freedom of assembly against interference from its other organs. This implies that we must be cautious not to reduce the state to just its penal function while neglecting its enabling role. While Louis Althusser exclusively focuses on the repressive state apparatus, Gramsci highlights the ambivalent and contradictory nature of the state, which lacks a stable core. We must guard against the ontology of the state as essentially coercive and violent, as this ends up reifying the state *as if* it existed.

An oft-forgotten Gramscian insight challenges the assumption that an empowered civil society inherently bolsters democracy; rather, civil society is, in fact, the very arena where hegemony is entrenched. Elite groups within civil society accumulate substantial political influence and gain access to transnational public spheres without being directly elected by the populations they claim to represent. The vanguardism of civil society actors, who function as the organic intellectuals of global capitalism, is characterized by an inherent paternalism. To exert pressure on states, nonstate actors often seek support from international allies and engage with external forums. However, this tactic raises concerns about postcolonial sovereignty.

I would propose that subaltern groups are caught between what the postcolonial feminist Shalini Randeria (2003) calls "the cunning state," which deploys the rhetoric of sovereignty strategically to prevent international intervention in certain realms such as human rights, yet is willing to implement economic policies and trade rules prescribed by international institutions. On the other side are civil society actors who appeal for external intervention regarding human rights issues but are highly critical of external involvement in national economic and social policies.

One of the most pressing challenges in global ethics is the disparity between those who administer aid and those who are merely categorized as victims of wrongs, thereby positioned as recipients of solidarity and justice (Spivak 2008, 15, 266n14). Any effort to fulfill global ethical obligations must urgently address the historical mechanisms that have relegated certain individuals to positions from which they extend global solidarity. When progressive activists and intellectuals altruistically support subaltern struggles for recognition and rights, they inadvertently perpetuate the very power dynamics they aim to dismantle. Interestingly, Spivak explains that it is the subalterns who teach the intellectuals about power. Inadvertently, intellectuals erode the ability of subalterns to resist. It is imperative to undertake a self-inventory of how our worldview is constituted while cultivating a critical imagination at the same time. Subalterns do not fantasize about saving the world; they do not have an understanding of themselves as political subjects. This marks an international division of labor of imagination between those who see themselves as resistant subjects and those who are cognitively disenfranchised and do not perceive themselves as rights bearers.

This alludes to the nonperformativity of critical practices in counterpublic spheres. As argued previously, Sara Ahmed (2006, 104) explains that although progressive politics are not completely ineffective, they do not necessarily lead to the effects they name or promise, while still being perceived as performative. This generates power effects, in that the nonperformative rhetoric prevents the combating of that which it pretends to abolish. This negative relation between rhetoric and reality, between claim and practice, confirms that the exercise of critique can stabilize hegemonic relations even as it claims to disrupt them. Protest politics and public assemblies can contribute to processes of subalternization instead of rearranging social, political, and economic relations. The state-phobic politics of social movements masks that they are not necessarily outside or beyond the state and its coercive apparatus.

Contrary to prevailing sentiments, I contend that, despite the crisis of legitimacy facing the nation-state, it is perilous to ignore the political consequences of state-phobic stances. State violence is juxtaposed against the nonviolence of civil society, which is constructed as the sphere of conviviality. Despite persistent strife over common goals, the civil society stages itself *as if* there is a collectivity. What is disregarded is that the state extends its influence through civil society even as it functions as a site where hegemony is fashioned. For Gramsci (2011b, 75; Q6 §88), hegemony is consensus protected by the "armor of coercion," and this is expressed by the state through civil society. In Gramsci's view, civil society is the domain of intellectuals (not necessarily a positive term for Gramsci), wherein they consolidate their hegemony by staging their particular class interests as the common interests of all. Civil society cannot disable the coercive apparatus of the state; it is complicit in the production of hegemony. An excellent example of this are the demonstrations against the coup in Myanmar in early 2021. There were no comparable protests in the face of the killing of thousands of Rohingya people and their displacement. As Kenan Malik (2021) rightly asks, "Where were the protesters when the Rohingya were being murdered?" Without dismissing the critical function of protest politics and counterpublics, I would argue that civil society stages itself as anti-state and oppositional while ironically consolidating hegemony. It is notable that in some countries in the global South, the nongovernmental organizations (NGOs) are more powerful than the postcolonial states. For instance, BRAC, the largest nongovernmental development organization in the world, is a global player from Bangladesh.[7] Interestingly, BRAC is described as a parallel, franchise, and shadow state in Bangladesh (Fink 2018, 222). Unsurprisingly, in rural Bangladesh the NGOs are described as *sarkar*, the Bengali and Urdu word for both government and master (Fink 2018, 222).

Following Gramsci and Spivak, civil society functions as a safety valve of the state; it releases pressure and deescalates the situation without always transforming exploitative structures. In the fragile democracies of the Third World, the state is a *pharmakon*, both poison and medicine—or, as Spivak (2008, 71) remarks, "What could have been medicine turned into poison." Rather than endorsing statism, it serves as a caution against the potential risks associated with replacing the state with nonstate actors. In India, we have a joke that the only democratic right the Indians take pleasure in exercising is the right to criticize the state; all other rights are considered a colonial hangover. In that spirit, the politics of the governed in the era of neoliberal globalization lies not beyond the state but in its reconfiguration. It lies in taking the state not as *monstre froid* but as *pharmakon*: The challenge is transforming poison into counterpoison, into medicine. In conclusion, I outline the difference between the importance of criticizing the state and the dangers of state phobia.

The Death of Leviathan

In the face of the state's monopoly on violence, along with its patriarchal, racist, and imperialist tendencies, queer feminists and religious and racial minorities face a dilemma: Should they bypass state institutions and instead focus their efforts on pursuing progressive political goals through nonstate activism? Considering the legitimate concerns surrounding the state's coercive powers, can the state be repositioned as an instrument of justice? Or should progressive politics prioritize learning the "art of not being governed," as suggested by James Scott (2010a), who advocates for state evasion as a survival strategy for subaltern classes? Describing state making as a form of internal colonialism, Scott suggests that the stateless peoples of the Zomia highlands in Southeast Asia pursue alternative forms of self-determination by withdrawing from the nation-state. These communities intentionally maintain their statelessness and develop strategies to deter states from annexing them into their territories. However, in a 2010 interview, Scott clarifies that choosing not to be incorporated into the state as a deliberate act of evasion has its limitations. He rejects the premise of the movie *Avatar*—that you can sever ties and keep modernity at bay—as purely idealistic and instead suggests that a better alternative may be "taming the state" (Scott 2010b).

This indicates that progressive political initiatives are ensnared in a double bind with respect to the state and its repressive powers (Dhawan 2019). The political ramifications of circumventing the state as a means for addressing economic, racial, and sexual injustice should be carefully considered. It is paramount to identify the risks associated with downplaying the affirmative role of the state and to understand the potential consequences of anti-statism for disadvantaged groups. Rather than proposing an ideal theory of the state, my aim is to reconsider and refine our understanding of it. This confronts us with the following questions: Is it possible to harness the state's coercive power to accomplish emancipatory objectives? Alternatively, might particular protective measures inadvertently harm minorities by inherently depicting them as vulnerable, thereby diminishing their autonomy and simultaneously reinforcing the state's coercive authority? Should extra-state spaces become repositories for abolitionist politics? Are nonstate forms of power distinct from state power? If the state were to cease to exist, how would progressive politics operate in a nonstate framework? If the state generates and perpetuates disparities among different groups, should it be responsible for addressing and remedying these issues, or could such accountability merely contribute to the entrenchment of its authority (Cooper et al. 2019)?

In the subsequent discussion, I contend that addressing the role of the state effectively requires consideration of two key insights to respond to these questions. First, as previously examined in relation to subalternity, one must avoid conflating an effect with its underlying cause, or committing metalepsis (Spivak 2006, 281). Rather than viewing the state as the source of a will to violence, it should be understood as a manifestation of diverse, discordant, and incongruous forces. Second, instead of pitting state institutions against nonstate entities, one must understand that the state's power draws on the institutionalization of social norms, and the two cannot be decoupled. The state can serve both as a tool for dominant groups to safeguard their interests and as a weapon of the weak to empower the marginalized. It is imprudent to adopt a clear-cut stance for *or* against the state's coercive powers (Dhawan 2020). As I have consistently highlighted, drawing on Jacques Derrida's concept of *pharmakon*, the state functions simultaneously as both poison and remedy.[8] To quote Derrida (1981a, 127): "If the *pharmakon* is ambivalent, it is because it constitutes the medium in which opposites are opposed, the movement and the play that links them among themselves, reverses them or makes one side cross over into the other (soul/body, good/ evil, inside/outside, memory/forgetfulness, speech/writing, etc.)."

Discussions, for instance, surrounding same-sex marriage legislation within postcolonial queer scholarship highlight the dangers inherent in a state-phobic stance. By dismissing progressive sexual politics as a red herring for neoliberal and neocolonial agendas, postcolonial queer scholars and activists risk reducing the state to its coercive functions while overlooking its potential as an enabling force. Recent developments, such as the backlash against reproductive rights exemplified by the overturning of *Roe v. Wade* in the United States and pushback against LGBTQI+ rights, as seen in Hungary, underscore the necessity for anti-imperialist and antiracist critiques of queer politics to address both state and nonstate mechanisms of reproductive heteronormativity. Neglecting one in favor of the other not only hinders but may even undermine the broader goals of decolonization.

In past decades, sharp critiques have emerged of queer racism, homon-ationalism, and the imperialist underpinnings of global gay politics (Mas-sad 2007; Puar 2007). Western states have been accused of exploiting emancipatory legislation, such as same-sex marriage, as a tool to margin-alize minorities domestically while portraying populations in the global South as inherently repressive and backward. There is concern that queer politics is being weaponized as an alibi for both internal discrimination within Euro-American borders and military interventions abroad. Queer emancipatory politics is faulted for reviving colonial narratives, framing *the Orient* as a site of gender and sexual oppression, in contrast to the sup-posedly egalitarian West that champions sexual freedom. Just as colonial rulers once deemed the colonized unfit for self-rule due to their alleged barbarism toward women, gay and lesbian identities now symbolize both Western modernity and Oriental backwardness. The perceived failure of queer emancipation in non-Western cultures reinforces Euro-American superiority. While Europe once excoriated *the Orient* for sexual excess, the modern West now condemns its repression of sexual freedoms, con-veniently ignoring its own history of criminalizing homosexuality in the colonies. This self-perception of sexual enlightenment justifies the forced modernization of *the Orient* in the name of liberation.

Neocolonial agendas persist through interconnected yet contradic-tory practices. On the one hand, Evangelical missionaries from countries such as the United States and South Korea actively campaign against homosexuality in postcolonial nations such as Uganda (Rao 2020). On the other hand, migrants in Europe face mandatory integration tests and classes to gain citizenship. These tests require demonstrating alignment with European values of sexual freedom and tolerance, effectively assess-ing applicants' suitability as ideal citizens. Notably, Germany's leading LGBTQI rights organization, Lesben- und Schwulenverband in Deutsch-land (LSVD), supports these tests, highlighting how emancipatory politics can reinforce neocolonial agendas. The supposed homophobic migrant is viewed as the primary barrier to queer justice, rather than addressing is-sues such as inequality, discrimination, violence, and harassment in the workplace, medical settings, educational institutions, housing, public services, and social spaces (Harithaworn and Petzen 2011). The narrative frames Europe as needing to protect its sexual minorities from allegedly homophobic migrants, particularly Muslims, integrating sexuality into security discourses. This casts migrants as obstacles to sexual progress, erasing the existence of queers of color by pitting gay-friendly Europeans against purportedly homophobic migrants. As noted by diasporic queer scholars, European gays and lesbians often secure their place in the nation through the Orientalization of homophobia, which leads to the demonization of migrants (Harithaworn and Petzen 2011).

Along similar lines, Western media frequently reports on the persecution of sexual minorities in countries such as Iran, Uganda, and Afghanistan. These dynamics foster paternalistic rescue narratives, where "white queers save brown queers from brown homophobes" (to paraphrase Spivak)." Consequently, Eurocentric homonormative politics extends beyond Western borders with support from leading LGBTQI rights organizations.

These examples raise a critical question: What happens when emancipatory politics are used to harass and discriminate against minorities, especially religious ones (Puar 2007, 15)? In the past decades, progressive sexual politics have served as an alibi for Western imperial projects, celebrating queer liberal subjects while reducing queers of color to mere victims of postcolonial state violence. At the same time, scholars such as Joseph Massad and Jasbir Puar overlook nonstate forms of heteronormative violence in families, communities, and public spaces. Their anti-homonationalist politics often dismiss legal recognition for sexual minorities as mere appeasement. They disregard how queer activists in the global South seek constitutional recognition of sexual rights, such as same-sex marriage, as crucial for sexual justice. These efforts are frequently dismissed by radical queer theorists in the global North as assimilationist, with Puar (2007, 27, 30), for example, describing gay marriage as "a demand for reinstatement of white privileges and rights" and "attendant citizenship privileges."

Even as I share the anti-homonationalist critique, I am wary of the unidimensional understanding of violence's operations that underpins these positions. Power and coercion do not flow only from Western liberal states; rather, they have multiple sources that are deeply entangled. A sole and limited focus on queer racism and homonationalism in the global North makes it difficult to address homophobic and heteronormative practices and structures in diasporic communities, as well as the broader postcolonial world. Despite homonationalism and the integration of queers into state building, nations—whether Western or non-Western—are thoroughly heteronormative. Heterosexuality is ritually (re)invoked to narrate and maintain the postcolonial nation. It is no surprise that many hard-won sexual rights, such as the right to abortion, are being rolled back even in the global North. This highlights the short-sightedness of anti-homonationalist politics, which disregards the grave issue of democratic backsliding.

Feminist historians of colonialism have shown that anticolonial nationalism was built on the creation of a middle class and respectable sexuality, key to bourgeois nationalist identities. Compulsory heterosexuality has played a central role in forming gendered, colonial, and nationalist subjects in postcolonial nation building. Both the empire and its anticolonial opposition are fundamentally heteronormative. Fanon (1986 [1952], 156) viewed homosexuality as a Western disorder tied to white supremacy, suggesting that "the negrophobic man is a repressed homosexual," and he imagined non-Western races as free from homosexuality. Kobena Mercer (1996, 125) argues that Fanon's fear and avoidance of Black homosexuality reflect a homophobic fixation and a refusal to address masculinity issues within Black liberation discourse.

The Chicana feminist Gloria Anzaldúa highlights the intertwined nature of native heteropatriarchy and colonial racism. She states, "As a Mestiza I have no country, my homeland cast me out; yet all countries are mine because I am every woman's sister or potential lover. (As a lesbian I have no race, my own people disclaim me; but I am all races because there is the queer of me in all races)" (Anzaldúa 1987, 182). Similarly, Hanif Kureishi's film *My Beautiful Laundrette* (1985) provoked controversy in South Asian communities in the United Kingdom for its portrayal of queer interracial desire. These examples highlight the complex interplay among various nationalisms and patriarchies, complicating any straightforward understanding of oppression and emancipation. Spivak (2008, 129) notes that "reproductive heteronormativity" is a pervasive institution used by both colonizers and anticolonial nationalists. Focusing solely on Western homonationalism ignores the heterosexist violence faced by queer people in the global South, including lifetime imprisonment or even the death penalty. Trivializing the struggles against homophobia in postcolonial contexts as mere mimicry of the West is disingenuous. Anti-homonationalist politics requires a more nuanced, multidirectional approach to address coercive sexual practices across the postcolonial divide.

Theorists such as Puar effectively draw on Foucault to examine how non-normative sexualities are instrumentalized within the biopolitical organization of populations—notably, how European queer identities are depicted as needing protection from threats such as presumed homophobic migrants and supposed regressive Muslim cultures. However, anti-homonationalist politics, which reject state engagement as mere cooptation, are deeply problematic. In my view, it is essential to address other forms of violence beyond Western racism and imperialism.

Neglecting homophobic violence within migrant communities can harm sexual minorities by ignoring their intersecting experiences of racism and homophobia. Labeling advocates for sexual equality, freedom, or emancipation in the global South as either allegedly Westernized or pawns for neoliberal political agendas delegitimizes their struggles for social recognition and legal protection. It is imperative to understand decolonization as more than just undoing the coercive legacies of modernity.

Anti-homonationalist politics often dehistoricize, demonize, and essentialize the state, reducing it to its penal functions. In discussions of *pinkwashing* in Israel or the decriminalization of homosexuality in India, Puar disregards the historical differences between countries like Israel and India, or between the United States and Germany.[9] Foucault's warning about state phobia is also neglected. He critiques various ideological positions—including Marxists, ultra-left radicals, liberals, and neoliberals—that view the state as a predator that must be contained and "defanged" (Foucault 2008, 188). His historical investigations outline how experiences with fascism and totalitarianism during National Socialism and Stalinism contributed to the rise of state phobia in Europe. Efforts to overcome totalitarianism sought to replace despotic or police states with a system governed by the rule of law and a constitutional framework, thereby reconfiguring the relationship between government and society.

According to Foucault, starting in the late 1970s and manifesting primarily as a critique of securitization and the repressive apparatus, anti-statism rapidly became the basis of liberal, left-leaning politics. This translated into uncritical solidarity with Soviet dissidents. Among both liberals and the left, the idea of the state as a threat gained traction, particularly in the context of fears of atomic war. Foucault problematizes state phobia in both liberal and leftist politics, arguing that they fail to distinguish among the administrative state, the welfare state, the bureaucratic state, the fascist state, and the totalitarian state. He distances himself from this inflationary form of liberal and left state phobia (Foucault 2008, 6).

The dynamic and ambivalent function of the state is dangerously ignored by scholars such as Puar, whose critique of the state quickly devolves into state phobia. This results in every attempt by queer individuals and groups to negotiate with the state being condemned as reinforcing homonationalism. It is important to recognize the fine lines among a critique of the state, state phobia, and anti-statism. The last is characterized by a deep distrust of state institutions per se. As Foucault compellingly argues, state phobia forms a foundational premise for the emergence of neoliberal governmentality, conflating anti-statism with resistance against repression, in which the state is portrayed as the origin of all violence.

The challenge for postcolonial queer feminist theory is to formulate a critique of the state and hegemonic heteronormativity without reproducing state phobia. Liberal and left-leaning state phobia is often informed by Eurocentrism, as a particular European experience with fascism is universalized, thereby reducing the complexity of diverse historical processes of state formation and nation building in postcolonial contexts. Puar's critique of the United States, Israel, and India, for instance, homogenizes distinct antidiscrimation policies and laws into a simplistic politics of appeasement. This reductive approach is risky in its oversimplification.

Interestingly, Puar neglects states such as Saudi Arabia and Mauritania, where homosexual acts are punishable by death. Moreover, she equates the decriminalization of same-sex acts in India with the repeal of sodomy laws in the United States, presenting both as examples of homonationalism. This comparison disregards the significant differences between the two distinct historical and regional contexts. Both legal reforms are the result of complex social and legal struggles, producing ambivalent and diverse effects that are questionably overlooked.

If Europe universalized its norms and epistemologies through colonialism, then decolonization remains incomplete without the de-universalization and provincialization of Euro-American experiences and politics. This requires a nuanced historical analysis of diverse configurations. In this regard, the specific German experience with fascism and totalitarianism must not be projected onto postcolonial contexts to justify a transnational state-phobic queer politics. Such an approach would be disastrous.

This raises the question: Why is Foucault's critique of state phobia often disregarded, not only by radical queer politics, but even by Foucauldians themselves? In my view, this stems from an inconsistency and ambivalence in Foucault's own position. He identifies sexuality as a key site of regulation in liberal-capitalist states, where threat and securitization, danger and protection, family and nation operate as central elements of governmental practices. Consequently, when it comes to the legislation of sexuality, Foucault harbors distrust of the state, even as he cautions others against state phobia.

A concrete example of this ambivalence is Foucault's (1988, 201) controversial proposal during a 1977 roundtable discussion, when he suggested treating rape like a "punch in the face." He advocated for the "desexualization of rape" as a strategy to counteract disciplinary power, arguing that the sexual definition of rape reinforces the genitalization of the body, thus justifying the state's disciplinary focus on sexuality. Foucault (1988, 200–202) provocatively questioned why an assault involving a penis should be legally distinguished from one involving any other body part. His goal was to decouple desire from crime, and sexuality from the law, in an attempt to shield sexuality from becoming a target of state intervention. I perceive an inconsistency in Foucault's stance, as he himself exhibits elements of state phobia. By proposing the reclassification of rape as a civil offense, punishable by monetary sanctions rather than imprisonment, Foucault aims to shield sexual acts from state punishment, specifically preventing the incarceration of rapists. In his view, modern law functions as a tool of discipline, surveillance, and normalization. By advocating for a legal redefinition of rape, Foucault proposes a shift in juridical discourse that no longer victimizes women and protects sexuality from the disciplinary reach of the law (Dhawan 2013b). In light of Foucault's reflections on governmentality, one could argue that the construction of women as vulnerable subjects in discourses and policies serves to position them as objects of governance. This rationalizes the regulation of their bodies and movements while deploying paternalistic forms of protection that reinforce gender stereotypes. Foucault presents a compelling case for the desexualization of rape, which would place sexuality outside the scope of state intervention. While one might understand his distrust of the judiciary, Foucault's efforts to remove sexuality from the realm of legislation risk misjudging the essential role of law. Departing from legal frameworks would mean abandoning many of the structures that safeguard individuals from violence and discrimination—structures enabled by the state's monopoly on violence.

Foucault (2008, 188) appears just as state-phobic as the neoliberals and anarchists he castigates. His remark, "From the strategic point of view of resistive struggle, the aim is to make the state disappear" (quoted in Cook, 2018, 30), echoes the Marxist vision of a stateless society, which promises not only freedom *within* the state but also freedom *from* the state. Friedrich Engels famously proclaimed that, with the realization of socialist ideals, the state would cease to exist and ultimately disappear. In such a stateless society, people would govern themselves without the need for coercive law enforcement: "State interference in social relations becomes, in one domain after another, superfluous, and then dies out of itself; the government of persons is replaced by the administration of things and by the conduct of processes of production. The state is not 'abolished.' It dies out" (Engels 2010 [1877], 268).

Although abolishing the state remains a popular trope, Foucault's warning against state phobia—which, he argues, is deeply embedded in liberal and neoliberal conceptions of civil society—is, in my view, highly compelling (Dhawan 2019). Many critical discourses juxtapose the state's perceived wickedness with the inherent goodness of civil society, framing the abolition of the state as the ultimate goal. This anti-state-centric approach to power situates radical politics in an extra-state space of innovation. The rejection of so-called pragmatic politics, such as same-sex marriage or antidiscrimination legislation, in favor of civil society campaigns such as *pinkwatching*—which increasingly rely on surveillance strategies to, in this case, expose and shame states' attempts at *pinkwashing* by the weaponization of progressive queer politics—can at times verge on state phobia.[10] While contesting neoliberal capitalism's appropriation of gender and sexuality is crucial, the outright rejection of all feminist and queer politics that engage with the state as part of a biopolitical agenda is self-defeating. A nuanced approach that acknowledges the potential of state-oriented efforts, while maintaining a critical stance toward biopolitical forces, is indispensable for postcolonial queer feminist politics.

The recent recriminalization of homosexuality in Uganda and Nigeria, along with backlash against LGBTQI legislation in the United States during the Trump era and in countries such as Hungary and Russia, underscores the indispensable role of negotiations with the state for emancipatory transnational queer feminist politics. This is not an argument for statism but a caution against replacing the state with nonstate actors as the primary engines of sexual justice. In this context, the growing anti-statist stance within postcolonial queer scholarship is concerning, as it overlooks the critical role of the state for citizens who lack access to transnational counterpublic spheres to address their grievances.

Decolonization cannot be achieved solely through strategies of state shaming. Rather, following the Gramscian-Spivakian framework, it is imperative to grant vulnerable and disenfranchised individuals and groups access to the state. The more pressing question is not about abandoning the state but about reimagining it so that it better serves its most vulnerable citizens. The challenge lies in pursuing a queer politics that resists state phobia without rationalizing the biopolitical state project or leaving queer bodies governable.

The issue at hand is whether the state can be restructured to advance the interests of precisely those whose lack of power constitutes the very foundation of its authority. Can the relationship among the state, the market, and disenfranchised (non)citizens be reconfigured (MacKinnon 1989, 161)? The skepticism toward the notion of employing the state's coercive powers for progressive ends stems from the Althusserian assertion that the state is fundamentally defined by its repressive apparatus, which must be opposed. This approach overlooks a significant critique of Marxist and anarchist theories of the state—specifically, that abolishing the state would not ensure a nonviolent form of politics among nonstate actors (Dhawan 2019). The assumption that dominant groups can be persuaded to willingly support anti-heterosexist and antiracist politics, allowing the bureaucratic and regulatory functions of the state to be replaced by collective and decentralized negotiations among nonstate actors, fails to account for the fact that social conflicts and antagonisms in nonstate contexts remain contentious and conflictual, albeit in forms distinct from state-sanctioned violence. The intention here is not to equate state and nonstate violence but to emphasize their interconnections.

Anti-state perspectives rely on a specific ontology of the state, conceptualized as "a single, gravity-like mechanism with causal powers that generates a corresponding set of 'actual' effects" (Jessop 2014, 483). This reduces conflicting and heterogeneous forces that produce a range of state effects to a unified entity with a deliberate and calculative will. However, as the Marxist state theorist Bob Jessop (2014) explains, the state is a "heterogeneous institutional ensemble (comprising, minimally, a territory, apparatus, and population) that has no agency *per se* but does have various capacities and action-relevant biases inscribed in itself when considered as a strategic terrain." This resonates with Pierre Bourdieu's (2015, 32) structuralist understanding of the state as a field riven by difference and an arena of struggle where a plurality of actors and institutions clash with one another, employing varied resources and strengths, pursuing and pushing different agendas. Thus, instead of focusing on the functions of the state and its bureaucracy, the state is understood in terms of an array of positions that are linked relationally to others. Although Bourdieu differentiates between left hand (welfare, education, the lower courts) and right hand (financial institutions and ministerial cabinets), both are involved in the formulation, as well as the implementation, of policy. George Steinmetz applies Bourdieu's ideas to analyze colonial states. Supplementing Bourdieu's mainly conventional, democratic, bureaucratic, Western nation-state, Steinmetz (2016) understands colonial empires as asymmetrically structured assemblages of states comprising a multiplicity of state fields. Similarly, in Mahmood Mamdani's (1996) view, indirect rule in the colonies led to the coexistence of the European alongside Indigenous states with diminished powers. All of them highlight the contradictory and indeterminate nature of the state.

Approaches that view state power as the primary threat to individuals often overlook the dynamics of intersubjective (racialized and sexual) violence, where more powerful groups coerce vulnerable (non)citizens. Promoting interactions among nonstate actors as a remedy for state violence overlooks a critical aspect of the state's role: mediating between citizens and noncitizens. If the state itself cannot maintain impartiality, then negotiations among nonstate actors, characterized by unequal power dynamics, are also unlikely to be free from (racialized and sexual) coercion. Jessop highlights that stereotypes about state power often foster the misconception that the state functions as a unified, monolithic entity. In reality, the state frequently becomes a convenient projection screen for the complex and pressing issues faced by communities and societies. It seems that anti-state positions would need to invent the state if it did not exist (see Hay 2014). Instead of treating the state as an ontological given, it may be more productive to employ it heuristically as a tool for advancing justice and addressing discrimination, inequality, and disenfranchisement. Relying solely on noninstitutionalized mechanisms within nonstate arenas for economic, racial, and sexual justice does not guarantee that the politics of contestation will be free from coercion or violence.

We must be vigilant against the fallacy of viewing the state as either omnipotent or impotent. The concept of state phobia serves as a discerning critique of political ideologies that amplify the state's coercive function through a specific narrative of state power (Foucault 2008, 284–86). Although anarchist and neoliberal viewpoints exhibit notable differences, both ontologize the state rather than perceiving it as a "site of strategic dilemmas as well as structural contradictions" (Jessop 2013). In his subsequent writings, Foucault appears to diverge from his earlier anti-statist exhortation to "cut off the king's head" (Foucault 1990, 89). The conceptualization of sovereignty as a "right of death" suggests an innately malevolent state, characterized by omnipotence, genocidal tendencies, and a necropolitical orientation. Foucault elucidates the limitations of this critical stance toward the state and its essential functions, which denounces the state's inherent authority as oppressive (Dean and Villadsen 2016, 2). This "assault against the state" (Foucault 2003, 135) represents a tactic rooted in neoliberal rationality that seeks to coopt state power by curtailing, disassembling, and reorganizing its functions. Neoliberalism advocates for a model of governance akin to business management, where citizens are regarded as clients. Consequently, neoliberal techniques influence the formation and conduct of subjects, weaponizing the norms of freedom and choice. An excellent example of this is the Department of Government Efficiency (DOGE), initially led by Elon Musk under the second Trump presidency, which aims to cut regulations, spending, and personnel within the federal government. While neoliberalism purports to champion individual freedom, it paradoxically coopts state power for its own ends. The skepticism toward state institutions fosters a demand for a hands-off approach within the political realm, mirroring neoliberal advocacy for minimal governmental interference in the marketplace. Adam Smith's metaphor of the invisible hand aptly illustrates this dynamic. Nonetheless, as meticulously examined by postcolonial, queer, and feminist scholars, the state remains neither impartial nor dormant.

Anti-state politics frequently conceptualize nonstate spaces as beyond the reach of the repressive state apparatus. Foucault cautions that the radical left's reaction to neoliberal governmentality may, paradoxically, bolster the very forces it contests. The proposed strategy for opposing state repression often involves retreating from state structures and forgoing state power, thereby attempting to create alternative arenas that fall outside the state's jurisdiction. Instead of seeing the nation solely as an adversary to be defeated, Mitchell Dean and Kaspar Villadsen (2016, 19) suggest that one should also recognize its role in fostering both individual and collective capabilities. Those who foreground the agency of nonstate actors and oppose state intervention often obscure the indispensable infrastructural support afforded by the state, without which nonstate actors would not be capable of effectively conducting these activities or building their capacities (Dean and Villadsen 2016, 177). Civil rights, public education, and universal health care are among the welfare services guaranteed by a stable and functioning state within its territorial jurisdiction, yet these are often disregarded by state-phobic positions (Dean and Villadsen 2016, 5).[11] The portrayal of the state as a destructive force and the idealization of nonstate spaces and actors position their supposedly benign political agency within structures such as the family, community, or marketplace, which are intimately connected to the state (Dean and Villadsen 2016, 30).

An illustrative historical case for the interlinkages between state and nonstate violence is the lettre de cachet: a royal decree issued directly by the king, frequently used to execute arbitrary decisions and enforce judgments without a trial and a possibility of appeal. During his archival research, Foucault discovered a collection of lettres de cachet that had been requested by ordinary citizens to curtail the liberty of a close family member, typically through measures such as house arrest, exile, or imprisonment (Farge and Foucault 2012, 178). What had previously been the exclusive domain of religious authorities was now being implemented from the ground up, with ordinary individuals taking on the role of surveilling and punishing those perceived as sinful or deviant (Dean and Villadsen 2016, 61–62). The king's sovereign exercise of authority was, in reality, a reaction to petitions from the populace, who collectively governed intimate social conduct and practices. Foucault carefully examines what is referred to as *poison-pen letters* alongside the responses provided by official institutions (Rocha 2012, 189). His conception of power experienced a profound transformation as he examined how the personal matters of ordinary people were deeply connected to and impacted the functioning of political institutions and state governance (Rocha 2012, 189). Instead of adhering to a top-down model of power, Foucault investigates how the social body—comprising neighbors, priests, and tenants—functioned as a locus from which denunciation was enacted (Rocha 2012, 184). By persuading the king to issue a lettre de cachet to punish a relative, individuals legitimized private repression, bypassing the formal judicial system. The populace called on the sovereign's coercive power to act against the marginalized and vulnerable, resulting in the intertwining of political authority with the fundamental aspects of social existence and daily life (Foucault 1994, 167–68). Routine practices of denunciation, surveillance, and control embedded within society underpinned the ruler's governance strategies, which later evolved into modern state institutions such as schools, prisons, and hospitals (Dean and Villadsen 2016, 63). Rather than exemplifying nonviolence and tolerance, these social groups were forerunners in parajudicial policing and surveillance through the enforcement of local norms. Later, state-led biopolitics used these grassroots microtechnologies (Dean and Villadsen 2016, 63). The extensive scope of legal and disciplinary dispositifs originated modestly within the family, community, and social fabric. In this context, Foucault's perspective appears to align with the materialist state theory's conception of state power as the "form-determined (institutionally mediated) condensation of a shifting balance of forces oriented to the exercise of capacities and powers associated with particular political forms and institutions as these are embedded in the wider social formation" (Jessop 2014, 485).

Foucault's later writings provide a meticulous analysis of the implications of situating politics outside the state. Echoing Gramsci's understanding of civil society as an arena for building hegemony, Foucault contends that a liberal art of government permeates civil society, thereby rendering the regulation of life effective within everyday spaces (Dean and Villadsen 2016, 24). In this framework, individuals are governed not solely as economic actors or legal subjects but as social entities connected through networks of association and community (Dean and Villadsen 2016, 138). Instead of relying on discipline and punitive measures, neoliberalism leverages and amplifies diversity and difference, shaping individuals through promises of freedom and tolerance. The valorization of civil society as a realm that liberates individuals from state domination belies the fact that it is, in fact, an augmentation of the state rather than merely its adversary. At the same time, civil society plays a crucial role in shaping and framing the ways in which state institutions wield their authority. Staging itself as oppositional to the state, civil society actually disingenuously conceals its implication in state structures. A dynamic civil society can thrive only through the sovereign state's regulation of conflicts among its actors and groups (Dean and Villadsen 2016, 36). Conversely, civil society regulates the exercise of power by state institutions. As diagnosed by Foucault, contrary to being a singular domain of ethical relations and democratic deliberations, civil society is imbued with mutual surveillance, strategies of control, and tactics of normalization (Dean and Villadsen 2016, 64). Instead of being suffused with lofty ideals of conviviality and social cohesion, civil society is marked by unrelenting struggles for power and domination. The state, however, as Foucault (2008, 4) explains, is not a coherent and centralized locus of power; rather, it is an effect of multiple and contradictory strategies and tactics. For instance, the modern state is not only a lawmaking but also a law-governed entity (Dean and Villadsen 2016, 174). The state is inflected by institutional contingencies and diverse rationalities and thus is capable of both coercion and protection. Butler (2002, 27), too, seems to admit that

> we do not always know what we mean by "the state." . . . The state is not a simple unity, and its parts and operations are not always coordinated with one another. The state is not reducible to law, and power is not reducible to state power. It would be wrong to understand the state as operating with a single set of interests or to gauge its effects as if they were unilaterally successful. I think the state can also be worked, exploited, and that social policy, which involves the implementation of law in local instances, can very often be the site where law is challenged, where it is thrown to a court to adjudicate.

One of the most instructive examples of the ambivalent nature of states is offered by the historian Timothy Snyder in his book *Black Earth: The Holocaust as History and Warning* (2015a). Snyder demonstrates how while colonialism was about destroying native sovereignty, Nazism was an ideology of state destruction. As proclaimed by the German legal theorist Carl Schmitt, a prominent member of the Nazi Party, "The epoch of statehood has come to an end" (quoted in Snyder 2015a, 144). Snyder claims that instead of being a nationalist or authoritarian who wanted an enlarged German state (Snyder 2015a, 241), Hitler was a "racial anarchist" (Snyder 2015b).

When Germany annexed Austria in 1938, conditions were created that made the extermination of Austrian Jews possible. Snyder analyzes the image of Jews forced to scrub the streets of Vienna and wipe away the word *Österreich* (Austria) (Snyder 2015a, 82–83). Austrian Jews were being made to unwrite the name of the state of which they had been citizens. Similarly, when Czechoslovakia was demolished in 1939, Jews suffered a level of persecution not possible in Germany at that time. When Germany invaded Poland in 1939 and destroyed legal and social structures, the persecution of Polish Jews was taken to a new level (Snyder 2016). Snyder (2015a, 117) speaks of "a double destruction of the state" and outlines how, during the Soviet occupation in Estonia, Latvia, and Lithuania, the legal code was eliminated, property rights were abolished, and state apparatuses were dismantled. By obliterating all forms of institutional protection, the Soviets, despite being guided by very different ideologies, unintentionally made it easier for Nazis to persecute Jews. Another compelling example Snyder gives is of the survival rates of Jews in countries where the state was not dismantled. In Denmark, 99 percent of the Jews who had Danish citizenship survived, unlike Jewish refugees who were denied state protection (Snyder 2015a, 217). In Estonia, 99 percent of Jews were killed—not because Danes were less antisemitic than Slavs and Baltic peoples, but because the institutional frameworks of the sovereign state obstructed the implementation of the Final Solution (Snyder 2015a, 212–13). Similarly, the survival rate of French Jews was higher than that of Dutch Jews. Although France had a bigger problem with antisemitism, 75 percent of French Jews survived, whereas 75 percent Dutch Jews were killed. Where the state was destroyed or sovereignty was eroded, Jews were killed (Snyder 2015a, 242–43).

Drawing on Arendt, and in light of these starkly different statistics, Snyder (2015a, 117) concludes that the first step toward the mass extermination of the Jews during National Socialism was to render them stateless. He explains that "state destruction did not alter politics, but rather created a new form of politics, which enabled a new kind of crime" (Snyder 2015a, 146). Destroying the state was inextricably linked to killing the juridical person, by which one takes away the protection of law, enabling the regime to more easily kill the person (Snyder 2016). Snyder (2016) warns against the assumption that if you destroy the state, you create a beautiful tabula rasa from which freedom and democracy can grow. He argues that if one understands the Holocaust in terms of a totalitarian German state, then one comes to the conclusion that one should destroy authoritarianism. However, if one understands the German rule under the Nazis as a special kind of racial regime, in which ideology and practice obliviated the remnants of states, then one links state destruction directly to the Holocaust (Snyder 2016).

With regard to current events, Snyder argues that although people are also being killed within the borders of states such as the United States and Russia, death, destruction, and displacement are taking on a completely different scale in places where state structures have been destroyed by these powers, such as in Syria, Yemen, Libya, and Ukraine. State destruction in a small territory does more harm than authoritarianism in a larger country. Snyder concludes by warning us to be vigilant about state destruction (Snyder 2016). The counterintuitive historical lesson is that bureaucracies and papers can also save lives. Steve Bannon, the architect of Trump's MAGA (Make America Great Again) ideology and former executive chairman of Breitbart News—a platform for the alt-right to promote racist, antisemitic, and sexist viewpoints—articulated that the objective was an ongoing struggle for the "deconstruction of the administrative state" (quoted in Rucker and Costa 2017). Project 2025, the Musk–inaugurated DOGE, and Argentine President Javier Milei all follow this mantra. Foucault anticipated the convergence of left- and right-wing anti-statism through his concept of state phobia. Contrary to Nietzsche's portrayal of the state as a *monstre froid*, Foucault (2008, 77) characterizes the state as "the mobile effect of a regime of multiple governmentalities" that intersect and occasionally conflict with one another. By dismantling the myth and monstrous image of the Leviathan, Foucault reconceptualizes politics as a dynamic interplay among various rationalities (Dean and Villadsen 2016, 103).[12] He argues that the state is perpetually in formation, existing simultaneously as what is and what is yet to be fully realized (Foucault 2008, 4).

It is important to note that, unlike Scott, Foucault does not advocate the art of not being governed; rather, he suggests avoiding being governed in a particular manner. In his words: "How not to be governed *like that*, by that, in the name of these principles, in view of such objectives and by means of such methods, not like that, not for that, not by them?" (Foucault 2007, 44). Instead of being governed to such an extent and at such a cost, Foucault (2010, 33) argues, Enlightenment requires a redistribution of relations between the governance of self and the government of others (Cook 2018, 85). Following Kant, Foucault explains that both critique and Enlightenment involve "the art of voluntary insubordination, that of reflected intractability" (Foucault 2007, 47). In my reading, Foucault emphasizes the important difference between criticizing the state and succumbing to state phobia. By understanding the state and law merely as sources of commands issued by the sovereign, anti-state positions overlook the fact that the state is also regulated by law (Dean and Villadsen 2016, 174). The state is shaped by institutional contingencies and is constantly engaged in the struggle to achieve internal coherence. The disparity between the existing state and the state yet to be constructed exposes the state as a continually unfinished project (Foucault 2008, 4). In conclusion, let us take a closer look at the concept of *pharmakon*, which is highly valuable for understanding the ambivalent legacies of the European Enlightenment, including the role of the state.

The ancient Greek word *pharmakon* is a paradoxical composite of three meanings: remedy, poison, and scapegoat. In ancient Athens, *pharmakos* referred to a ritualized sacrifice, a kind of societal catharsis, used to purge evil from the body and the city. *Pharmakon* was the name given to a symbolic scapegoat, invested with the sum of the corruption of a community that needed to be rendered benign. Society's problems are projected onto this wrongdoer, such that their destruction would bring an end to suffering. The ideological killing of a *pharmakon* was an act of societal cleansing. *Pharmakon* as poison was to be expelled from the system, leading to *katharsis*. *Pharmakos* was the solution to society's ills—a purifier by way of debasement. As a remedy for the city, an outsider—for instance, slaves or outlaws—was expelled at times of crises, such as natural catastrophes or wars, from the community. It is noteworthy that accepting the status of scapegoat was voluntary and consensual. It was believed that this would bring about purification in that the evil that had infected the city would be forever removed and returned to the outside. *Pharmakos* signifies that link among catharsis, sacrifice, and purification (Girard 1986, 37–38). Related to this was the political process of *ostracism* that was common in fifth-century BCE Athens, wherein those individuals who were considered too powerful or dangerous to the city, such as politicians, were exiled for ten years by popular vote. Thus, *pharmakos* (scapegoat) is a tonic *pharmakon* (antidote, cure) for purging the toxic *pharmakon* (poison, disease) that plagues the community. Socrates is a good example of scapegoat-poison-remedy. He was found guilty of impiety and corrupting the young, sentenced to death, and then required to carry out his own punishment by consuming a deadly potion of the poisonous plant hemlock. Socrates rejected the offer to flee, consenting to his execution. With his voluntary death, Socrates, the scapegoat, functions as counter-poison/medicine, healing Athens.

In his essay "Plato's Pharmacy," Derrida focuses on the word chain *pharmakeia-pharmakon-pharmakeus* and its link to the missing term *pharmakos*, which is nonetheless always already present in the word chain *pharmakeia-pharmakon-pharmakeus*. In Derrida's view, *pharmakon* alludes to the indeterminacy and ambiguity of identifying it as either cure *or* poison. In translating *pharmakos* (drug) either only as remedy or only as poison, one chooses one signification over the other, thereby disregarding the plurality of potentials (Derrida 1981a, 129–30). Instead of either-or, Derrida focuses on both-and, such that he defers choosing between one and the other.

Pharmakon is a magical dose that causes destruction and healing. It is poisonous cure and remedying poison. This alludes to the productive potential of medicines and their capacity to reconfigure bodies and diseases in multiple, unpredictable ways. Citing the example of some human immunodeficiency virus (HIV) patients taking antiretroviral therapy, Asha Persson (2004, 49) states: "The ambivalent quality of pharmakon is more than purely a matter of 'wrong drug, wrong dose, wrong route of administration, wrong patient.'" Drugs, as is the case with antiretroviral therapy, have the capacity to be beneficial and detrimental to the same person at the same time. Another good example is chemotherapy that deploys potent poisons to kill a pathogen and destroy deviant, outside cells while saving the host. Chemotherapy is a dialectic between killing and healing, with modern medicine mimicking the purification rituals of the ancients Greeks, where the *pharmakon* was the poison used properly, revealing its potential as cure. Similarly, *pharmakos* was the scapegoat who was invested with the sins of the entire community and whose ritual expulsion left the community purified.

When I speak of the state as a *pharmakon*, I mean it in all three senses—poison (state monopoly on violence), medicine (the enabling structures of the state), and scapegoat (fitting foil onto which all societal problems are projected). This highlights the state's intrinsic contingencies, as its institutions and structures are characterized by slippages, ambivalences, and inconsistencies. The state, functioning as a *pharmakon*, lacks a stable essence and is defined by contradictions: It embodies both violence and justice, ideology and emancipation, law and repression. The indeterminacy, fluidity, and dual nature of the state—its Manichaean quality—suggest that it inherently embodies contradictions, holding the potential to transform poison into remedy and curse into cure (Derrida 1981a, 127). Focusing exclusively on the negative aspects of the *pharmakon*—namely, death and destruction—obscures and neglects its enabling and empowering potential. To transform poison into medicine, it is crucial to develop a critique of the state that goes beyond mere state-phobic rhetoric and politics. This necessitates recognizing the ambivalences inherent in state formation and the inconsistent functions of its institutions and apparatus. This is a particularly valuable lesson for postcolonial sovereignty and struggles for decolonization. In conclusion, I echo Edward Said's prescient observation: "I will be the first critic of the state of Palestine once it is established" (quoted in Spivak 2018b).

This chapter is devoted to outlining that, despite sympathies with the current postcolonial-queer-feminist opposition to state violence and its understanding of decolonization in terms of abolitionism, including the defunding and dismantling of the racist-patriarchal-capitalist state, I am concerned about the state phobia present in emancipatory movements and critical scholarship. As I have argued, rather than viewing civil society as simply oppositional to the state, we must understand how it is both an extension of *and* antagonistic to the state. For me, approaching the state as *pharmakon* means that decolonization involves desubalternization— namely, enabling subaltern groups to access both the state and civil society.

In the next chapter, I address in greater detail the contentious role of violence and nonviolence in the process of decolonization. Gandhi famously advocated for nonviolent resistance against colonialism because he feared that violent struggle risked the oppressed becoming like their oppressors. The ethics of means and ends haunts critical theories of decolonization. Can one overcome violent regimes nonviolently, or is revolutionary counterviolence indispensable? Does violence endlessly perpetuate itself, with each violent act reinforcing its power? Can one combat gender or racial injustice nonviolently? In the next chapter, I focus on the dynamic between critique and (non)violence.

5

Critique of Violence—Violence
of Critique

Determination to fight for one's life which characterizes the native's reply to oppression are obviously good enough reasons for joining in the fight. But you do not
carry on a war, nor suffer brutal and widespread repression, nor look on while all
other members of your family are wiped out in order to make racialism or hatred
triumph. Racialism and hatred and resentment—"a legitimate desire for revenge"—
cannot sustain a war of liberation.—FRANTZ FANON, *The Wretched of the Earth*

In the face of ongoing wars and conflicts, the contentious correlation between political violence and resistance once again looms large. Since the
brutal attacks by Hamas on Israel on October 7, 2023, postcolonial studies
has been accused of providing the ideological foundation for legitimizing
the atrocities committed in the name of decolonization and liberation. The
very credibility of postcolonial thought seems to be at stake, for it is excoriated for glorifying violence. While Mohandas K. Gandhi, Martin Luther
King Jr., and Nelson Mandela were previously seen as icons of nonviolent
decolonization, Frantz Fanon and Malcolm X are now vilified as advocates
of postcolonial vindictiveness and barbarity. What the backlash against
postcolonial thought disregards is that Fanon would have strongly rejected
any form of violence and terrorism against civilians (Shatz 2024). To follow

up on the insight in the chapter's epigraph, Fanon (1963 [1961], 139) astutely warns against the "giddiness, where my blood calls for the blood of the other, where by sheer inertia my death calls for the death of the other." He avers that the detoxifying effects of anticolonial violence are, at best, fleeting.

What, then, is the appropriate and adequate strategy to oppose slavery and colonial subjugation? If, as Immanuel Kant argued, failed political acts of rebellion are aesthetically equivalent to disgust and repulsion, how can revolt be uplifting and heroic (Ross 2004, 384)? What are the norms that frame our judgment of legitimate and illegitimate resistance? While Hannah Arendt challenges Fanon's understanding of violence as an emancipatory force, views violence as a substitution for power, and distinguishes between imperial violence and that of totalitarian regimes such as National Socialism, Fanon claims that armed struggle is "disintoxicating" (*la violence désintoxique*) (quoted in Shatz 2023). Although Fanon notoriously asserted that "decolonisation is always a violent phenomenon," he also lamented that Europeans understood only the language of war. In contrast to Arendt, Jean Améry tends to agree with Fanon that, for the oppressed, violence is indeed a means to gain affirmation of their humanity. Gandhi, however, feared that colonized Indians would become like their masters—brutal and inhuman. For him, the tragedy of decolonization would be to gain independence through violent means. In response to the imperative to exercise nonviolence, Malcolm X (1965) famously remarked: "I don't favor violence. If we could bring about recognition and respect of our people by peaceful means, well and good. Everybody would like to reach his objectives peacefully. But I'm also a realist. The only people in this country who are asked to be nonviolent are black people." This diversity of perspectives on the role of violence and nonviolence in processes of decolonization within anticolonial and postcolonial thought is the focus in this chapter. The effort is to understand the conflictual dynamics between critical thought and violence while also defending postcolonial studies against blanket accusations of "terrorism washing."

Albert Einstein famously wrote to Sigmund Freud asking how to reduce violence in the world and tame the latent instincts of hate in man (Einstein 2018). The question was whether the destructive (nationalist) drives could be contained if states were to cede sovereignty to global institutions, preventing war and guaranteeing peace by mediating conflict between nations. In place of supranational political arrangements that would draw on juridical power to deliver justice and counteract against violence, Freud (2019) recommended a "community of interests." This would supersede divisive attitudes while fostering non-nationalist sentiments of solidarity, thereby resisting the seductions of war. In his contemplations on group psychology, Freud asserted that destructive impulses flourished when the critical faculty is inhibited. This implies that nurturing critical reflection can mitigate the *Todestrieb* (death drive) through deliberate forms of self-restraint. Freud seems to make a direct link between critical practice and nonviolence.

Taking inspiration from these contemplations, this chapter engages with the following question: In the face of the brutality and dehumanization inherent to the mechanics of occupation and slavery, is a nonviolent transition from colonialism to postcolonialism possible or are those brutalized by colonialism inevitably inclined to violence? One could put forth the example of the Indian freedom struggle as an instance of nonviolent revolution, but, as discussed in the chapter, the conflict between two of India's most important anticolonial thinkers—namely, Gandhi and B. R. Ambedkar—illustrates the complexities of defining nonviolence and of practicing it in the context of decolonization.

Comprising four sections, the chapter begins by juxtaposing Gandhi, Arendt, and Judith Butler with Fanon and Ambedkar to examine the complex dynamic between violence and nonviolence. The second section focuses on how the exercise of critique not just contests violence but can also perpetuate it. The third section outlines how emancipatory norms such as democracy, justice, and rule of law, which are legacies of the Enlightenment, exercise normative violence—namely, how the norms themselves exert violence even as they promise emancipation. The chapter ends with the conundrum of postcolonial critique of state violence.

Violence. Symptom or Remedy?

One of the biggest challenges facing critical theorizing of violence is how to define it. Are these accounts universal and ahistorical or are they specific to time and space? How do different practices of violence constitute bodies and spaces? Through what physical, structural, discursive, normative, and affective means and modalities is violence staged and enacted? Which forms of violence are justified and which remain illegitimate? How do we respond to the ethical demands that these issues raise?

The complex dynamic between politics and violence has long been a major point of contention among critical theorists. While some, such as Fanon, emphasize the cathartic and rehabilitating function of revolutionary violence, others, such as Gandhi, mobilize the strategy of nonviolence to compromise the opponent's capacity to resist (Caygill 2013, 11). Another important challenge is the ethics of means and ends, of political goals and the legitimate means to achieve them. Writing in defense of the Paris Commune of 1871, which was accused of being brutally violent, Friedrich Engels (1978 [1874], 733) asserts: "Have these gentlemen ever seen a revolution? A revolution is certainly the most authoritarian thing there is; it is the act whereby one part of the population imposes its will upon the other part by means of rifles, bayonets, and cannon."

Distrusting the instrumentalist defense of violence, Gandhi, Arendt, and Butler all warn that violence at times exceeds and flouts its intentions and risks getting out of hand. Although violence may be tactically necessary, it is not a neutral tool that can be put to use, then simply discarded; rather, its employment constitutes and shapes the world in specific ways (Butler 2020, 12). Instead of being a sign of weakness, naïve idealism, or moral calculus, nonviolence is a means without an end and a recognition of interdependence and shared vulnerability. Scholars of nonviolence such as Gandhi and Butler firmly believe that our co-implicated interdependence makes us nonviolent, for there is a link between the destruction of the other and self-destruction. If, as they argue, it is impossible to be indifferent to the suffering of others, then the ethos of nonviolence is not an individual choice or attitude but a collective political practice of imagining how to cohabitate less violently.

Arendt, like Gandhi, views violence not as inevitable in politics but as a threat to it. For Arendt (1970, 56), power and violence are opposites such that "it is not correct to think of the opposite of violence as nonviolence; to speak of nonviolent power is actually redundant. Violence can destroy power; it is utterly incapable of creating it." Arendt contends that while violence can dismantle illegitimate power, unlike Fanon, she does not believe that violence is the appropriate means to achieve power. In her critique of Fanon, Arendt (1970, 80) argues that violence exceeds the end and has unintentional consequences, thereby making the world as such only more violent. Thus, even as violence may be a remedy, it can end up being worse than the illness, in perpetuating endless spirals of violence.

One of the recurring arguments for the justification of violence in politics is that it is intrinsic to human nature—as presumed, for instance, by Thomas Hobbes in his idea of *bellum omnium contra omnes* (the war of all against all). Even Fanon (1963 [1961], 61) famously remarked that "colonialism . . . is violence in its natural state, and it will only yield when confronted with greater violence." Rejecting this idea, Butler (2020, 177) turns to Freud to explore how certain presumptions about human nature undermine while others strengthen the political critique of violence. Butler (2020, 148) proposes that precisely because we are capable of violence and destruction, we are obligated to curb our destructive capacity. Drawing on Freud's reflections on Eros and Thanatos, as well as the bonds that hold a community together, Butler (2020, 154) explores the question of what can be done to keep in check the cruelty that jeopardizes "future possibility of peaceful coexistence." The Freudian imperative to "murder your own murderous impulse" (Freud, quoted in Butler 2020, 177), wherein the super-ego renounces its violent drives, evokes the promise of a society beyond violence.

Butler, following Melanie Klein, suggests that identification and empathy undergird principles of solidarity and radical equality. This offers an alternative to paternalistic approaches that emphasize the protection of the so-called needy from political and social violence. At the same time, nurturing disidentification, as proposed by Freud, with tyrannical and authoritarian forces can enable a critical distancing from brutal regimes (Butler 2020, 164). Cultivating our pacifist impulses through fostering the critical faculty can arouse aversion against the thrills of war, thereby undermining destructive tendencies. While guilt and conscience are usually negatively connoted, Butler (2020, 93) explains that, by holding one's ego accountable, we can overcome our own grievances against others. However, this process of mindfulness can also result in self-aggrandizement (Rose 1998, 144). In addition to rectifying past harms, we must strive to prevent future damage in the form of "an anticipatory form of repair" (Butler 2020, 100). This would involve constituting economic structures and institutions that would forestall a differentiated production of vulnerability.

One of the greatest skeptics of this normative approach to nonviolence was Fanon, who notably argued that nonviolence is just as much a matter of political calculus for both colonial and colonized elites as violence. Fanon (1963 [1961], 61–62) remarks:

At a decisive moment, the colonialist bourgeoisie . . . introduces that new idea which is in proper parlance a creation of the colonial situation: non-violence. In its simplest form this non-violence signifies to the intellectual and economic elite of the colonized country that the bourgeoisie has the same interests as they and that it is therefore urgent and indispensable to come to terms for the public good. Non-violence is an attempt to settle the colonial problem around a green baize table, before any regrettable act has been performed or irreparable gesture made, before any blood has been shed. But if the masses, without waiting for the chairs to be arranged around the baize, listen to their own voice and begin committing outrages and setting fire to buildings, the elite and the nationalist bourgeois parties will have be seen rushing to the colonialist to exclaim, "This is very serious! We do not know how it will end; we must find a solution—some sort of compromise."

Even someone like Kant, who declared as illegitimate any government that relegates a citizen to a position of servitude and slavery, rebuked the colonizeds' right to revolution (Kant 1991c [1797], 138–39). Kant's rejection of the right to revolt presumes that one lives in a well-functioning republican constitutional state (*Rechtsstaat*); the same does not necessarily apply to a colonial state that dehumanizes and enslaves the native population, such that violent revolution is sometimes the only possibility of overthrowing a tyrannical regime to gain freedom. To this end, Fanon understands violence to be imperative for politics; he focuses on the strategic element within violence, which must be both contained and channeled toward certain goals. Fanon's reflections on the inextricable intimacy between violence and freedom draws on G. W. F. Hegel's master-slave dialectic, which was written during Europe's transition from feudalism to capitalism. In his reading of Hegel's *The Phenomenology of Spirit*, Fanon shows the limits and lures of Hegel's master-slave dialectic for anticolonial radical thought. Unlike Hegel's claim that the master seeks recognition from the slave, Fanon argues that the Black slave is not even fully human to the colonial master. Thus, there is no reciprocity between the two: "The master laughs at the consciousness of the slave. What he wants from the slave is not recognition but work" (Fanon 1986 [1952], 220). In Fanon's view, the white master sees the Black slave only as a conduit of labor. The Black slave, unlike the slave of Hegel, finds no emancipation in his work.

For Hegel, risk and freedom are interconnected such that by not staking one's life for recognition, enslavement comes about. Fanon bemoans that the master paternalistically grants the presumed gift of freedom and supposedly acknowledges the latter without the slave struggling for recognition. Thus, "The black man knows nothing of the cost of freedom, for he has not fought for it" (Fanon 1986 [1952], 221). To achieve true freedom, the subjugated must demand recognition by taking power in his own hand; violence becomes the cleansing force that liberates the slave. Fanon (1963 [1961], 94) is often seen advocating for violence because it "frees the native from his inferiority complex and from his despair and inaction; it makes him fearless and restores his self-respect."

Defenders point out that, instead of glorifying violence for its own sake, Fanon was painfully aware of the costs of resorting to counterviolence as a means, mindful that it both surpasses the ends and is self-perpetuating (Caygill 2013, 100). He is cognizant that anticolonial violence aimed at destroying colonial power does not end with decolonization but continues to dominate the postcolonial world: "We see that violence used in specific ways at the moment of the struggle for freedom does not magically disappear after the ceremony of trooping the national colors" (Fanon 1963 [1961], 75). As a psychiatrist, Fanon is acutely aware that the subject, as well as the world that comes into contact with violence, is not immune to the impact of its unleashing. Colonial violence provokes a response from the colonized, who are fighting for their destiny as well as their future; for this reason, Fanon had an ambivalent position on the issue of resistant violence. The complex and dilemmatic relation between means and end, between violence and freedom in Fanon's approach, are at times misrepresented as straightforward and unambiguous, with him being demonized as "The Patron Saint of Political Violence" (Beckerman 2024). Fanon was acutely aware that emancipation *from* the colonial past was not the same as liberation *for* a postcolonial future (Caygill 2013, 103). We must not forget that Fanon was a doctor and a healer, not just a revolutionary.

Despite Fanon's influential contemplations on numerous topics, the seventy-one-page chapter "Concerning Violence" has received disproportionate attention (Gordon 1995, 68). In particular, his remarks on the redemptive function of armed resistance and on the psychological liberation experienced by the colonized when exercising violence against the oppressor have been a source of dispute. Lewis Gordon (1995, 82) instead reads Fanon's contemplations as a "tragic text about a tragic world." Positions such as Fanon's are less advocacy for violence than an effort to trace the calamitous conditions that incite violence. With an unequal distribution of agency, the colonized were driven to counterviolence, for which they were demonized. In *The Black Jacobins*, C. L. R. James (2001 [1938], 75) explains:

> The slaves destroyed tirelessly. . . . They knew that as long as these plantations stood their lot would be to labour on them until they dropped. The only thing was to destroy them. From their masters they had known rape, torture, degradation, and, at the slightest provocation, death. They returned in kind. For two centuries the higher civilization

had shown them that power was used for wreaking your will on those whom you controlled. Now that they held power they did as they had been taught. . . . And yet they were surprisingly moderate, then and afterwards, far more humane than their masters had been or would ever be to them.

Gordon (1995, 83) observes that, although James's remark "And yet they were surprisingly moderate" evoked consternation, James stood by it. Tracing the spectrum of positions vis-à-vis violence in the context of the civil rights struggle, Gordon (1995, 79) draws attention to Malcolm X's rejection of both Mao Zedong's "only the gun" stance and King's "never the gun" approach to propose a "don't rule out the gun" doctrine. In Gordon's reading, Fanon and Malcolm X converge insofar as they emphasize the impossibility of knowing either the ends or the means to get there in advance. Violence, for them, is not only a symptom of oppression but also a remedy against it, when channeled strategically and appropriately. Instead of nonviolence being an ethical doctrine to aspire to and violence being the last resort for political resistance, the inextricable link between the two is foregrounded. In our everyday understanding, nonviolence's failure leads to a descent into violence. Fanon, however, interrupts this temporal narrative to unveil the dynamic between violence and nonviolence (Marasco 2015, 160). He further deconstructs the positioning of rational nonviolence versus irrational violence.

Like Fanon, Mao claims that violence is cathartic and indispensable in the constitution of a revolutionary subjectivity (Caygill 2013, 63). Drawing on Carl von Clausewitz, Mao, in his reflections on people's war, observes: "Politics is war without bloodshed while war is politics with bloodshed" (Mao, quoted in Caygill 2013, 63). Mao favors the tactics of deferral, prolongation, and nonengagement to those of confrontation and escalation. Unlike Lenin, who focuses on the resistant subject as bearer of a clear and distinct class-consciousness, or Rosa Luxemburg's emphasis on the emergent historical consciousness, Mao recommends the strategy of frustrating the opponent's initiatives, which requires a tactical understanding of the enemies' strategies (Caygill 2013, 66–69). The intentional and judicious deployment of violence toward emancipation is a tactical option.

While Mao foregrounds victory with the use of violence if necessary, Gandhi warns that retaliatory violence risks destructive reciprocity and recurring terror. Despite Gandhi's name being synonymous with anticolonial freedom struggle, the role of violence and nonviolence in processes of decolonization remains a contentious one. This also bears on the relationship between postcolonialism and Enlightenment norms of emancipation, justice, and equality. The ensuing section is crucial for my contemplations on the politics and ethics of decolonization.

There is no better example of the ambivalent and impossible relationship of the postcolonial world to the European Enlightenment than Gandhi's and Ambedkar's divergent attitudes toward the West and their hostility against each other. Gandhi's most formidable adversary, Ambedkar was one of the most important intellectuals of India: He was the architect of the Indian Constitution, a champion of the Dalits, and the author of the hugely influential book *Annihilation of Caste* (1936).[1] Deeply inspired by European Enlightenment, Ambedkar found Gandhi's critique of modernity and his romantic *Swadeshism* (of one's own country) counterproductive for marginalized groups. Ambedkar lamented that there was no hope for the common man in Gandhism and emphasized that the Dalits have no nostalgia for the precolonial past, which, with its caste system, was a brutal experience of humiliation and exploitation for them. Despite their common commitment to forging an independent India as an egalitarian society, Gandhi and Ambedkar had irreconcilable differences on equality and freedom. The acrimonious relationship between them is not just about disagreements over caste reform or the struggle against empire. The dispute concerns the fundamental dynamic between politics and violence.

While some revere Gandhi as a saintly figure and prophet of peace and nonviolence, others mock him as a hopelessly naïve idealist (Lal 2009, 281). It speaks in his favor that, despite the Gandhi-initiated boycott of mill-manufactured clothing and its harmful impact on the livelihoods of English workers, Gandhi received a rousing welcome when he visited the cloth mills in Lancashire (Butler 2020, 281). It is pointed out, however, that Gandhi succeeded against the supposed gentlemanly British but would have failed miserably against a totalitarian regime such as Nazism. The other accusation against Gandhi is that by bringing religion into politics, Gandhi harmed the entrenchment of secular norms in postcolonial democratic India (Sharma 2021). Whether one idolizes or vilifies Gandhi, what is undeniable is that he is a deeply ambivalent and inconsistent figure in postcolonial thought (Pratinav 2023). An epitome of Homi Bhabha's (1994) "mimicry man," Gandhi in his youth strove to emulate the British gentlemen, dressing in British style and taking lessons in violin, dancing, and elocution (Lal 2009, 285). Gandhi observes that he learned from the

British "punctuality, reticence, public hygiene, independent thinking and exercise of judgment" (quoted in Lal 2009, 285). Hallmarks of modernity such as rational thinking and the scientific outlook were formative in his intellectual development. As is widely known, he was deeply inspired by Western intellectuals such as Henry David Thoreau, Leo Tolstoy, and John Ruskin, and his staunchest friends and supporters were Europeans, including European Jews, acquaintances made during his time in South Africa (Lal 2009, 284). Gandhi's *Satyāgraha* (holding on to truth) was famously influenced by Thoreau's *On the Duty of Civil Disobedience*. Although Mignolo cites Gandhi as an inspiration for the decolonial option, Gandhi departed from the decolonial strategy of "epistemic delinking" insofar as his thought and practice was profoundly inspired by Western thinkers. At the same time, Gandhi was no blind imitator of Western values and norms and questioned European self-representation as superior. Vinay Lal (2009, 284) compellingly argues that Gandhi sought to rescue the West from itself: "Should not Gandhi's encounter with the West also be read as a parable of his strongly held view that victors need to be liberated as much as the vanquished, the colonizers as much as the colonized?"

Given that Gandhi's intellectual and political formation occurred in England and South Africa, it is a challenge to address the question of what is Indian about him, for he was, in many ways, a stranger in India (Devji 2012, 9–10). While Howard Caygill (2013, 71) contends that Gandhi's understanding of nonviolent action was not theoretically rigorous, Jyotirmaya Sharma claims that his *ahiṃsā* (nonviolence) cannot be read back into any available past Indian tradition, whether Jain or Hindu (Sharma 2021, 8). On the contrary, I would argue that Gandhian nonviolence was deeply influenced by *Anekāntavāda* (the doctrine of non-absolutism), which is central to the heterodox Jain approach to epistemology, politics, and ethics (Dhawan 2007, 43–53). For the Jains, *dhárma* (duty) is synonymous with *ahiṃsā*. In keeping with their spirit of *ahiṃsādhárma*, the *Anekāntavādins* guard against *bhava hiṃsā* (epistemic violence) by avoiding categorical assertions or negations and by upholding an attitude of nonabsolutism (*anekānta*). *Anekāntavāda* as part of the Jain practice of "epistemic *ahiṃsā*" is an effort to pursue nonassimilative, no-exclusionary politics of truth (Dhawan 2007, 43–53). In the journal *Navajivan*, Gandhi (1999 [1926], 410) explained: "The seven blind men who gave seven different descriptions of the elephant were all right from their respective points of view, and wrong from the point of view of one another, and right and wrong from the point of view of the man who knew the elephant. I very much like this doctrine of the manyness of reality. . . . My *Anekāntavāda* is the result of the twin doctrine of *Satyāgraha* and *Ahiṃsā*."

Gandhi's tactics of nonviolence were critical in achieving a moral advantage for the Indian independence movement (Hardiman 2003, 60). Even as he followed Thoreau's advice that it was one's duty not to cooperate with immoral rule, he went beyond mere noncooperation in the struggle against the British Raj and argued that one must move the British to repentance and reconciliation by adapting altruistic forbearance. Lal (2009, 283) explains poignantly that the British were at a loss as to how "to respond to a man who appeared keener on punishing himself than on chastising the British." Faced with nonviolence, the colonizers were left in a predicament, as their repression of peaceful resistance became a sign of their rule's "moral bankruptcy" (Lal 2009, 59). In fact, several British officials resigned from their positions, as they did not want to have to sanction violence against unarmed, nonviolent resisters (Lal 2009, 59). Gandhi (2009 [1927], 293) claimed that the British rule in India was possible not because of British military strength but because Indians consented to it. The renowned scholar of nonviolence Gene Sharp (2013, 14) took up this insight when he argued that regimes of violence feed on the complicity of ordinary people. By withholding consent and through disobedience nonviolent struggles emerge.

Gandhi's affirmative attitude toward the West underwent a dramatic change later. His ambivalent and inconsistent relationship with the West is exemplified in *Hind Swaraj* (Indian Home Rule), which pillories modern civilization (Lal 2009, 291). Although it rejected armed insurrection, the text was still considered seditious by the British and thus censored. The central tenet of the book is that modern civilization had corrupted England, and it was morally imperative to end British colonialism before it also damaged India (Lal 2009, 292). However, Gandhi did not want freedom at any cost, and he was especially concerned that Indians would end up being like the British. He famously objected to this mindset of mastery and servitude: "In effect it means this: that we want English rule without the Englishman. . . . [T]hat is to say, you would make India English" (Gandhi 1939, 27).

Tracing the provenance of nonviolence to Hindu civilization, Gandhi contends that following "the path of violence would be to Europeanize India" such that decolonization without nonviolence would be a failure (Gandhi 1939, 193). Gandhi rejected a vision of India's future that drew on Europe's past, which was his worst nightmare. His understanding of self-rule went beyond "replacing white faces with brown ones, or merely gaining for Indians the political freedoms that Englishmen possessed" (Devji

2012, 2–3). India, rather, by overcoming violence, was to be an experiment in the universal practice of nonviolence that would enable a moral and political transformation of all of mankind (Devji 2012, 2–3).

Paradoxically, even as Gandhi fought for Indian independence and self-rule, he rejected the nation-state as a coercive form of organizing collectivities (Lal 2009, 306). Gandhi's assassin, a Hindu ideologue, condemned Gandhi's alleged betrayal of the Hindus and the idea of the Hindu nation. Sharma, by contrast, assails Gandhi for bringing religion into politics, thereby paving the path for the Hindu nationalism. Gandhi's self-description of Hindus as essentially nonviolent and Hinduism as a religion that had perfected itself with nonviolence (Sharma 2021, 78) stereotyped Hindus as tolerant and peaceful. Although violence is ubiquitous and unavoidable, Hindu civilization, by confining the use of force to the warrior caste, in Gandhi's view, regulated violence and nurtured nonviolence (Sharma 2021, 95). Ahiṃsā can be practiced only by those capable of killing (Sharma 2021, 177). Simply abandoning violence, according to Gandhi, does not translate into overcoming the desire to kill; rather, a true warrior is not one who kills, but one who dies defending the weak (Sharma 2021, 179, 192). And because the soul is eternal and the body is merely a transient vehicle, members of the warrior caste are willing to sacrifice their own bodies in the service of nonviolence (Sharma 2021, 233). Gandhi's teleology of nonviolence converges with his theology.

The Gandhian practice of Satyāgraha is an ineliminable element in the exercise of ahiṃsā. However, he does not proffer a universalized account of resistance or a theory of truth; he only provides guidelines for practice and speaks of his "experiments with truth" (Gandhi 2009 [1927]). Ahiṃsā is characteristically understood as the strategy of those considered weak and powerless, of those who do not have the strength to fight back. Nonviolence is not lack of courage or capacity to resist but an effort to end violence, such that "nonviolence cannot be taught to a person who fears to die" (Gandhi 1969, 103). The Gandhian practice of ahiṃsā emphasized the desubjectivation of the act of violence. This implies that the deed is detached from the doer or performer of the action and the focus is crucially shifted from the subject to the act of violence itself. This does away with the need for a supposed enemy while offering other tactics to deal with one's hatred and rage. The exercise of nonviolence involves collective practices and rituals, such as public vows of fasting and prayer meetings. Satyāgraha is thus both a strategy of resistance and a way of life. Gandhi advocates nonviolence, even at the cost of death and suffering for the resister. Rather than merely being a weapon of the weak, the *satyāgrahi*—the resister—nurtures not only the capacity for nonviolence but also, surprisingly, the capacity to love, instead of resorting to hate or coercion.

There have been controversial discussions about the gendering of nonviolent resistance, with Gandhi claiming that women were supposedly naturally predisposed to nonviolence. This has also been reinforced by ecofeminists such as Vandana Shiva (2017). Feminist critics focus on the deep link between masculinity and violence. Fanon (1963 [1961], 36–37), for instance, claims that it is through violence that "the 'thing' colonized becomes a man" by healing the violated. From a postcolonial-queer-feminist perspective, it is important to note that both violence and nonviolence are gendered, racialized, and caste- and class-biased in historically and geopolitically specific ways. This safeguards against both lofty condemnations of violence and naïve proclamations of nonviolence as ethically preferable. In many postcolonial contexts, colonialism was perceived as a form of emasculation, such that anticolonial violence becomes a means to remasculinization. Thus, Hindu nationalists lamented nonviolence as a form of the feminization of the nation; the assassin of Gandhi justified his killing as liberation from this disarming effeminate nonviolence (van der Veer 1994, 96).

Thus, the role of violence in anticolonial struggle is more complex than one of simple negation or overcoming; it is only against the foil of violence that the moral superiority of nonviolence becomes evident (Devji 2012, 3–4). By foregrounding dying over killing as more virtuous, Gandhi was reconfiguring the very idea of sovereignty (Devji 2012, 6). While Michel Foucault, Judith Butler, and Achille Mbembe focus on the genocidal and necropolitical state and its capacity to kill, Gandhi avers that even if "individuals might be unequal in their ability to kill they were all equally capable of dying, demonstrating therefore the universality of suffering and sacrifice over violence of all kinds" (Devji 2012, 6). Faisal Devji astutely points out that, instead of juxtaposing the violent state against the nonviolent nonstate actor, the rival to Gandhi's nonviolent protagonist is the violent revolutionary who is willing to kill for freedom and independence (Devji 2012, 6).

Gandhi's position on the Indian Mutiny of 1857, which he initially supported but later condemned, is a case in point. While other nationalists celebrated the mutiny as India's first war of independence that brought together Hindus and Muslims, and Karl Marx compared it to the French Revolution, Gandhi dismissed it as an orgy of violence (Devji 2012, 12). As with the Haitian Revolution, the India Mutiny, which occurred some decades later, was condemned by the Europeans as proof of the barbarity and brutality of the natives. Gandhi was of the conviction that as long as Indians resorted to violence they were not ready for freedom (Devji 2012, 93). When mass violence occurred on his watch, Gandhi often took responsibility for the atrocities committed by his followers, performing penance for others' acts (Devji 2012, 86). Rather than a mere means toward a goal temporally deferred to the future, nonviolent protest was an end in itself (Devji 2012, 94). An act of violence in the present cannot be legitimized in the name of lofty ideals to be realized in the future. Gandhi decouples moral action from political expediency and calculus and understands virtue in terms of necessity. In place of setting norms to guide moral choices, Gandhi counterintuitively subtracts choice from moral action, making it superfluous to ethical practice (Devji 2012, 108). If the future is indeterminate, then choice is meaningless and delusionary, making instrumentalism and political opportunism irrelevant to ethics. Gandhi advises that one should not expect the results or rewards of practicing nonviolence in one's lifetime (Sharma 2021, 23). This flies in the face of liberal Western approaches to ethics, where norms of freedom and choice are at the heart of a moral responsibility exercised by an autonomous rational agent.

Challenging the efficacy of violent resistance, Gandhi observed that counterviolence validates the coercion exercised by the adversary. Through unleashing destructive violence, escalation can usher in the end of politics itself. However, by refusing to resort to retaliatory violence, the relation among power, coercion, and justice can be reconfigured. Once a society goes down the path of violence, it has repercussions that persist even when the goal has been accomplished, no matter how justified the cause. To achieve independence through violent means would result in the constitution of violent subjectivities, which would haunt the postcolonial world.

But as Arundhati Roy (2017, 24) rightly points out, one of the biggest challenges in reading Gandhi is "that Gandhi actually said everything and its opposite." Thus, even as he claimed to be a champion of the downtrodden, Gandhi was popular with neither the Marxists nor the anti-caste movement. The Marxists accused him of being a factotum of the bourgeoisie and argued that Gandhian nonviolence deflected armed class warfare, dissuading workers from pursuing their class interests (Lal 2008, 61). While the train incident in South Africa has been immortalized as the moment of Gandhi's political birth, critics point out that he was interested in protecting and promoting only the interests of the so-called passenger Indians and not indentured laborers from India (the so-called coolies) or the native Africans (Roy 2017, 70).[2] Gandhi insisted that he wanted to live like the poorest of the poor, but his strategy of hunger strikes and sexual abstinence were not part of a systematic critique of capitalism. There is an ideological difference between fasting and starving. The Indian political activist and poet Sarojini Naidu infamously quipped: "If Gandhi only knew how much it costs us to keep him in poverty!" (quoted in Lal 2008, 61). Given the ascetic tradition in India, Roy (2017, 62) argues "that the act of renunciation by someone who has plenty to renounce . . . appealed to the popular imagination. Gandhi would eventually discard his Western suit and put on a dhoti in order to dress like the poor. Ambedkar, on the other hand, born unmoneyed, and denied the right to wear clothes that privileged-caste people wore, would show his defiance by wearing a three-piece suit." While Gandhi was deploying the spinning wheel as a political weapon and rejected machines and industrialization as signs of Western depravity, his ashrams were financed by the industrialist G. D. Birla (Roy 2017, 73). Ambedkar was similarly supported by privileged-caste Hindus, but unlike Gandhi, he was not deterred from his fight to dismantle the Hindu caste system and its systematized violence.

Gandhi is accused of merely staging himself as a renunciant, uninterested in political power while wielding it strategically and tactically. His sway drew on populism without constitutional accountability (Devji 2012, 124–25). Although he claimed to be a champion of the Dalits, Gandhi never categorically renounced his belief in *cāturvarṇa* (the caste system). He rejected inter-dining and intermarriage, thereby upholding caste and communal practices (Sharma 2021, 116–17). Gandhi feared that any challenge to the caste system would lead to turmoil: "I believe that caste has saved Hindus from disintegration. To destroy the caste system and adopt the Western European social system means that Hindus must give up the principle of hereditary occupation, which is the soul of the caste system. Hereditary principle is an eternal principle. To change it is to create disorder" (quoted in Ambedkar 2014b, 275–76). The decolonial approach, in idealizing precolonial epistemologies, must address these conundrums when scripting their vision of decolonization.

Despite concerns about communal bloodshed and his unconditional commitment to nonviolence, Gandhi insisted that the British leave India to its fate, proclaiming that chaos and disorder were preferable to colonial rule. The partition of India—the ensuing riots, with their estimated loss of life of two million people; displacement of ten million–twelve million people along religious lines; and creation of an overwhelming refugee crisis—was the tragic and violent legacy of India's nonviolent struggle for independence. As feared by Gandhi, in waging nonviolent struggle against the British, Hindus and Muslims violently turned against each other (Devji 2012, 163).

Ironically, even though Gandhi did not have faith in democracy and the state, when the displaced refugees started arriving in camps just before India's partition, Gandhi rejected help from private individuals and charitable organizations. On the one hand, he wanted the government to take responsibility, while on the other, he wanted the refugees to be treated, and to behave, like citizens in a democracy (Devji 2012, 188). In his view, without citizens' claiming their political rights and the state being accountable to its citizens, a robust democracy could not emerge (Devji 2012, 189). The sacrifice of lives and suffering were a price Gandhi was willing to pay to ensure that refugees would be treated as citizens rather than as victims and to establish a political relation between the state and the subalterns (Devji 2012, 189). Interestingly, Gandhi rejected the idea of inalienable rights, which formed the basis of the Universal Declaration of Human Rights (UNDHR), proposing instead the vision of citizenship of the world, which foregrounds duties over rights. In place of citizenship rights, which can be guaranteed only by individual states, Gandhi emphasized the idea of duties not limited by borders that could never be stripped or alienated by any political entity (Devji 2012, 190–91).

In his insistence that morality was universal without allowing exceptions, as this would compromise its legitimacy, Gandhi sounds surprisingly Kantian. Devji (2012, 132) avers that Gandhi "held nonviolence to be not only the rational, but also [the] inescapable conclusion of any ethics claiming universality for itself." Gandhi's most controversial position was his emphasis on nonviolent resistance against Nazism. Fighting violence and brutality with the same weapons, in Gandhi's view, were useless in saving humanity, suggesting instead that noncooperation would vanquish Nazism without armed opposition. Instead of defeating colonizers and fascists, Gandhi was interested in converting them to the cause of nonviolence (Devji 2012, 132). The endeavor was to confront violence with the force of suffering, and thereby transmute it into nonviolence (Devji 2012, 7). As Sharma (2021, 10) explains: "The practitioner of *ahiṃsā* pits his soul against the body of the tyrant in the hope of awakening the oppressor's soul. One can, therefore, never overdo *ahiṃsā*."

Gandhi (1977 [1939], 122) questioned the moral legitimacy and hypocrisy of the British war against German fascism in the name of freedom while Britain continually refused to give up its colonies. He appeals in a letter to

Hitler "in the name of humanity to stop the war" (Gandhi 1978 [1940], 253–55), which is cited as evidence of his naïve politics. Gandhi's warning of how matching Nazi violence with the armed intervention of the Allies would put the whole of humanity at risk came true in the bombing of Hiroshima and Nagasaki. When asked whether the atom bomb had antiquated nonviolence, Gandhi (1982 [1946], 371) responded, to the contrary, that "unless now the world adopts non-violence, it will spell certain suicide for mankind."

Instead of putting faith in state violence to defeat fascism, Gandhi encouraged private individuals, particularly those considered too vulnerable and oppressed to be vanguards, to act as moral agents of change. Some of Gandhi's closest friends were Jewish; he advised them to "not allow themselves to become the passive victims of Nazism" (Devji 2012, 135). When mocked for dangerous naïveté, Gandhi defended alleged pointless resistance for not only safeguarding the moral integrity of its agent in the present but also serving as an ideal for future practices (Devji 2012, 142). While violence has historical limits, nonviolence is universal, without exception, and thus abiding. Gandhi's approach demilitarizes resistance, rendering it quotidian and ubiquitous. Everyone might not have the capacity to access weapons or the ability to commit violence, but there is no one who cannot not be nonviolent.

The Bollywood actress Kangana Ranaut triggered controversy in India by remarking that, because the anticolonial struggle was achieved nonviolently, "freedom was given to us in Gandhi's begging bowl" (quoted in The Hindu 2021). Warning Indians to choose their heroes wisely, Ranaut mocks Gandhi by observing that "offering the other cheek gets you bheekh (alms) not azaadi (freedom)" (quoted in The Hindu 2021). In her view, India got true independence only in 2014, when the Hindu nationalists came to power. This reminds me of Hegel's (1988 [1837], 33) warning about history's revenge on revolutionary heroes, who are disgraced not because of their actions, but because they are rendered redundant, such that they "fall off like empty hulls from the kernel." The lament seems to bemoan the absence of Indian Jacobins and condemn Gandhian nonviolence for not being particularly heroic. What Ranaut fails to understand is that, like the Haitian insurgents', Gandhi's rallying cry for the anticolonial struggle in India was "liberty or death." But as King's (1959) reading of Gandhi elucidates, "Rivers of blood may have to flow before we gain our freedom, but it must be our blood." The relation between decolonization and nonviolence is a conundrum. In contrast to the political calculus of military strategy and biopolitical regimes that sacrifice life for the sake of race, religion, or national interest, nonviolence is experimental beyond the constraints of victory and defeat. Paradoxically, Gandhi (1976b [1937], 361) argues, only through willingness to suffer and mastering the art of "throwing away one's life" does one have the courage to practice nonviolence.

Gandhi placed particular emphasis on the voluntary sacrifices and nonviolent struggles of minorities, such as the Jewish people in Nazi Germany and Black people in the United States within the context of the civil rights movement. In his view, minorities could transform world history by being exemplary moral agents (Devji 2012, 59). Gandhi was of the opinion that the character not only of individuals, but also of collectivities, could be built through selfless suffering (Devji 2012, 3–4).

In contrast to Gandhi's understanding of vulnerable groups as the epitome of a nonviolent, resistant subjectivity, Ambedkar (2002 [1948], 487) avers: "Minorities are an explosive force which, if it erupts, can blow up the whole fabric of the state." It is notable that Arendt (1944, 108) speaks of "the pariah quality of Jewish existence." Originally, the term *pariah* referred to the lowest caste or outcasts in Hindu society. Arendt borrowed the concept to characterize the rebellious and oppositional stance of non-assimilated Jews. In her view, the pariah acts as a defiant critic and "champion of an oppressed people" (Arendt 1944, 108).

As a young boy, Ambedkar wished to study Sanskrit, but because he was a so-called untouchable, he was banned from learning the presumed holy language. He went on to get his graduate degree in English and Persian, his only available options. On the basis of his excellent English, he was offered a scholarship to study at Columbia University in New York, where he was a student of John Dewey (Omvedt 2005, 19). As pointed out by Roy (2017, 27), millions of Ambedkar statues all over India hold a book in the hand—namely, the Indian Constitution, which he played a vital role in conceptualizing. Gandhi's statues, by contrast, have him reading the Bhagavad Gita, a pivotal Brahmanical text on righteous war, which he called his "spiritual dictionary." Against Gandhi's highly idealized view of India as being spiritually superior to the West, Ambedkar highlights the violence of the Hindu caste system. For him, decolonization is a much more complex process than one of de-Westernization. As Ambedkar (2014b, 202) rightly points out, those who were fighting for the freedom of India were not necessarily fighting for the freedom "of the lowest of the low."

Ambedkar's positive attitude toward modernity stands in stark contrast to Gandhi's rejection of industrialization, Western medicine, and systems of education. Like Gandhi, Ambedkar drew on thinkers such as Marx and

Jean-Jacques Rousseau, even as he was unpopular with both the communists, who were mostly Brahmins unwilling to address the intersections of caste and class, and the secularists in India. A staunch constitutionalist and republican thinker, Ambedkar helped compose the constitution of free India, serving as the elected chairman of its drafting committee between 1947 and 1950 (Kumar 2015, 4). Prior to that, in December 1927, Ambedkar publicly burned a copy of the *Manusmṛti*, considered one of the oldest legal texts in the world, which had been used to formulate the Hindu law by the British colonial government. In contrast to Gandhi's *Hind Swaraj*, which is a rejection of Western civilization as (self-)destructive, Ambedkar's *Annihilation of Caste* is a treatise of resistance against the Hindu caste order, which he saw as violent and thus warranting eradication.

For Ambedkar, *Hind Swaraj* was testimony to Gandhi's unwillingness and inability to see the inextricable link between the caste-based division of labor and violence, which formed the foundation of capitalism in India (Kumar 2015, 12). Ambedkar critically links Gandhi's unwillingness to promote labor and caste reform to the marginalization of impoverished so-called untouchable communities from the political realm of civil disobedience (Kumar 2015, 13). Thus, Ambedkar (2014a, 72) condemns not only colonialism but also the Hindu caste system as inimical to norms of freedom and equality.

Regarding *Annihilation of Caste*, whose publication Ambedkar funded himself, Gandhi (1976a [1936], 135) remarked that the cost of the book should have been lower. Aishwary Kumar (2015, 13) wonders whether Gandhi suggested reducing the price so that the book might reach the masses or to trivialize Ambedkar's scholarship by suggesting the book was overpriced. Gandhi's hostility to Ambedkar was "a war against equality, which undercuts anticolonialism's emancipatory promise" (Kumar 2015, 14). When the British conceded to the provision of separate electorates for so-called untouchables, Gandhi threatened that he would fast to death. Ultimately, the provision was revoked, with Ambedkar being villainized for endangering both Gandhi's life and anticolonial unity by making such a demand. Commenting on the incident, Ambedkar (2014b, 259) wrote: "There was nothing noble in the fast. It was a foul and filthy act. . . . It was the worst form of coercion against a helpless people to give up the constitutional safeguards of which they had become possessed under the Prime Minister's Award and agree to live on the mercy of the Hindus. It was a vile and wicked act. How can the Untouchables regard such a man as honest and sincere?" Instead of enfranchising the so-called untouchables, Gandhi's strategies included victimizing or romanticizing them, attempting to include them in Hinduism by granting them entry into the temples. While Ambedkar perceives the untouchability question as a political one, for Gandhi it is a question of religious and social reform (Sharma 2021, 17).

Gandhi, the self-professed anarchist, dreamt of sovereignty without a state in the form of decentralized peasant economy (Mantena 2012). He idealized a stateless, nonviolent polity, while locating violence squarely in the realm of the state: "The State represents violence in a concentrated and organized form. The individual has a soul, but as the State is a soulless machine, it can never be weaned from violence to which it owes its very existence" (Gandhi 1974 [1934], 318). Against Gandhi's anti-statism, Ambedkar, the anti-caste radical and constitutionalist, was profoundly cognizant of the exclusionary nature of modern citizenship and "could apparently dream only in the language of the state" (Kumar 2015, 15). His statement "Gandhiji, I have no homeland" (quoted in Kumar 2015, 16) problematizes the anarchist enchantment with statelessness. As the first law minister of independent India, Ambedkar was acutely aware of both the enabling and the coercive aspects of constitutional power when envisioning "the conditions of egalitarian citizenship" in the "juridical and institutional languages of the state" (Kumar 2015, 17). He conceived the restitution of dignity for the so-called untouchables, who had suffered centuries of humiliation and exploitation "in terms of constitutional safeguards and juridical regulations against caste cruelty and religious oppression" (Kumar 2015, 20). While Gandhi foregrounded the moral over the political, Ambedkar interlinked the juridical, social, and political with the ethical. Gandhi's Western influences are celebrated as evidence of his ability to embrace the supposed enemy, whereas Ambedkar's commitment to republican constitutionalism is regrettably often dismissed as Eurocentric. Kumar (2015, 22, 260) points out that, while Gandhi and Fanon are celebrated as anticolonial thinkers and activists par excellence, Ambedkar's understanding of decolonization has not received the same global recognition. Gandhi and Fanon focused on freedom by overthrowing colonial rule. Ambedkar, by contrast, was committed to equality through the constitution of an independent state as guarantor of civic rights, resulting in the world's longest constitution (Kumar 2015, 25). When Gandhian and Fanonian revolutionary force is juxtaposed to Ambedkarite constitutional power, the tension between freedom and equality, "revolution and Constitution, popular sovereignty and shared vulnerability" remains unresolvable (Kumar 2015, 25). Gandhi's anticolonialism is state-phobic, while

Ambedkar's resistance to imperialist caste and class-based subjugation translates into constitutionalism. Kumar argues that Ambedkar's notion of "constitutional morality" opens up the "productive space between Constitution and insurrection, between civic virtue and civic disobedience" (Kumar 2015, 260). How can citizens—particularly, the weakest and most vulnerable—strike the right balance of obedience and resistance vis-à-vis the constitution, which can both protect and persecute them (Kumar 2015, 264)? Insofar as Ambedkar questions the sanctity of the very document he helped to compose, the designation of "insurrectionary constitutionalist" is indeed fitting (Kumar 2015, 265).

Gandhi's and Ambedkar's divergent relationship with Hinduism is also instructive. Gandhi's last words were *O Ram,* which stand inscribed on his memorial.[3] Ambedkar (2007 [1935], 271) famously declared: "It was my misfortune to be born a Hindu. I do not have the capacity to eliminate this defect in me. However, I do have the strength to not accept the humiliating practices that I was subjected to as an Untouchable. It is within my capacity to reject the Hindu religion. I will say this publicly, that even though I was born a Hindu, I will not die a Hindu." Ambedkar's utopia, in Roy's (2017, 32) reading was "an enlightened India . . . that fused the best ideas of the European Enlightenment with Buddhist thought." Gandhi, however, was wary of Western modernity: "God forbid that India should ever take to industrialism after the manner of the West. The economic imperialism of a single tiny island kingdom is today keeping the world in chains. If an entire nation of 300 millions took to similar economic exploitation it would strip the world bare like locusts" (Gandhi 1970 [1928], 311). Gandhi indeed rightly anticipated the brutality to which modernization, industrialization, and technology would lead, even as his nostalgia for "Indian pastoral bliss" disregarded how it dehumanized and humiliated the downtrodden, who were victims of the Hindu caste system on which his idealized villages stood (Roy 2017, 33). While Gandhi's village *swaraj* was a stateless ideal of enlightened anarchy of self-rule, on November 4, 1948, during the Constituent Assembly Debates, Ambedkar (1948, 486) made the remark: "What is the village but a sink of localism, a den of ignorance, narrow-mindedness and communalism?"

Gandhi preached the virtues of hereditary occupation to the so-called untouchables, while Ambedkar, in contrast, radically addressed the question of caste and untouchability by linking them to political economy and exploitation, going beyond the purity-pollution dynamics. Drawing on the European Enlightenment tradition and Buddhism, Ambedkar outlines how the disenfranchised have been cut off from both democracy and revolution through cognitive servitude (this resonates with Gayatri Chakravorty Spivak's position). He remarks:

> Why have the mass of people tolerated the social evils to which they have been subjected? There have been social revolutions in other countries of the world. Why have there not been social revolutions in India is a question which has incessantly troubled me. . . . On account of the Chaturvarnya, they could receive no education. They could not think out or know the way to their salvation. They were condemned to be lowly and not knowing the way of escape and not having the means of escape, they became reconciled to eternal servitude, which they accepted as their inescapable fate. (Ambedkar 2014a, 63).

Unfortunately, even as Ambedkar fought for the dignity of the depressed castes, his attitude toward the Adivasis—namely, the Indigenous—echoed the vocabulary of Western liberalism: He described them as "uncivilized" and "primitive" (Roy 2017, 102). Accordingly, the Indian Constitution of 1950, while giving the Adivasis the right to vote, made the state custodian of Adivasi homelands in the name of protecting them (Roy 2017, 102). This signals the difficult relation among revolution, constitution, and democracy.

Kumar (2015, 51) reads Ambedkar's approach to both imperialism and nationalism as one of "affirmative negativity" or "nonnegative negation." This involves "insurrectionary engagement" with both European Enlightenment and vernacular traditions to contest their coercive impulses. Importantly, Ambedkar had an equally "rebellious relationship with the document to which he has given the most productive and crucial years of his political life"; he declared his readiness to burn the constitution he had written if it failed to protect the minority from the majority (Kumar 2015, 342). For Ambedkar, this is the severest test of a democracy, which he describes as "revolutionary nonviolence" (Kumar 2015, 342).

In this section, I have outlined the deeply ambivalent dynamics between emancipation and violence, as well as between means and ends. Vis-à-vis the difficult task of decolonization, this leaves us with the challenging questions: How does power inform the exercise of critique? And how does critique feed power? One intuitively presumes that critical thought is contra violence; that it exposes and contests it. But what if the practice of critique itself produces and reinforces violence? What if the medicine kills the patient? In the next section, I show how critical thought can sustain and subvert power at once.

The Weapon of Criticism and
the Criticism of the Weapon

Critical thinking should expose the oppressive mechanisms within contemporary society while bolstering resistance efforts against discriminatory political, economic, social, and cultural frameworks. Ernst Bloch (1995 [1954–59]) invokes the notion of utopia to elucidate the role of critical practice, which involves the intertwining of immanent critique and the transformation of the present system to envision what is yet to come. This perspective requires an analysis of current social conditions to articulate the potential for a profoundly different future that emerges from existing struggles and contradictions. In positioning itself as a challenge to coercive exercise of power, critical practice can be "heroic" (Asad 2009a, 49). Jacques Derrida (1985, 87) suggests that critique is fundamentally an act of love rather than merely a negating force. However, while critique can both subvert and reinforce hegemony, it can also manifest as a form of cruelty, even as it advocates for emancipation.

In an era marked by planetary devastation, the rise of right-wing and white-supremacist ideologies, and multiple crises and conflicts leading to immiseration, dispossession, and disenfranchisement on a global scale, one of the most urgent and essential tasks for critical scholarship is to clarify the role of thinking. Building on Hegel, Marx (1992a [1843], 209) conceptualizes critique as "the self-clarification (critical philosophy) of the struggles and wishes of the age." Engels and he (1956 [1844–45]) disparage "critical criticism" that emerges from frustration and leads to inaction. This provokes pressing questions about whether critical theory has a responsibility to provide effective political responses to the problems it identifies and whether all optimism would be lost if it did not, consigning us to hopelessness in the face of intractable conditions that seem resistant to any effort at transformation.

An additional difficulty in examining the purpose of critique concerns the interplay between intellectual contemplation and political action. Theoretical pursuits are often spurned for failing to address the immediacy of current events or to provide timely guidance for policy and advocacy, provoking disaffection. Marx and Engels (1998 [1845], 253–54) notably remarked that "philosophy and the study of the actual world have the same relation to one another as onanism and sexual love." Critical thought is frequently disparaged as an impotent, self-serving, solitary endeavor detached from more transformative collective political practices.

Yet does our political attachment to the question "What to do?" obstruct rather than facilitate change? What happens to critical theory when it is freed from the imperative to provide normative blueprints for others, who are then relieved of the need to think for themselves? Critique, for Kant, involves contemplation of the possibilities and limits of thought. For Foucault (2007, 44), a "critical attitude" means transgressing the boundaries not only of how we think but also of how we live. By opening up space for previously foreclosed thought and action, critique entails *"the art of becoming a little less cowardly"* (Marasco 2015, 182).

In ancient Greek legal discourse, the terms *kritikos* and *krinein* encompassed the practices of dividing, sifting, distinguishing, and making judgments in response to crises, controversies, and disruptions within the polis (Koselleck 1988). Critique, as a manifestation of free and candid expression (*parrhesia*), was particularly linked to the Cynics. The Greek term *kynikos*, from which it originates, means dog-like. It is therefore fitting that the Cynics were referred to as the watchdogs of humanity, given their explicit intention to challenge prevailing norms and beliefs. Diogenes (2012, 24) famously stated, "Other dogs bite their enemies, I bite my friends to save them." Through the rigorous detection of fallacies over the ensuing centuries, critique increasingly came to represent the process of distinguishing reason from speculation. The most notable advocate of this approach was Kant, who, in reaction to Hume's skepticism, which challenged the certainty of epistemology, sought to prevent conjectural errors by confining pure reason within appropriate boundaries. Kant eventually termed his transcendental philosophy *critical,* delineating between the internal limits and possibilities of the knowledge process and the constraints imposed by external authority. Another facet of the Kantian approach is its emphasis on the deliberative process of engaging with others through the public exercise of reason. The tribunal of reason serves as the arena for both epistemological and ethical self-correction. Kant contends that everything, including reason itself, must be subjected to critique. This challenges the demand for absolute compliance and subjects every command to a process of rational and reflective scrutiny. Kant, drawing inspiration from Horace, invokes the courage of reason through the motto *Sapere Aude,* or "dare to know," as emblematic of the Enlightenment (Kant 1991a [1784], 54). If the primary barriers to freedom and emancipation are merely cowardice, inertia, or restrictions on the public exercise of reason, then individuals can alter their conditions by recognizing that their own lack of resolve and courage to use reason constitutes the source of their oppression. For Kant,

Enlightenment represents "man's emergence from his self-incurred immaturity." Ignorance, he argues, is not merely an absence of knowledge but a deficiency in will, reflecting "man's inability to make use of his understanding without direction from another" (Kant 1991b [1795], 54).

Hegel's (1968 [1802]) concept of immanent critique centers on the historical process from which critique emerges through the clash of internal contradictions and antagonisms. Rather than adopting an external standpoint as a point of departure, these fissures create the potential site for oppositional thought to arise. Marx drew inspiration from Hegelian philosophy, though he profoundly altered the concept of immanent critique. In his view, immanent principles serve as essential tools in the pursuit of progressive social transformation, as they offer a foundation for critique grounded in historical context. This immanent foundation became central to his groundbreaking critique of capitalism. Marx's analysis further elucidates the intricate relationship between society and the critical consciousness of its members. He asserts that the emancipation of the working class must be achieved through their own, collective efforts. Moreover, Marxist critical theory connects the public act of criticism to its revolutionary purpose. Transcending the boundaries set by traditional epistemology, Marx redefines critique as a tool for those striving to alter reality rather than merely to interpret it. Friedrich Nietzsche's (1998 [1889]) phrase "to philosophize with a hammer" is particularly useful here. For Nietzsche, critical thinking involves liberating oneself from borrowed conventions and accepted beliefs, and it is closely tied to the courage required to transgress these norms (Nietzsche 2019, 57). A fundamental aspect of critical thinking is the skepticism toward inherited ideas.

Edmund Husserl (1970 [1935]) explores the profound connection between critique and crisis, cautioning that the most significant crisis lies in the failure to recognize it. He posits that the true danger is forgetfulness, in which the past, if regarded solely as something that has occurred, loses its capacity for critical influence. The Nietzschean-Foucauldian notion of genealogy as countermemory assumes great significance. Genealogy, as a form of critique, functions as an inventory of our discourses and their power effects. If coercive regimes subjugate individuals, then for Foucault (1996a, 386), critique becomes the "art of voluntary inservitude, of reflective indocility." The essential function of critique is desubjectification. This critical attitude does not entail a categorical rejection of the art of government; rather, it challenges the technologies, tactics, and rationalities that make us governable.

Critical contemplation involves a rigorous examination of the deficiencies and limitations within its own processes. The Frankfurt School of critical theorists notably advanced this concept of self-reflexivity, illustrating how the antiauthoritarian ethos of Enlightenment reason inadvertently led to new modes of domination. Theodor Adorno and Max Horkheimer argue that, despite the failures of the Enlightenment, it should be not discarded but reconfigured. The role of critical theorists is to contest the dominance of positivist and instrumental frameworks that shape modern society and to activate forces of resistance in the pursuit of human liberation.

Despite significant differences, a dominant assumption within the Western paradigm is that critical discourse inherently fosters progressive politics. However, the well-known philosophical debate between Derrida and Foucault demonstrates that critical practice can serve both as a tool of coercion and as a means of emancipation. Derrida (1978, 33–34) rebuts Foucault's effort to transcend the Western mode of reason and the violence inherent within it. He notes that Foucault interrogates reason on behalf of those it has silenced; however, Derrida asserts that Foucault relies on the very language of reason he aims to surpass. The paradox is as follows: "The misfortune of the mad, the interminable misfortune of their silence, is that their best spokesmen are those who betray them best; which is to say that when one attempts to convey their silence itself, one has already passed over to the side of the enemy, the side of order, even if one fights against order" (Derrida 1978, 35–36).

If one must rely on the language of reason to advocate for the silenced, then avoiding complicity in reason's exclusions becomes impossible. By using language, one inevitably participates in the act of silencing and, consequently, engages in violence. There is no exception, which means that reason in itself cannot be overcome. Derrida (1978, 41–42) contends that Foucault is aware of this conundrum: Reason is not dispensable, and the language of violence cannot be employed to counteract exclusion. Derrida finds Foucault's assertions misleading because they deny the extent of their reliance on Western reason.

Despite the compelling nature of Derrida's criticisms, Foucault (1979) cautions that Derrida's stance undermines the emancipatory potential of contesting Western reason. If, as Derrida argues, language is intimately linked to exclusion and violence, then critical discourse inevitably replicates these mechanisms of violence. This suggests that violence is inescapable and nonviolence is elusive.

Derrida responds to Foucault by invoking Ludwig Wittgenstein's famous dictum, "About that which one cannot speak, one must remain silent," but contends that this should not deter us from speaking (Derrida 1996, 11). Derrida (1978, 358) observes that, while the language of reason is inherently conflicted, it also contains the imperative for its own critique. The central issue in the Foucault-Derrida debate is how to address and critique violence without perpetuating it in the process. Notably, in *Critique of Hegel's Philosophy of Right*, Marx (1992b [1843–44], 251) cautions that "the weapon of criticism cannot replace criticism of the weapons."

A notable historical instance of employing criticism as a tool was undertaken by the *nāstikas*, proponents of heterodox schools within classical Indian philosophy. Their theory and practice of *ahiṃsā* meticulously address the dynamics of power involved in the act of critique. In doing so, they seek to cultivate a nonviolent ethical framework for political intervention (Dhawan 2007, 301–5). As discussed earlier in this chapter, Gandhian anticolonial critique integrated the Marxist strategy of the general strike with *nāstika* (heterodox) ethics. It has been posited that Gandhi's nonviolent tactics were crucial in securing a moral high ground for the anticolonial struggle. Confronted with nonviolence, the colonizers found themselves in a difficult position; their own brutality came to symbolize the moral decay of their authority. However, as previously noted, Gandhi's experiments with nonviolence faced considerable opposition. For instance, in the context of the antiapartheid struggle, Nelson Mandela contended that Gandhian nonviolence might not always be practicable. He remarked: "Non-violent passive resistance is effective as long as your opponent adheres to the same rules as you do" (quoted in Hardiman 2003, 60). Similarly, Antonio Gramsci (2011b Q6 §78, 61) characterizes Gandhian tactics as a form of passive nonresistance, likening them to a "mattress against the bullet." Despite its favorable reception in some quarters, nonviolence as a method of critique has not universally resonated. Thus, the tension between critique and violence remains a complex and challenging issue.

An additional crucial dimension is the role of categories such as class, race, and gender. For example, in critical race theory, the term *critical* serves a dual role: It not only identifies *race* as a category of discrimination that must be addressed but also, following Kantian principles, defines the conditions of meaning and the boundaries of the concept of race. W. E. B. Du Bois's sharp analysis of the color line in *The Souls of Black Folk* (1996 [1903], 13) exemplifies this double function. His critique extends beyond challenging prevailing racist discourses to question the very framework of racial analysis itself. Thus, central to Du Bois's critical race theory is a metacritique of the theoretical approach to *race*.

Critical race feminists and intersectional feminists (Collins 2019; Crenshaw 1989; Davis 2019; hooks 1990; Lorde 2007) offer a nuanced analysis of the interlinkage among racial, gender, and sexual politics. They warn that addressing only one facet of domination risks perpetuating violence by neglecting other sources and manifestations of oppression. This underscores the necessity for anti-imperialist and antiracist critique within feminist and queer politics, while postcolonial studies must also incorporate a critique of reproductive heteronormativity. Addressing one without the other reinforces mechanisms of violent oppression (Castro Varela and Dhawan 2017).

This raises several critical questions: How can feminist, queer, and postcolonial theories stake a claim on the Enlightenment while also challenging it? If the critical tradition historically has been monopolized by Europeans and men, what role can their Other play in the task of critique? Given the conflation of Enlightenment with critique in the Western philosophical tradition, how can Enlightenment ideals be extended beyond their European origins and adapted to benefit marginalized groups? If the primary function of critique is to foster intellectual maturity, transforming individuals into autonomous thinkers who reject external authority, Talal Asad (2009b, 141) questions why, in the name of the critical tradition, the global North continues to impose its normative frames on the global South. Conversely, it is not enough simply to denounce Western racism and imperialism; the postcolony must also confront its own shortcomings and complicities. Historically, however, such self-critique has often been weaponized—used to delegitimize postcolonial, queer, and feminist perspectives—or condemned as anti-national and as undermining the broader struggle against neocolonialism.

The function of the critical thinker in society also demands closer scrutiny. On one hand, the role of the professional critic involves a rigorous framing of the task of critique, delineating its objectives, methodologies, and scope (Asad 2009a, 55). On the other hand, the freedom to critique is enshrined as both a right and an obligation of every modern individual, whose unceasing quest for truth epitomizes their political agency. Nonetheless, as Asad (2009a, 54) underscores, all critical practices are situated within the material conditions that shape their manifestation. The practice of critique, while challenging and reinforcing certain aspects, is itself facilitated and constrained by corporate and state power, which constitute the very conditions of criticism (Asad 2009a, 54). A case in point is the manner in which, within the current culture war–inflected social media platforms, right-wing ideologues and conspiracy theorists position themselves as public intellectuals, critics of the so-called deep state, self-proclaimed defenders of free speech, and purported victims of liberal regimes, mobilizing opposition to DEI (Diversity, Equity, and Inclusion) initiatives and what they label as gender ideology.

In light of these considerations, it can be contended that establishing appropriate criteria for a critique of violence remains both elusive and contentious. In addition, the Freudian belief that cultivating critical faculties can temper destructive impulses suggests a causal link between nonviolence and the practice of critique, a relationship that, in Western social and political thought, is often traced back to the Enlightenment. However, as has been argued throughout this book, the Enlightenment critical tradition is not solely emancipatory but also has coercive aspects; it not only is enabling but also bears elements of violence.

A good example of the normative dilemmas confronting processes of decolonization is the inconsistent approach of the postcolonial world to international legal, economic, and security order. The unspeakable tragedy of the entanglements between colonialism and National Socialism is unfolding in the wake of the 2023 Israel-Hamas war. South Africa's genocide allegation against Israel has resulted in the International Court of Justice (ICJ) in The Hague becoming a historic site of collision between narratives about law and justice, war and peace, legitimate and illegitimate violence. While some commend the trial as a postcolonial litmus test of the extent of the decolonization of the Western-led order, others view it as yet more evidence of alleged postcolonial antisemitism. The stakes could not be higher, for what stand on trial are the legitimacy of international law and the universal validity of human rights (Murithi 2024). Given that the ICJ's donors are predominantly from the Western countries, the reputation of the global rules-based order is being judged. However, it is an unparalleled example of the postcolonial world's ambivalent relationship with the Enlightenment, whose cursed long shadow is cast over current geopolitics.

On January 26, 2024, the ICJ ruled that some allegations of Israel committing genocide are plausible; however, the court stopped short of ordering a ceasefire. Although the genocide convention is a cornerstone of international law, the ICJ has no enforcement mechanism. As the ICJ's ruling resonated globally, the role of Judge Julia Sebutinde of Uganda, the first African woman to sit on the ICJ, who voted against all of the provisional measures South Africa sought against Israel, became a focal point of discussion. While countries such as the United States, United Kingdom, and Germany belittled South Africa's case, Sebutinde's dissent highlights the plurality of approaches in the postcolonial world. Sebutinde claimed that the conflict between Israel and Palestine was "political," and not a legal dispute to be resolved through "judicial settlement by the Court" (ICJ 2024a). While some hailed her as the "voice of reason" (Higgins 2024) on the ICJ, others pilloried her, even as Uganda distanced itself from Sebutinde, stating that her position did not reflect Uganda's stance on Palestine. It has been reported that Sebutinde is affiliated with Watoto Church, one of the largest and most influential Evangelical Christian churches globally. The church is noted not only for its support of the death penalty for LGBTQI people but also for its adherence to Christian Zionist doctrine. Moreover, Sebutinde's husband is among the founding members of Watoto Church, prompting human rights advocates to question her impartiality (Schlindwein 2024).

Another example of the cognitive dissonance of the postcolonial condition is reflected in the relationship between the Arab world and the United States. Despite professing solidarity with Palestinians, Arab states actively court figures like Donald Trump, who is openly Islamophobic and proclaims unwavering support for Israel, as demonstrated by the repression of pro-Palestinian advocacy on US campuses. The United States, in turn, sells billions of dollars' worth of military equipment to Arab states that Israel perceives as threats to its sovereignty. This dynamic reveals ideological inconsistencies and political opportunism that define the postcolonial condition, highlighting the extent to which emancipatory ideals such as human rights and humanitarianism are not universally upheld but are instead strategically and selectively deployed by both global powers and regional actors to serve shifting political and geopolitical interests.

The Postcolonial Critique of Normative Violence

Postcolonial scholars are mindful of how lofty critical discourses, from Kant to Marx, all legitimized colonial violence. This is the very reason that the postcolonial world has difficulty trusting the Enlightenment's promises of peace and order. Fanon (1963 [1961], 43) avers:

During the period of decolonization, the native's reason is appealed to. . . . But it so happens that when the native hears a speech about Western culture he pulls out his knife—or at least he makes sure it is within reach. The violence with which the supremacy of white values is affirmed, and the aggressiveness which has permeated the victory of these values over the ways of life and of thought of the natives mean that, in revenge, the native laughs in mockery when Western values are mentioned in front of him. . . . In the period of decolonization, the colonized mock these very values, insult them, and vomit them up.

Instead of accepting European rhetoric at face value, Fanon (1986 [1952], 224) argues that the oppressed are capable of reflecting on their lived experiences of colonial subjugation and the farce of Western ideals. While violence exerted by the West is sublimated through justificatory narratives, liberation struggles are demonized as reckless terror and destructive hatred.

A concern often raised in the face of postcolonial-queer-feminist criticism of Enlightenment values of reason, secularism, and human rights is that this approach reinforces anarchic violence, religious conservatism, moral relativism, and ethnocentric nativism. It is argued that, instead of emancipating us from fascism and nationalism, the critique of Enlightenment rationality has ironically strengthened anti-Enlightenment ideologies. An extreme example of antimodernity ideology is the Islamic State in West Africa commonly known as Boko Haram, which loosely translates as "Western education is forbidden." All that is associated with the West is rejected as sacrilege and sin. From climate change denial to white supremacism, antirational, antiliberal, and antiscience ideologies are thriving in the current political climate. Critics of the Enlightenment, such as the postmodernists, intersectional feminists, and postcolonial scholars— or what, in France, is labeled Islamo-leftism (*islamo-gauchisme*) (Dacher 2021)—are being held responsible for the rise of so-called post-truth politics. Assailing Enlightenment norms and ideals is considered dangerous and a threat to progressive and emancipatory politics. Leftist critical theory is accused of dovetailing with right-wing ideologies in their distrust of democratic institutions, such as the judiciary, as well as the demonization of the free press as a handmaiden of neoliberal capitalism. The indictment of the Enlightenment as the source and origin of modernity's horrors, it is contended, fails to recognize its accomplishments.

However, as has been outlined in the previous chapters, Enlightenment-inspired institutions are themselves entrenched in, and therefore perpetuate structures of, violence. Democracy, human rights, and transnational justice are not only beacons of progressive politics; they are also deeply complicit in dynamics of violence. Adorno (2005c [1963], 90) astutely remarked: "I consider the survival of National Socialism within democracy to be potentially more menacing than the survival of fascist tendencies against democracy."

Although the idea of democracy is rooted in ancient Greece, it is a preeminent Enlightenment norm linked to the emergence both of the modern administrative state and liberal constitutionalism (Bohman 2005, 357). The collective will of the people promises to regulate social, political, and economic processes justly. Furthermore, liberal approaches to democracy, going back to Hobbes, tout their ability to tame violence and guarantee peace and justice for the polity, who, in exchange for their obedience of law, receive security and liberty through the state's monopoly on violence. In the face of objections, the oft-quoted adage by Dewey (1946, 144) is cited: "The cure for the ills of democracy is more democracy." What is often disregarded is Dewey's stipulation—namely, that the ills can be remedied only by becoming a democracy that is genuinely of a different kind. One of the difficulties with this liberal, modern narrative is that it sounds like an "engineering problem," (Bohman 2005, 357) in which the entire system would function well if informed and trained citizens were to make optimal, rational decisions and choices. The formalization of reflexivity and judgment in democratic procedures promises the smooth exercise of normative and deliberative powers, where persuasion prevails instead of coercion (Bohman 2005, 358).

Postcolonial-queer-feminist scholars, however, warn that the current phase of populism and nationalism has embedded the most pernicious and coercive aspects of democracy within the system, leading to the tyranny of the majority. Instead of becoming weapons of the weak, democracy, justice, human rights, and rule of law increasingly function as instruments of coercion. Here Butler's (1999, xx) notion of normative violence—namely, a violence of norms—is extremely relevant. When certain subjects cannot fulfil the norms of citizen or human, they are vulnerable to violence in its varied forms. However, those privileged subjects who qualify as citizen or human are protected by democratic norms and international laws concerning human rights. Postcolonial-queer-feminist scholars particularly focus on the weaponization of norms of gender justice and women's human rights by Western states to wage wars and legitimize violence against the non-Western Others. Despite such misuses and abuses, postcolonial critique does not advocate renouncing norms of freedom or justice. Instead, it attempts to resist their coercive instrumentalization.

Ironically, colonialism and, subsequently, neocolonialism are classic cases of victim blaming, with the (formerly) colonized being constituted as the source of violence, threatening Western norms and values along with the rule of law and order. The defense of land and life by the Indigenous was an affront to the European colonizers, who claimed that they had come bearing the gifts of the Enlightenment and expected the natives' gratitude and appreciation in return. Kant, for instance, argued that "one is authorized to use coercion against someone who already, by his nature, threatens him with coercion" (Kant 1991c [1797], 122). If Europe's others are characterized as those who embrace a lawless freedom, then preemptive strikes against them are justified. Accordingly, it is permissible to use unilateral coercion against non-Europeans if the end is to compel them into a juridical state of society (Kant 1991c [1797], 127). Here the crucial categories of legitimate and illegitimate violence become decisive in justifying colonialism. Antony Anghie (2007, 13) gives the historical example of the jurist and theologian Francisco de Vitoria (1492–1546), who is considered the father of international law for his theories on the law of war. According to Vitoria, the difference between Spaniards and *Indios* was that the latter, due to their alleged barbaric cultural practices and lack of a legal personality, were not capable of being sovereign (Anghie 2007, 27). Incapable of confirming to universal laws—specifically, Spanish laws—Indigenous people forfeited their autonomy, while the Spaniards were justified in imposing their norms, practices, and identity on them (Anghie 2007, 29). Anghie demonstrates how Vitoria's arguments significantly informed the development of international law on three counts. First, certain groups of people could justifiably be excluded from the sphere of sovereignty by virtue of not fulfilling European norms, which were declared to be universal. Second, those who possessed sovereignty are therefore justified to dominate the nonsovereign. And third, refusal to assimilate provided further justification for colonialism (Anghie 2007, 31).[4]

In the current situation, Anghie's arguments gain significance in the context of the International Criminal Court (ICC), which so far has pursued only prosecutions in African countries (Kimani 2009). Among the ICC's stated objectives is improving national justice systems and the rule of law in so-called developing countries. Critics point out that in cases such as northern Uganda, the prosecution by the ICC has ironically weakened the local justice system, thereby undermining long-term stable peace. The legitimacy and efficiency of local mechanisms and practices have been eroded through top-down Eurocentric norms that ignore the singularity of the context in which they are to be operationalized (Mbeki and Mamdani 2014). The constitution of the non-Western world as incapable of self-governance, as in the case of Libya, justified Western intervention and sanctions in the name of protecting the liberal international order.

Postcolonial feminists highlight how imperialism mobilized and continues to mobilize specific discourses about gendered violence to (re)legitimize itself ever anew. Spivak (1999, 287), for instance, examines how, as a civilizing mission in which "the white man saves the brown woman from the brown man," colonial regimes instrumentalized gender violence and, in a key maneuver, reduced native women to the status of supposed victims. This justified the imposition of the presumed modernizing and liberating regime of empire—a process that also consolidated imperial Europe's self-image as civilizationally superior. This kind of victim talk continues to justify "rescue narratives" in which native subjects are constituted and depicted as in need of deliverance (Abu-Lughod 2013). The fact that this is still employed to legitimize contemporary interventions—for instance, in Afghanistan—proves that gender continues to function as an alibi for neocolonialism. The Sri Lankan feminist Malathi de Alwis (2010) highlights how the "injured body of the Third World woman," especially in the case of "rape narratives" in conflict and post-conflict contexts, becomes a site of "victim spectacle" and focuses on how national and international elite consume the pain of others. The production of a form of transnational solidarity functions through identification with the Third World woman's suffering. De Alwis questions whether we are capable of empathizing with the pain of others at all. Or does that pain serve only to affirm our humanity and our capacity to care, and should we even be allowed to witness their grief? This, of course, is accompanied by the need for supposed authentic victims who truly deserve our benevolence. What do we do with our will to empower the presumed weak and the vulnerable? How is the distance between the supposed victims and the saviors to be negotiated?

The ideological conflict and collaboration between colonial and native patriarchies are equally important to consider. Similarly, the complicity of Western feminism in colonialism, as well as in neocolonialism, risks being obscured by discourses of alleged global sisterhood. Here it is particularly important to investigate the processes by which specific gender norms become hegemonic and thereafter frame the discourses of gender justice and women's human rights. Postcolonial feminists explore ways to address issues of sexual violence and gender injustice, particularly in the global South, without reinforcing Orientalist and Eurocentric impulses in the global North. Since the incidents in Cologne in 2016, when hundreds of women reported sexual assaults and thefts on New Year's Eve, primarily attributed to groups of men of North African and Arab descent, and the onset of the #MeToo movement, the issue of gender violence is increasingly receiving attention in the media and in policy discourses, as well as in feminist scholarship in the global North. Previously, these issues were deemed relevant only in the global South. At the same time, justified concerns are being voiced by postcolonial-queer-feminist scholars and activists regarding the weaponization of sexual violence by hegemonic forces to stigmatize migrant communities and postcolonial societies as inherently violent and misogynistic. The troubled relationship among violence, law, and justice indicates the challenges of decolonizing geopolitics. A closer look at the issue of legitimate violence is needed to understand the normative dilemmas of postcolonial jurisprudence.

According to the Hobbesian understanding of *social contract*, entering state sovereignty replaces the primitive violent condition of the state of nature with rule of law, which guarantees peace and order. Any contestation of state authority, it is warned, risks a relapse into anarchic extrajuridical violence. Against this prevailing doxa, Walter Benjamin's influential essay *Critique of Violence* reflects on the normative relation between law and justice as they intersect in violence. Benjamin (1996 [1921], 236) explores the different conditions under which an action may be judged to be violent. An instrumentalist approach, often provided by the state and the legal system, seeks to furnish grounds for distinguishing between legitimate and illegitimate means and ends. The state tries to establish a monopoly on violence by restricting others from exercising it. As Benjamin (1996 [1921], 238) argues: "From this maxim it follows that the law sees violence in the hands of individuals as a danger undermining the legal system." What is most threatening to the state is not the legality or illegality of people's ends, but whether these ends are pursued with violence; thus, it is the mere existence of violence outside the law that constitutes a threat (Newman 2004, 571). Distinguishing between lawmaking and law-preserving types of violence, Benjamin contends that both lead to a reinforcement of the juridical and, consequently, of power. Law-preserving violence, either in the implementation of existing laws or the amendment of particular laws, preserves the authority of the legal system and the state. Lawmaking violence, directed toward the toppling of existing laws, simply substitutes new laws for old ones. The symbolic place of the law is preserved and reinforced in both forms of violence (Newman 2004, 574). For Benjamin (1996 [1921], 243), every juridical or legal contract is founded through violence. There is no contract that does not have violence as both an origin (*Ursprung*) and an outcome (*Ausgang*). In his view, revolution as the destruction of the state apparatus, and thereby of all law, is to be associated not with violence but, rather, with a utopian moment of nonviolence (Avelar 2005, 98). The depravity of an institution occurs when it disregards the violent origin from which it emerged (Avelar 2005, 97). In other words, it is in the silencing of a primordial violence that the worst form of violence occurs, as this legitimizes the most brutal forms of prevailing violence (Avelar 2005, 97). One of the greatest contributions of Benjamin's analysis is his critique of the erasure of "originary violence."

A "union without violence" (*gewaltlose Einigung*), in Benjamin's (1996 [1921], 244) view, is possible only in the private world, when ruled by a "culture of the heart" (*die Kultur des Herzens*), wherein cordial courtesy, sympathy, love of peace, trust, and friendship are present. However, the nonviolent resolution of conflicts is plausible only so long as the possibility of violence is not totally excluded in principle (Benjamin 1996 [1921], 244–45). Along similar lines, one of the most important lessons Foucault (1978, 95) teaches us is that "resistance is never in a position of exteriority in relation to power." That is, resistance, by its nature, arises from power, in both its productive and its repressive and violent manifestations.

The justification of violence in the name of peace and justice is also addressed by Emmanuel Levinas, who proposes nonviolence-oriented ethics that unconditionally privilege peace over war. Both Gandhi and Levinas understand justice in terms of nonviolent encounters with alterity, where love and compassion are bestowed even on enemies. This is the origin of unlimited responsibility, even for one's persecutor, which leads to the rejection of the brutality of violence. For Levinas, not a fear *of* the Other but a fear *for* the Other's death and suffering binds us to the Other through speech, where the Other is just an interlocutor and not an opponent or enemy. Thus, according to him, insofar as entering the realm of speech and coming face to face with alterity is inextricably linked to the renunciation of violence, language is nonviolent (Tahmasebi-Birgani 2014, 131–32). Responding to Levinas's claim that peace, and not violence, was the originary state, Derrida (1978, 147) maintains that all discourse is primordially violent, such that "violence appears with articulation." Accordingly, a nonviolent language would have to be one that goes without a verb, without predication, without *to be*. Predication is the first violence, such that Levinasian absolute peace could exist only in the realm of absolute silence, in a utopia without language. For Derrida, "Pure non-violence, like pure violence, is a contradictory concept," in which both pure violence and pure nonviolence are equally impossible (Derrida 1978, 147).

Taking inspiration from Benjamin and Derrida, the feminist political theorist Drucilla Cornell explains how power struggles and violence masquerade as the rule of law. She argues that even as law aspires to be just, justice, in falling back on violence, always eludes law. This inescapable paradox makes justice an aporia. Cornell (1992, 167) warns that what is "rotten" in a legal system is its erasure of its violent origins, so that it dresses itself up as justice. This is particularly instructive in the context of the discussion about the genealogy of international law and its involvement in the continued disenfranchisement of postcolonial states, which—even after the achievement of formal independence—continue to be caught in a relation of structural inequality with their former colonizers. Because this historical complicity in colonial violence is erased, it is possible for international law—for example, human rights law—to "dress up" as a mechanism for justice. On the one hand, ideals of progress, development, and rights, which are all promoted by international institutions, continue to justify the West's humanitarian and military intervention in the non-Western world and may be read as neocolonialism by other means. On the other hand, fragile postcolonial states often abdicate their responsibility for protecting their most vulnerable citizens in the name of their powerlessness vis-à-vis the growing clout of international institutions.

In "Force of Law," Derrida (2002 [1994]) insists on the undecidability, discontinuity, slippages, and incommensurability between justice and law. Even as one is necessary for the operation of the other, and even as they are co-implicated, each is distinct from the other. Law, as the exercise of justice, is a system of regulated and coded prescriptions—both closed and calculable—that thereby ensures stability, regularity, and consistency (Derrida 2002 [1994], 250). Derrida (2002 [1994], 233) unfolds how there can be no law without force. Justice compels us to engage persistently with the law vis-à-vis the particular situation, which differs from case to case, and to engage with that which is overlooked, excluded, erased, and silenced by the law. This demands permanent revision, reinvention, and rejustification of law in the course of its effort to exercise justice (Derrida 2002 [1994], 251). United

Nations Security Council Resolution (UNSCR) 1325 on women, peace, and security is a case in point. In the aftermath of the transitional justice processes for Rwanda und Yugoslavia, UNSCR 1325 was ratified on October 31, 2000; it reaffirmed sexual violence as both a crime against humanity and a crime of genocide. This revision and inclusion came as a response to criticism of previous laws' inability to implement justice on behalf of survivors of sexual violence, which testifies to their agency. Law cannot insulate itself from the ethical interventions of justice, from the call to respond to the specific and particular. The challenge is to navigate the tension between a justice responsive to singularity and the normative imperative of justice grounded in universality. It is about being not only within legality or right but also within justice (Derrida 2002 [1994], 245).

Law functions as both a conduit to justice and a potential instrument of violence. Consequently, when demands placed on the state and the rule of law inadvertently bolster their coercive capacities, a critical question arises: How should (antiracist and postcolonial) feminism engage with law and the state? In the effort to leverage legal frameworks for the benefit of marginalized groups, does postcolonial feminism risk capitulating to the very power structures it seeks to challenge? Moreover, can the state's coercive mechanisms truly eradicate the violence inflicted on vulnerable citizens and noncitizens? The British sociologist Carol Smart (1989, 12, 161) argues, "Just as medicine is seen as curative rather than iatrogenic, so law is seen as extending rights rather than creating wrong. . . . [W]e need to consider that in exercising law we may produce effects that make conditions worse, and that in worsening conditions we make the mistake of assuming that we need to apply more doses of legislation." Medicine not only addresses and cures disease but also fosters the development of a medical profession and a pharmaceutical industry. Similarly, law does more than resolve disputes; it also cultivates a legal profession and a legal industry, which, in turn, reinforce patriarchal and racist systems.

As Derrida (2002 [1994], 244) insightfully notes, "Law is not justice[, although] it is just that there be law." While law and justice are fundamentally interconnected, law is continually interrupted by the elusive and incalculable nature of justice. Each legal decision aims to implement justice but is perpetually confronted by indeterminacy (Derrida 2002 [1994], 252); hence, it must be continually revised to address what it excludes, silences, and neglects. Justice surpasses law, even though it cannot be fully realized without the regulatory structure of law. This necessitates deconstructive vigilance and meticulous effort from those who dispense justice. Spivak famously notes that while law may not always deliver justice, one "cannot not want" (Spivak 1999, 84) the empowering potential that it offers, even as its coercive and violent aspects must be critically challenged. As Spivak (2018a) suggests, "Let's focus on the law, but think justice." This perspective does not advocate for the judicialization of politics, where judicial mechanisms are employed to resolve moral and social conflicts, or for judicial supremacy. However, I remain skeptical of arguments that call for legal and institutional passivity in addressing social, political, and economic issues (Dhawan 2019, 2020). I do not support the idea of allowing legal procedures to replace public deliberation and nonjudicial negotiations, as this could lead to judicial overreach and the dominance of law over social and political relations. The right of (non)citizens to engage in constitutional resistance against the state's coercive powers must always be safeguarded. The aim, however, is for legal frameworks to do more than shield victims of racial and gender-based violence; they should also provide vulnerable communities with pathways to redress. This vision aspires to create a more democratic and just society in which marginalized (non)citizens can depend on the state to rectify inequalities. Such an approach would not stop at merely defending against homophobia, antisemitism, racism, and sexism. It would actively work to secure dignity and equal status for all members of society. Given the commitment of postcolonial-queer-feminist scholarship and activism to combating discrimination, demanding state passivity in the face of racist and sexist violence would be politically counterproductive. While concerns about the state's coercive power are valid, rejecting state intervention to protect vulnerable groups carries significant risks. Although there is an inherent discontinuity between law and justice, attempting to shield justice from law by confining mechanisms of racial and sexual justice to informal, extrastate spaces is not a viable approach to political contestation. Dismissing the rule of law as an essential avenue for redress would mean abandoning several systems that safeguard against racialized sexual violence and discrimination, which are sustained by the state's monopoly of violence. The critical question is whether the state can function as a conduit for the interests of those whose powerlessness has supported its authority. Interestingly, Butler (2012, 94–98) concedes in an interview: "Of course, I want legal protections for certain kinds of freedoms. . . . The point is not to be against all law, nor is it to live without any laws. The point, in my view, is to develop a critical relation to law which is, after all, a field of power, one that is differentially applied and supported." The double bind and aporia of law, justice, and violence, then, is not to be resolved. This once again confronts us with the state and its monopoly on violence.

While social contract theorists such as Hobbes link anarchic violence with lawlessness and foresee the end of violence through the social contract, Foucault, Butler, and Mbembe trace an alternative genealogy that links sovereign power with genocidal violence and biopolitics. The complex and ambivalent dynamic among the state, law, and violence is astutely captured by King (1987 [1967], 202):

> As I have walked among the desperate, rejected, and angry young men, I have told them that Molotov cocktails and rifles would not solve their problems. I have tried to offer them my deepest compassion while maintaining my conviction that social change comes most meaningfully through nonviolent action. But they asked . . . , "What about Vietnam?" They asked if our own nation wasn't using massive doses of violence to solve its problems, to bring about the changes it wanted. Their questions hit home, and I knew that I could never again raise my voice against the violence of the oppressed in the ghettos without having first spoken clearly to the greatest purveyor of violence in the world today: my own government.

This confronts us with the following conundrum: If the means to ending (colonial) violence is through the establishment of the (postcolonial) state and rule of law, what is to be done when the (postcolonial) state itself is violent? If the very purpose of the (postcolonial) state is to put an end to (colonial) violence, opposing the existence of the postcolonial state would be counterproductive. Tragically, the founding of postcolonial states has not ushered in an overcoming of coercion and violence. Lofty anticolonial ideals of freedom and equality and the promise of peace, progress, and order regrettably resulted in the unfinished project of decolonization. The role of the state in this process remains debatable.

In the previous chapters, I discussed postcolonial critique of European Enlightenment, and in chapter 4 I presented a detailed analysis of the conundrums of anti-state politics. In this final section, I argue that, despite the genocidal violence that accompanied state making in Europe and beyond, one "cannot not" (Spivak 1989, 214) favor norms of sovereignty and constitutionalism, which are pivotal for subaltern groups. It is important to focus once again on the state as recent abolitionist approaches condemn it as the sole source of violence and coercion.

The Genocidal Versus the Missing State

The long-touted claim that democratic forms of rule promote and protect peace and justice is at variance with the historical experience of how the emergence of liberal democracies and rule of law in Europe went hand in glove with genocidal violence in the colonies. Despite proclamations of norms of equality and freedom, Western capitalist societies continue to be the locus of repression and surveillance, within their own territories but also globally. Linking disciplinary power and biopolitics, Foucault (1978, 149–50) provides an astute analysis of how states exercise the power to decide life and death. He considers Nazism the epitome of state racism in that it generalized "the sovereign right to kill" (Foucault 2003, 259–60). In his analysis of state racism, Foucault, however, misses a chance to consider colonialism. This is taken up by Mbembe, whose notion of necropolitics expands Foucault's ideas of biopolitics (politics of life), thanatopolitics (politics of death), and biopower. Combining Foucault's insights with Fanon's, Mbembe (2019a, 92) highlights the creation of "death-worlds" globally. Technologies of state terror and institutional racism have pushed certain racialized populations into "a permanent condition of 'being in pain'" (Mbembe 2019a, 91). A continuity between plantation slavery and contemporary forms of resource extraction and destruction of the biosphere can be traced (Mbembe 2019b). Furthermore, colonial racism is mutating into digital racism, with machine learning and "the cult of data" (Mbembe 2019b) replacing critical thought.

In contrast to a commonsense understanding of sovereignty as framing norms of democracy, peace, and justice, Mbembe, following Foucault, argues that politics as war by other means implies that sovereignty resides above all in the power to determine who is disposable (Mbembe 2019a, 80). The parameters for this are determined on the basis of an understanding of friend-enemy relations that underwrite the state and its wars, reducing certain populations to the status of "the living dead" (Mbembe 2019a, 92). Necropolitical power is about the abolishing of protections and guarantees such as law, rights, freedom, and responsibility to be able to kill with impunity, revealing the constitutive and latent violence underlying democracies (Mbembe 2019a, 27).

In the face of state racism and terror, Mbembe pleads for justice without vengeance. Taking inspiration from Fanon's reflections on healing and repairing the world as an antidote to enmity and destruction, Mbembe

(2019a, 139–41) suggests that "radical decolonization" could be achieved if the postcolonial world were "the origin of the future." This is not a mere undoing or reversal of colonial logic but an opening up of the unexpected and incalculable, the new and the not yet. It is a move away from brutality (*brutalisme*) and enmity to a politics of care and repair. Those denied subjectivity and humanity can contribute to the project of a shared planetarity. However, to chart postimperialist futures, the issues of restitution, repatriation, and reparation must be addressed. Engaging with Afrocentric, Afropessimist, and Afrofuturist trends, Mbembe (2019a, 161) alludes not only to the impossibility, but also to the never-ending process, of undoing and overcoming historical violence, which goes beyond formal political, economic, and social independence and self-rule in the postcolonial world. To this end, one must "recover the faculty of critique, re-educate our desires and rehabilitate reason as a key faculty for any project of freedom or emancipation. Reason is under siege, reduced as it is to its instrumental dimension. . . . [D]emocracy cannot survive in the absence of reason, that we cannot share the world, repair it or properly take care of life in the absence of a reformed notion of reason, one that marries thinking, feeling and projecting" (Mbembe 2019b). Such arguments contradict the accusations that postcolonial thought is anti-Enlightenment and anti-reason. As argued throughout the book, decolonization entails not only a multidirectional critique of the exclusionary aspects of Western reason, but also essentialist claims to difference in anticolonial radical thought such as Négritude and the decolonial option. This involves exploring possibilities of reason in non-Orientalist, nonracist, and nonsexist terms, which is much more complex than overcoming Eurocentrism. Thus, even as I have outlined the violent trajectory of European norms, I am wary of forsaking principles of justice, democracy, and human rights—all legacies of European Enlightenment.

As outlined in chapter 4, postcolonial scholars present a compelling critique of the genocidal state as a continuation of colonial terror. Sovereign power exercised by the state involves both instituting and suspending law through the declaration of exception (Banerjee 2017, 27). Advocates of abolitionist politics focus on camps, prisons, internment, occupation, segregation, and apartheid—common manifestations of how states exercise their monopoly on violence. For abolitionists, decolonization is understood as the defunding and dismantling of the racist-patriarchal-capitalist state, along with the demonopolization of its coercive powers. Unfortunately, in foregrounding anti-state politics, advocates of the abolitionist approach seem to disregard an important lesson that Foucault imparted: that violence has multiple sources. By presuming the state to be inherently necropolitical, abolitionists are unable to account for the differential forms of state building and governmental techniques that produce varied forms of subjectivities.

In the first volume of *The History of Sexuality*, Foucault (1978, 94) asserts that "power comes from below," with "no binary all-encompassing opposition between rulers and ruled at the root of power relations." Making use of the Gramscian notion, Foucault speaks of hegemonic effects to explain the manifold relations of force and power struggles that come into play in families and institutions. As discussed in detail earlier, Foucault thereby debunks the top-down approach to power, which understands resistance and critique in terms only of being against the state and its institutions. Foucault traces the "negative theology of the state as the absolute evil" back to German Ordoliberalism (Cook 2018, 33) from which state phobia emerges. The market becomes the "economic tribunal" to test governmental action (Foucault 2008, 247) "as a site of truth for governmental practice" (Cook 2018, 33). In this context, Foucault (2008, 187) calls the neoliberal view of the state "inflationary" on the grounds that it postulates "a kinship . . . between different forms of the state, with the administrative state, the welfare state, the bureaucratic state, the fascist state, and the totalitarian state all being . . . successive branches of one and the same great tree of state control in its continuous and unified expansion."

Taking inspiration from Foucault, I would argue that in addition to the repressive state apparatus, we must consider how states create other forms of infrastructure such as hospitals, schools, universities, and clinics. Although early Foucault condemned these as sources of disciplinary power and, accordingly, Mbembe would associate them with necropower, these sites present a deeper ambivalence regarding the liminal relation of life to death. Otherwise, given their staunch condemnation of state power, neither Foucault nor Mbembe would have worked at a university or visited a hospital when ill.[5] As argued previously, reducing the state to its genocidal drive obscures its enabling capacities. The COVID-19 pandemic is an instructive lesson in how, even as some states, such as the United States, Brazil, and Sweden, prioritized economy over life, others, such as Taiwan, New Zealand, and South Korea, mobilized the state apparatus, including the bureaucracy and public health-care system, to provide targeted economic and medical assistance to shield its most vulnerable citizens.[6] The disparity in mortality rates is indicative of how the sovereign right "to make live and to let die" (Foucault 2003, 241) can counter the biopolitical project of letting the old, infirm, and presumably economically nonproductive subjects die.

The deployment of the state's monopoly on violence in numerous forms—whether it is in the closing of its borders, lockdowns, or the enforcement of mandatory mask wearing in the name of fighting the virus—ironically protected some sections of the supposedly weak from the indifference of the purportedly healthy neoliberal subjects, who prioritized their freedom over the vulnerability of their fellow citizens. The hoarding of toilet paper became emblematic of the neoliberal subject's panic and anxiety in times of crisis. Other notable phenomena were the anti-restriction protests against pandemic protection measures, including the storming of the German Reichstag, the symbol of postfascist Germany. Thus, we witnessed *freedom rallies* (mostly in the global North) against the pastoral state's purported "corona fascism," when it implemented quarantine measures and curtailed the right to mobility and assembly. By foregrounding the genocidal state, abolitionists disregard aspects of social security, public health, and education—namely, strategies of fostering life. Necropolitics and sovereignty are conflated and become analytically indistinguishable. With technologies of death as the main focus, politics of care and welfare are ignored.

By contrast, there is the example of what I refer to as the missing state in India. For its May 2021 edition, *Outlook India* magazine printed a blank white page on its cover, resembling a missing poster. The cover stated that the government of India was missing amid the devastating second COVID-19 wave. It also specified that, if the government were found, the citizens of India should be notified.[7] With funeral pyres burning around the clock and cremation grounds running out of space, images of bodies floating in the Ganges or buried in the sand of its banks circulated globally, evidence of what happens when the state fails not only in its most fundamental function of protecting the lives of its citizens, but also in granting some basic dignity in death. While the living could not be heard in India, the dead could not be silenced. During the devastating second wave, India, the biggest vaccine producer in the world, had no vaccines left to inoculate its most vulnerable and needy (Yeung and Mitra 2021). Paradoxically, while some of the citizens in the global North were protesting against their states' disciplinary and normalizing powers, these richer states were pursuing "vaccine nationalism" or "vaccine apartheid" (Ivanova 2021). Germany strongly rejected the proposal to temporarily waive patent protections on COVID-19 vaccines, a move that would have allowed broader global access to vaccine production and distribution during the pandemic (Hecking et al. 2021), while celebrating the Turkish German "dream-team" behind the BioNTech vaccine as the new face of Europe

(Oltermann 2020). In June 2021, it was reported that Germany regretted colonial acts of terror and would return the looted Benin bronzes to Nigeria that were on display in German museums. It was also announced that Germany would start vaccinating German children older than twelve. At this point, most doctors and health workers on the African continent had not received even the first vaccination. This indicates the cynicism of the proclamations of global solidarity and cosmopolitanism (*Weltoffenheit*) (Senate Department for Culture and Social Cohesion 2024).

In my view, the terror of the genocidal state parallels the tragedy of the missing state. We must, of course, not disregard that many states have weaponized the pathogen to consolidate their coercive powers vis-à-vis policing and surveillance. This has had long-term repercussions after the pandemic (Hannah et al. 2020). At the same time, we must not lose sight of the differential power effects of various governmental rationalities. Surprisingly, Foucault scholars disregard one of his most astute observations about the exercise of critique—namely, that it is a rejection of not all governmental rationalities but, rather, of "how not be governed like that, by that, in the name of those principles, with such and such an objective in mind and by means of such procedures, not like that, not for that, not by them" (Foucault 2007, 44). Here, Foucault is drawing attention to different strategies, mechanisms, techniques, and instruments of coercion deployed by different governmental rationalities, without flattening or homogenizing their various tactics. This allows a nuanced analysis of which forms of coercion and power relation are acceptable under what circumstances and for whom. Thus, even as subjects are made governable and govern themselves and others, the possibility of not being governed "like that" opens up the potential to negotiate coercion. When Foucault tells us "Where there is power, there is resistance," he is arguing not that the resistance eliminates power and violence but, rather, that it shifts and forces power to govern in a different way.

My effort is to question the thinking of political violence in terms of a universal violent state-resistant civil society binary. This approach reduces the state to its repressive apparatus, such that the birth of the modern state is defined in terms of sovereign violence. The state as origin of terror, which intentionally unleashes violence on its subjects, is juxtaposed with a resistant and redemptive violence emerging from the oppressed. In reducing the state to its punitive function, it is understood as monopolizer of violence, selectively wielding it in the name of ensuring life and property. My attempt has been to pluralize this state-centric focus when thinking about political violence in its various manifestations. In Western thought, the loss of state

monopoly on violence is read in terms of presumed failed or weak postcolonial state making. In contrast, the extreme episodes of violence in the
postcolony—for instance, against minorities and women in the form of riots
and rape—indicate the inability, perhaps even the unwillingness, of the state
to assume full sovereign power (Banerjee 2017, 28). The state outsources and
delegates the exercise of violence to (global) extra-state actors to reinforce
its gender, caste, race, and religious ideologies. At the same time, the state itself becomes a weapon in the hands of dominant groups to terrorize minorities. Political and social violence mediate each other such that, instead of
the state being a coherent and unified source of terror, a network of agents
carries out atrocities against vulnerable groups while the state abdicates
both its monopoly on violence and its responsibility vis-à-vis its citizens
(Banerjee 2017, 28). The poor and vulnerable in the postcolonial societies
are confronted with the multidirectionality and transnationalization of violence—that is, they experience terror from multiple sources, and violence
is exercised by diverse actors, state as well as extra-state. The decentralized
sources of regulative and punitive power in postcolonial societies provide
a counterpoint to mainstream theories of state violence, which view it in
terms of centrality and coherence. These insights expose the fictive nature
of universal theories of state sovereignty and territorial integrity (Banerjee
2017, 28). This is an important lesson for critical theories of decolonization.

   With a focus on international law and postcolonial sovereignty, I conclude this chapter by showing the challenges faced by the postcolonial
world in rescuing the Enlightenment from the Europeans.

Who's Afraid of Postcolonial Sovereignty?

Perhaps there is no better illustration of postcolonial efforts to rescue the
Enlightenment and its norms, such as Kantian understanding of sovereignty and cosmopolitanism, than Third World Approaches to International Law (TWAIL). Scholars of TWAIL (Anghie and Chimni 2003; Chimni
2006; Mutua 2000) seek to reform international law by laying bare its colonial and neocolonial framings. Decolonizing international law necessitates
reversing the selective and racialized application of national sovereignty established during colonialism, which justified the domination of colonized
peoples by declaring them nonautonomous (Anghie 2007, 99, 109). Precolonial legal and economic systems—as seen in the Americas, for example—
were invalidated, stripping natives of their right to self-determination.

To rectify unjust international legal practices, disputes about jurisdiction, or reparations, TWAIL scholars insist that Western leaders and societies must be willing to listen and learn from the experiences of the global South. Rather than rejecting international institutions and discourses, the attempt is to reconfigure the Eurocentric understanding of sovereignty and rights, offering alternative paradigms. A pertinent example of TWAIL in action is its criticism of structural adjustment programs imposed by the World Bank and International Monetary Fund on the so-called developing countries during the 1980s and 1990s. The TWAIL scholars outline how these policies perpetuated neocolonialism by entrenching economic dependence and thereby eroding the sovereignty of newly independent former colonies (Pahuja 2011). The privatization of state-owned enterprises and the liberalization of trade and commerce in the global South undermined state autonomy, cementing an imbalance of power. However, instead of forsaking international law, which served as a handmaiden to international economic institutions, TWAIL scholars endeavor to reshape postcolonial sovereignty, encompassing both political and economic dimensions. For instance, this entails postcolonial states' asserting permanent sovereignty over natural resources (Anghie 2007, 211).

Turning to current international human rights, the Kenyan American TWAIL scholar Makau Mutua (2002) traces how, under the pretext of doctrine of Responsibility to Protect, human rights and democracy often serve as a smokescreen for Western imperialist interests. This was exemplified in the case of Libya, where the territorial integrity and sovereignty of an African nation was undermined by North Atlantic Treaty Organization (NATO) forces. The TWAIL scholars examine the tension between human rights and the right to self-determination of postcolonial states, aiming to uphold territorial integrity and sovereignty without succumbing to Eurocentric norms of universality. Despite decades of scholarly and activist interventions, postcolonial efforts to rescue the Enlightenment from the Europeans remain a frustrating and exigent task. The alarming disputes about the role of the ICJ and the ICC concerning territorial jurisdiction during the 2023 Israel-Hamas war serve as a case in point.

On May 20, 2024, the ICC prosecutor Karim Khan applied for arrest warrants for Israeli Prime Minister Benjamin Netanyahu and Hamas officials for war crimes and crimes against humanity (Khan 2024). Khan clarified that, under the principle of complementarity, if Israel were to investigate the war crimes, the ICC would reconsider the charges. Four days later, on May 24, 2024, the ICJ ordered Israel to stop the Rafah offensive

(ICJ 2024b). On July 19, 2024, the ICJ ruled that Israel had no right to sovereignty over the Palestinian territory, and its settlements violated international law by impeding Palestinians' right to self-determination (ICJ 2024c). Although nonbinding, the court's findings carry political weight insofar as, if adopted as a resolution, they can set the legal parameters for a future negotiated settlement.

The United States, United Kingdom, and Germany have declared near-unconditional support for Israel. In fact, in anticipation of the arrest warrants, twelve US Republican senators warned in a letter dated April 24, 2024, and addressed to Khan, that any potential arrest warrants against Netanyahu and other top officials were illegitimate and lacked legal basis. They threatened ICC members and their families with severe sanctions if they went ahead with their plan to issue arrest warrants (TRT World 2024). Interfering and intimidating in a judicial matter constitutes obstruction of justice and is a crime (*Democracy Now!* 2024e). The ICC is strafed for overreaching and for undermining Israeli sovereignty.

It is noteworthy that neither the United States nor Israel is a signatory to the Rome Statute, which is the international treaty that established the ICC; adopted on July 17, 1998, it came into force on July 1, 2002. In fact, the Hague Invasion Act, passed by the US Congress in July 2002, just a few weeks after the creation of the ICC, authorizes the US president to use any means available to release any detained or imprisoned person "by, on behalf of, or at the request" of the ICC (Wikipedia 2024c). In addition to US citizens acting for the US government or allies such as NATO member states, the law extends to non-NATO allies. As a result, numerous other countries have declined to acknowledge the jurisdiction of the ICC and have opted not to cooperate with it, as they are reluctant to defy the United States.

Palestine did become a signatory to the ICC after an agreement with Hamas, thus, as many argue, granting the ICC jurisdiction over the current war. Previously, the ICC issued an arrest warrant for Russia's Vladimir Putin over alleged war crimes in Ukraine, although Russia is not a signatory to the Rome Statute. Interestingly, in this case, the United States endorsed the ICC's jurisdiction and provided details of alleged Russian war crimes in Ukraine to the ICC (*Democracy Now!* 2024e).

In response to the charges against Netanyahu, both US President Joe Biden and Netanyahu expressed outrage, with Biden unilaterally declaring that there is no genocide in Gaza, although this is currently under review by the ICJ. Hamas, too, denounced the indictment request for arrest warrants, insisting on the right to armed resistance to occupation. Israel, the

United States (Foreign Relations Committee 2024), the United Kingdom, and Germany (Federal Foreign Office 2024) have taken umbrage with the ICC, pointing out that it is creating a false moral equivalency between democratic Israel and Hamas. Notably, Gazans also object to the false equivalence within the ICC charges and criticize the disproportionality of Israeli military operations, arguing that these actions contravene the Geneva Conventions and international humanitarian law. Others highlight that, instead of equating the two, the ICC is underscoring that commission of war crimes by one side does not legitimize war crimes of the other side (Fulford et al. 2024). Every state has the right to defend itself; rules of war determine how this war is to be carried out (Panel of Experts in International Law 2024). The United States has repeatedly threatened to once again sanction the ICC, as it did in 2020 to thwart ICC investigations in Afghanistan (Human Rights Watch 2020). Khan is being accused of going "rogue" (John 2024). Hungary hosted Israeli Prime Minister Benjamin Netanyahu on April 3, 2025, and announced its withdrawal from ICC on the same day. While some EU member states voiced concern, others openly supported Hungary's position.

My deepest concern is that the Western countries' inconsistent response will cause enormous damage to their claim of being principled supporters of the rule of law. If they do not change course, international institutions such as the ICJ and ICC will be deemed illegitimate, inefficacious, and irrelevant. This appears to be a defining moment for the international rules-based order, as it sends the message that nobody will be granted global legal exception and impunity. It could turn out to be a pivotal moment in the history of international law and a game changer, considering the ICC's dubious reputation of only pursuing war criminals in Africa to date while deploying norms of justice and human rights against adversaries of Western regimes (Benvenuto 2013). In the statement, Khan asserted: "If we do not demonstrate our willingness to apply the law equally, if it is seen as being applied selectively, we will be creating the conditions for its collapse." As of summer 2025, a three-judge panel is reviewing the request, and reports have already indicated that there are attempts to exert pressure on the countries from which the judges originate (*Democracy Now!* 2024d).

The day after Khan's request, Spain, Ireland, and Norway announced that they would formally recognize the Palestinian state. Since 1988, about 140 of the 193 UN member states have acknowledged Palestinian statehood. Although some decry this as merely a symbolic gesture, others welcome it as a tangible step toward affirming the Palestinian right to self-determination.

As a sovereign state, Palestine could pursue legal rights over its territorial waters and air space.

In his talk at the Wiener Festwoche, Omri Boehm (2024) revealed the contradictions between national sovereignty and human dignity. He argued that instead of protecting the universal inviolability of human rights, the foregrounding of national sovereignty compromises human dignity. He provided the example of postcolonial and Jewish sovereignties, both emerging from experiences of persecution and extermination. While colonized societies have focused on territorial integrity and national sovereignty as the ultimate vehicle of liberation, the sovereign Jewish state, in the aftermath of the Holocaust, was seen as the way forward to restore dignity for the Jewish people. Although Boehm (2024) stressed that these were the right responses, they are now, in his view, on a "collision course." The narrow framings of postcolonial and Jewish sovereignty have ended up disregarding the human rights of the other.

As a way forward, Boehm (2024) argues that the European Union (EU) offers a compelling answer to the question "What to do after empire?" Drawing on Timothy Snyder, he recommends Europe's ethical answer to its former victims. Boehm claims that by instating a strong concept of citizenship, irrespective of race or ethnicity, the EU successfully managed to restrict national sovereignty in favor of the universality of human dignity by entering a federative constellation and by submitting to international law. By questioning and replacing national sovereignty, Europe has successfully answered to its violent past. Boehm contests the accusation that European ideas of cosmopolitanism and humanism are being imposed on postcolonial societies as a form of neocolonialism. Rather, in his view, Europe's accomplished move to "deconstruct sovereignty and assert human dignity" could provide a way out of the violation of human rights faced by those who "seem to stand in the way" of postcolonial and Jewish sovereignty (Boehm 2024).

Boehm does concede that Europe at times betrays its own principles. For example, he points out how Germany has, in the past, challenged the investigation of war crimes by Israel in Palestine by arguing that the ICC does not have jurisdiction in Palestinian territories. As the main benefactor of the ICC, Germany has compromised the court's autonomy and authority to protect Jewish sovereignty. Boehm (2024) condemns this as an "irresponsible way of speaking about historical responsibility."

As stated at the beginning of the book, considering its shameful history, Germany's efforts at *Wiedergutmachung* are commendable. German

Chancellor Angela Merkel's doctrine of Israel's security as Germany's *Staatsräson* (reason of state), first articulated on March 18, 2008, and the singularity thesis, arising from the *Historikerstreit* in 1986–87, serve as evidence of this commitment. While both have significantly influenced intellectual and public debates in Germany, unlike legal measures that criminalize Holocaust denial or trivialization and the denial of Nazi war crimes, they are not codified in German law. Furthermore, claiming responsibility for another state, as Germany does for Israel, is to identify with that state. Daniel Marwecki (2020, 2024) calls this "surrogate nationalism" (*Ersatznationalismus*). This contrasts sharply with the optimistic picture of EU cosmopolitanism that Boehm paints.

As a member of the Rome Statute and a signatory to the Genocide Conventions, Germany faces a contradiction between its *Staatsräson* and its obligation to comply with international law. Germany's evasive response to the arrest warrants against Netanyahu confirms Boehm's concern that national sovereignty supersedes human dignity. Ironically, Western states are undermining the credibility of international law by delegitimizing its institutions, while postcolonial states such as South Africa and Nicaragua are turning to international law to address the war crimes in Gaza.

In his dismissal of territorial integrity and sovereignty, Boehm overlooks their significance as a cornerstone legacy of the Enlightenment. As I have posited, using the example of Ambedkar, postcolonial state sovereignty and constitutionalism were influenced by the Enlightenment, albeit undergoing significant transformation in the process of decolonization. For instance, Indigenous peoples' ideas of plurinational sovereignty in countries such as Bolivia, the ideas of Pan-Africanism and Pan-Arabism, and the Non-Aligned Movement were all postcolonial attempts to experiment with Eurocentric understandings of sovereignty. In addition to promoting solidarity among African nations, the formation of the African Union and the Pan-African Parliament seeks to assert African interests on a global platform. The Palestinian case shows that, without territorial integrity and sovereignty, Gazans have no "right to have rights" (Arendt 1962 [1951], 296). It is precisely the discontinuity between the rights of citizens and the rights of man that Arendt foregrounds with respect to the plight of the stateless. She examines the disenfranchisement after World War II of Jewish refugees, who, without citizenship or legal status in a nation-state, lacked the basic rights and protections afforded to citizens. They were stripped not only of German citizenship, but also of the fundamental right to belong to a political community, and thereby of the protections this offered. Statelessness poses an intractable conundrum for Boehm's contention that postcolonial sovereignty and universal human rights are inherently oppositional.

Boehm not only does a disservice to postcolonial studies; he also disregards Kant's foremost principle of consistency. In celebrating the EU, he fails to mention its betrayal of thousands of stateless people, whom international law so far has failed to protect. In focusing only on European, postcolonial, and Israeli citizens, Boehm neglects to address the distress of those with uncertain legal status and lacking citizenship in any recognized state. These individuals are unprotected not only by postcolonial and Israeli national sovereignty, but also by international institutions, despite the existence of various conventions, covenants, and legislation. As Arendt compellingly argued against the background of the Holocaust, stateless people cannot be legitimate political subjects because they have no addressee for their grievances, which could guarantee them their rights. Without citizenship or membership in a political community, they lack the institutional framework necessary to assert their rights effectively. This absence of a legal personality as rights-bearing citizen within a nation-state renders them politically precarious. This brings to mind the passage from Bertolt Brecht's *Flüchtlingsgespräche* (*Refugee Conversations*) (2019 [1940/41], 7, my translation from German): "The passport is the most precious part of a person. It does not come into being as easily as a human being. A person can come into being anywhere, in the most careless way and for no good reason, but not a passport. That's why it is recognized, if it is a good one, while a person can be ever so good and still not be recognized."

Boehm also fails to mention that Kant, his favorite Enlightenment thinker, was not in favor of a single, all-encompassing republican world state and insisted on the right of territorial integrity and sovereignty of individual states. Notwithstanding his commitment to universal cosmopolitan rights, abolishing state sovereignty was anathema to Kant. Despite the universal validity of human rights, there is no standing international police force that has the power to rectify the violation of rights. This raises the question of power of enforcement of international law.

Furthermore, rather than communicating in a unified language of justice and humanity, global governance increasingly resembles the Tower of Babel, where we appear destined to speak at cross-purposes. For instance, when the United States proposed a resolution at the UN Security Council calling for an immediate and sustained ceasefire in Gaza, Russia and China vetoed it (Psaledakis and Brunnerstrom 2024). Previously, the United States had vetoed three draft resolutions for humanitarian ceasefires proposed by Brazil, Algeria, and the United Arab Emirates (Nichols 2024). While, as stated by the ICJ, a plausible genocide is unfolding in Gaza, with thousands of deaths, widespread starvation, and extensive destruction of infrastructure, powerful states that have pledged compliance with international humanitarian laws are pursuing Machiavellian realpolitik. "Giving one party weapons and the other party bread" (Marwecki 2024) is not the recipe for "perpetual peace." Paradoxically, the party that has most benefited so far from the 2023 Israel-Hamas war is the arms industry, which has profited from global militarization. After 247 days of war in Gaza, the Security Council adopted Resolution 2735 (2024), aimed at reaching a comprehensive ceasefire deal. Although it is legally binding, the resolution, unfortunately, has not led to immediate ceasefire in Gaza.

It must be noted that nineteen Arab states are parties to the Genocide Convention, but unlike South Africa, they did not file a case against Israel at the ICJ. A likely reason is that their severe human rights violations undermined their credibility. In addition, they were reluctant to defy the United States. One could conclude that, while the Arab world rhetorically supports the Palestinian cause, it has not done enough in practice for Palestinian independence (Bishara 2023). It is no surprise that Edward Said faced censorship for condemning authoritarian regimes in the Arab world. In *Peace and Its Discontents*, Said (1996, 110) remarks about Hamas: "For any secular intellectual to make a devil's pact with a religious movement is, I think, to substitute convenience for principle. It is simply the other side of the pact we made during the past several decades with dictatorship and nationalism." This long and rich intellectual history of postcolonial critique of nationalism, including anticolonial nationalism, is regrettably ignored by Boehm.

I do not aim here to propose remedies to the current conflicts or to take a stance on whether a one-state or two-state solution for Israel and Palestine is more viable. Instead, the purpose of my arguments is to highlight the double bind of the postcolonial world in relation to Enlightenment norms of territorial integrity, sovereignty, human rights, and humanitarianism. For centuries, the West preached the rule of law to the postcolonial world, shaming it for corruption, arbitrariness, lack of accountability, and disregard for human rights. Now the roles are reversed. When it comes to the relationship between postcolonial sovereignty and international law, the tides seem to be turning. The postcolonial world is drawing on international institutions, despite their flaws and failings, to deliver justice. In an opening statement in The Hague, where South Africa's case against Israel is being reviewed at the ICJ, the Irish barrister Blinne Ní Ghrálaigh KC, representing South

Africa, warned: "Some might say that the very reputation of international law—its ability and willingness to bind and to protect all peoples equally—hangs in the balance" (quoted in Wintour 2024). The judgment will determine the postcolonial world's future relationship to international law, one of the most important legacies of the Enlightenment.

The chapter began with Einstein's question to Freud about whether and how it is possible to reduce violence in the world and engaged with diverse approaches to and contemplations of the role of violence and nonviolence in the processes of decolonization. We understood that a critique of violence does not lead to a critique beyond violence. The antinomies and aporias of critical practice are that, in fighting violence, it can destroy that which it seeks to preserve. Thus, even when critical practices are guided by emancipatory norms, they reproduce normative violence. When confronted with the contradictions and inconsistencies inherent in norms of democracy, justice and rule of law, the postcolonial world is tempted to reject them for being flawed and deficient. Yet, as has been argued throughout the book, even if Enlightenment norms are inadequate, they are also indispensable for processes of decolonization. Critical theories of decolonization cannot circumvent the normative dilemmas that confront them.

An excellent example of postcolonial aporias is proferred by Derrida in his contemplations on the struggles with democracy in his homeland, Algeria. In 1992, with the prospect of overwhelming victory for the Islamist Front Islamique du Salut party, the democratic government was dissolved to be replaced with military rule. Democracy in postcolonial contexts, as Derrida (2005, 87) points out, is not just a form of governance but an exercise of radical critique: "Democracy is the only system, the only constitutional paradigm, in which, in principle, one has or assumes the right to criticize everything publicly, including the idea of democracy." Yet the constitutive death drive implicit in democratic rule alludes to the capriciousness of decolonization. Derrida (2005, 45) explains that "democracy's suicide is an autoimmune reaction," in which democratic processes in Algeria were interrupted and temporarily suspended by democratically elected leaders to safeguard and preserve democratic structures from being permanently harmed by their enemies, "a suicide to prevent a murder" (Thomson 2005). Thus, even as he previously declared "No deconstruction without democracy, no democracy without deconstruction" (Derrida 1997, 105), Derrida is acutely cognizant of the autoimmunity of norms, which carry within themselves the seeds of their own destruction. This malfunction results in the body that, instead of protecting itself from external threats, compromises its own immunity.

In arguing that every democratic state is also a rogue one, Derrida (2005, 156) clarifies that it is not that particular states fail to approximate the ideals of democratic governance. Rather, state power is "originally excessive and abusive." In the moment that the state defines its legitimate demos, it is immediately undemocratic to those who do not qualify. Thus, democracy is always inadequate and comes up short against the norm. Yet instead of jettisoning these ideals, Derrida holds on to the promise and ambiguity of the norm. Democracy, for him, is perpetually deferred in the mode of "to come" (*la démocratie à venir*), not in terms of its future perfectibility, but in its impossibility and unforeseeability. Peace, security, and equality are delivered through violence and coercion. Instead of resignation or rejection, democracy, with all its contradictions, is "an empty name" (Derrida 2005, 86). Yet even though it cannot impart to us in advance what is to come and where this will take us in the future, it remains a necessary idea to which we must continually hold fast.

This encapsulates the normative dilemmas facing the project of decolonizing the Enlightenment. The Czech poet and immunologist Miroslav Holub's (1977) poem "Brief Thoughts on Maps" is a brilliant lesson in the contingency and unpredictability of the dynamic between goals and how to get there (Phillips 2015b):

> Albert Szent-Gyorgyi, who knew a lot about maps
> according to which life is on its way somewhere or other,
> told us this story from the war
> due to which history is on its way somewhere or other:
> The young lieutenant of a small Hungarian detachment in the Alps
> sent a reconnaissance unit out into the icy wasteland.
> It began to snow
> immediately, snowed for two days and the unit
> did not return. The lieutenant suffered: he had dispatched
> his own people to death.
> But the third day the unit came back.
> Where had they been? How had they made their way?
> Yes, they said, we considered ourselves
> lost and waited for the end. And then one of us
> found a map in his pocket. That calmed us down.
> We pitched camp, lasted out the snowstorm and then with the map
> we discovered our bearings.
> And here we are.

The lieutenant borrowed this remarkable map
and had a good look at it. It was not a map of the Alps
but of the Pyrenees.
Goodbye now.

Norms such as justice, democracy, peace, and nonviolence give us a sense of direction and orientation as to what the ethically and politically appropriate and desirable response in a particular situation may be. This explains our rage and frustration when, instead of delivering what they promise, norms mutate into their antithesis; when necropolitics masquerades as democracy and justice brings conflict. Norms are like maps: There are no guarantees that they will get us where we want to go. And sometimes, when we are lost without orientation and guidance, when our norms fail us, we must get inventive; we must reconsider, reimagine, and reconfigure both our political goals and the ways to achieve them. When norms sabotage what they aspire to uphold, when we become unmoored, this vagrancy can entice us to think critically, to look for other anchors for our thought and action. Norms, like maps, can reassure and guide, but they can also over-determine the outcome and ultimately foreclose other possibilities. Sometimes, knowing where one is or where one wants to go and how to get there is the most dangerous and threatening issue for ethics. However, feeling lost is sometimes imperative for progressive politics, when our norms of justice, nonviolence, democracy, and peace are tested. Thus, rather than sustaining the illusion that ethics and politics are only about efficaciously implementing hand-me-down norms of nonviolence, justice, and democracy, the capacity to feel lost reveals one of its critical virtues: It can allow us the space necessary to reimagine our relationship with those norms.

In the introduction to an edited volume featuring contributions by, and interviews with, Habermas and Derrida, Giovanna Borradori (2003, 15) claims, "As is the case with clinical medical practice, for Critical Theory diagnosis is not a speculative enterprise but an evaluation oriented toward the possibility of remedy.... Habermas calls this demand the 'unfinished project of modernity.' Begun by Kant and other Enlightenment thinkers, this project requires belief in principles whose validity is universal because they hold across historical and cultural specificities." In complete disregard of postcolonial-queer-feminist critique, Borradori rehearses a Eurocentric eulogy that highlights the accomplishments of the Enlightenment and obscures European colonialism's violent legacies. In her account of the Enlightenment and Critical Theory, she repeats the traditional demand to underwrite struggles with ethical principles, implying that an individual or group must provide proof that their theoretical papers are in order before they can embark on an emancipatory mission. However, as argued by post-structuralists and postcolonial scholars, one cannot choose the supposed correct political position from a preexisting set of ready-made possibilities, nor is there an immediately pregiven subject of struggle, such that there are no absolute good or bad causes, appropriate strategies, or resistant subjects. Politics is no longer a set of practices derived from the alleged interests belonging to ready-made subjects. In the face of a lack of stable identities and metanarratives, the conventional theories of political action must be replaced with experimental norms, ones with unexpected and unpredictable outcomes. Norms such as justice, democracy, and nonviolence are good servants but bad masters, so that one needs persistently to recalibrate our relationship to them. Norms in this sense are rogue, infidel, and vagrant, inadequate yet indispensable, never quite what we make of them. We never know "whether we have chosen well or ill, whether something will turn out good or bad, whether it will have shown itself to be a threat or an opportunity" (Naas 2008, 134). As a double bind of chance and risk, norms, even as they have the capacity to destroy ethics and politics by way of suicidal autoimmunity, can also open up the possibility of a new ethics or politics. Derrida (2005, 157) concludes *Rogues* by observing that, given the lack of a reliable prophylaxis against violence, Enlightenment must come to terms with "this poisoned medicine, this *pharmakon* of an inflexible and cruel autoimmunity that is sometimes called the 'death drive.'"

Finally, let us turn our attention to how aesthetics negotiate the tension between the politics and the ethics of decolonization. In contrast to having faith in democratic processes, Adorno argues that the rise of mass culture consolidates capitalist structures while eroding democratic speech, as well as publics as a whole, ultimately being counterproductive to the engendering of a critical attitude. The confluence of art and entertainment by the culture industry drains society of all critical and utopian content, producing unthinking, isolated individuals (Adorno 1975 [1967], 19). Rather than being thought-provoking and mind changing like the Greek tragedies, the culture industry numbs and sedates, becoming consoling and mollifying. In the concluding chapter, I once again demonstrate the affinities between the first generation of Critical Theory and postcolonial studies—in particular, between Adorno and Spivak—while outlining the differences between the decolonial option and postcolonial studies. Finally, the chapter addresses the issues of desubalternization and the important role of aesthetic education.

6

Aesthetic Enlightenment and the Art of Decolonization

For a philosopher to say, "The good and the beautiful are one," is infamy; if he goes on to add, "also the true," one ought to thrash him. Truth is ugly. We possess art lest we perish from truth.—FRIEDRICH NIETZSCHE, *The Will to Power*

During World War II, there were 105 performances in concentration camps in Germany of the play *Dakghar* (The Post Office). Written in Bengali by the anticolonial thinker and Nobel laureate Rabindranath Tagore while he was grieving after the death of his young son, the play was also translated into French by André Gide and was read by him on the radio the night before Paris fell to the Nazis (Kellman and Chakrabarti 2021). The story revolves around a young orphan named Amal who suffers from an ailment and is quarantined at home. In his quest to explore the world beyond, he sits near a window facing a road and talks to people passing by. He becomes fascinated by the newly constructed post office near his window and imagines receiving a letter from the king informing him that he will send his personal physician to cure Amal. The play presents a vivid picture of Amal's longing and his fears.

Perhaps one of the most noteworthy stagings was by Janusz Korczak (the pen name of Henryk Goldszmit), a Polish Jewish educator who ran an orphanage in the Warsaw Ghetto that housed nearly two hundred children age seven to fourteen (Mukherjee 2015). Chronic shortages of food meant that starvation and illness, as well as the threat of mass deportations, were ever present (Wiener Holocaust Library 2024). In this time of uncertainty and suffering, one wonders why Korczak had the orphans stage a play by an Indian playwright (Chakrabarti 2021). In the abysmal conditions of the Warsaw Ghetto, Korczak helped emaciated children prepare their costumes from old bedsheets and torn socks, defying the ban by the Nazis on cultural activities inside the ghetto. If caught, the performers would have received extreme punishments (Wiener Holocaust Library 2024). It is reported that the children were excited by the prospect of the entire community coming to see them perform. Three days later, mass deportations to the Treblinka concentration camp began, and neither Korczak nor the orphans survived. The most obvious explanation for performing a tragic play about an ailing child on the verge of an untimely death would be that Korczak was preparing the orphans in his care for their eventual death. However, a more compelling idea is that he was attempting to give the children dignity through aesthetics when they had been robbed of it.

I begin this chapter with this historical example to highlight the possible role of aesthetics in transforming politics and ethics. Given that colonialism was not only about economic exploitation and military intervention, but also about the production of imperial and subaltern subjects, it is imperative not only to address the challenges of economic redistribution and political recognition, but, as argued in this chapter, also to engage with the role of aesthetics in processes of decolonization and desubalternization. In what follows, I juxtapose Walter Mignolo with Theodor Adorno and Gayatri Chakravorty Spivak to present their contrasting positions on aesthetics. The first section outlines the decolonial option's understanding of "aesthetic disobedience." This extends the idea of "epistemic delinking" by advocating non-Eurocentric approaches to aesthetics. The next section engages with Adorno's and Spivak's foregrounding of aesthetics as a possible site of inculcating critical intelligence. Drawing on Immanuel Kant and Friedrich Schiller, Spivak compellingly argues that an aesthetic education trains the imagination to engage ethically with alterity in a nondominant manner.

From war and political conflict to natural catastrophes and environmental destruction, we are flooded daily with images of suffering. While some respond to the pain of others (Sontag 2004) with solidarity and empathy, many complain of compassion fatigue. The question is whether art can make us political and ethical by provoking us out of our indifference and irresponsibility. Could creative and affirmative artistic practices facilitate the nurturing of democratic principles, the meting out of transnational justice, and, ultimately, the protection and promotion of human rights? Or should art be autonomous and nonpurposive and not be yoked in service of political and ethical imperatives?

Considering the historical role of art in colonial and fascist regimes, can one entrust art with the task of decolonization? In contrast to Nietzsche's quote from *Will to Power*, which focuses on the redemptive function of aesthetics, Adorno's (1997, 34) famous assertion, "To write poetry after Auschwitz is barbaric," bears witness to the disillusionment with the promise of both art and artists as agents of transformation. How could a society with such sublime art, music, poetry, literature, and philosophy commit such heinous crimes against humanity? It is a struggle with the puzzle: How could the land of Bach, Goethe, and Kant also bring forth the likes of Hitler, Goebbels, and Eichmann? Furthermore, given that art functions within structures of capitalism and neocolonialism, the political, social, and economic roles of art, as well as artistic practices and art institutions, remain ambivalent and controversial under the current conditions of global inequality.

The key question for postcolonial scholarship is whether the political labor of training the imagination would mitigate imperialist, racist, Orientalist, antisemitic, and heteronormative structures and practices. While decolonial scholars suggest a break from Western aesthetics, thinkers such as Spivak draw on Kant and Schiller to posit an aesthetic education as a step toward decolonization. Instead of rejecting the Enlightenment and its legacies, she suggests "sabotaging" it to realize the process of desubalternization through aesthetic agency.

Drawing on Kant, Schiller proposes the pedagogical function of the aesthetic in preparing subjects to imagine and dwell in ideal worlds. Kant claims that enlightened political action results from the circulation of ideas and commerce (*Bücher* [books] and *Geld* [money]) (Kant 1991a, 55). As the public can achieve Enlightenment only slowly and must be guided by the self-liberating actions of critical minds, in his view, the diffusion of knowledge must proceed gradually. Thus, political transformation is enabled through disseminating progressive ideas promulgated by the intelligentsia (Kester 2012, 91). Interestingly, aesthetics is granted a key role in this process, which Schiller takes up in his notion of an "aesthetic education." According to him, mature participation in the public sphere is made possible through the supposed civilizing influence of aesthetic experience. In contrast to viewing civil society as a realm of debate in which consciousness is formed and from which change emerges, Schiller (2016b [1795], 6) argues that no meaningful political change can take place until human consciousness undergoes a transformation through a process of aesthetic education: "If one is to resolve this political problem one must in practice take the aesthetic path, for it is by way of beauty that one approaches liberty."

This approach shifts the focus from thinkers to artists and poets as agents of Enlightenment. While Schiller analyzes how modern life damages civic subjects, Spivak focuses on the epistemic violence of colonialism. Kant, Schiller, and Spivak all argue that an aesthetic experience can nurture critical intelligence, which would contribute to a more lasting and comprehensive transformation of a given social structure, one beyond a fleeting moment of resistance. The emphasis here lies in the pedagogical function of the aesthetic in preparing us to read and inhabit our worlds responsibly. The cognitive pliancy induced by such an experience unfolds complex articulations of politics, ethics, and aesthetics. Adorno (2005a [1951], 39) astutely remarks that "wrong life cannot be lived rightly" (*Es gibt kein richtiges Leben im falschen*). Spivak would add that you cannot have good politics in a context framed by bad ethics. The hope is that aesthetics can come to the rescue.

Aesthetic Disobedience and Decolonial Options

The decolonial scholars Walter Mignolo and Rolando Vazquez (2013) consider "aestheTics" to be part of the colonial matrix of power that accompanied the colonization of the New World. The modern/colonial project not only encompassed economic, political, epistemic, and military domination but also regulated the aesthetic faculties; this was accomplished by means of a Eurocentric normativity that devalues and disqualifies other aesthetic practices, notions of the beautiful, and good taste. "Modern aestheTics" universalized European standards of beauty and the sublime, ultimately shaping and dominating global aesthetic experiences. "AestheTics" replaced "poetics" and "poiesis" in eighteenth-century Europe, de-localizing and universalizing a Western sensibility and norm and playing a crucial role in the constitution of the modern rational subject. Through a decolonial reading of Kant's *Observations on the Beautiful and the Sublime* (2011 [1764]), Mignolo and Vazquez elucidate the difference between "aestheTics" and "aestheSis." They describe the former as a regional invention of European Enlightenment, while the latter offers alternatives to Eurocentrism but goes beyond a straightforward de-Westernization of the arts.

Decolonial options claim to subvert the colonial/modern order by proffering alternatives to the Western canon, not as supposedly superior options, but as suggestions that foreground the legitimacy of alternative understandings of beauty and the sublime. Through a "geopolitics of sensing and knowing" (Mignolo 2013), decolonial aestheSis counteracts the colonial/modern impulse to rank and hierarchize people and societies while affirming difference and thereby healing colonial wounds. Decolonial aestheSis contests the Western canon and liberates decolonial subjectivities not by way of a metacritique expressed in abstract concepts but through embodied practices of "aesthetic disobedience" and a recovery of alternative memories, knowledges, and sensibilities that engender a "re-existence" of previously marginalized and silenced subjectivities (Mignolo and Vazquez 2013). Drawing on aesthetic concepts and practices beyond the European canon, decolonial work de-universalizes Eurocentric concepts, opening up other non-European options to the world of the sensible (Mignolo and Vazquez 2013). "Decolonial transmodern aesthetics is intercultural, inter-epistemic, inter-political, inter-aesthetical and inter-spiritual but always from perspectives of the global south and the former-Eastern Europe" (Transnational Decolonial Institute 2024). To contest the so-called colonialization of the mind that polices, negates, standardizes, and homogenizes difference and entrenches hegemonic languages and institutions, the decolonial option attempts to facilitate democratic and tolerant epistemic and aesthetic practices that operate from multiple geopolitical sites of enunciation (Mignolo 2009, 18).

To retrieve aesthetic practices beyond the normative modern framing, the focus is shifted to masses of people who have not been exposed to Western education and have creative skills that bring pleasure to their community. Mignolo (2014, 204) proposes "delinking" as a strategy of opening up opportunities to explore modes of thinking, doing, and being that were previously disqualified by both Christian theology and modern secular science. Decolonial aestheSis is the ability of the colonized subjects to decolonize their sensibilities through a transgression of the European framing of universality by retrieving precolonial memories, sensibilities, skills, and knowledge (Mignolo 2014, 201–2). Concomitantly, "decolonial healing" is a communal enterprise practiced by Indigenous people in Abya Yala, the Indigenous name for the American continent. This involves moving away from European ways of thinking, hearing, seeing, feeling, and doing and "learning to be" decolonial subjects (Mignolo 2014, 207). Mignolo clarifies that, as a non-Indigenous thinker, scholar, activist, and artist, he is not in a position to determine whether the "decolonial option" is meaningful or helpful for Indigenous projects (Mignolo 2014, 208).

In an astute critique of the decolonial project of "delinking," Achille Mbembe (2021, 79–80) points out that the secessionist imperative of the decolonial approach disregards the entangled and interdependent nature of the worlds in which we live. He warns that if "decolonial acts" are to be more than mere "gestures by which one is cut off, or one cuts oneself off, from the world," then "they must work through connectivity and elasticity" of our globalized condition (Mbembe 2021, 89). Furthermore, Mbembe (2021, 78) laments that in most discourses on decolonization, *Africa* is reified and essentialized "as if there were no other grounds for an African identity than the 'indigenous' and the 'ethnic.'" He bemoans the lack of critique of Indigenous epistemologies and their conflation with "traditional cosmogonies or vernacular *arts de faire*, including crafts, narratives, and proverbs" (Mbembe 2021, 78). Drawing on Yambo Ouologuem, Mbembe (2021, 210) not only questions "the very notions of origins, birth, and genealogy that are so central to the discourse of Négritude" but "relativizes the fetishism of origins by showing that every origin is bastard and that every origin rests on a heap of filth [*un tas d'immondices*]." This is a call for deontologizing notions such as *Black* and *Africa*.

Along similar lines, in contrast to the decolonial option, which celebrates the community over the state and understands decolonization as subversion and reversal of both modernity and coloniality, I am unconvinced of de-Westernization or delinking as the formula for decolonization. It is dubious to propose that decolonization is a simple process of return to pristine, authentic, and unadulterated precolonial epistemologies and aesthetics. Resisting the temptation to romanticize non-European subjectivities and practices, we must be cognizant of the complicated relationship among decolonization, desubalternization, and European Enlightenment. Against an unequivocal exaltation of the aesthetic, drawing on Spivak, I focus on the ambivalent nature of aesthetic education. Kant (2002 [1790], 90–91) proposes that, while aesthetic disinterest is both redemptive and prefigurative, it is different from normative political discourse, which provides parameters for enlightened agency. Similarly, Adorno, following Kant, argues that autonomous aesthetic practice enables a critical distance to self-centered social and political action

(Kester 2012, 91). Let us now trace how Spivak draws on Kant, Schiller, and Adorno, even as she departs from them, to propose that the aesthetic can change minds away from mere self-interest toward decolonization.

Aesthetic Education and Desubalternization

Adorno (2002 [1970], 1) begins his *Aesthetic Theory* by questioning the right of art to exist. Prior to Adorno, different scholars have given a variety of responses to this issue. In the fourth century BCE, Plato claimed that art is dangerous as it distorts truth/reality and manipulates emotions. Plato's *Republic* (2012) banishes artists from the ideal state; they, unlike philosophers, are accused of being meddlers and irresponsible critics who deserve to be censored. Similarly, Stoic philosophers such as Seneca (2010), who wrote in the mid-first century CE, warned that emotions could be manipulated and artistic practices could be unpredictable in their impact, thereby recommending the state of being emotionless as the appropriate basis for ethical practice. The Stoics rejected compassion in favor of apathy, or the freedom from all affects, as a desired state of being. The historical role of art in fascist and colonial regimes seemed to confirm the misgivings of Stoics vis-à-vis aesthetics and affect. The promise of art producing *mündige* and *aufgeklärte Bürger* (active and enlightened citizens) appeared untenable in the face of the failure of the Eurocentric civilizational ideal of *Bildung* in the context of European colonialism and fascism.

Others, however, claim that art nurtures an ethical engagement between the spectator and the afflicted, thereby evoking sympathetic agency. The theatrical scene of suffering invites the gift of compassion and empathy—namely, sharing and participating in the pain of others; in the place of schadenfreude or hopelessness in the face of others' hardship, art encourages responsibility. Instead of feeling impotent or overwhelmed by the enormity of the painful spectacle (Sontag 2004), aesthetic practices can mobilize affect toward justice and freedom. In his *Poetics*, Aristotle (1997), writing in the latter part of the fourth century BCE, reflects on the purgative power of tragedy and, in contradiction to Plato, claims that a perfect tragedy incites emotions of fear and pity in the spectator, leading to catharsis. Furthermore, Aristotle argues that catharsis is not only purifying; it also reconciles art and ethics, all while producing knowledge. This greatly influenced Martha Nussbaum's (2015) contemplations on the positive role of political emotions.

Rather than relying on positivist approaches such as pie charts and statistics to convey information about poverty or war and raise awareness of global issues, one could argue that aesthetic practices, by provoking us out of our indifference and irresponsibility, are a more effective means of making us both political and ethical. Spivak argues that art not only familiarizes us with the unfamiliar by "productively undoing" (Spivak 2012a, 1) the opacity of the obvious and the given, it also, and more importantly, defamiliarizes the familiar (Spivak 2012a, 116). This resonates with Sigmund Freud's (1999 [1919], 195, 220-21) contemplations on the dialectics between *heimlich* (familiar, tame, and intimate but also secret and obscure) and *unheimlich* (unhomely, unfamiliar, uncomfortable). In a counterintuitive move, Freud explains that *unheimlich* is an unexpected self-revelation, the negation of the hidden and concealed. It is the unhomey and eerie that inadvertently reveal the familiar and the intimate that the self conceals from itself. In the realm of the aesthetic, instead of mirroring or testing reality, aesthetic practices metamorphose the ordinary into the uncanny, and vice versa. The aesthetic bears the promise of revealing to us what we are unwilling to confront and thus has the power to surprise us with the ordinary. The promise is that an uncanny politics of representation, in terms of both *Darstellung* and *Vertretung*, can forge new political subjectivities and take us beyond the checklist concept of justice and democracy.

One would think that one could achieve decolonization by securing economic independence, social empowerment, and political enfranchisement of subaltern classes. Although all of these aspects are necessary, they are, in Spivak's (2012a, 41) view, nevertheless insufficient for undoing subalternity and have to be supplemented by an aesthetic education that transforms "the way in which objects of knowledge are constructed; perhaps also shifting desires in the subject." This is not about a policy-oriented plan for the promotion of the arts and their education or setting standards for judgments of taste. Rather, the focus is on the importance of the critical value of an aesthetic education, which is the practice of teaching and learning to train the imagination. An indispensable aspect of decolonization involves "productively undoing another legacy of the European Enlightenment—the aesthetic" (Spivak 2012a, 1). An aesthetic education goes beyond the imparting of information and skills. It is related to "the habit of the ethical" (Spivak 2012a, 9) in that it shifts "belief onto the terrain of the imagination" (Spivak 2012a, 10). In her readings of the Western canon, Spivak's attempt is to "sabotag[e] Schiller" (Spivak

2012a, 2) by intentionally misreading his contemplations on the aesthetic to contribute to the project of desubalternization and, consequently, decolonization.

Before elaborating Spivak's position, let me briefly rehearse the arguments of authors on whom she draws. Within Western philosophical thought, Kant's influential position focuses on the link between human cognition and aesthetic judgments. In contrast to the gratification drawn from moral action, aesthetic experience, for Kant, produces a "disinterested satisfaction" that is neither anchored in reality nor burdened with moral or political imperatives. This is not causally evoked by a work of art. It is, instead, a state of mind unconstrained by self-interest. In Kant's view, an aesthetic judgment, which is different from private sensual pleasure, is a reflection of the beautiful. This causes disinterested and universal pleasure, which, although apart from the objective judgment of reason, nevertheless rests on the link between the individual and the universal (Eriksson 2008–9, 36–37). Aesthetics emancipates us from private self-interestedness and makes "intersubjectivity" possible; it fosters a transition from "I" to "we" (Eriksson 2008–9, 40). One of the most important lessons of *The Critique of Judgment* (Kant 2002 [1790]) is that the divide between individuality and humanity is bridged through aesthetics. Kant scholars argue that the greatest achievement of his aesthetic theory lies in its liberation of aesthetic judgment, challenging the feudal monopoly on what is considered good taste, which had been the exclusive domain of the aristocracy. This democratizes the process of acquiring and cultivating aesthetic judgment.

This claim is contested by Pierre Bourdieu, who points out that Kant's and Schiller's bourgeois challenge to aristocracy did not undo the role of class in the sphere of the aesthetics. In *Distinction*, Bourdieu (1979) disputes the claim of universality and disinterested nature in Kantian aesthetics. He outlines the aesthetic divide between elite and privileged classes and the distaste of the privileged vis-à-vis working-class aesthetics (Eriksson 2008–9, 39). Thus, instead of intersubjectivity and universality, aesthetics cements social status and class privileges. This abrogates the promise of aesthetic judgment, leveling hierarchies by democratizing taste. Kant stands accused of proposing aesthetic elitism, wherein privileged people legislate and set standards on questions of beauty and the sublime, thereby determining who qualifies as civilized.

Against the charge that only select aesthetically cultivated men can adjudicate matters of taste and beauty, it can be argued, aesthetic judgment for Kant is not based on singular experience of the beautiful or the sublime. Despite maintaining the subjective nature of taste, Kant (2002 [1790], 114) insists on a common ground of judgment based in our shared human condition. The capacity to experience beauty is a core human capability that is not limited to those with refined sensibilities or evolved appreciation for fine arts. This implies that aesthetic pleasure is not reserved for an exceptional few to be experienced in private or some other manner of elitist seclusion. Kant instead emphasizes the role of the aesthetic in the formation of the intellectually active and morally responsible citizen. The rift between reason and inclination, between intellect and will, is negotiated through the "enlarged mode of thought" (Kant 2002 [1790], 174) nurtured by aesthetic experience.

It is important to bear in mind that, for Kant (1991a [1784], 55), the exercise of reason as a form of autonomous thinking, which is an antidote to subservience as well as arbitrariness, is not a solitary endeavor. A private individual cannot expect to escape "immaturity"; rather, autonomy in thinking is always intersubjective and exercised through the public use of reason. For the emergence of an enlightened public, the freedom to make public use of one's reason is more significant than political reform or revolution.

A form of homage and response to Kant's *Critique of Judgment*, Schiller's *On the Aesthetic Education of Man* letters (2016b [1795]) were written in the aftermath of the Reign of Terror during the French Revolution. Reflecting on the question of true political freedom, the text explores the tension between the opposing forces of the sensuous and the rational. Anticipating Adorno's thoughts on instrumental reason, Schiller (2016a [1793]), in a letter dated July 13, 1793, outlines the pitfalls of overrationalization, which he links to barbarism: "However, man can be at odds with himself in two ways: either as savage, his feelings ruling his principles, or as barbarian if his principles destroy his feelings" (Schiller 2016b [1795], fourth letter). As a means to reconcile sense and thought, an aesthetic education functions as an antidote: "If one is to resolve this political problem one must in practice take the aesthetic path, for it is by way of beauty that one approaches liberty" (2016b [1795], second letter). The link between beauty and freedom is such that the experience of the former is indispensable for the attainment of the latter. The liberation that follows revolutions will be unsuccessful without an aesthetic education; without a sense of the beautiful, freedom from tyranny can quickly end in barbarism. The failure of the Enlightenment, for Schiller, is that the focus was predominantly on educating the intellect without cultivating capacity for feelings and desires (Schiller 2016b [1795], 15). The sensibilities of people have to be shaped such that they are inclined to act in accordance with the principles of reason. Any progress in the political sphere is possible only by ennobling the character of citizens through art (Schiller 2016b [1795], 29). Beauty can be redemptive, such that a cultivated aesthetic taste is a prerequisite for the constitution of upstanding citizens. Rather than serving a merely instrumental function, aesthetics nurtures a person's capacity and capability for moral and political action.

Schiller focuses on the link between an aesthetic and a playful attitude in humans, who play and create, both of which are nonpurposive but not frivolous. The free play of the imaginative—namely, *Spieltrieb* (play drive)—is prior to the emergence of reason in human subjects (Schiller 2016b [1795], 51). Rule-governed and yet without a purpose beyond itself, the sensuous pleasure derived from playing transports one to the realm of beauty (Schiller 2016b [1795], 56). For Schiller, following Kant (2002 [1790], 27), the aesthetic lies between the sensuous pleasure of purposiveness/purposelessness of play and the law of reason governing ethical action (Chesney 2014, 63). What is free has no purpose beyond itself and beauty is the form freedom takes in the realm of sensory experience. Through its particular education, the aesthetic consequently can prepare man to be truly free for a moral life. Furthermore, a person becomes rational through the aesthetic in that it prepares subjects to choose and exercise their will. By teaching man to accept formal rule through the training of the senses and the imagination, man is set free. The aesthetic mediates between man's sensuous and rational natures, giving us access to the epistemic (Chesney 2014, 64).

Schiller's subordination of political liberation to the process of aesthetics is assailed for promoting a Eurocentric idea of beauty. Spivak rebukes the universalist aspirations of Kant's and Schiller's aesthetic theories, as well as the ahistorical, humanist model of aesthetic education in their writings. However, instead of censuring or boycotting him, Spivak (2012a, 2) explicitly aims to "sabotag[e] Schiller" by reading him against the grain. This entails rethinking the role of an aesthetic education in processes of decolonization, not to justify aesthetics in political or ethical terms, but to outline how the pursuit of liberatory politics and an ethical life is impossible without nurturing the imagination. Training the intellect is not just about programming human beings into universal reason through education; rather, as Schiller (2016a [1793], 126) remarks in his July 13, 1793, letter to his patron, the Duke of Augustenburg, "One has to begin with the creation of the citizens for a constitution, before these citizens can be granted a constitution." Lest we forget, *sapientia* (wisdom) has its root in *sapor* (taste): a faculty of feeling, intuition, and sensibility. Another important point to note is the discontinuity between utility and value, such that art has worth not just in terms of its supposed use value and practical function; given the irreducible nature of aesthetic experience and pleasure, it is significant on its own terms (*für sich*). In place of a purely rational subjectivity, Spivak agrees with Schiller that an aesthetic education is indispensable in cultivating an intuition of the public sphere in citizens. This must be achieved not by promulgating a code of laws for aesthetics, but by nurturing political and moral virtues in the constitution of a person, ultimately leading to a free and just society.

At the same time, we must be wary of an idealized account of education and of aesthetics as ineluctably redemptive (Spivak 2012a, 19–20). Postcolonial scholars, such as Edward Said and Spivak, highlight the role of the arts during colonialism and the elitism within the aesthetic realm, with aesthetic judgment serving as a marker of European civilization. They analyze the role of race, religion, gender, and sexuality in colonial construction of aesthetics. Ironically, in the past decades one can trace a shift in elitist taste, particularly in the West, from snobbish exclusion, dismissal, and devaluation of non-European practices to exoticization, Orientalization, and cannibalization of the Other. From cinema to cuisine, from artworks to apparel, the commodification and fetishization of non-European aesthetics is a multibillion-dollar industry. Instead of celebrating this as de-universalization of colonial aesthetics, we must focus on the "cultural industry" as a failure of the decolonization of aesthetics. The dethroning of Western hegemony is insufficient to decolonize the arts. While emphasizing the teaching and educability of taste, postcolonial scholars question the opposition between presumably cultivated and refined norms of the elite versus the masses indulging in purportedly base and vulgar pleasure. At the same time, instead of dismissing Kant as the spokesperson of white, upper-class Europe and romanticizing popular culture as revolutionary and radical, it is imperative to understand how both can be critical and uncritical. The challenge lies in reconciling the two ends.

At the core of Spivak's understanding of an aesthetic education is the capacity to negotiate the paradoxes prominent in the current era of globalization. Drawing on Gregory Bateson's theory of the double bind, which Spivak (2012a, 3) explains as "learning to live with contradictory instructions," she explores how this impossible situation is to be negotiated. While Bateson recommends play therapy as a means of coping with these double binds, Spivak (2012a, 2) proposes an aesthetic education to prepare subjects epistemologically to counter the "mind-numbing uniformization of globalization." This epistemological shift implies reconsidering what one knows and how one knows it. The tension among reason, politics, and ethics is mediated through the "training of the imagination for epistemological performance" (Spivak 2012a, 122). The imagination negotiates between the inherited ways of knowing and the possibility of epistemic change.

Like Schiller, who proposes that women do not have the capacity to access truth yet are superior to men in the realm of imagination and of sensibility, Paul de Man claims: "Philosophy . . . is the domain of men; art is—basically, the beautiful is—the domain of women" (quoted in Spivak 2012a, 32). Deconstructing the discontinuity between access to truth and beauty, Spivak seeks to displace the gender binary without attempting to erase sexual difference (Spivak 2012a, 32). Without essentializing or biologizing the feminine as redemptive, Spivak addresses the possibilities for aesthetic/gender as a site of possible epistemic change that contests rationalized empiricism. But this potential of the aesthetic is contingent, as it can only offer "hope against hope" (Spivak 2012a, 28), with no guarantees. Unlike the assurances from scholars such as Nussbaum, who claim that the humanities will bring Enlightenment, Spivak (2012a, 189) argues that "change is hardly ever possible on grounds of reason alone." It is an impossible but necessary task of undoing the epistemological and ethical consequences of globalization, of capital and data, such that "information command has ruined knowing and reading. Therefore, we don't really know what to do with information" (Spivak 2012a, 1). Let us now take a more detailed look at the role of aesthetic education in the processes of decolonization.

The Art of Decolonization

The goal of colonial education was to produce Western-educated natives, who would function as conduits between Europe and the colonies, forging a class alliance between the elite natives and Europeans (Sharpe 2014, 512; Spivak 2012a, 105). For instance, the aim of the British Raj, as outlined in Thomas Babington Macaulay's (1952 [1835], 729) infamous 1835 minutes on Indian education, was to create "a class of persons, Indian in blood and colour, but English in taste, in opinions, in morals, and in intellect." Drawing on the power of the Enlightenment, the aspiration was to encourage the pursuit of truth and reason in so-called uncivilized societies. At the same time, there were also concerns that exposure to European literature and poetry could feed the allegedly untamed imagination of the natives, thereby inciting anticolonial sentiments (Sharpe 2014, 512). As Gauri Viswanathan (1989, 157) points out, "The fact that educated Indians were reading Goethe in translation caused infinitely greater concern in British administrative circles than their reading the works of political liberals like Locke or Hume, whose appeal to reason and constitutionalism rather than imagination presumably posed fewer dangers of shaping a unified nationalist sentiment." Interestingly, while political philosophy promised to insert the natives into modernity's colonial episteme, romantic poetry posed the threat of inspiring resistance and revolution. Instead of having a supposedly modernizing effect, English-style education ironically resulted in solidifying social stratification in India rather than undoing caste affiliations (Viswanathan 1989, 151).

This colonial gesture of forging native subjectivities in the episteme of modernity was repeatedly pursued in subsequent approaches to education. The aim was to interpellate the neocolonial subject who, having received a Western education, would contribute to the project of modernization in postcolonial societies and nations (Sharpe 2014, 513). Postcolonial citizens received training in the episteme of global finance and were inserted into the grid of international electronic capital. The deterritorialization and virtualization of data and capital has resulted in the "computation of the globe into the abstract" (Spivak 2012a, 105). Here, aesthetics can serve as a tool for electronic capitalism, not only in relation to the global art market, but also by positioning creativity as a resource that further drives the globalization of capitalism. The corporatization of universities implies the instrumentalization of science, with thought becoming commodity and language a vehicle of commerce. Along with the decline of the ability to exercise judgment, critical thinking is dismissed as an old-fashioned luxury. Knowledge becomes a means to uphold the status quo, thereby abandoning its critical and oppositional functions. Instead of allowing the imagination to go places beyond and envisioning the not yet, it is measured against the standard of efficiency and utility.

A counterpoint to the strategy known as artwashing—in which aesthetics are coopted by capitalist and neoliberal agendas—is artivism, which represents the intersection of art and activism: the harnessing of militant aesthetic practices to facilitate progressive agendas. The discussion in the introduction of the controversial documenta fifteen exhibition serves as an illuminating example of the complexities inherent in political art. Adorno's juxtaposition of Bertolt Brecht and Samuel Beckett is an instructive lesson in the dynamic between aesthetics and politics. Brecht's aesthetics seeks to negotiate the gap between a work of art and the socio-economic and political problems of the masses. Adorno dismisses Brecht's attempt to bridge aesthetics and politics as purposive. Precisely for these reasons, Adorno objects to an ethical or political role for aesthetics. In a conversation in 1967, Beckett informed Adorno that Brecht intended to write an *Anti-Godot*. Adorno jotted down in his notebook, "My God, what a piece of crap that would have been" (quoted in Klasen 2018, 1024). This incident is demonstrative of his position on "committed" versus "autonomous" art (Adorno 1980 [1965], 177; Klasen 2018, 1024). In addition to the famous question of "whether works of art can still come into being at all after the catastrophes that had taken place" (Tiedemann 1994, 18), Adorno explored the (non)function of art in society. Even as "autonomous"—that is, detached from social obligations—art was indefensible for Adorno; he belittled art in the service of political and ethical imperatives as sheer propaganda. "Commitment" is not merely an effort to improve a given situation; rather, it seeks to transform the very preconditions that engender the situation in the first place (Adorno 2002 [1970], 246). However, when aesthetic practice translates into direct political action, it ironically reproduces that against which it struggles (Klasen 2018, 1025). Art, then, becomes a distraction from the very conditions it seeks to highlight, thereby functioning as an alibi and substitute for substantial transformation.

Adorno accuses Brecht of disregarding the autonomy of art, whereby, in its efforts to social and political transformation, his art becomes purposive. When art is reduced to a social function, this functionality robs it of its critical potential. "Aesthetic autonomy" is the hope that rescues us from the barbarism of modern Enlightenment, in that it resists appropriation by politics and integration into society and its norms (Adorno 2002 [1970], 12–13). Autonomy of art enables new worlds to emerge that offer counterfactual possibilities (Hohendahl 1985, 25). Contrary to this is "socialist realism," the doctrinal art of the Soviet Union since the 1930s (Adorno 2002 [1970], 254; Klasen 2018, 1025). A lack of distance between art and social praxis is anathema to Adorno, who famously proclaimed: "Rather no art than socialist realism" (Adorno 2002 [1970], 53). He derides Brecht's proximity to party communism, as well as the conscious connection he makes between art and society in his *Lehrstücke* (learning-play). In Adorno's view, the result of Brecht's desire to educate the masses is the instrumentalization of his art for a political purpose, by which he succumbs to realism. Yet despite Brecht's political commitments, Adorno (2005e [1969], 275) accuses him of being more interested in theater than in changing the world. In concerning himself with the real world, Brecht fails to abstract from reality, ultimately undermining the integrity of his art. Brecht's lack of ambivalence and "infantile simplification" (Adorno 1991, 222) results in his art managing only to depict reality superficially. Brecht thereby fails in his intentions by resorting to didactics in the representation of social suffering.

Political art, for Adorno, is the manipulation of art as it tends toward the propagandistic while sacrificing the aesthetic. Irrespective of the content, art with a political message is reactionary rather than radical, for it reduces aesthetics to a mere instrument (Marasco 2015, 105). Dismissing Brecht's "manipulative technique," (Adorno 2002 [1970], 242) which prioritizes doctrine over form, Adorno foregrounds the ambiguity of autonomous art that inspires rather than sermonizes. Gauged against committed art stands autonomous art, which has no obvious use value. It performs dialectical critique through abstraction, absurdity, and parody. In Adorno's (1991 [1958], 269) reading, autonomous art is self-critical and reflexive, like the works of Beckett, which, while being "historico-philosophical sundials" (geschichtsphilosophische Sonnenuhren), also go beyond merely mirroring empirical reality and documenting history. Rather than promoting a specific ideology or being "socially useful" (Adorno 2002 [1970], 226), the radicality of autonomous art lies in providing a counterpoint to existing social norms (Klasen 2018, 1027). Without being intentionally oppositional or transgressive, autonomous art "criticizes society by merely existing" (Adorno 2002 [1970], 225–26). In expressing the social experience of loss of meaning, Beckett's art refuses the temptation to distill meaning from meaninglessness (Klasen 2018, 1029). By transforming language into an instrument of its own absurdity, Beckett frees the subject from purposive activity. The senselessness of an action becomes the reason for doing it. Given that language historically has functioned as an instrument of domination, Beckett short-circuits it through his absurd logic. Without "a single political word" (Adorno 2002 [1970], 234), Beckett's art still embodies radicality for Adorno. Insofar as it does not aspire to be logical, Beckett's art undermines positivism and inspires hope even while denying it (Klasen 2018, 1031). In outlining the absurdity of action, it fuels change. In the face of disenchanted aesthetics, only art that evades the principle of utility can withstand instrumentalization. Adorno is, of course, aware that autonomous art can become politically and socially inconsequential (Klasen 2018, 1035) and can become an alibi for the avoidance of intervening practice. At the same time, he warns of falling into the trap of empiricism while working toward political transformation (Adorno 2002 [1970], 91, 2009 [1959–60], 195).

The contrast Adorno draws between the aesthetic structure of modern art and reified everyday reality stands accused of an elitism that further widens the gap between aesthetics and the general public (Hohendahl 1985, 23). Max Horkheimer and Adorno's hostility toward popular culture was denounced by students as a sign of bourgeois elitism and snobbery toward consumers of Hollywood movies, musicals, jazz, radio shows, and magazines. Their contempt for the "pleasure industry" (Horkheimer and Adorno 2002 [1947], 116) reflects the bias of an elite cultural milieu. The claim that the "pleasure industry" annuls critical thought disavows popular culture's role in enabling new subjectivities and political practices to emerge. The critical potential of popular culture is even evident to the right, given their vehement backlash against it. As discussed in chapter 2, jazz, for instance, was a crucial site for the formation of Black women's political agency. In her inspiring book *Blues Legacies and Black Feminism*, Angela Davis (1999), who studied with Adorno, analyzes the role of the blues tradition as powerful articulations of an alternative Black consciousness that is contrary to mainstream American culture. Davis compellingly demonstrates how the aesthetic practices of Black working-class female singers and artists challenged moral, social, and sexual mores of middle-class respectability. Imaginations, bodies, pleasures, and desires are shaped and constituted through these historically devalued and delegitimized aesthetic practices that have both ethical and political ramifications.

Against the utility and marketability of art, wherein art embodies political slogans, Adorno (1980 [1965], 193) counterargues that when art is made to serve social causes, it becomes political propaganda assimilating to that against which it protests. Rather than nurturing nuanced aesthetic judgment, the "culture industry" produces unthinking and docile audiences through the commodification of artistic practices. Instead of experimenting with the audience's assumptions, challenging their normative frames and common sense, art becomes reassuring and uncritical insofar as it renders the audience passive consumers of prepackaged, standardized products (Adorno 1975 [1967], 19). Purposive art renders critical intelligence unthinkable and promotes indulgent contemplation. In contrast, for Adorno, following Kant, the purposeless of art implies that it serves no useful function, which makes it critical of instrumental reason.

The principle of idealist aesthetics, Kant's paradoxical formulation that the beautiful is what is purposive without a purpose, is inverted in the model of usefulness adopted by bourgeois art, which provides entertainment and leisure: "purposelessness for purposes dictated by the market"

(Horkheimer and Adorno 2002 [1947], 127). Dismissing popular culture, Adorno considers good art only that which, in its form and content, resists and destabilizes the commodification and homogenization that pervades late capitalist culture. He draws a distinction between false and genuine art, with the former being merely an instrument of ideology, and the latter refusing any form of appeasement or affirmation of finite conclusions.

Contrary to György Lukács' focus on partisan art and socialist realism, for Adorno the truth of an artwork lies in an autonomous aesthetic logic (Adorno 2002 [1970], 225–26). Ironically, the presumed uselessness of the artwork safeguards it from commodification (Adorno 2002 [1970], 237). Functionlessness of art for Adorno is a symbol of freedom that resists how the commodity form tries to functionalize nearly everything. Art is economically nonautonomous if it is dependent on marketing, branding, and advertising to survive. Similarly, it is politically nonautonomous if it is commissioned by dominative powers to glorify their power. Abstract and experimental art strengthens the audiences' imaginations, making it anti-ideological.

In response to accusations of elitism, it is crucial to emphasize that Adorno distinguishes between autonomous and committed art in the aftermath of the Holocaust, drawing on his experiences with fascism. Rather than romanticizing or glorifying aesthetic practices, he encourages critical understanding of how art can become a handmaiden of authoritarian regimes. While I appreciate Adorno's emphasis on critical analysis of aesthetic practices, the juxtaposing of autonomous versus committed art risks disregarding that the boundaries between the two are not as clear-cut as he considers them. This can oversimplify aesthetic practices as transparent and intentional, disavowing the multifacetedness of artistic process, motivation, and reception. For instance, while Adorno's views on jazz reflect his disdain for passive consumption of popular culture and fears of commodification of art, they also demonstrate a lack of understanding of jazz's rich history: of how jazz has transgressed conventional norms of harmony, rhythm, and form and pushed the boundaries of aesthetic experience through creative improvisation. Instead of being merely entertaining or a symptom of cultural decline, jazz embodies the artistic and cultural expression of oppressed communities. To dismiss this as identity politics does it great disservice. I would quote Thelonius Monk to Adorno: "Jazz is freedom. You think about that."[1]

Like Adorno, who rebukes conformity and standardization, Spivak is wary of the utilitarian exigencies of global capitalism, such that aesthetics, for her, can alter how we think, thereby changing what we know and, consequently, what we want (Chesney 2014, 61). In an effort to counter the homogenizing processes of globalization, Spivak (2012a, 116) hopes that an aesthetic education can sabotage "the repeated construction of the colonial subject." To achieve this, emancipation for subaltern classes should be redefined from mere access to financial capital to a mode of education that empowers subalterns to become problem solvers rather than victims in need of rescue. The iniquitous dynamics between hegemonic and subaltern classes must be rectified to mitigate "the necessity of 'good' rich people solving the world's problems. . . . Beggars receive material goods to some degree and remain beggars" (Spivak 2012a, 135). The agency of subjects, who have been deprived of the Enlightenment's enabling legacies, must be activated through aesthetics.

A journalist once asked James Baldwin (2009) whether being poor, Black, and gay had made him feel disadvantaged as a young writer. "No," Baldwin replied. "I thought I had hit the jackpot. It was so outrageous, you had to find a way to use it." Spivak mobilizes the same words and speaks of "using the Enlightenment" by way of a renegotiation with the colonial episteme of modernity. Rather than abandoning European thought, the goal is to "sabotage" the Enlightenment, in which we "learn to use the European Enlightenment from below . . . to counteract the fact that the Enlightenment came, to colonizer and colonized alike, through colonialism" (Spivak 2012a, 3–4). Using the Enlightenment "from below" does not signify a stance of subordination or deference; rather, it represents the complex dilemma faced by the postcolonial world in relation to European Enlightenment. The postcolonial approach is one of "critical intimacy," such that the effort is to turn around from within the Enlightenment, as opposed to delinking. Instead of eschewing the Enlightenment, Spivak's "affirmative sabotage" (Spivak 2012a, 4) is an attempt to wield the master's tools to undercut his goals. The capacity to engage in intellectual labor through access to these empowering critical tools would provide subalterns with the potential to transform hegemony (Spivak 2012a, 436). Furthermore, it would reconfigure the relationship between the elite and the (gendered) subaltern, with the latter no longer simply being objects of knowledge or native informant-style subjects patronizingly considered incapable of epistemological performance (Spivak 2012a, 60). In place of being the "*subject* of crisis," the subaltern is embedded into the "logic of *agency*" (Spivak 2012a, 436).

This brings us to the challenging dynamic between the subaltern and the intellectual, between "ordinary people" and "the *Gelehrte*" (Kant 1991a

[1784], 57), "the hero of Kantian Enlightenment, in being 'oppositional' to every system, the individual who resists systems" (Spivak 2012a, 391). In this context, intellectuals, especially upper-class diasporic and native women from the global South, must question their self-perception as role models for impoverished rural women. To establish an ethical relationship between intellectuals and subalterns, the former must gain the confidence of the latter through "the patient effort to learn with the goal of transmitting that learning to others" (Sharpe and Spivak 2003, 619–20). Instead of harvesting data about others, the elite must relinquish the notion of themselves as the preeminent subjects of knowledge (Sharpe 2014, 516). To unlearn epistemological presuppositions, or what Spivak calls uncritical habits of the mind, requires being prepared to renounce a will to knowledge. Here the intellectual no longer sees herself as an agent of social change but, instead, recognizes herself as being part of the problem rather than the solution. This recognition of being implicated in hegemonic structures can enable a transformation in how (intellectual) elites view the world. It opens the imagination to the radically other instead of assimilating it into the self. Not just the subaltern but the elite, too, are in need of an aesthetic Enlightenment.

One of the biggest challenges of social and political theory lies in understanding why oppressed groups accept their subjugation and exploitation. How does one persuade a rural, illiterate tribal woman in the poorest corner of the world that she has the same rights and dignity as the richest, most powerful men and women in the world? How do you convey the democratic principle of one person equals one vote as a formula for robust and active citizenry? Spivak, who runs schools in the remotest villages of India for the poorest children of the biggest democracy in the world, speaks of her experience with the teachers of her school supporting the local right-wing politician. When she asked them about their ideological affiliation, one of the teachers scratched his head and responded that democracy was too complicated. He just casts his vote.

In their insightful essay "Can the Subaltern Vote?" Leerom Medovoi, Shankar Raman, and Ben Robinson (1990, 134–35) examine how electoral processes in the global South can reinforce subalternity even as they seem to empower marginalized collectives. They question the idea of elections as transparent representations of the people's will and reveal how the discourse of self-determination and democratic legitimacy often silences disenfranchised collectives while claiming to give them voice. The authors argue that, although elections are framed as political speech—reflected in the German word *Stimme*, meaning both voice and vote—this idealized portrayal of voters as coherent and homogeneous subjects actually undermines the promise of genuine democratic postcoloniality through parliamentary elections.

The postcolonial world struggles with the following questions: How does one frame voting as an arithmetic operation of democracy and citizenship such that each citizen has a voice through the vote? How does one train the imagination of those exiled from intellectual labor to understand themselves as part of an abstract entity of the demos? How can one explain the significance of their participation in an election and the counting of votes as integral to the performance of citizenship? Education as a "slow cooking of the soul" (Spivak 2016) is the opposite of easy and speedy learning and can rearrange people's desire, so they do not act against their own interests and those of their fellow citizens. The contradictory and complex dynamic between self-interest and desire challenges the rational choice model as well as the understanding of humans as mere *Homo economicus*. When what subalterns *want* is changed, what they *do* will follow. Education here goes beyond literacy and numeracy, which does not automatically nurture democratic judgment. Democracy is "the tug of war between autonomy and rights of others" (Spivak 2013). Nurturing critical intelligence transforms self-interested subjects with unreflected political motives into citizens capable of thinking beyond the self.

Desubalternization is intended not to make the poor employable but to create the "subaltern intellectual" (Spivak 2012b). Furthering Antonio Gramsci—who argues that everyone is an intellectual, but not everyone has the function of an intellectual in society—Spivak argues that subalterns are exiled from intellectual labor, such that undoing subalternity involves unlearning the impulse to obey by nurturing reflective insight in the imagination of those who have never been taught to question. As Kant (1991a [1784], 57) explains: "This would also mean that each citizen . . . would be given a free hand as a scholar to comment publicly, i.e. in his writings, on the inadequacies of current institutions." While scholars of the Enlightenment believe that the bringing to consciousness of the unenlightened can be instigated only by those who possess critical insight, Spivak, in a counterintuitive move, argues that the intellectual must learn from the subaltern how to best facilitate the transformation of their desires and imagination—namely, "learn to learn from below" (Spivak 2004, 563). This decenters the mastery of intellectuals, wherein they become the disciples of the subaltern and their circumstances. The intellectual must learn from the subterranean subaltern practices and their underlying insights regarding the constitution of power and subjectivity. In contrast to presuming that the intellectual possesses a uniquely privileged capacity to comprehend the totality of domination, the intellectual must learn from the subaltern how to criticize and transform the conditions and processes of subalternization. The principle of critical autonomy is reconfigured by infusing into it the significance of quotidian subaltern insights and practices.

The intellectual's role is to cultivate democratic impulses in marginalized citizens who have been excluded from political participation. For Spivak (2004, 48–49), "It is more important to develop a critical intelligence than to assure immediate material comfort." Such an approach could be accused of being indifferent to the pressing existential needs of the impoverished. However, in this view, overcoming global inequality and injustice is not simply a matter of attending to the so-called basic needs of the disenfranchised; rather, the effort is to redistribute agency transnationally. It is worthwhile to recall W. E. B. Du Bois's disagreement with Booker T. Washington following the American Civil War and end of slavery. Two of the most important Black intellectuals of their time had a conflict over the form of education best suited for recently liberated collectivities. Washington believed that the key to emancipation of African Americans was through education in vocational and industrial training, which would allow them to be financially independent by earning a living wage as plumbers, carpenters, mechanics, builders, and electricians. In his view, previously uneducated groups must quickly acquire literacy and numeracy to become equal members of society through economic empowerment. Du Bois, however, argued that emancipation entailed much more than becoming employable as a skilled laborer. The forty acres and a mule that were promised to newly freed African Americans in the aftermath of the Civil War as compensation for unpaid labor during slavery was insufficient to guarantee either rights or dignity. Du Bois claimed that freed slaves needed to train their imagination; it was not enough to have freedom *from* until one understood what freedom was *for*. Washington accused Du Bois of mimicking whiteness when promoting arts and humanities, which he considered luxuries beyond the means of the poor and disenfranchised. Du Bois, by contrast, championed training the mind for abstract thinking, especially for vulnerable groups, as key to human emancipation and full citizenship for people who had previously been denied this right.

Drawing on Du Bois and Adorno, Spivak warns against providing subaltern classes with an education that reduces knowledge to brute facts that are calculable, quantifiable, and instrumental: the utopia of logical positivists. This form of intellectual formation of subalterns serves the interests of the capitalist structures of society; such knowledge is complicit in the system that oppresses and causes suffering. Facilitating critical consciousness in the oppressed makes them aware of the significance of their disenfranchisement instead of simply accepting their supposed fate as natural and inevitable. Education should be about "changing minds" of subalterns to develop the habits and reflexes of democracy, not through formulas designed to engineer them into good, law-abiding citizens, but into citizens capable of critical thought. Preparing subaltern subjects for "epistemological performance" (Spivak 2012a) creates active citizens involved in a democratic process that goes beyond the formal procedures of electing a body of representatives. Imagination must be prepared such that the subalterns see themselves as part of an abstract entity of the demos, wherein every citizen is equal, irrespective of differences in class, gender, sexuality, age, race, and religion. In a democracy, whether one is the richest citizen in the country or the poorest, everyone gets one vote—no more, no fewer. Despite differences, everyone is formally equal. To grasp and reflect on this abstract idea of equality, education must be understood to be much more than impact assessment, effective teaching, nongovernmental organization tool kits, and knowledge management. Bad education destroys the mind, robbing subalterns of their right to refuse to obey, even as submissiveness is rewarded. In contrast, an aesthetic education, which is much more than an ends-means curriculum or effective pedagogy, disrupts the "class apartheid," thereby producing subalterns as citizens (Spivak 2012a, 513 fn. 23).

The formation of the rational economic subject under capitalism emerges in conjunction with developing indifference to the subjectivity of the radically other. This ethical deficit reduces social relations to instrumental reason. The aesthetic can serve as a powerful tool to reshape these entrenched, self-interested ways of thinking. One must, of course, be vigilant about how the aesthetic can be manipulated to promote the dominant ideologies of fascism, capitalism, nationalism, and patriarchy. Ideology critique is implicit in an aesthetic education.

The capitalist celebration of creative imagination is caught in individualist ideology. The "class-marked" bias of aesthetics (Spivak 2012a, 6) implies that, instead of mitigating it, an aesthetic education could consolidate the relation between class formation and subjectivation. However, an aesthetic education can also enable access to freedom for subaltern groups by disrupting hegemonic class formations. In place of consciousness-raising, "patient epistemological care" (Spivak 2012a, 519, fn. 57) can train the imagination to abstract one's experience, enabling one to connect to others, instead of self-righteously pronouncing the superiority and universality of the self. "Radical alterity," Spivak (2012a, 391) explains, is "an otherness that reason needs, but which reason cannot grasp," one that interrupts the monotonous reproduction of the same. Critical aesthetic intelligence can cultivate sensibility toward differences. This is not about putting ourselves in other people's shoes but about being cognizant of the limitations of our own perspectives. Aesthetics allows the momentary bringing together of incommensurable realities.

An aesthetic education can thus nurture the ability to leave one's self behind and "enter another's text" (Spivak 2012a, 6). Using the literary term *metonymy*, Spivak (2012a, 436) highlights the ability to replace one's own position with another's. Similarly, *synecdoche* alludes to a part of oneself that can identify as a member of a collective (as in workers, women, or migrants) such that, by way of "necessary fiction," one supports collective action *as if* one's interests were completely represented by the collective. This is different from identity politics or groupthink insofar as these collectives, for Spivak, are always strategic and contingent interpellations. The alignment of the self and the collective is made possible through aesthetic training that enables identifications and analysis of the limits of one's subject formation. One is thereby capable of reading another's narrative without appropriating or dismissing it. Instead, one imagines oneself being inserted into another's world. By suspending and resisting self-interest and unlearning the urge to take oneself as the norm, this reflexive capacity allows reimagining the relationship between self and other. This offers the chance not only to intervene in the habits of the imperial self, but also, at the other end of the spectrum, ultimately to undo subalternity. To noninstrumentally access the episteme of another person or group, training the imagination is ineluctable. However, an ethical relationship between the subaltern and the hegemon is not merely an anthropological exercise in which the hegemon learns the language of the subaltern solely for the purpose of data extraction. A grim example of such cannibalistic extractivism is the work of the German anthropologist Eva Justin, a senior member of the Race Hygiene Research Center who played a crucial role in contributing to Nazi crimes against the Roma and Sinti (SintiundRoma.org 2024). She argued that Roma and Sinti people could not be educated or assimilated into German society because their purportedly primitive thinking could not be changed. Contributing to racial hygiene laws, she recommended their sterilization supposedly to safeguard the German population from presumed impure elements (Benedict et al. 2018). Justin spoke Romani, thereby earning the trust of Roma and Sinti people, whom she interviewed extensively. In fact, the deportation of children to Auschwitz-Birkenau was delayed to allow Justin to complete her research on them (Barth 2005, 122).

Spivak (2009a, 32) warns that accessing the "lingual memory" of subaltern groups is integral to both colonialism and decolonization. In contrast to Justin, for Spivak learning the language of the other holds the promise of "setting aside" one's own ideologies. This obliges another ethics of listening, which reconfigures the relation between rights and responsibility. While "the . . . Enlightenment-model social engineering on the Left as well as the liberal, capitalistic center—cannot think responsibility and right together" (Spivak 2012a, 342), the concept-metaphor of *al-haq*, which is translated as "the birthright of being able to take care of other people" (Spivak 2012a, 294), implies both my right *to* and my responsibility *for* the other. This resists reducing the subaltern to a recipient of neocolonial benevolence. Other epistemes not only enable us to think differently, but, more important, they are "defective for capitalism" (Spivak 2012a, 344). In deploying an alternative episteme, Spivak is not pursuing a decolonial agenda of promoting Indigenous epistemologies and cosmologies as political models; the non-European Arabic/Bengali/Urdu/Hindi concept-metaphor of *al-haq* to conceive of radical alterity is an effort to "learn from below" from subaltern worlds, yet without presenting them as best practices or foolproof recipes for decolonization.

Aesthetic enlightenment facilitates another politics of reading and listening, not through formulas or blueprints, but through intellectual labor that is "destined for errancy" (Spivak 2012a, 28) yet must be pursued nevertheless. The most important lesson to be learned is that the aesthetic short-circuits our habit of disregarding our habits. Merely following a different set of rules will not guarantee social and political change. It is tempting to forget that habits are at the core of our subject formation, and it is aesthetics that teaches us to reflect on our habitual forms of thinking. This mindfulness nurtures the capacity to both Other oneself and acquire an aesthetic sensibility, making it possible for us to learn how to learn. The undoing of habitual forms of thinking is made possible through an aesthetic education that is based on neither instrumental reason nor self-interest. It thereby opens up possibilities of other forms of desire and imagination.

The focus on the capacity to exercise one's imaginative faculties, as the "great in-built instrument of othering" (Spivak 2003b, 13), allows us to relate imaginatively with alterity. The aesthetic gives access to epistemic insights that escape the natural and social sciences. Outlining the limits of reason and its epistemic reach, the aesthetic can transgress the structures of reason to make us ethical subjects: "Ethics are not a problem of knowledge but a call of relationship" (Spivak 1993b, 32). According to Seyla Benhabib (1986, 342), "Relations of solidarity, friendship, and love are not aesthetic but profoundly moral ones." In contrast, Spivak would argue against the separation of politics, ethics, and aesthetics. This reminds one of the controversial staging of Beckett's *Waiting for Godot* by Susan Sontag during the Siege of Sarajevo in 1993 in a theater with twelve candles and a cast of malnourished and fatigued actors. While some assailed Sontag for being frivolous for putting on (such) a play in a conflict zone, others claim that it drew so much attention to the city's plight that it helped end the war. Whether one reads the staging as an act of solidarity or self-indulgence, what is indisputable is that, unlike the accusation that putting on a play in the middle of war is akin to fiddling while Rome burns, this example confirms that the aesthetic *is* indeed political and ethical.

Finally, following Marx's third Feuerbach thesis, which proclaims that "it is essential to educate the educator himself," the elite must see themselves as disciples who must learn from subalterns how to contribute to the process of desubalternization. By imagining the Other as at once similar to and yet different from the self, the encounter between the subaltern and the intellectual must produce a "mindchanging encounter on both sides" (Spivak 1999, 384). This aporia or logical impasse cannot be resolved; rather, it is the discontinuity between our imagination of the Other and the figure of the Other that must be negotiated (Sharpe 2014, 516). The ethical imperative in the aesthetic consists of imaginatively acknowledging the limits of the epistemic; it is incumbent to resist the temptation of reducing the ethical to the rationalist sense of "doing the right thing" and the "desire to be good," and this is possible only through the aesthetic (Spivak 2012a, 111). As Spivak (1994c, xxv) explains the aporia of the ethical: "Please note that I am not saying that ethics are impossible, but rather that ethics is the experience of the impossible." Aesthetics enables "the habit of mind" (Spivak 2012a, 111) to experience this ethical and epistemic impossibility not as defeat, but as a Beckettian opportunity to keeping trying and failing and failing better. Or in Spivak's ominous words about the double bind: "Who wins loses" (Spivak 2012a, 3).

Conclusion

Affirmative Sabotage
of the Master's Tools

We live in a world in which we can no longer imagine a better one. The consolation that the utopian impulse offers, as opposed to the mere wish for a better world, is its capacity to grasp the thought that something fundamentally different from the given could be possible. —THEODOR ADORNO, *Lectures on Negative Dialectics*

How to Imagine a Postimperial World

The unprecedented advances in science and technology and rapid social and political transformation promise the protection and promotion of equality and freedom globally. At the same time, we are also facing un-paralleled challenges: ecological destruction and immiseration, the rise of right-wing movements across the globe, conflict and war, transnational dispossession and disenfranchisement. The list goes on. Although we seem to be barreling toward planetary destruction and ruin, we are also on the cusp of previously unimaginable global movements striving for economic, political, social, and cultural justice. Importantly, the situation in which we currently find ourselves is in many ways shaped by the legacies of colonialism. From climate change to the refugee crisis, from the controversies around the role of religion in politics to minority rights and citizenship, colonialism has left its traces on contemporary geopolitical, social, and economic questions. It is thus appropriate that across the disciplines, from scholarship on robotics to social media, from food sovereignty to peace and conflict studies, from fashion to music, postcolonial perspectives cannot be disregarded or evaded, despite repeated efforts to delegitimize them. To the contrary, they enrich and expand our understanding of our entangled pasts and futures. Unless we are able and willing to learn from our failures and crimes, we are condemned to repeat our mistakes.

The term for past and future in many non-European languages, such as Mandarin, Urdu, and Hindi, is the same. The Chinese word for "the day after tomorrow" literally means "behind day," whereas "the day before yesterday" is referred to as "front day." The words *yesterday* and *tomorrow* both translate to the same word in Hindi and Urdu: कल (*kal*). In *Midnight's Children*, Salman Rushdie (2021, 142) remarks: "No people whose word for 'yesterday' is the same as their word for 'tomorrow' can be said to have a firm grip on the time." What Rushdie is alluding to is the tenuous relation between temporality and hope, the desire and imagination for nondominant futures, and the impossibility of utopian thinking. Achille Mbembe (2021, 53) explains that colonialism not only negated the past and the history of the colonized but eroded their capacity for futurity, which is monopolized by Europe. This brings to mind two significant German words: *Vergangenheitsaufarbeitung* and *Zukunftsfähigkeit*. The former can be roughly translated as "working through the past," and the latter implies "future viability." I would argue that to be *Zukunftsfähig* one has to be able to undertake *Vergangenheitsaufarbeitung*, which involves taking stock of how we got to this state of affairs. It is my firm belief that our histories of the past should aid in strategic interrogations of the present as a way to help us envision the possibilities for postimperialist futures.

Given the link between colonial utopian experiments and the ensuing violence, it seems paradoxical to speak of postcolonial utopias. Yet, how is one to envision a post-imperial world? Or does the world in which we live preclude the potential to imagine postcolonial utopias? For centuries, European colonizers have combed the globe in search of adventures, chasing the allure of pristine, untouched land and people. Colonies served as fantastic projection screens onto which Europe mapped its forbidden desires and fears even as they functioned as laboratories for European hopes and imaginations. Originally published in 1516, Thomas More's *Utopia* is both a conceptual novelty and one of the earliest examples of imperialistic worlding and imagined geography. More describes a fictional island society in the South Atlantic Ocean off the coast of South America. Previously, when Christopher Columbus first encountered the New World and its Indigenous inhabitants, he believed he had found the Garden of Eden. However, as is known, the term *utopia* is a compound of the syllable *ou-* (no) and *topos* (place) from ancient Greek. But the homophonic prefix *eu-* (good) also resonates in the word, with the implication that the perfectly *good place* is really *no place*, so that the imagined ideal place does not exist (yet). This unviability of the future is not defeatism or cynicism but a melancholia for the yet to be. It is a yearning for that which is perpetually deferred. In the face of the unfulfilled desires that haunt the postcolonial world, how are we to overcome the acute paralysis of will and sheer lack of vision such that we may once again aspire to nondominant futures?

Given that Europe universalized its values, norms, and epistemologies through colonialism, decolonization seems a simple enough matter of de-universalizing Europe. But as has been argued throughout this book, this aspiration is impossible yet necessary; the gift and curse of the European Enlightenment's legacies are unavoidable. Although Europeans have proved to be the worst betrayers and abusers of the Enlightenment and its ideas of equality, liberty, justice, human rights, and democracy, the lofty post-colonial ambitions to salvage the legacies of the Enlightenment from the Europeans remains a daunting challenge.

The postcolonial critique of the Enlightenment, as I have shown, is not a rejection of the Enlightenment but an effort to locate the role of critique in processes of decolonization. Anticolonial revolutions held the promise of emancipation by vanquishing the brutality of colonialism. The painful past was to be supplanted by a healing present, driven by the restorative force of anticolonialism (Scott 2004, 6). Colonialism's totalizing dehumanization shaped the militant vocabulary of anticolonial struggles. However, the driving force of the past no longer serves to guarantee the opening of an emancipated future. Notions of resistance and dissidence have to be reimagined in face of multiple crises.

The postcolonial world must come to grips with the fact that anticolonial revolutions have fallen short of expectations. David Scott's (2004, 7) lamentation, "We live in tragic times," marks the failure of decolonization, such that "anticolonial utopias have gradually withered into postcolonial nightmares." With problems of global economic, social, and political inequality, reiterating earlier slogans of anticolonialism seems misplaced (Scott 2004, 167). Decolonization must be recast in other terms that imagine emancipation beyond anticolonial posturing and narratives of vindication

(Scott 2004, 7). To chart postcolonial futures, we need to reappraise the conviction that, to decolonize, undoing European colonialism would be sufficient to usher in a world without injustice and oppression.

Non-Europeans were not conscripted to Enlightenment's and modernity's project as volunteers but, rather, were coercively obliged to render themselves its objects and agents (Scott 2004, 9). Modernity was not an option for non-Europeans to either accept or disregard but "one of the fundamental conditions of choice" (Scott 2004, 19). As discussed in the previous chapters, the tragedy of the Haitian Revolution lies in the fact that colonial power circumscribed the conceptual and institutional conditions under which the slaves were obliged to fight for freedom (Scott 2004, 119). This paved the way for the postcolonial impasse, wherein colonial structures and subjectivities were inscribed into the postcolonial world in new ways. Commenting on Haiti and Liberia as republics emerging from plantation experiences—the former, a failed experiment of "self-liberation," and the latter, of "planned decolonization"—Mbembe (2021, 50) similarly laments that, in both cases, "servitude survives the process of abolition, emancipation having produced the exact inverse of what it wanted."

The tragic gift and curse of the Enlightenment is that it simultaneously enables and disables, strengthens and weakens; its script is intimately familiar yet elusive. The Enlightenment's inheritance cannot be rejected; it must be negotiated. Postcolonial subjects cannot *not* be conscripts of Enlightenment, such that we must "seek freedom in the very technologies, conceptual languages and institutional formations in which modernity's rationality" sought our oppression (Scott 2004, 168). The challenge is to unsettle and subvert the mastering ambitions of the Enlightenment without an outright rejection of its claims. Insofar as we are historically determined by it, it remains unavoidably one of the conditions of the analysis of ourselves (Foucault 1984, 45). We must not submit to the demand of loyalty to its doctrinal elements; instead, we must practice a continual questioning of its rationalities (Butler 2009). The postcolonial world's paradoxical relationship with the Enlightenment emerges from the conundrum that our mode of critique, as well as our constitution as critical subjects, is itself a legacy of the Enlightenment. Caught between instrumental one-sided reason and the enabling critical judgment, the challenge we face is in holding on to the contradictions of Enlightenment in a productive tension. What we need is to develop a "patience of paradox" and an acknowledgment that the "colonial past may never let go" (Scott 2004, 220). If the former slaves have become conscripts of the Enlightenment, inadvertently reinforcing its coercive legacy, what is the direction and grammar of postcolonial critique?

In light of these impossible conditions, how do we script our hopes, desires, and imaginaries to overcome the disillusioned present? The lofty postcolonial ambitions of envisioning an alternative future is revealing itself to be a missed appointment with history. For Antonio Gramsci (2011a, 276; Q3 §34), however, this presents an opening: "The old is dying and the new cannot be born: in this interregnum, morbid phenomena of the most varied kind come to pass." How should one imagine nondominant futures while retaining a certain pessimism of the intellect and an optimism of the will? What are the challenges of scripting a post-imperial politics from the (non)place of planetarity?

In place of an eschatological tradition that lends claims of directionality and purpose, complete with promises of salvation and fulfillment, a planetary approach to thinking about utopias facilitates multidirectional flows of hopes, desires, and imaginaries without reproducing hegemonic paradigms of globality that offer romantic longings for transnational conviviality and solidarity. The Greek term *eschaton* contains two meanings of the notion of an *end*: one as the finishing of a process as *finis*, and the other as the completion of a goal as *telos*. In contrast to investing futures with a purposiveness (Immanuel Kant's *Zweckmäßigkeit*), we need to be cognizant of the non-formulaic openness of planetary utopias that involves reflecting not only on what is to be hoped, desired, and imagined, but also on the limits of our best efforts to do so. For imagining the unimaginable and hoping in the face of hopelessness is precisely the task of utopias, a nostalgia for that which is yet to be, the not yet.

The postcolonial queer scholar José Esteban Muñoz (2009) suggests that queer futurity is an attempt to intervene in "straight time" that normalizes temporality. Countering a linear, progressive narrative, Muñoz (2009, 1) remarks: "We must dream and enact new and better pleasures, other ways of being in the world, and ultimately new worlds. . . . Queerness is essentially about the rejection of a here and now and an insistence on potentiality for another world." In contrast to Lee Edelman (2004), who rejects the politics of reproductive futurism and links queerness to the death drive, Muñoz presents a compelling rejoinder to queer apocalypse, which Edelman proposes in place of a forward-looking, reproductive, and heteronormative politics of hope that animates many political projects. The queer subject, Edelman argues, has been epistemologically bound to negativity, to nonsense, to antiproduction, and to unintelligibility; instead of fighting this characterization by dragging queerness into recognition, he proposes that we embrace the negativity that we structurally represent. Muñoz, by contrast, proposes a queer world making that hinges on the possibility of mapping a world in which one is allowed to cast pictures of utopia in the form of "performing impossibility in the face of the pragmatic" (Muñoz 2009, 40). But these utopian gestures are marked by the damaged past and present of heterosexist, racialized colonial violence and postcolonial loss. This only further begs the question, "What is to be (un)done?"

What Is to Be (Un)done?

Nikolay Chernyshevsky's 1863 novel *What Is to Be Done?*, which is often described as a handbook of radicalism, serves as a so-called textbook for life.[1] Implicit in the question is the expectation that radical thought is obliged to provide satisfactory answers to the pressing problems confronting individuals and societies. The question presupposes an objective or a proper goal, wherein the aim is already determined and one's future is plotted in advance. Although it seems reasonable to demand reconciliation between theory and practice, it is not always possible to offer an adequate blueprint of how to strike the balance between these two without foregrounding one over the other. A thinker's response to the question "What is to be done?" is often considered a litmus test of their political and intellectual integrity. It is impossible to answer, yet one cannot not respond to it. The quest is inherently unfulfillable, yet it cannot be disavowed. As one can neither resolve nor evade the question, a double bind is created for every thinker. Cogitation without a plan of action is considered self-indulgent.

Kant's reply to the question "What must I do?" moves away from a preposited understanding of morality and ethics to allude to a form of doing *as if* a universal goal could be outlined. Friedrich Nietzsche calls this "regulating fiction," alluding to the fabricated nature of the goal, which decouples the doing of the action from its goal. Despite being ultimately unrealizable, it is a doing that is nevertheless pursued. Along similar lines, the act of thinking as contemplation must be freed from purposiveness to preserve its autonomy over against the imperative to provide formulas. Theodor Adorno rebukes the "primacy of praxis" and warns that "the question 'what is to be done?' is an automatic reflex to every critical thought before it is fully expressed, let alone comprehended" (Adorno 2005e [1969], 268, 276). The danger of the imperative to act urgently and immediately can result in "actionism" (*Aktionismus*), a term used by Adorno (2005e [1969], 262, 269) to express his disapproval of the radical activism of the 1968 generation and their anti-intellectualism. It is an excessive emphasis on social action, activity, or change in lieu of contemplation, reflection, and intellectual labor. The disjunction between theory and practice must not be sublated; the gulf and contradiction (*Widerspruch*) between the two must be upheld to prevent theory from becoming *mere* interpretation and practice becoming "restless impatience" in its attempt to transform the world without the political labor of interpreting it (Adorno 2005e [1969], 265). Theory as the oppositional force against the onslaught of positivism must be defended by freeing it from the demand of pragmatically responding to social problems. In my reading, by highlighting how actionism embodies an antipathy and hostility toward theory, Adorno refutes Karl Marx's *Thesis Eleven on Feuerbach*. This rejects the idea of theory as abstract and passive, in contrast to which praxis is staged as concrete and transformative (Cook 2004, 58). Questioning the impulse to assess the value of an idea by its "use-value" for action, Adorno urges us to consider thinking itself as a "force of resistance" (Adorno 2005g [1969], 293). To revisit Adorno's reflections in the epigraph, the pathway to postcolonial utopias is to be charted through rigorous critical thought.

This resonates with Vladimir Lenin's (1987 [1929], 28) remark: "Without revolutionary theory there can be no revolutionary movement. This idea cannot be insisted upon too strongly at a time when the fashionable preaching of opportunism goes hand in hand with an infatuation for the narrowest forms of practical activity." The dialectic between theory and practice is not about deriving "the right practice from the correct theory" (Bosteels 2005); rather, in place of harmonizing or reconciling theory and practice, the tension and contingency between the two must be accepted. The unpredictability and uncertainty of "What is to be done?" ought to be reckoned with. Even Marx (1992a [1843], 207–8) concedes that "every individual must admit to himself that he has no precise idea about what ought to happen. However, this very defect turns to the advantage of the new movement, for it means that we do not anticipate the world with our dogmas but instead attempt to discover the new world through the critique of the old."

From a postcolonial-queer-feminist perspective, the revolutionary function of theory and practice is to facilitate the formation of critical consciousness, which offers subalterns the opportunity to exercise political agency. It allows the subaltern to dream, to hope, to desire, to imagine the impossible as the possible. It nurtures the capacity for thinking the future without top-down master plans. According to Jacques Derrida, the only ethical response to the question "What is to be done?" is to avoid responding to it or to follow Lenin's proposition: "We must dream!" (Bosteels 2005). In place of efficient mapping of desires, pursued by algorithms in the digital realm, the incalculable inadequacy, disjunction, interruption of the teleological must be observed so as not to foreclose the future of that which is to come. In an effort to undo mastery, the answer to Lenin's question must necessarily remain suspended; we must avoid responding to it (Derrida 2007, 62). Likewise, when asked, "What is to be done?" Adorno (2010, 234) explains that he would never be presumptuous enough to tell people how to act and responds: "I usually can only answer 'I do not know.' . . . In the process, I am reproached in the following manner: 'If you criticize, you have to say how to do better.'" Adorno warns against "the noisy optimism of immediate action" and suggests that at times, despair may be politically more efficacious (Adorno 2002 [1970], 17). This is not a plea not to act; it exposes the fictive nature of the goal of the doing of the action.

But if thinking and acting are not commensurable, then how can change happen? Let us address the dynamic between critical thought and the racist, sexist, heterosexist, and imperialist conditions in which radical ideas and practices of decolonization emerge.

The Unbearable Slowness of Change

Max Horkheimer (1993 [1931], 5) takes umbrage with Hegelian social philosophy for rationally explaining individual oppression in terms of an overarching movement of the "eternal life of Spirit." This kind of metaphysical view seeks to explain human suffering without making efforts to alleviate it. As discussed in the previous section, one of the biggest challenges for those who seek to transform unjust social, political, and economic relations is undoing the discontinuity between thinking and doing. Invariably, one gets prioritized over the other, with the risk of either producing theory that is detached and depoliticized, with little relevance to the everyday lives of the disenfranchised and dispossessed, or reifying experience, where self-reflection and self-critique are sacrificed in the face of the urgency of immediate action. In conclusion, I draw inspiration from postcolonial queer feminist scholarship to outline my understanding of the tangled relation between critical thought and processes of decolonization.

In her powerful talk "How Does Change Happen?" Davis shares experiences of racism that were formative in her political and intellectual endeavors (Coleman 2017). At a time when there were separate drinking fountains and restrooms for nonwhite people, Davis's mother told her, "This is not the way things are supposed to be . . . (and) they will not always be this way" (quoted in Jones 2006). It was an instructive lesson of not accepting *what is* simply because *it is so*. To change the world, we need to rethink the role of thinking and doing and the relation between the two. Theory and action are always immanent, framed by the context and conditions in which they are exercised, even as they shape and are shaped by subjects who think and act. Davis explains, "It's only depressing if you assume that the way things are today is the way they will be tomorrow" (quoted in Coleman 2017). At the same time, Davis warns against tales of heroic individualism and the Messiah model of leadership that erases the contribution of collectives as agents of social change: Segregation came to an end, she remarks, not because "presidents or legislators or judges one day had epiphanies . . . (but) because ordinary people became collectively aware of themselves as potential agents of social change . . . (with) the power to create a new world" (quoted in Jones 2006). Instead of sublating the incongruence between theory and practice, this discontinuity must be nurtured to prevent theory from becoming a tool to deliver formulas for solving the world's ills and practice being measured according to its effectiveness. When theory cannot provide blueprints for political action, when activism does not facilitate the change to which was aspired, disillusionment and cynicism follow. Furthermore, prioritizing one over the other can lead to anti-intellectualism. Instead of facilitating social and political transformation, the hierarchical opposition between theory and practice obstructs emancipation. The imperative to act urgently cannot circumvent the task of thinking, for every practice exceeds the mere implementation of a plan of action. Thus, action must be reimagined as more than just the execution of thought, which will inevitably be deemed deficient and ineffectual if it fails to deliver on its promises. Critical thinking is indispensable for social and political transformation and is not just a means to an end; rather, thinking is an end in itself. To make change happen, we need to change how we think.

bell hooks (1994) offers a similar approach, arguing that theory can function as a liberatory practice: "I came to theory because I was hurting—the pain within me was so intense that I could not go on living. I came to theory desperate, wanting to comprehend—to grasp what was happening around and within me. Most importantly, I wanted to make the hurt go away. I saw in theory then a location for healing." This goes against the understanding of theory as an elite pursuit and alludes to the deeply transformative power of critical thought.[2] Black feminists such as hooks and Audre Lorde highlight the complex relation between personal experience and political transformation, between words and deeds, and between survival and revolution. Social and political transformation is inextricably linked to the power of words. After being diagnosed with breast cancer, Lorde realized that her biggest regret in life was her silence. Lorde's (2007, 41) advice is that one must confront one's fears in the face of power and domination, for "your silence will not protect you." With this statement, Lorde insightfully addressed various themes, such as the relation between language and action and between violence and silence and the importance of recognizing the differences between women and overcoming the evasion of responsibility. The fight against inequality and injustice, in her view, will not be successful unless the fury and rage that Black feminists and feminists of color have against white feminists is taken seriously. While well founded, their distrust and misgivings about claims of so-called global sisterhood and transnational solidarity are not always heeded. An instructive illustration of feminist academic arrogance is Lorde's experience in 1979 at a New York University Institute for the Humanities conference, where the insights of Black, lesbian and Third World women were allotted the last, separate slot at the event with merely two contributors. This blatant disregard of the strength of difference, Lorde (2007, 110) explains, led to her iconic indictment: "The master's tools will never dismantle the master's house." Lorde bemoans the disconnect between academic scholarship and the struggles for survival of marginalized subjects. She rebukes the practices of exclusion, tokenism, and invisibilization of minorities within elite feminist scholarship.

However, instead of being incapacitated by their pain and suffering, Lorde advises Black women and women of color to channel their bitterness, frustration, and fury to resist the abject position of victimhood that is ascribed them by dominant structures and discourses. In disavowing their privilege and ignorance, white feminism obfuscates how it is complicit in racism and imperialism. At the same time, Black feminists and feminists of color have to bear the so-called double burden of educating white women while struggling to build coalitions across experiences of discrimination. This is brilliantly captured in the paradoxical and ironic title of the collection *Sister Outsider*, in which Lorde reclaims the position of nonbelonging as one of strength instead of weakness.

Her powerful remark, "There is no hierarchy of oppressions" (Lorde 1983, 9), anticipates the most important insights of intersectional feminism. As a Black lesbian woman, Lorde could not afford the luxury of opposing only one form of oppression; the fight against sexism, heterosexism, racism, and capitalism must be contested on multiple fronts, without prioritizing one over the others. Lorde shares experiences of discrimination she faced in the Black community as a lesbian as well as in the queer community as a Black woman. Racism is as much an issue for the queer community as heterosexism and homophobia is for the Black community. Hostility toward and intolerance of difference comes in all guises, so that one's own experience of marginalization does not automatically evoke solidarity with other discriminated groups. At the same time, oppressed communities are pitted against each other, and this division serves the interests of hegemonic groups, who profit from disrupting joint political action. This makes a common fight against multiple axes of inequality imperative.

Lorde (2007, 51) also highlights her experiences of discrimination at the hands of heterosexual Black women who claim that accepting lesbianism would amount to endorsing "the death of our race." And in a forceful exchange with James Baldwin, she describes the violence faced by Black women at the hands of Black men (Lorde and Baldwin 2014). When Baldwin attempts to explain Black men's violence as a response to white terror, alluding to a difference between a family and public quarrel, Lorde compellingly counterargues that, despite shared experiences of racism, there are "power differences" between Black men and women such that at times Black women must struggle against Black men for their very survival. "Don't shed my blood" (Lorde and Baldwin 2014), Lorde pleads with Black men, arguing that instead of turning against each other, it is imperative to focus on the joint battle against racism and sexism. Lorde (2007, 112) urges that "divide and conquer must become define and empower." Ironically, Lorde was involved in a significant dispute with Caribbean-American poet June Jordan, stemming from Lorde's support of Jewish feminist author Adrienne Rich and her initial silence on the question of Palestine. While both Lorde and Rich would later articulate criticisms of Zionism, it was Jordan who consistently and unequivocally expressed solidarity with the Palestinian people and affirmed their right to life and self-determination (Burden-Stelly 2024, Fitzgerald and Swift 2024, Magloire 2024).

As a child of immigrant parents, Lorde was intimately aware of the fragility of political belonging and citizenship, of the precarity of concepts such as home and security, which disenfranchised subjects can never take for granted. For her, struggles against exclusion and disenfranchisement are never-ending, such that revolution is a process, "not a one-time event" (Lorde 2007, 130). Linking politics and ethics with aesthetics, her poetry and prose celebrate the erotics of writing and the joy at the survival of those who were not meant to live. Lorde's writings are a commemoration of life, love, and language, which is by no means a straightforward task. As she puts it beautifully, "Every line I write shrieks there are no easy solutions" (Lorde 2007, 78). Above all else, in the face of fear and despair, her writings offer hope for a livable future. Despite the innumerable challenges, her unwavering commitment to the struggles of the dispossessed holds the promise of resilience. As Lorde (2009, 89) rightly points out, "I will never be gone. I am a scar, a report from the frontlines, a talisman, a resurrection. A rough place on the chin of complacency."

Like Lorde and Davis, Sara Ahmed, in her work *Living a Feminist Life* (2017), focuses on how collectivities are built through shared experiences of loss and pain. Resignifying terms such as resignation and complaint to take away their negative and paralyzing connotations, Ahmed proposes that personal crises and traumas can instigate political resistance and renewal. Drawing on Lorde's "A Litany for Survival" (1978), Ahmed (2017, 236) observes that "feminism is a killjoy survival kit," emphasizing that staying alive is a politically ambitious act that involves nurturing hope while holding on to the projects that remain unfulfilled. Living a feminist life entails embracing the role of agitator, misfit, and troublemaker who also persistently gets into trouble. But "sometimes a feminist has to go on strike. To strike is to put your tools down, to refuse to work by working with them" (Ahmed 2017, 242).

The ambivalent postcolonial-queer-feminist relationship with the (master's) tools is also addressed by Gayatri Chakravorty Spivak, who recommends the strategy of affirmative sabotage (Dhawan 2014). She characterizes the access to the European Enlightenment through colonization as an "enabling violation" and advocates for strategically leveraging this enablement while simultaneously renegotiating the nature of the violation (Spivak 2008, 259). Spivak (1994b, 279) considers the postcolonial in terms of "child of rape": Rape cannot be justified under any condition; ostracizing the child of rape, however, is unacceptable. Similarly, without condoning colonial violence, the postcolonial world must reconceptualize its relationship with the Enlightenment and its enduring legacies. The challenge is: "How is one to learn to love a child of rape, an act of violence?" Spivak (2007, 180) advocates the *ab*-use of the Enlightenment.

Ab-use can be a misleading neographism that can be misread simply as "abuse" (Spivak 2012a, 4). However, this is neither a mistreatment nor an ill usage, but a critical relationship with the structures that we cannot evade. When oppressed minorities fight for civil and political rights, they are invoking the principles of the Enlightenment.

Against a culturally relativistic denouncement of the legacies of the Enlightenment, or an ethnocentric search for presumed authentic non-Western knowledge systems, the focus should be on the entanglements of Western and non-Western theory productions. In numerous postcolonial contexts, selectively dismissing certain elements of modernity has often bolstered authoritarian and nationalist regimes. The critical project of decolonization involves preserving the best aspects of the Enlightenment while rethinking its relationship with delegitimized knowledges. The binary between Enlightenment and postcolonialism is disingenuous, as it obscures how our sense of critique is shaped by the Enlightenment, even as it extends beyond it. Postcolonial thought offers inspiring directions for future critical theories. To draw an analogy: As we know from the history of inoculation, the vaccines are mostly tested in countries of the global South on the very poor, who, after the vaccines are declared safe and successful, are unable to afford them. Similarly, while emancipatory critique emerges from struggles against oppression and marginalization, ironically, the disenfranchised often do not reap the rewards of revolutions.

Whereas postcolonial elites denounce the Enlightenment while profiting from it, disenfranchised groups are denied access to the Enlightenment's fruits while their presumed authenticity is exalted. Given the simultaneously imperial and counter-imperial nature of the Enlightenment, it is imperative to mobilize anti-paternalistic forms of Enlightenment in the service of the disenfranchised. This supersedes nativist denunciations of the Enlightenment's legacies or ethnocentric return to precolonial cosmologies and epistemologies. Enlightenment ideals, while inherently marked by racial, class-based, and gendered biases, are nonetheless indispensable. It remains essential to rigorously scrutinize their weaponization in perpetuating imperialist agendas (Spivak 1999, 84). Derrida (1981b, 21–25) draws on the metaphor of vomit, which is a revolt against the proper trajectory of digestion, to unsettle the binarity between disgust and taste. This, in my view, is an apt description of the postcolonial relationship with European Enlightenment. Despite its disenchantment, the postcolonial world is stuck with "vomit in the mouth" (Ross 2004, 378)—namely, the consequences of the entanglements between colonialism and modernity.

The dilemmatic postcolonial condition is that the vomit resists both assimilation and ejection. The legacies of the Enlightenment cannot be simply purged from the body or fully incorporated into the system; they can be neither swallowed nor disgorged. The irresolvability of the postcolonial conundrum is that it exceeds empty gestures of rejecting modernity that earn the resisting subject a good conscience. It strips anti-Enlightenment approaches of their disruptive and redemptive force. At the same time, the coercive aspects of the Enlightenment cannot simply be undone by recuperative logics of righting historical wrongs. Any attempt at neutralizing the violence of colonialism must come to terms with this aporia.

For Spivak (2012a, 4), decolonization entails an "affirmative sabotage" of those Enlightenment principles "with which we are in sympathy, enough to subvert!" One etymology of *sabotage* traces the word back to *sabot* (wooden shoe). Workers in fifteenth-century Holland would throw their clogs into the gears of textile looms to break their cogs, lest the automated machines render the human workers obsolete. The saboteur aimed to subvert through obstruction and disruption, through intentionally withdrawing efficiency. This opposition to technology might seem backward and irrational; however, the workers were keenly aware of the capitalists' attempts to exploit their labor even more through automation.

Sabotage was employed by the General Confederation of Labor of France in 1897 as a weapon for the workers in their efforts to pressure their employers and gain bargaining power. The strategy was initially received skeptically by the workers; while some questioned its morality, others denounced it as cowardice. The American labor leader, activist, and feminist Elizabeth Gurley Flynn (1916, 1) explained that the necessity of the strategy made it ethical. As a deliberate interference or creative reconfiguration of work assignments, sabotage sometimes draws on the law, abiding by the rules, while at other times it must break the law (Gurley Flynn 1916, 22). Gurley Flynn (1916, 25) gave the example of the worker who took a vital part of an engine with him, making it impossible to operate a machine. While a boycott or general strike may not always be feasible due to extreme misery and disorganization, sabotage, by contrast, serves as a tactic to make the employer vulnerable. In doing so, it redefines the dominant narrative between capital and labor, shifting the worker from a victim to an active agent of production. Work may continue, but it does so according to the terms set by the workers and not the masters. The slogan of the Glasgow dock workers was *ca canny* (go slow). Production corresponds to the wages rendered. Spivak supplements the term with the adjective *affirmative*, devising a strategy in which the instruments of colonialism are turned around into tools for transgression, poison used as medicine. She explains: "The invention of the telephone by a European upper class male in no way preëmpts its being put to the use of an anti-imperialist revolution" (Spivak, quoted in Alcoff 1991–92, 29). This alludes to the ambivalent and unforeseeable role of the "master's tools" in processes of decolonization (Dhawan 2014).

Those who condemn postcolonial scholarship for both drawing on and questioning the Enlightenment fail to understand that it is not contestation and transformation of Enlightenment principles but unquestioning fidelity and blind servitude to them that is its truest betrayal. Adorno (2005a [1951], 52) remarks that "one must have tradition in oneself, to hate it *properly* [um sie *recht* zu hassen]." In place of an "improper hating" (Agnani 2013, 183), which would entail a naïve rejection or opposition, the challenge is the practice of criticism of that which one cannot not love (Spivak 1989, 214)—namely, Enlightenment norms such as democracy, equality, freedom, and justice. Adorno warns that it "would be poor psychology to assume that exclusion arouses only hate and resentment; it arouses, too, a possessive, intolerant kind of love, and those whom repressive culture has held at a distance can easily become its most diehard defenders (*Schutztruppe*)" (Adorno 2005a [1951], 53). As Sunil Agnani (2013, 185) points out, the *Schutztruppe* were German military forces in colonial Africa, some of whom were natives, who loyally defended European imperial interests. Hate and resentment can lead to a possessive, intolerant love (Adorno 2005a [1951], 53). Spivak turns this around and says that the postcolonial world must learn to love the Enlightenment "properly." This involves a critical relation to both the coercive and the enabling aspects of the Enlightenment.

As has been argued in this book, the critical project of decolonization understands the Enlightenment as both a memory and a hope that can incite us to act responsibly and move toward transforming the world to make it less violent and unjust. This book has been an effort to respond to the question "What does the imperative 'decolonize!' entail?" Do we know what we are doing, when we attempt to decolonize Enlightenment? Must one know what must be done in advance before actually doing it? Derrida (2019, 1) asks, "When I say *faut le faire* [it must be done], what am I doing?" He explains that the "'must' is not a command or a prescription that would be attached to doing, to a doing whose meaning would be known" (Derrida 2019, 17). Drawing on Derrida's (1997, 114) insight that "no politics has ever been adequate to its concept," Jean-Luc Nancy (2014, 107–8) points out that no practice is always faithful to its principle. In this infidelity lies the promise of practice, which always exceeds the mere implementation of a plan of action.

We are confronted with the contradictory imperatives of Marx's *Thesis Eleven on Feuerbach*: "The philosophers have only interpreted the world in various ways; the point, however, is to change it." How does one infiltrate the enigma of the link between interpretation and change in Marx's last thesis on Feuerbach? To borrow from Kant's reflections on empty thought and blind intuitions, is critique without revolution *empty* and revolution without critique *blind*? In disavowing one or the other, is one not ironically also affirming that one without the other is impossible (Derrida 2019, 15)? The insistence on "practicism" (Derrida 2019, 22) must at once acknowledge its unforeseeability. Derrida (2019, 14) agrees with Gramsci's criticism of Benedetto Croce, who claims that Marx foregrounds transformation over interpretation. In Gramsci's reading, instead of repudiating critical thought and prioritizing revolutionary practice, Marx's *Thesis Eleven on Feuerbach* is a "vigorous affirmation of a unity between theory and practice" (Gramsci, quoted in Derrida 2019, 15). Kant's three key questions: "What can I know?" "What should I do?" and "What am I permitted to hope?" hint at the precarious link among knowing, doing, and hoping, which cannot be harmonized.

In failing to provide straightforward blueprints in the face of multiple global crises, these *nonanswers* may be frustrating. The current political climate of post-truth politics has once again raised suspicions about the poststructuralist influence on postcolonial studies, and we are witnessing a comeback of postmodernism bashing. This has a long backstory, with Bruno Latour's lecture "Why Has Critique Run Out of Steam? From Matters of Fact to Matters of Concern" (2004) being a case in point. Latour (2004, 230) asks whether critique can be efficacious if facts are relativized as social constructs and objectivity is forsaken. In the face of the current crisis of truth, the concern is that the "critical arsenal" is weaponized by conspiracy theorists and irrational ideologues in the postfactual era. Latour (2004, 240–41) mocks *"critical barbarity"* for its cavalier and chauvinistic attitude toward "indisputable facts." He asks, "What were we really after when we were so intent on showing the social construction of scientific facts? . . . There is no sure ground even for criticism. . . . But what does it mean when this lack of sure ground is taken away from us by the worst possible fellows as an argument against the things we cherish?" (Latour

2004, 227). As a solution, Latour recommends circumventing both positivism and social constructivism to move toward a "fair position," which not only debunks but also "gathers" and "assembles" to foster epistemological capaciousness. The word *criticism*, in this view, should be mostly associated with positive metaphors that broaden our epistemological horizon.

Against the call for return to *facts* as a way out of the post-truth era and the accusation that, in questioning Enlightenment norms of reason and universalism, postcolonialism is contributing to the crisis of truth, I want to draw attention to Otto Neurath's (1983 [1935]) idea of "pseudorationalism." In a Kantian vein, Neurath argues that while rationalism is an acceptance of the limits of knowledge, pseudorationalism is a refusal to acknowledge the limits of reason as well as the disregard of the impossibility of making final claims on facts *and* values. Unless any given problem is approached and analyzed from a multiplicity of perspectives, the result is pseudorationalism, which reduces the plurality of ethical, social, historical, and aesthetic dimensions to a monolithic form of reason.

My postcolonial-queer-feminist response to Latour would emphasize that critical theories of decolonization are not about always being right or feeling self-satisfied for having a critical perspective. Rather, they are an exercise in survival, rooted in the historical experience of resisting oppression. The motivation for critique does not come from the sense of superiority that accompanies faultfinding or the gratification of proving others wrong or misguided; it is associated with the imperative to contest the deprivation of rights and dignity. One commits to critical thought not because of the prestige and status that it grants the critic, but because it offers the possibility of hoping for and living a less exploitative existence. Cultivating a critical attitude is less about pursuing facts than about transforming relations of power. I use the phrase "care to know" to address the issue of painful truths and shameful secrets. It is tempting to avoid uncomfortable realities and remain ignorant of traumatic histories. In contrast to Kant's "dare to know," critical theories of decolonization create opportunities to confront what is troubling and unsettling. Instead of letting old wounds fester, these theories advocate for addressing difficult topics responsibly, offering self-critical and introspective approaches to understanding and rectifying historical injustice. Taking inspiration from Marx's (1992b [1843–44], 247) remark that "these petrified conditions must be made to dance by having their own tune sung to them," critical theories of decolonization seek to transform entrenched social structures by exposing and exploiting their inherent contradictions through critical analysis, thereby enabling revolutionary change.

In the introduction I asked whether our political attachment to the question "What to do?" impedes rather than facilitates radical change. What happens to critical thought when it is freed from the imperative to furnish solutions to social, political, and economic problems? How can one practice critique without having to provide reassuring answers and positivist solutions for global problems? If the medicine caused the illness, then the dose must be adjusted so that it may become a remedy. The how much and when depends on the condition of the patient. Thus, instead of universal prescriptions, this book encourages tailoring answers to fit singular contexts depending on the aspirations of the particular collective in its struggle for a post-imperialist world.

The Cambridge economist Joan Robinson (1964, 46) famously said, "The misery of being exploited by capitalists is nothing compared to the misery of not being exploited at all." As argued in this book, the only thing worse than being dehumanized and disenfranchised by the European Enlightenment is not having access to its enabling tools. If decolonization is a "strategy of reversing, displacing, and seizing the apparatus of value-coding" (Spivak 1993a, 63), then it is imperative to reconfigure the relationship between the Enlightenment and the subaltern. In chapter 1, I outlined how, through a Black radical appropriation of Kant, Charles Mills shows postcolonial critical thought a way forward toward decolonizing the Enlightenment. I also argued that critical theories of decolonization entail not rejecting the Enlightenment and its legacies but reimagining and recalibrating Enlightenment norms of justice, democracy, human rights, secularism, freedom, and equality. Chapter 2 engaged with the convergences of concerns and strategies between first-generation Critical Theory and postcolonial studies, as well as the unfinished conversations between the two. Another focus was the case of mistaken identity wherein the differences between postcolonial studies and the decolonial option are often disregarded. The effort has been to defend postcolonial studies against the accusation of being anti-Enlightenment *and* Eurocentric. In chapter 3, I analyzed how the twin project of decolonizing Europe and the Enlightenment involves questioning the sufficiency and adequacy of European critical thought's conceptual arsenal to best understand the postcolonial condition. To forge postimperialist critical thought, one must revisit the question, "Who qualifies as a critical intellectual?" As argued in chapter 4,

critique remains nonperformative unless previously disenfranchised subjects can exercise intellectual labor through access to the Enlightenment's
enabling tools. Instead of normative foundationalism, commitment to
the ideals of human rights and justice would be immanently justified. As
argued throughout the book, to counter the top-down implementation
of normativity, the epistemic agency of disenfranchised groups must be
enabled so they are in a position to provide normative legitimacy for the
ideals they deem relevant for their lives and the particular sociopolitical
and economic contexts in which they live. In my view, unless conditions
are made conducive for subalterns to exercise epistemic agency, the project of decolonization will remain incomplete. As argued in chapter 5, the
unchallenged assumptions and exclusions implicit in our understanding
of both *critical* and *theory* must be contested to make them both less coercive and violent. This book outlines how critical theories of decolonization neither romanticize non-European thought nor vilify the Enlightenment; they facilitate interaction among diverse epistemic communities.
Extractivism of knowledge, which entails mining the global South for
data and information in the name of intercultural competence and global
learning, is replaced by planetary ethics and transnational literacy. Chapter 6 explored how aesthetics can nurture the political labor of training
the imagination to contest imperialist, racist, Orientalist, and heteronormative structures and practices.

Throughout the book, I have drawn extensively on Spivak's valuable insights regarding the significance of desubalternization and of undoing the
divide between the hegemon and the subaltern. However, in my view, she
falls short in addressing how to effectively foster alliances across differences.
While, on the one hand, postcolonial studies is equated with "identity
politics" and "tribalism" (Neiman 2021), Spivak (1990, 17), on the other
hand, paradoxically proclaims that "in postcolonialism we don't know our
friends." In my view, the biggest hope for democratic politics lies in building bridges among different epistemic communities by forming coalitions
across distinct forms of vulnerabilities and agencies. The focus should not
be only on one's own discrimination and disenfranchisement but also on
others' suffering. An inspiring example of this are queer groups calling for
a ceasefire in the context of the 2023 Israel-Hamas war. They have faced
mockery, with critics often arguing that, by aligning with the Palestinian
cause, queers are endorsing or supporting ideologies or regimes that are
anti-LGBTQI+ and oppressive to queer people (Huggins 2024). Solidarity
with Palestine is set against the rights and safety of LGBTQI+ individuals

in the region, particularly in territories controlled by Hamas. This criticism suggests that queers in solidarity with Gaza are misguided or hypocritical in their advocacy. For instance, in an address to the US Congress on July 24, Netanyahu mocked ceasefire protesters holding signs "Gays for Gaza," likening them to "Chickens for KFC" (quoted in *Economic Times* 2024). Queers for Palestine are often met with the question: Will Palestine ever be for queers? What the critics fail to understand is that this solidarity is not transactional; rather, it is unconditional. Even at the risk of their own persecution, queers calling for a ceasefire are challenging the violation of rights and dignity.

In today's political landscape, echo chambers abound in which people are primarily exposed to information or viewpoints that reiterate and affirm their own. One of the cursed legacies of neoliberalism is its tendency to set one vulnerable group against another. It is crucial not to prioritize one struggle over others and to simultaneously combat various forms of discrimination, including, among others, racism, antisemitism, sexism, transphobia, and ableism. Here we confront the challenge of the so-called attention economy, in which minorities are pitted against one another in a struggle to gain recognition for their individual causes and issues. In such a scenario, there is the danger of inverting the feminist principle of the "personal is political" to "only the personal is political." This approach reduces politics to self-interest, both individual and collective. As an antidote to neoliberal *divide-and-rule* tendencies, it is urgent to actively and effectively foster alliances by focusing on the intertextuality of our narratives and struggles. What comes to mind is the Parents Circle–Families Forum, a joint Israeli-Palestinian organization of more than seven hundred families, which attempts reconciliation between Palestinians and Israelis who have lost loved ones in the conflict. To achieve sustained peace, hostility and rage must be overcome through tolerance and respect (Parents Circle–Families Forum 2024).

In the final chapter of *The Origins of Totalitarianism*, Hannah Arendt (1962 [1951]) warns that isolating individuals and groups from one another renders them politically impotent and robs them of agency. It is my firm belief that political friendships (Castro Varela and Oghalai 2023) can be a bulwark against atomization and the erosion of trust between communities. Shared experiences and affinities create collectivities in which we listen to one another and find our own voice. The antidote to tyranny and terror is to connect with one another and to share not only anger, fear, and anxiety but also laughter and joy. The task at hand involves building, nurturing, and consolidating relationships across difference. This is neither compliancy nor opportunism; rather, it is about recognizing and being vigilant that every time we censure others for their flaws and blank spots, we should not disregard our own. Critique without self-critique is lazy politics.

The book started with the postcolonial dilemma of whether the Enlightenment should be renounced or rescued. Although the fault lines emerge in the moment of conception of Enlightenment norms, instead of discarding these ideals, the postcolonial world must aspire to rescue these legacies of the Enlightenment by overcoming their androcentric and Eurocentric biases. Instead of mobilizing history for self-vindication and self-congratulation, tracing the coercive effects of the Enlightenment can safeguard against repeating its violent tendencies. By questioning the self-aggrandizement of Western critical thought, I have outlined how its deployment as an alibi for Western imperialism can be interrupted. In his talk "A Europe of Hope," Derrida (2006, 410) describes Europe as an unfulfilled promise that "sets the example of what a politics, a thinking, and an ethics could be, inherited from the passed Enlightenment and bearing the Enlightenment to come." The book ends with the Spivakian suggestion of the Enlightenment's affirmative sabotage, which, instead of coding decolonization as simply an undoing of colonialism, attempts to reimagine our use of the master's tools to dismantle the master's house. As has been argued throughout this book, insofar as the postcolonial present is historically determined by the Enlightenment, it remains unavoidably one of the conditions of its analysis. However, if European thought is both indispensable and inadequate to the process of decolonization, then the task of appropriating and transforming the European Enlightenment *from* and *for* the postcolonial world is never-ending. Postcolonial critical thought faces the aporia of thinking the unthinkable. As Ernesto Che Guevara proclaimed, "Be realistic, demand the impossible!" Spivak (1990, 41) explains that the critical project of decolonization is like brushing one's teeth: You are never able to clean your teeth once and for all; it is a repetitive and persistent task that is nevertheless a losing battle against mortality. And yet, although there are no guarantees about how long we will live, we practice dental hygiene as an act of optimism, one ultimately doomed to failure because we are going to die. Toiling in the face of the certainty of failure, for Spivak, is akin to the practical politics of the open end. The futile act of brushing one's teeth, the practice of dental hygiene as a critique of mortality, teaches us important lessons about working without guarantees. One cannot future-proof critical practices: The future is a risk that masquerades as a promise. Despite the seemingly insurmountable challenges, we must persevere in our pursuit of the critical project of decolonization by working for the best and preventing the worst. This calls on each of us to examine what is being done in our name and who is paying the price for our privileges and security. The task of postcolonial critique is to allow suffering to speak; even as critical theories of decolonization are an exercise in imagining nondominant futures, of harvesting utopias out of hopeless conditions, they entail transforming the impossible by mastering the art of the possible. As Lorde (2007, 123) poignantly writes in a poem that befittingly describes the fraught relationship of European Enlightenment to postcolonial thought:

> We have chosen each other
> and the edge of each other's battles
> the war is the same
> if we lose
> someday women's blood will congeal
> upon a dead planet
> if we win
> there is no telling
> we seek beyond history
> for a new and more possible meeting.

Acknowledgments

I would like to thank the following institutions for their support: Volk-swagenStiftung; Technische Universität Dresden; Duke University Press; Campus Verlag; Siglo XXI; transcript Verlag; Routledge; Goethe Institute; Thomas Mann House, Los Angeles; ICI Berlin Institute for Cultural Inquiry; Institut für Auslandsbeziehung (IFA); Justus Liebig University Giessen; The EU-funded Push*Back*Lash project; Research Platform "Gender Research: Identities—Discourses—Transformations," University of Innsbruck; Excellence Cluster "The Formation of Normative Orders," Cornelia Goethe Center for Gender Studies, and AFRASO—Africa's Asian Options, Frankfurt Inter-Centre, Goethe University Frankfurt; Interdisciplinary Research Training Group "Dynamics of Space and Gender," University of Kassel and University of Göttingen; University of California, Berkeley; Columbia University; the University of Melbourne; Stanford University; Mumbai University; SNDT Women's University; Indian Institute of Technology; Jawaharlal Nehru University; Central University of Punjab; Pusan National University; Universidad de La Laguna; Universidad de Costa Rica; Universidad Nacional Autónoma de México; FLACSO Ecuador.

I am grateful to the following people for supporting the publication: Courtney Berger, Laura Jaramillo, Livia Tenzer, Susan Deeks, Chad Royal, Chris Robinson, Judith Wilke-Primavesi, Alwin Jorga Franke, Tatjana Schönwälder, Mark Arenhövel, Gwendal Lamay, Antje Millan, Didi Herman, Natalia Fomina, Ana Maria Miranda Mora, Roberto Luis Ellis, Franz Knappik, Leyla Sophie Gleissner, and the anonymous reviewers.

My gratitude goes to the following family members, friends, and colleagues: Suresh Dhawan, Nalin Dhawan, Estrella Varela Pazos, Carlos Castro Pena, Rahul Warke, Shwetha Warke, Juliet D'Souza, Teresa Orozco, Priyadarshi Jetli, Nutan Sarawgi, Gisela Ott-Gerlach, Uschi Wachendorfer, Birgit Rommelspacher, Putul Sathe, Jyoti Sabharwal, Manisha Ghatage, Gayatri Chakravorty Spivak, Judith Butler, Angela Davis, Shalini Randeria, Chandra Talpade Mohanty, Tejaswini Niranjana, Belén Martín Lucas, Avishek Ganguly, Sundhya Pahuja, Sara Ahmed, Manuela Picq, Davina Cooper, Janet Newman, Rahul Rao, Banu Subramaniam, Ilan Kapoor, Ratna Kapur, Malathi de Alwis, Dipesh Chakrabarty, Wendy Brown, Ann Laura Stoler, Ursula Apitzsch, Jamila Mascat, Manjeet Ramgotra, Dirk Rupnow, Manuela Picq, Sruti Bala, Thomas Lindenberger, Bélen Martín Lucas, Eva Darias Beautell, Emma Wolukau-Wanambwa, Randi Elin Gressgård, Nivedita Menon, Shuddhabrata Sengupta, Christoph Holzhey, Antke Engel, Volker Woltersdorff, Greta Olson, Sonia Correa, Philipp Schulte, Nina Tabassomi, Ana Vujanović, Jochen Schmon, Ayça Çubukçu, Hasret Cetinkaya, Mithu Sanyal, Anja Besand, Elad Lapidot, Emilia Roig, Rirhandu Mageza-Barthel, Johanna Leinius, Elisabeth Fink, Luisa Hoffmann, Hanna Al-Taher, Daniel James, Daniel Heinz, Eleonora Hummel, Susanne Bernhart, Julia Redmann, Refqa Abu-Remaileh, Achille Rossini, Madhusree Mukherjee, Sandra Chatterjee, Walter Anyanwu, Valerie Gaugl, Teresa Blasi Marti, Kira Kosnick, Uta Ruppert, Katharina Mückstein, Sylvia Nagel, Silvia Osei, Dimitria Clayton, Anuja Phadnis, Cigdem Esin, Denise Gigante, Isabel Raabe, Uriel Orlow, Noemi Smolik, Saraswati Patel, Reema Khanna, and the Wadhawan family.

Notes

Introduction. Postcolonial Dilemmas. To Renounce or Rescue the Enlightenment?

1 Throughout the text, I use the unhyphenated form of the term (except in direct quotes), as the hyphenated form seems to suggest the existence of something called Semitism, which anti-Semitism opposes.
2 For a critical analysis of the debate, see Brumlik 2021; Rothberg 2020.
3 The *Historikerstreit* (Historians' Dispute) was an intellectual and public debate in West Germany during the late 1980s, involving scholars such as Ernst Nolte and Jürgen Habermas, about how to interpret and represent Nazi Germany and the Holocaust. The controversy centered on questions of historical responsibility, the uniqueness of the Holocaust, and whether it should be studied comparatively.
4 I thank Doreen Mende for reminding me of *The Unfinished Conversation* (2012), a three-screen installation by John Akomfrah that explores the work of Stuart Hall. It was initially shown at Tate Britain, London; see https://www.tate.org.uk/art/artworks/akomfrah-the-unfinished-conversation-t14105.
5 Written by the Jewish American songwriter Abel Meeropol under his pseudonym Lewis Allan, the poem *Strange Fruit* was a protest against racist lynchings and was inspired by Lawrence Beitler's photograph of the 1930 lynching of Thomas Shipp and Abram Smith in Marion, Indiana. Billie Holiday's iconic rendition of the song is considered a rallying cry of the Civil Rights Movement (Wikipedia 2024a).

Chapter 1. Who Financed the Enlightenment?
Colonialism and the Age of Reason

1 The Kant monument stands in front of the main building of the Immanuel Kant Baltic Federal University in Kaliningrad, formerly the German city of Königsberg.

2 In December 1783, Johann Friedrich Zöllner asked, in the *Berlinische Monatsschrift*, "What is enlightenment?"—a question he felt was as crucial as "What is truth?" but had yet to be answered (Schmidt 1996, 2). On December 17, 1783, J. K. W. Mohsen presented a paper at the Mittwochsgesellschaft, a secret society of Enlightenment supporters, titled, "What Should Be Done to Enlighten Fellow Citizens?" (Schmidt 1996, 3). Within a year, the *Berlinische Monatsschrift* published responses from Mendelssohn and Kant.

3 Feminists highlight how the Kantian distinction between public and private uses of reason is inherently gendered.

4 My use of terms such as *European* and *non-European*, *West* and *non-West*, and *Occident* and *Orient* is informed by the idea of writing "under erasure" (Dhawan 2007, 330). Martin Heidegger often crossed out (*kreuzweise Durchstreichung*) the word *Being* to emphasize both the necessity and the impossibility of discussing it. Derrida suggests that such erasures (*sous rature*) are not merely negative; they signal that a concept is essential, despite its inherent limitations. This approach cautions readers not to take these terms at face value, revealing their simultaneous necessity and inadequacy. In a similar way, terms such as *European* and *non-European*, while constructs, still have considerable purchase.

5 In his famous talk and essay "Politics as a Vocation," Max Weber (2004 [1919]) discusses "the disenchantment of the world" (*die Entzauberung der Welt*). He borrowed the term *Entzauberung* (de-magification) from Friedrich Schiller to describe the modernized, bureaucratic, and secularized Western society.

6 *Vacuum domicilium* and *terra nullius* are sometimes used interchangeably, both terms referring to lands considered to be empty or to belong to no one.

7 I consider liberal thinkers such as Tocqueville and Mill to be part of the broader intellectual movement that emerged during the Enlightenment.

8 By failing to explicitly state that her focus is solely on European women, May Schott inadvertently perpetuates the notion of a universal category of women.

9 I thank Mark Arenhövel for this insight.

10 The Kant scholar Dieter Schönecker (2021) argues that, in addition to white Europeans, "Moors (Mauretanian from Africa), the Arabs (following Niebuhr), the Turkish-Tataric ethnic tribe and the Persians" qualified as the "white race" for Kant.

11 Rebuking Foucault's and Deleuze's claim that oppressed groups can speak for themselves, Spivak (1994a, 80–81) cautions against abandoning the task

of representation, arguing that "there is no unrepresentable subaltern subject that can know and speak itself."

12 Despite the presence of Black people and migrants in Europe for centuries, racism has not diminished; thus, it is clearly not merely a lack of direct contact that fuels prejudice and hatred.

13 Baucom (2010, 337) argues that post-9/11 US national security agencies have revived this conceptual framework to support a nexus of international law, global warfare, and speculative finance.

14 In the context of recent discussions on responsibility to protect and humanitarian intervention, Mathew Altman (2017, 187) points out that, drawing inspiration from Kantian cosmopolitanism, it has become common to justify military intervention in totalitarian states and enforcement of international law in the name of protecting the rights of world citizens. Altman cites Habermas as an example, noting that despite his commitment to discourse ethics, he supported both the US-led Persian Gulf War in 1991 (Habermas 1994) and the invasion of Kosovo by the North Atlantic Treaty Organization (NATO) in 1999 (Habermas 1999). According to Habermas, the justification for the former was to support the United Nations and protect Israel (despite the near-total destruction of cities such as Basra and the extremely high number of civilian casualties in Iraq), while the latter was to prevent the genocide of ethnic Albanians.

15 The burkini, combining the words *burka* and *bikini*, is a type of modest swimwear designed for Muslim women. In 2016, some municipalities in France banned it from public beaches, citing secularism and public order concerns.

The slogan "Rapefugees not Welcome" was coined by the right-wing group Pegida (Patriotic Europeans Against the Islamization of the West) in Germany.

Chapter 2. The Self-Barbarization of Europe. Enlightenment and Nazism

1 Widely used as a battle flag during the American Civil War, the Confederate flag is an enduring symbol of racism, white supremacy, and intimidation of African Americans. *Arbeit macht frei* (Work Brings Freedom) was written on the entrance gate to Auschwitz.

2 The *Positivismusstreit* (positivism dispute) in 1961 was between critical rationalists such as Karl Popper on one side and "the Frankfurters"—such as Horkheimer, Adorno, and Habermas—on the other, who focused on the limitations of positivism.

3 In his opening lecture of the sixteenth Deutscher Soziologentag, held in Frankfurt am Main in 1968, Adorno (2003b [1968], 116, 121) remarks that

"theories of imperialism have not been rendered obsolete by the great powers' withdrawal from their colonies" and that "the relations of production . . . are responsible for the fact that human beings in large parts of the planet live in penury."

4 When speaking of missed encounters, postcolonial studies and Holocaust studies should both be faulted for not adequately engaging with the Russian empire and the question of decolonization in post-Soviet territories. Scholars in both colonialism and Holocaust studies have concentrated predominantly on Europe and the non-European world, often overlooking the so-called Second World and its complex intermediary position. Unfortunately, I am unable to explore this in greater detail here.

5 I am grateful to Daniel James for sharing this article with me.

6 Rolf Tiedemann wrote his dissertation under the supervision of Adorno and Horkheimer and subsequently served as Adorno's research assistant at the Institute for Social Research in Frankfurt. He later became the director of the Adorno archives in Frankfurt and was one of the editors of Adorno's *Gesamtausgabe* (Collected works). His roles provided him with firsthand knowledge of the dispute.

7 Habermas's use of the concepts of consistency and contradiction differs significantly from the way the concept of contradiction is used in, for example, heterodox Indian philosophical systems. For instance, *Saptabhaṅgīvāda*, or *Syādvāda*, the Jaina seven-valued logic, constitutes a system of argumentation with seven distinct semantic predicates that transcends binary logic (Burch 1964).

Chapter 3. Europe. What Can It Teach Us?

1 The title of this chapter, "Europe: What Can It Teach Us?" draws on the Indologist Friedrich Max Müller's lecture "India, What Can It Teach Us?" delivered at the University of Cambridge in 1883.

2 Felipe Guaman Poma de Ayala, also known as Waman Puma (his Quechua name), was born around 1534 in present-day Peru. He chronicled pre-Columbian Andean history, the Spanish conquest, and colonial rule, offering a rare Indigenous perspective on colonial Peru. In his writings, he condemned Spanish colonial practices and called for justice for the Indigenous population.

Ottobah Cugoano (ca. 1757–ca. 1791), born in present-day Ghana, was a pioneering abolitionist and one of the first formerly enslaved Africans to publish a powerful critique of slavery and the transatlantic slave trade in English.

3 Central to African ethical philosophy is *Ubuntu*, the idea of people's allegiances to and relations with one another, as summarized in the phrase

"I am what I am because of who we all are." *Pachamama*—"World Mother" or "Mother Earth"—is considered sacred in the cosmology of the Indigenous people of the Andes. *Dhamma* is the political theology of Dalit (so-called untouchables) Buddhists in India that encompasses moral action for social change.

Chapter 4. The Nonperformativity of Critique. Protest Politics, State Phobia, and the Erotics of Resistance

1 The term *Gewalttouristen* was invoked to discredit protestors during the Group of 20 meeting in 2017 in Germany.
2 A good example of the entrenchment of the Enlightenment in modern Europe is the right to resist: *Widerstandsrecht* (Grundgesetz 2024, art. 20, para. 4), which since 1968 has been ensured by the German Constitution. Critics, however, point out that this enables the state to maintain the status quo instead of empowering citizens to resist state violence.
3 Although, as discussed in chapter 1, Kant would not support anticolonial independence movements against legitimate colonial rule.
4 Johann Erich Biester, the editor of *Berlinische Monatsschrift*, wrote about his relief on reading Kant's rejection of the right to revolution: see Biester to Kant, October 5, 1793, in Kant 1970, 208–9. There has, of course, been speculation as to whether Kant was being cautious in his published writings in deference to the Prussian censors. In the past, when he was ordered not to express his views on Christianity publicly, Kant obeyed. Others argue that he truly did not support revolutions in theory and practice. In a letter to Moses Mendelssohn, Kant (1970, 54) wrote: "Although I am absolutely convinced of many things that I shall never have the courage to say, I shall never say anything I do not believe."
5 George Floyd was a Black American man whose death at the hands of Minneapolis police officers in May 2020 sparked global protests against police brutality and systemic racism. Mahsa Amini was a twenty-two-year-old Iranian woman who died in police custody in September 2022 after being arrested by Iran's morality police for allegedly violating the country's mandatory hijab laws; her death triggered widespread protests across Iran and internationally.
6 The right to exercise the freedom of assembly is documented in international law, and the International Labour Organization makes explicit that the right to assembly and associational rights are tied to rights of collective bargaining (Butler 2015, 156). In human rights discourses, the right to assembly is described as a fundamental form of freedom that deserves to be protected by governments.

7 Called the Bangladesh Rehabilitation Assistance Committee at its founding in 1972, the organization now has the name Building Resources Across Communities and operates in many countries.

8 An excellent example of *pharmakon* is facial recognition software. The technology used for racial profiling, which reproduces the biases of its programmers, is the same technology used by visually impaired people to navigate space. So, on the one hand, racist technology is deployed for mass surveillance, which can be weaponized by law enforcement against marginalized communities, while, on the other hand, the enabling function of facial recognition technology aids visually impaired people during social interactions.

9 The term *pinkwashing* is used to describe a variety of marketing and political strategies aimed at promoting corporations or countries as queer-friendly to stage them as progressive, modern, and tolerant, thereby distracting from coercive practices and policies pursued by these entities.

10 For an example of pinkwatching, see the Facebook account with the name "Pinkwatching Israel," accessed August 1, 2024, https://www.facebook.com/pinkwatchingisrael.

11 Anticolonial movements sought to achieve independence and sovereignty by establishing postcolonial states.

12 This subsection's title, "The Death of Leviathan," is inspired by Anish Kapoor's artwork *Death of Leviathan*, 2011–13, PVC, dimensions variable. For images of the work installed in 2013 at the Martin-Gropius-Bau, Berlin, see https://anishkapoor.com/963/death-of-leviathan.

Chapter 5. Critique of Violence—Violence of Critique

1 The Marathi word *Dalit* (broken/scattered) is a self-applied concept for people belonging to the lowest caste in India, characterized as "untouchable."

2 "Passenger Indians" were immigrants of the merchant class who went to South Africa to trade and not as indentured laborers.

3 Ram is one of the most important deities of Hinduism and has become the face of Hindu nationalism. Hindu nationalists envision a Hindu India as *Ram Rajya* (kingdom of Ram).

4 As we know, this reasoning continues to be employed to legitimize present wars in the name of spreading democracy.

5 Foucault died in a hospital in Paris from complications of HIV/AIDS.

6 It must be noted that, for instance, undocumented migrants and prisoners continue to be on the margins of the state's priority of providing protection.

7 Ironically, the cover page is no longer available on the magazine's website (Krishnan 2021).

**Chapter 6. Aesthetic Enlightenment
and the Art of Decolonization**

1 I thank María do Mar Castro Varela for reminding me of this remark and of
   another significant Black-Jewish friendship—that between Monk and Pan-
   nonica de Koenigswarter, a member of the Rothschild family who supported
   Monk unwaveringly through all ups and downs.

**Conclusion. Affirmative Sabotage
of the Master's Tools**

1 The title of this section is a variation of Albert's (1974) *What Is to Be Undone:
   A Modern Revolutionary Discussion of Classical Left Ideologies.*
2 I am grateful to María do Mar Castro Varela for reminding me of hooks's
   powerful insight.

References

Abandon Biden. 2024. "Ceasefire Now." Accessed August 1, 2024. https://abandonbiden24.com.

Abbas, Ackbar. 2012. "Adorno and the Weather: Critical Theory in an Era of Climate Change." *Radical Philosophy* 174: 7–13. https://www.radicalphilosophy.com/article/adorno-and-the-weather.

Abu-Lughod, Lila. 2013. *Do Muslim Women Need Saving?* Cambridge, MA: Harvard University Press.

Adorno, Theodor W. 1975 [1967]. "The Culture Industry Reconsidered." *New German Critique* 6: 12–19.

Adorno, Theodor W. 1980 [1965]. "Commitment." In *Aesthetics and Politics*, edited by Fredric Jameson, 177–95. London: Verso.

Adorno, Theodor W. 1989–90 [1936]. "On Jazz." *Discourse* 12, no. 1: 45–69.

Adorno, Theodor W. 1991 [1958]. "Extorted Reconciliation: On Georg Lukács' Realism in Our Time." In *Notes to Literature*, vol. 1, 216–40. New York: Columbia University Press.

Adorno, Theodor. 1993. "Messages in a Bottle." *New Left Review* 200, July–August 2024. https://newleftreview.org/issues/i200/articles/theodor-adorno-messages-in-a-bottle.

Adorno, Theodor W. 1997 [1955]. *Prisms*. Cambridge. MA: MIT Press.

Adorno, Theodor W. 2002 [1970]. *Aesthetic Theory*. London: Continuum.

Adorno, Theodor W. 2003a [1953]. "Individuum und Organisation." In *Gesammelte Schriften, Band 8: Soziologische Schriften*, vol. 2, 440–56. Frankfurt am Main: Suhrkamp.

Adorno, Theodor W. 2003b [1968]. "Late Capitalism or Industrial Society?" In *Can One Live After Auschwitz? A Philosophical Reader*, edited by Rolf Tiedemann, 111–25. Stanford, CA: Stanford University Press.

Adorno, Theodor W. 2003c [1973]. *Dissonanzen. Einleitung in die Musiksoziologie*. In *Gesammelte Schriften*, vol. 14. Frankfurt am Main: Suhrkamp.

Adorno, Theodor W. 2004 [1966]. *Negative Dialectics*. London: Routledge.

Adorno, Theodor W. 2005a [1951]. *Minima Moralia*. London: Verso.

Adorno, Theodor W. 2005b [1962]. "Introduction." In *Critical Models: Interventions and Catchwords*, translated by Henry W. Pickford, 3–4. New York: Columbia University Press.

Adorno, Theodor W. 2005c [1963]. "The Meaning of Working Through the Past." In *Critical Models: Interventions and Catchwords*, translated by Henry W. Pickford, 89–104. New York: Columbia University Press.

Adorno, Theodor W. 2005d [1969]. "Progress." In *Critical Models: Interventions and Catchwords*, translated by Henry W. Pickford, 143–60. New York: Columbia University Press.

Adorno, Theodor W. 2005e [1969]. "Marginalia to Theory and Praxis." In *Critical Models: Interventions and Catchwords*, translated by Henry W. Pickford, 259–78. New York: Columbia University Press.

Adorno, Theodor W. 2005f [1969]. "Critique." In *Critical Models: Interventions and Catchwords*, translated by Henry W. Pickford. New York: Columbia University Press: 281–88.

Adorno, Theodor W. 2005g [1969]. "Resignation." In *Critical Models: Interventions and Catchwords*, translated by Henry W. Pickford, 289–94. New York: Columbia University Press.

Adorno, Theodor W. 2006 [1964–65]. *History and Freedom: Lectures 1964–1965*. Edited by Rolf Tiedemann. Cambridge: Polity.

Adorno, Theodor W. 2008 [1965]. *Lectures on Negative Dialectics*. Edited by Rolf Tiedemann. Translated by Rodney Livingstone. Cambridge: Polity.

Adorno, Theodor W. 2009 [1959–60]. "Vorlesung über Ästhetik." In *Nachgelassene Schriften, Abteilung IV: Vorlesungen*, vol. 3, edited by Eberhard Ortland, 7–343. Frankfurt am Main: Suhrkamp.

Adorno, Theodor W. 2010. "Appendix: Who's Afraid of the Ivory Tower: A Conversation with Theodor W. Adorno." In *Language Without Soil*, edited by Gerhard Richter, 227–38. New York: Fordham University Press.

Adorno, Theodor, Else Frenkel-Brunswik, Daniel J. Levinson, and Nevitt Sanford. 1950. *The Authoritarian Personality*. New York: Harper and Brothers.

Adorno, Theodor W., and Herbert Marcuse. 1999 [1969]. "Correspondence on the German Student Movement." *New Left Review* 233: 123–36.

Agnani, Sunil. 2013. *Hating Empire Properly: The Two Indies and the Limits of Enlightenment Anticolonialism*. New York: Fordham University Press.

Aharony, Michal. 2019. "Why Does Hannah Arendt's 'Banality of Evil' Still Anger Israelis?" *Haaretz*, May 11. https://www.haaretz.com/israel-news/2019 -05-11/ty-article-magazine/.premium/why-does-hannah-arendts-banality -of-evil-still-anger-israelis/0000017f-db1a-df9c-a17f-ff1a90bc0000.

Ahmad, Aijaz. 1992. *In Theory: Classes, Nations, Literatures*. Oxford: Oxford University Press.

Ahmed, Sara. 2006. "The Nonperformativity of Antiracism." *Meridians* 7, no. 1: 104–26.

Ahmed, Sara. 2017. *Living a Feminist Life*. Durham, NC: Duke University Press.

Albert, Michael. 1974. *What Is to Be Undone: A Modern Revolutionary Discussion of Classical Left Ideologies*. Boston: Porter Sargent.

Alcoff, Linda. 1991–92. "The Problem of Speaking for Others." *Cultural Critique* 20: 5–32.

Allen, Amy. 2016. *The End of Progress: Decolonizing the Normative Foundations of Critical Theory*. New York: Columbia University Press.

Altman, Mathew. 2017. "The Limits of Kant's Cosmopolitanism: Theory, Practice, and the Crisis in Syria." *Kantian Review* 22, no. 2: 179–204.

Ambedkar, Bhimrao R. 1968 [1936]. *Annihilation of Caste: Speech Prepared for the 1936 Annual Conference of the Jat Pat Todak Mandal of Lahore But Not Delivered*. Jalandhar: Bheem Patrika.

Ambedkar, Bhimrao R. 2002 [1948]. "Motion on the Draft Constitution (4-11-1948)." In *The Essential Writings of B. R. Ambedkar*, edited by Valerian Rodrigues, 473–94. New Delhi: Oxford University Press.

Ambedkar, Bhimrao R. 2007 [1935]. "Speech at the All Bombay Province Depressed Classes Conference." In *Dr. Babasaheb Ambedkar*, edited by Vasant A. Dahake, 271. New Delhi: Planning Commission, Government of India.

Ambedkar, Bhimrao R. 2014a. *Babasaheb Ambedkar: Writings and Speeches*, vol. 1. New Dehli: Dr. Ambedkar Foundation.

Ambedkar, Bhimrao R. 2014b. "What Congress and M. K. Gandhi Have Done to the Untouchables." In *Babasaheb Ambedkar: Writings and Speeches*, vol. 9, 1–297. New Delhi: Dr. Ambedkar Foundation.

Améry Jean. 1980 [1966]. *At the Mind's Limits: Contemplations by a Survivor on Auschwitz and Its Realities*. Bloomington: Indiana University Press.

Améry, Jean. 2005 [1968]. "Die Geburt des Menschen aus dem Geiste der Violenz." In *Aufsätze zur Politik und Zeitgeschichte, Werke* 7, edited by Stephan Steiner, 428–49. Stuttgart: Klett-Cotta.

Amo, Anton W. 2020 [1734]. "Inaugural Dissertation on the Impassivity of the Human Mind." In *Anton Wilhelm Amo's Philosophical Dissertations on Mind and Body*, edited by Stephen Menn and Justin E. H. Smith, 153–98. Oxford: Oxford University Press.

Anghie, Antony. 2007. *Imperialism, Sovereignty and the Making of International Law*. Cambridge: Cambridge University Press.

Anghie, Antony, and Bhupinder S. Chimni. 2003. "Third World Approaches to International Law and Individual Responsibility in Internal Conflicts." *Chinese Journal of International Law* 1: 77–103.

Anijdar, Gil. 2002. "'Once More, Once More': Derrida, the Arab, the Jew." In *Acts of Religion*, by Jacques Derrida, 1–41. London: Routledge.

Anker, Elizabeth S., and Rita Felski. 2017. *Critique and Postcritique*. Durham, NC: Duke University Press.

Anzaldúa, Gloria. 1987. *Borderlands/La Frontera: The New Mestiza*. San Francisco: Aunt Lute.

Arendt, Hannah. 1944. "The Jew as Pariah: A Hidden Tradition." *Jewish Social Studies* 6, no. 2: 99–122.

Arendt, Hannah. 1962 [1951]. *The Origins of Totalitarianism*. Cleveland: Meridian.

Arendt, Hannah. 1970. *On Violence*. New York: Harcourt Brace.

Arendt, Hannah. 1978 [1943]. "Portrait of a Period." In *The Jew as a Pariah*, edited by Ron Feldman, 112–21. New York: Grove.

Arendt, Hannah. 1994. *Essays in Understanding, 1930–1954: Formation, Exile, and Totalitarianism*. New York: Schocken.

Arendt, Hannah. 1998 [1958]. *The Human Condition*. Chicago: University of Chicago Press.

Arendt, Hannah. 2006 [1963]. *On Revolution*. London: Penguin Classics.

Aristotle. 1997. *Poetics*. Translated by Malcom Heath. London: Penguin Classics.

Asad, Talal. 1993. *Genealogies of Religion*. Baltimore: Johns Hopkins University Press.

Asad, Talal. 2003. *Formations of the Secular: Christianity, Islam, Modernity*. Stanford, CA: Stanford University Press.

Asad, Talal. 2009a. "Free Speech, Blasphemy and Secular Criticism." In *Is Critique Secular? The Townsend Papers in the Humanities*, vol. 2, by Talal Asad, Wendy Brown, Judith Butler, and Saba Mahmood, 20–63. Los Angeles: University of California Press.

Asad, Talal. 2009b. "Reply to Judith Butler." In *Is Critique Secular? The Townsend Papers in the Humanities*, vol. 2, by Talal Asad, Wendy Brown, Judith Butler, and Saba Mahmood, 137–45. Los Angeles: University of California Press.

Associated Press. 2023. "Colombia Plane Crash: Custody Battle Breaks Out Between Relatives of Children." *The Guardian*, June 13. https://www.theguardian.com/world/2023/jun/13/colombia-plane-crash-custody-battle-breaks-out-between-relatives-of-children.

Avelar, Idelber. 2005. *The Letter of Violence: Essays on Narrative, Ethics and Politics*. New York: Palgrave Macmillan.

Axinn, Sidney. 1971. "Kant, Authority, and the French Revolution." *Journal of the History of Ideas* 32: 423–32.

Bacon, Francis. 1779 [1620]. *Novum Organum*. Jo. Jac. Stahel: Würzburg: Jo. Jac. Stahel.

Baldwin, James. 2009. "The Price of the Ticket." *California Newsreel*, video, October 27. https://www.youtube.com/watch?v=4_hYraYI2J8.

Banerjee, Prathama. 2017. "State (and) Violence." *India Seminar* 691. https://www.india-seminar.com/2017/691/691_prathama_banerjee.htm.

Bardawil, Fadi A. 2018. "Césaire with Adorno: Critical Theory and the Colonial Problem." *South Atlantic Quarterly* 117, no. 4: 773–89.

Bartal, Yossi. 2024. "Die Wiederkehr des 'Schutzjuden.'" *nd*, September 15. https://www.nd-aktuell.de/artikel/1185261.antisemitismus-die-wiederkehr -des-schutzjuden.html.

Barth, Fredrik. 2005. *One Discipline, Four Ways: British, German, French, and American Anthropology*. Chicago: University of Chicago Press.

Baucom, Ian. 2009. "Cicero's Ghost: The Atlantic, the Enemy, and the Laws of War." In *States of Emergency: The Object of American Studies*, edited by Russ Castronovo and Susan Gillman, 124–42. Chapel Hill: University of North Carolina Press.

Baucom, Ian. 2010. "Financing Enlightenment, Part Two: Extraordinary Expenditure." In *This Is Enlightenment*, edited by Clifford Siskin and William Warner, 336–56. Chicago: University of Chicago Press.

BBC. 2020. "Halle Synagogue Attack: Germany Far-Right Gunman Jailed for Life." December 21. https://www.bbc.com/news/world-europe-55395682.

BBC. 2024. "Why Are There Riots in the UK?" August 10. https://www.bbc.com /news/articles/ckg55we5n3xo.

Beck, Lewis W. 1971. "Kant and the Right of Revolution." *Journal of the History of Ideas* 32, no. 3: 411–22.

Beckerman, Gal. 2024. "The Patron Saint of Political Violence." *The Atlantic*, March 28. https://www.theatlantic.com/books/archive/2024/03/frantz -fanon-adam-shatz-the-rebels-clinic/677904.

Benedict, Susan, Linda Shields, Colin Holmes, and Julia Kurth. 2018. "A Nurse Working for the Third Reich: Eva Justin, RN, PhD." *Journal of Medical Biography* 26, no. 4: 259–67. https://doi.org/10.1177/0967772016666684.

Benhabib, Seyla. 1986. *Critique, Norm, and Utopia*. New York: Columbia University Press.

Benhabib, Seyla. 2004. *The Rights of Others: Aliens, Residents, and Citizens*. Cambridge: Cambridge University Press.

Benjamin, Walter. 1996 [1921]. "Critique of Violence." In *Selected Writings*, vol. 1, edited by Marcus Bullock and Michael W. Jennings, 236–52. Cambridge, MA: Harvard University Press.

Benvenuto, Francesca Maria. 2013. "Fighting Impunity, but Only in Some Cases." *Le Monde Diplomatique*, November 5. https://mondediplo.com/2013 /11/05icc.

Bernasconi, Robert. 2003. "Will the Real Kant Please Stand Up: The Challenge of Enlightenment Racism to the Study of the History of Philosophy." *Radical Philosophy* 117: 13–22.

Bernasconi, Robert. 2011. "Kant's Third Thoughts on Race." In *Reading Kant's Geography*, edited by Stuart Elden and Eduardo Mendieta, 291–318. Albany: State University of New York Press.

Bhabha, Homi. 1994. *The Location of Culture*. London: Routledge.

Bhambra, Gurminder K. 2014. "Postcolonial and Decolonial Dialogues." *Postcolonial Studies* 17, no. 2: 115–21.

Bishara, Marwan. 2023. "Arab Leaders Must Walk the Talk on Palestine." *Al Jazeera*, October 30. https://www.aljazeera.com/opinions/2023/10/30/arab-leaders-must-walk-the-talk-on-palestine.

Biskamp, Floris. 2020. "Sollte man Kant als Rassisten bezeichnen? Kritik der Weißen Vernunft." *Tagesspiegel*, June 21. https://www.tagesspiegel.de/kultur/kritik-der-weissen-vernunft-4176256.html.

Bloch, Ernst. 1995 [1954–59]. *The Principle of Hope*, vols. 1–3. Cambridge, MA: MIT Press.

Boehm, Omri. 2015. "The German Silence on Israel and Its Cost." *New York Times*, March 9. https://archive.nytimes.com/opinionator.blogs.nytimes.com/2015/03/09/should-germans-stay-silent-on-israel.

Boehm, Omri. 2022. "Das Schreiduell. Antisemitismus bei der Documenta." *Die Zeit*, July 14. https://www.zeit.de/2022/29/documenta-antisemitismus-bds-judentum.

Boehm, Omri. 2024. "FRW 2024. Eine Rede an Europa." *Wiener Festwochen*, video, May 8. https://www.youtube.com/watch?v=NAxxpsNPNno.

Bohman, James. 2005. "We, Heirs of Enlightenment: Critical Theory, Democracy and Social Science." *International Journal of Philosophical Studies* 13, no. 3: 353–77.

Borradori, Giovanna, Jürgen Habermas, and Jacques Derrida. 2003. *Philosophy in a Time of Terror—Dialogues with Jurgen Habermas and Jacques Derrida*. Chicago: University of Chicago Press.

Bosteels, Bruno. 2005. "What Is to Be Dreamed? On the Uncommon Saying: That May Be Correct in Practice, but It Is of No Use in Theory." *Journal of Graduate Research* 1, no. 1. http://laic.columbia.edu/journal-graduate-research/what-dreamed-the-uncommon-saying-that-may-correct-practice-but-use-theory.

Bourdieu, Pierre. 1984. *Distinction: A Social Critique of the Judgment of Taste*. London: Routledge.

Bourdieu, Pierre. 2015. *On the State*. Cambridge: Polity.

Brecht, Bertolt. 2019 [1940/41]. *Flüchtlingsgespräche*. Frankfurt am Main: Suhrkamp.

Brock, Bazon. 2022. "Frau Schormann, bleiben Sie stark!" *Süddeutsche Zeitung*, June 30. https://www.sueddeutsche.de/kultur/bazon-brock-brief-documenta-1.5612434?reduced=true.

Brumlik, Micha. 2020. "Lasst das Denkmal stehen." *Die Tageszeitung*, June 26. https://taz.de/Immanuel-Kant-und-der-Rassismus/!5692764.

Brumlik, Micha. 2021. *Postkolonialer Antisemitismus? Achille Mbembe, die palästinensische BDS-Bewegung und andere Aufreger Bestandsaufnahme einer Diskussion*. Hamburg: VSA.

Buck-Morss, Susan F. 1977. "T. W. Adorno and the Dilemma of Bourgeois Philosophy." *Salmagundi* 36: 76–98.

Buck-Morss, Susan F. 2009. *Hegel, Haiti, and Universal History*. Pittsburgh: University of Pittsburgh Press.

Burch, George B. 1964. "Seven-Valued Logic in Jain Philosophy." *International Philosophical Quarterly* 4, no. 1: 68–93.

Burden-Stelly, Charisse. "The June Jordan-Audre Lorde Dispute, Kamala Harris, and Palestine." *Black Agenda Report*. August 14, 2024. https://www .blackagendareport.com/june-jordan-audre-lorde-dispute-kamala-harris -and-palestine.

Busia, Abena. 1989–90. "Silencing Sycorax: On African Colonial Discourse and the Unvoiced Female." *Cultural Critique* 14: 81–104.

Butler, Judith. 1999. *Gender Trouble: Feminism and the Subversion of Identity*. London: Routledge.

Butler, Judith. 2002. "Is Kinship Always Already Heterosexual?" *Differences* 13, no. 1: 14–44.

Butler, Judith. 2009. "Critique, Dissent, Disciplinarity." *Critical Inquiry* 35, no. 4: 773–95.

Butler, Judith. 2012. "On Anarchism: An Interview with Judith Butler." In *Anarchism and Sexuality: Ethics, Relationships and Power*, edited by Jamie Heckert and Richard Cleminson, 93–100. London: Routledge.

Butler, Judith. 2015. *Notes Toward a Performative Theory of Assembly*. London: Harvard Univesity Press.

Butler, Judith. 2020. *The Force of Nonviolence: An Ethico-Political Bind*. New York: Verso.

Butler, Judith, and Athena Athanasiou. 2013. *Dispossession: The Performative in the Political*. Cambridge, MA: Polity.

Camus, Renault. 2021 [2011]. *Le grand remplacement*. Paris: La Nouvelle Librairie.

Carey, Daniel, and Sven Trakulhun. 2009. "Universalism, Diversity and the Postcolonial Enlightenment." In *The Postcolonial Eighteenth Century*, edited by Daniel Carey and Lynn Festa, 240–80. Oxford: Oxford University Press.

Carter, J. Kameron. 2008. *Race: A Theological Account*. Oxford: Oxford University Press.

Cascardi, Anthony. 1999. *Consequences of Enlightenment*. Cambridge: Cambridge University Press.

Castro Varela, María do Mar, and Nikita Dhawan. 2017. "'What Difference Does Difference Make?': Diversity, Intersectionality and Transnational Feminist Politics." *Wagadu* 16: 11–39.

Castro Varela, María do Mar, and Bahar Oghalai. 2023. *Freund*innenschaft. Dreiklang einer politischen Praxis*. Münster: Unrast.

Caygill, Howard. 2013. *On Resistance, a Philosophy of Defiance*. London: Bloomsbury Academic.

Césaire, Aimé. 2000 [1950]. *Discourse on Colonialism*. New York: Monthly Review.

Chakrabarti, Jai. 2021. "The Post Office: A Play from India to Wartime Poland." *Jewish Book Council*, September 15. https://www.jewishbookcouncil.org/pb -daily/the-post-office-a-play-from-india-to-wartime-poland.

Chakrabarty, Dipesh. 2000. *Provincializing Europe: Postcolonial Thought and Historical Difference*. Princeton, NJ: Princeton University Press.

Chakrabarty, Dipesh. 2002. *Habitations of Modernity*. New Delhi: Permanent Black.

Chakrabarty, Dipesh, and Amitav Ghosh. 2002. "A Correspondence on Provincializing Europe." *Radical History Review* 82: 146–72.

Chatterjee, Partha. 1993. *The Nation and Its Fragments: Colonial and Postcolonial Histories*, Princeton, NJ: Princeton University Press.

Chatterjee, Partha. 2011. *Lineages of Political Society: Studies in Postcolonial Democracy, Cultures of History*. New York: Columbia University Press.

Chatterjee, Partha. 2013. "Subaltern Studies and Capital." *Economic and Political Weekly* 48, no. 37: 69–75.

Chernyshevsky, Nikolay. 1989 [1863]. *What Is to Be Done?* Ithaca, NY: Cornell University Press.

Chesney, Duncan M. 2014. "Aesthetic Education and Sympathetic Imagination." *Tamkang Review* 45, no. 1: 61–66.

Chibber, Vivek. 2013. *Postcolonial Theory and the Specter of Capital*. London: Verso.

Chimni, Bhupinder S. 2006. "Third World Approaches to International Law: Manifesto." *International Community Law Review* 8: 3–27.

Chow, Rey. 1993. *Writing Diaspora: Tactics of Intervention in Contemporary Cultural Studies*. Bloomington: Indiana University Press.

CNN. 2024. "Bernie Sanders: 'This May Be Biden's Vietnam.'" Video, May 2. https://www.youtube.com/watch?v=_6rQmvko18M.

Coleman, Angie. 2017. "How Does Change Happen: Angela Davis on Movements, Erasure, and the Dangers of Heroic Individualism." *Angie Coleman*, January 30. http://www.angiecoleman.me/music-tech/2017/2/2/how-does -change-happen-angela-davis-on-movements-erasure-and-the-dangers-of -heroic-individualism.

Collins, Patricia Hill. 2019. *Intersectionality as Critical Social Theory*. Durham, NC: Duke University Press.

Colpani, Gianmaria, Jamila M. H. Mascat, and Katrine Smiet. 2022. "Postcolonial Responses to Decolonial Interventions." *Postcolonial Studies* 25, no. 1: 1–16. https://doi.org/10.1080/13688790.2022.2041695.

Cook, Deborah. 2004. "Ein Reaktionäres Schwein? Political Activism and Prospects for Change in Adorno." *Revue Internationale de Philosophie* 58, no. 227.1: 47–67.

Cook, Deborah. 2018. *Adorno, Foucault and the Critique of the West*. London: Verso.

Cooper, Davina, and Didi Herman. 2019. "Doing Activism like a State: Progressive Municipal Government, Israel/Palestine and BDS." *Environment and Planning C: Politics and Space*, 38, no. 1. https://doi.org/10.1177 /2399654419851187.

Cooper, Davina, Nikita Dhawan, and Janet Newman. 2019. *Reimagining the State: Theoretical Challenges and Transformative Possibilities. Social Justice Series*. London: Routledge.

Cornell, Drucilla. 1992. *The Philosophy of the Limit*. New York: Routledge.

Coronil, Fernando. 2008. "Elephants in the Americas? Latin American Postcolonial Studies and Global Decolonization." In *Coloniality at Large*, edited by Mabel Moraña, Enrique Dussel, and Carlos A. Jáuregui, 396–416. Durham, NC: Duke University Press.

Crenshaw, Kimberlé. 1989. "Demarginalizing the Intersection of Race and Sex: A Black Feminist Critique of Antidiscrimination Doctrine, Feminist Theory and Antiracist Politics." *University of Chicago Legal Forum* 1, no. 8: 139–67.

Cummiskey, David. 2008. "Justice and Revolution in Kant's Political Philosophy." In *Rethinking Kant: Current Trends in American Kantian Scholarship*, 219–42. Cambridge: Cambridge Scholar.

Dabashi, Hamid. 2013. "Can Non-Europeans Think?" *Al Jazeera*, January 15. http://www.aljazeera.com/indepth/opinion/2013/01/2013114142638797542.html.

Dacher, Priscilla. 2021. "'Islamo-Leftism' Is Not a Scientific Reality." National Centre for Scientific Research, February 17. https://www.cnrs.fr/en/press/islamo-leftism-not-scientific-reality.

Dans, Paul, and Steven Groves, eds. 2023. *Mandate for Leadership: The Conservative Promise (Project 2025)*. Washington, DC: Heritage Foundation. https://static.project2025.org/2025_MandateForLeadership_FULL.pdf.

Daub, Adrian. 2024. "Psychozionism." *n+1*, July 3. https://www.nplusonemag.com/online-only/online-only/psychozionism.

Davis, Angela. 1999. *Blues Legacies and Black Feminism: Gertrude 'Ma' Rainey, Bessie Smith, and Billie Holiday*. New York: Vintage.

Davis, Angela. 2019. *Women, Race and Class*. London: Penguin.

Davis, Angela, Gayatari C. Spivak, and Nikita Dhawan. 2019. "Planetary Utopias." *Radical Philosophy* 205: 67–78. https://www.radicalphilosophy.com/article/planetary-utopias.

de Alwis, Malathi. 2010. "The Apparition of Rape and the 'Sisterhood' of International Feminists." Keynote speech delivered at Reimagining Gender and Politics: Transnational Feminist Interventions conference, Goethe University, Frankfurt, November 27–28, 2010.

Dean, Mitchell, and Kaspar Villadsen. 2016. *State Phobia and Civil Society: The Political Legacy of Michel Foucault*. Stanford, CA: Stanford University Press.

Deitelhoff, Nicole, Rainer Forst, Klaus Günther, and Jürgen Habermas. 2023. "Grundsätze der Solidarität. Eine Stellungnahme." *Normative Orders*, November 13. https://www.normativeorders.net/2023/grundsatze-der-solidaritat.

Deleuze, Gilles, and Félix Guattari. 2003. *Anti-Oedipus: Capitalism and Schizophrenia*. Minneapolis: University of Minnesota Press.

Democracy Now! 2024a. "'McCarthyism Is Alive and Well': Google Fires Employees for Protesting Contract with Israeli Military." Last modified April 18. https://www.democracynow.org/2024/4/18/headlines/mccarthyism_is

_alive_and_well_google_fires_employees_for_protesting_contract_with
_israeli_military.

Democracy Now! 2024b. "'Stop Weaponizing Antisemitism': Police 'Body-Slam'
Jewish Dartmouth Prof[essor] at Campus Gaza Protest." Video, May 7.
https://www.youtube.com/watch?v=7nYXYNj_1dY.

Democracy Now! 2024c. "Protests in Sweden Call Out Israel's Participation in
Eurovision." Last modified May 10. https://www.democracynow.org/2024
/5/10/headlines/protests_in_sweden_call_out_israels_participation_in
_eurovision.

Democracy Now! 2024d. "International Criminal Court Seeks Arrest Warrants
for Netanyahu, Gallant and Hamas Leaders for War Crimes." Video,
May 20. https://www.youtube.com/watch?v=Pwm4A_Eo68A.

Democracy Now! 2024e. "'A Watershed Event': ICC Charges Against Netanyahu
First Time Court Has Gone After Western Leader." Video, May 21. https://
www.youtube.com/watch?v=sAXNopi29js&t=5s.

Derrida, Jacques. 1978. *Writing and Difference*. Chicago: University of Chicago
Press.

Derrida, Jacques. 1981a. *Dissemination*. London: Athlone.

Derrida, Jacques. 1981b. "Economimesis." *Diacritics* 11, no. 2: 2–25.

Derrida, Jacques. 1985. *The Ear of the Other: Otobiography, Transference, Translation*.
Translated by Peggy Kamuf. New York: Schocken.

Derrida, Jacques. 1992. *The Other Heading: Reflections on Today's Europe*. Bloomington: Indiana University Press.

Derrida, Jacques. 1996. "How to Avoid Speaking: Denials." In *Languages of the
Unsayable: The Play of Negativity in Literature and Literary Theory*, edited by
Sanford Budick and Wolfgang Iser, 3–70. Stanford, CA: Stanford Univer-
sity Press.

Derrida, Jacques. 1997. *The Politics of Friendship*. London: Verso.

Derrida, Jacques. 1998. *Archive Fever: A Freudian Impression*. Chicago: University
of Chicago Press.

Derrida, Jacques. 2000. "Hostipitality." *Angelaki* 5, no. 3: 3–18.

Derrida, Jacques. 2002 [1994]. "Force of Law: The Mystical Foundation of
Authority." In *Acts of Religion*, edited by Gil Anidjar, 228–98. London:
Routledge.

Derrida, Jacques. 2005. *Rogues: Two Essays on Reason*. Translated by Pascale-Anne
Brault and Michael Naas. Stanford, CA: Stanford University Press.

Derrida, Jacques. 2006. "A Europe of Hope." *Epoché* 10, no. 2: 407–12.

Derrida, Jacques. 2007. "Que faire—de la question 'Que faire?'?" In *Derrida pour
les temps à venir*, edited by René Major, 45–62. Paris: Stock.

Derrida, Jacques. 2019. *Theory and Practice*. Chicago: University of Chicago Press.

Deutscher Bundestag. 2022. "Debatte über Antisemitismus-Skandal bei der
Documenta." July 7. https://www.bundestag.de/dokumente/textarchiv
/2022/kw27-de-documenta-900546.

Devji, Faisal. 2012. *The Impossible Indian: Gandhi and the Temptation of Violence.* Cambridge, MA: Harvard University Press.

Dewey, John. 1946. "The Public and Its Problems." In *The Later Works, 1925–1927,* 2. Carbondale: Southern Illinois University Press.

Dhawan, Nikita. 2007. *Impossible Speech: The Politics of Silence and Violence.* Sankt Augustin: Academia.

Dhawan, Nikita. 2013a. "The Empire Prays Back: Religion, Secularity, and Queer Critique." *boundary 2* 40, no. 1: 191–222.

Dhawan, Nikita. 2013b. "Postkoloniale Gouvernementalität und 'die Politik der Vergewaltigung': Gewalt, Verletzlichkeit und der Staat." *Femina Politica* 2: 85–104. http://nbn-resolving.de/urn:nbn:de:0168-ssoar-447317.

Dhawan, Nikita. 2014. "Affirmative Sabotage of the Master's Tools: The Paradox of Postcolonial Enlightenment." In *Decolonizing Enlightenment: Transnational Justice, Human Rights and Democracy in a Postcolonial World,* edited by Nikita Dhawan, 19–78. Opladen: Verlag Barbara Budrich.

Dhawan, Nikita. 2017. "Can Non-Europeans Philosophize? Transnational Literacy and Planetary Ethics in a Global Age." *Hypatia* 32, no. 3: 488–505.

Dhawan, Nikita. 2019. "The Death of Leviathan: Feminist Dilemmas and State Phobia." *Social Politics* 28, no. 3: 682–703.

Dhawan, Nikita. 2020. "State as Pharmakon." In *Reimagining the State: Theoretical Challenges and Transformative Possibilities,* edited By Davina Cooper, Nikita Dhawan, and Janet Newman, 57–76. New York: Routledge.

Dhawan, Nikita. 2023. "Gayatri Chakravorty Spivak." In *Rethinking Political Thinkers,* edited by Manjeet Ramgotra and Simon Choat, 427–44. Oxford: Oxford University Press.

Dhawan, Nikita, Elisabeth Fink, Johanna Leinius, and Rirhandu Mageza-Barthel. 2016. *Negotiating Normativity: Postcolonial Appropriations, Contestations and Transformations.* New York: Springer.

Dhawan, Nikita, and María do Mar Castro Varela. 2024. "Class, Capitalism and the Postcolonial Question." *Class and Capital* 48, no. 2: 273–86.

Diderot, Denis. 1876 [1751–72]. *Encyclopédie.* Paris: Garnier frères.

Diogenes. 2012. *Diogenes the Cynic: Sayings and Anecdotes, with Other Popular Moralists.* New York: Oxford University Press.

Djait, Hichem. 1985. *Europe and Islam: Cultures and Modernity.* Berkeley: University of California Press.

Dokumentations- und Kulturzentrum Deutscher Sinti und Roma. 2010. "Civil Rights Prize 2010." Accessed August 1, 2024. https://dokuzentrum .sintiundroma.de/en/participation/civil-rights-prize/civil-rights-prize-2010.

Doughan, Sultan, A. Dirk Moses, and Michael Rothberg. 2022a. "A New German Historians' Debate? A Conversation with Sultan Doughan, A. Dirk Moses, and Michael Rothberg (Part I)." Interview by Jonathon Catlin. *Journal of the History of Ideas* (blog), February 2. https://www.jhiblog.org/2022/02

/02/a-new-german-historians-debate-a-conversation-with-sultan-doughan
-a-dirk-moses-and-michael-rothberg-part-i.

Doughan, Sultan, A. Dirk Moses, and Michael Rothberg. 2022b. "A New German Historians' Debate? A Conversation with Sultan Doughan, A. Dirk Moses, and Michael Rothberg (Part II)." Interview by Jonathon Catlin. *Journal of the History of Ideas* (blog), February 4. https://www.jhiblog.org /2022/02/04/a-new-german-historians-debate-a-conversation-with-sultan -doughan-a-dirk-moses-and-michael-rothberg-part-ii.

Dubois, Laurent. 2004. *Avengers of the New World: The Story of the Haitian Revolution*. Cambridge, MA: Harvard University Press.

Du Bois, W. E. B. 1952. "The Negro and the Warsaw Ghetto." *Black Thought and Culture*. https://europe.unc.edu/wp-content/uploads/sites/314/2021/02 /DuBois-The-Negro-and-the-Warsaw-Ghetto.pdf.

Du Bois, W. E. B. 1996 [1903]. *The Souls of Black Folk*. New York: Penguin.

Economic Times. 2024. "US: Netanyahu Equates Pro-Palestine Protestors 'Gays For Gaza' to 'Chickens for KFC' in His Speech." Video. Accessed August 1, 2024. https://www.youtube.com/shorts/ycK1gubjL9I.

Edelman, Lee. 2004. *No Future: Queer Theory and the Death Drive*. Durham, NC: Duke University Press.

Eigen, Sara, and Mark Larrimore, eds. 2006. *The German Invention of Race*. New York: State University of New York Press.

Einstein, Albert. 2018. "Why War? A Letter from Albert Einstein to Sigmund Freud." *UNESCO Courier*, June 11. https://courier.unesco.org/en/articles/why -war-letter-albert-einstein-sigmund-freud.

EMMA. 2015. "Schamlos: Verschweigen von EMMA!" October 7. https://www .emma.de/artikel/fluechtlinge-was-jetzt-passieren-muss-330655.

Encyclopedia. 2024. "Aymara (Language)." Encyclopedia.com. Accessed August 1. https://www.encyclopedia.com/humanities/encyclopedias-almanacs -transcripts-and-maps/aymara-language.

Engels, Friedrich. 1978 [1874]. "On Authority." In *The Marx-Engels Reader*, edited by Robert C. Tucker, 730–33. New York: W. W. Norton.

Engels, Friedrich. 2010 [1877]. "Anti-Dühring: Herr Eugen Dühring's Revolution in Science." In *Marx and Engels: Collected Works*, vol. 25. London: Lawrence and Wishart.

Eriksson, Birgit. 2008–9. "On Common Tastes: Heterogeneity and Hierarchies in Contemporary Cultural Consumption." *Nordic Journal of Aesthetics* 36–37: 36–53.

Eze, Emmanuel C. 1997a. "The Color of Reason: The Idea of 'Race' in Kant's Anthropology." In *Postcolonial African Philosophy: A Critical Reader*, edited by Emmanuel Chukwudi Eze, 103–40. New York: Blackwell.

Eze, Emmanuel C. 1997b. *Race and the Enlightenment: A Reader*. Oxford: Wiley-Blackwell.

Eze, Emmanuel C. 2001. *Achieving Our Humanity: The Idea of the Postracial Future.* New York: Routledge.

Eze, Emmanuel C. 2008. *On Reason: Rationality in a World of Cultural Conflict and Racism.* Durham, NC: Duke University Press.

Fanizadeh, Andreas. 2022. "Antisemitismus auf der Documenta. Waterloo der Postkolonialen." *Die Tageszeitung*, June 21. https://taz.de/Antisemitismus -auf-der-Documenta/!5859650.

Fanon, Frantz. 1963 [1961]. *The Wretched of the Earth.* New York: Grove.

Fanon, Frantz. 1986 [1952]. *Black Skin, Whites Mask.* London: Pluto.

Fanon, Frantz. 2007 [1959]. *A Dying Colonialism.* New York: Grove.

Fareld, Victoria. 2021. "Entangled Memories of Violence: Jean Améry and Frantz Fanon." *Memory Studies* 14, no. 1: 58–67.

Farge, Arlette, and Michel Foucault. 2012. "'Présentation,' Le désordre des familles: Lettres de cachet des Archives de la Bastille au XVIIIe siècle." In *Foucault, the Family and Politics*, edited by Robbie Duschinsky and Leon A. Rocha, 178–88. London: Palgrave Macmillan.

Federal Foreign Office. 2024. "Federal Foreign Office on the Application for Arrest Warrants at the International Criminal Court." May 20. https://www .auswaertiges-amt.de/en/newsroom/news/-/2657664.

Festa, Lynn, and Daniel Carey. 2009. "What Is Postcolonial Enlightenmment?" In *The Postcolonial Eighteenth Century*, edited by Daniel Carey and Lynn Festa, 1–33. Oxford: Oxford University Press.

Fink, Elizabeth. 2018. *Transnationaler Aktivismus und Frauenarbeit: Social Movement Unionism in Bangladesch.* Frankfurt: Campus.

Fischer, Sybille. 2004. *Modernity Disavowed: Haiti and the Cultures of Slavery in the Age of Revolution.* Durham, NC: Duke University Press.

Fitzgerald, Joseph R., and Jaimee A. Swift. 2024. "On the Record: Barbara Smith on Palestine, June Jordan, Audre Lorde, and Adrienne Rich." *Black Women Radicals.* August 22. https://www.blackwomenradicals.com/blog-feed/on-the -record-barbara-smith-on-palestine-june-jordan-audre-lorde-and-adrienne -rich.

Flax, Jane. 1992. "Is Enlightenment Emancipatory? A Feminist Reading of 'What Is Enlightenment.'" In *Postmodernism and the Re-reading of Modernity*, edited by Francis Barker, Peter Hulme, and Margaret Iversen, 232–49. Manchester: Manchester University Press.

Flikschuh, Katrin. 2017. *What Is Orientation in Global Thinking? A Kantian Inquiry.* Cambridge: Cambridge University Press.

Flikschuh, Katrin, and Lea Ypi, eds. 2014: *Kant and Colonialism.* Oxford: Oxford University Press.

Foreign Relations Committee. 2024. "Bipartisan Senators Condemn ICC Action Against Israel." May 21. https://www.foreign.senate.gov/press/rep/release /bipartisan-senators-condemn-icc-action-against-israel.

Forsdick, Charles, and Christian Høgsbjerg. 2017. *Toussaint Louverture: A Black Jacobin in the Age of Revolutions*. London: Pluto.

Foucault, Michel. 1977. "Intellectuals and Power: A Conversation Between Michel Foucault and Gilles Deleuze." In *Language, Counter-memory, Practice: Selected Essays and Interviews by Michel Foucault*, edited by Donald F. Bouchard, 205-17. Ithaca, NY: Cornell University Press.

Foucault, Michel. 1978. *The History of Sexuality, Volume I: An Introduction*. New York: Pantheon.

Foucault, Michel. 1979. "My Body, This Paper, This Fire." *Oxford Literary Review* 4, no. 1: 9-28.

Foucault, Michel. 1984. "What Is Enlightenment?" In *The Foucault Reader*, edited by Paul Rabinow, 32-50. New York: Pantheon.

Foucault, Michel. 1988. "Confinement, Psychiatry, Prison." In *Politics, Philosophy, Culture: Interviews and Other Writings, 1977-1984*, edited by Lawrence D. Kritzman, 178-210. New York: Routledge.

Foucault, Michel. 1990. "Power and Sex." In *Politics, Philosophy, Culture: Interviews and Other Writings, 1977-1984*, edited by Lawrence D. Kritzman, 110-24. New York: Routledge.

Foucault, Michel. 1994. "Lives of Infamous Men." In *Power: The Essential Works of Foucault*, vol. 3, edited by James D. Faubion, 157-75. New York: New Press.

Foucault, Michel. 1995. *Discipline and Punish*. New York: Vintage.

Foucault, Michel. 1996a. "What Is Critique?" In *What Is Enlightenment? Eighteenth-Century Answers and Twentieth-Century Questions*, edited by James Schmidt, 382-98. Berkeley: University of California Press.

Foucault, Michel. 1996b. *Foucault Live, Collected Interviews 1961-1984*. New York: Semiotext(e).

Foucault, Michel. 1997. "Polemics, Politics, and Problematizations: An Interview with Michel Foucault." In *Ethics: Subjectivity and Truth; The Essential Works of Michel Foucault, 1954-1984*, 111-20. New York: New Press.

Foucault, Michel. 2000. "So Is It Important to Think?" In *Power: The Essential Works of Foucault, 1954-1984*, vol. 3, edited by James D. Faubion, 454-58. New York: New Press.

Foucault, Michel. 2001. "Space, Knowledge and Power." In *Power: The Essential Works of Foucault, 1954-1984*, vol. 3, edited by James D. Faubion, 349-64. New York: New Press.

Foucault, Michel. 2003. *Society Must Be Defended*. London: Penguin.

Foucault, Michel. 2007. "What Is Critique?" In *The Politics of Truth*, edited by Silvère Lotringer, 41-81. Los Angeles: Semiotext(e).

Foucault, M. 2008. *The Birth of Biopolitics: Lectures at the Collège de France, 1978-1979*. London: Palgrave Macmillan.

Foucault, Michel. 2010. *The Government of Self and Others: Lectures at the Collège de France 1982-1983*. Translated by Graham Burchell. New York: Palgrave Macmillan.

Foucault, Michel. 2013 [1959]. *Madness and Civilization*. New York: Vintage.

Francis, Matthew. 2017. "How Albert Einstein Used His Fame to Denounce American Racism." *Smithsonian Magazine*, March 3. https://www.smithsonianmag.com/science-nature/how-celebrity-scientist-albert-einstein-used-fame-denounce-american-racism-180962356.

Fraser, Nancy. 1992. "Rethinking the Public Sphere: A Contribution to the Critique of Actually Existing Democracy." In *Habermas and the Public Sphere*, edited by Craig Calhoun, 109–42. Cambridge, MA: MIT Press.

Fraser, Nancy. 1997. *Justice Interruptus: Critical Reflections on the "Postsocialist" Condition*. New York: Routledge.

Freud, Sigmund. 1981a [1925]. "Inhibitions, Symptoms and Anxiety." In *The Standard Editition of the Complete Psychological Works of Sigmund Freud*, vol. 20, 77–178. London: Vintage.

Freud, Sigmund. 1981b [1926]. "The Question of Lay Analysis." In *The Standard Editition of the Complete Psychological Works of Sigmund Freud*, vol. 20, 179–258. London: Vintage.

Freud, Sigmund. 1999 [1919]. "The 'Uncanny.'" In *The Standard Edition of the Complete Psychological Works of Sigmund Freud*, vol. 17, 217–56. London: Vintage.

Freud, Sigmund. 2019. "Why War? A Letter from Freud to Einstein." *UNESCO Courier*, July 6. https://courier.unesco.org/en/articles/why-war-letter-freud-einstein.

Fuchs, Christian. 2016. *Critical Theory of Communication: New Readings of Lukács, Adorno, Marcuse, Honneth and Habermas in the Age of the Internet*. London: University of Westminster Press.

Fulford, Lord Justice, Theodor Meron, Amal Clooney, Danny Friedman, Baroness Helena Kennedy, and Elizabeth Wilmshurst. 2024. "Why We Support ICC Prosecutions for Crimes in Israel and Gaza." *Financial Times*, May 20. https://www.ft.com/content/aa2089c5-6388-437d-bf5c-9268f3a788ce.

Gandhi, Mohandas K. 1939. *Hind Swaraj*. Ahmedabad: Navajivan.

Gandhi, Mohandas K. 1967. "Answer Men" (set of five miscellaneous quotations), *Reader's Digest*, vol. 91, September, 52.

Gandhi Mohandas K. 1969. "Ahimsa, or The Way of Non-violence." In *All Men Are Brothers: Life and Thoughts of Mahatma Gandhi as Told in His Own Words*. Paris: UNESCO.

Gandhi, Mohandas K. 1970 [1928]. "Discussion with a Capitalist (Before 10-12-1928)." In *The Collected Works of Mahatma Gandhi*, vol. 38, 311. Ahmedabad: Navjivan Trust.

Gandhi, Mohandas K. 1974 [1934]. "Interview with Nirmal Kumar Bose (9/10-11-1934)." In *The Collected Works of Mahatma Gandhi*, vol. 59, 316–20. Ahmedabad: Navjivan Trust.

Gandhi, Mohandas K. 1976a [1936]. "Dr. Ambedkar's Indictment (11-7-1936)." In *The Collected Works of Mahatma Gandhi*, vol. 63, 134–36. Ahmedabad: Navjivan Trust.

Gandhi Mohandas K. 1976b [1937]. "Interview to Capt. Strunk (3-7-1937)." In *The Collected Works of Mahatma Gandhi*, vol. 65, 360–62. Ahmedabad: Navjivan Trust.

Gandhi, Mohandas K. 1977 [1939]. "What to Do? (9-4-1939)." In *The Collected Works of Mahatma Gandhi*, vol. 69, 121–23. Ahmedabad: Navjivan Trust.

Gandhi, Mohandas K. 1978 [1940]. "Letter to Adolf Hitler (24-12-1940)." In *The Collected Works of Mahatma Gandhi*, vol. 73, 253–55. Ahmedabad: Navjivan Trust.

Gandhi, Mohandas K. 1982 [1946]. "Talk with an English Journalist (29-9-1946)." In *The Collected Works of Mahatma Gandhi*, vol. 85, 370–72. Ahmedabad: Navjivan Trust.

Gandhi, Mohandas K. 1999 [1926]. "Three Vital Questions (17-01-1926)." In *The Collected Works of Mahatma Gandhi*, vol. 22, 408–10. Ahmedabad: Navjivan Trust.

Gandhi, Mohandas K. 2009 [1927]. *An Autobiography or the Story of My Experiments with Truth*. Bangalore: Vasam.

Gani, Jasmine. 2017. "The Erasure of Race: Cosmopolitanism and the Illusion of Kantian Hospitality." *Millennium* 45, no. 3: 425–46.

Garraway, Doris L. 2009. "Of Speaking Native and Hybrid Philosophers: Lahontan, Diderot and the French Enlightenment Critique of Colonialism." In *The Postcolonial Eighteenth Century*, edited by Daniel Carey and Lynn Festa, 207–39. Oxford: Oxford University Press.

Garraway, Doris L. 2017. "Black Athena in Haiti: Universal History, Colonization, and the African Origins of Civilization in Postrevolutionary Haitian Writing." In *Enlightened Colonialism*, edited by Damien Tricoire, 287–308. New York: Springer.

Gasché, Rodolphe. 2009. *Europe or the Infinite Task: A Study of a Philosophical Concept*. Stanford, CA: Stanford University Press.

Gilmore, Ruth W. 2022. *Abolition Geography: Essays Towards Liberation*. London: Verso.

Gilroy, Paul. 2000. *Between Camps: Race, Identity and Nationalism at the End of the Colour Line*. London: Routledge.

Girard, Philippe. 2016. *Toussaint Louverture: A Revolutionary Life*. New York: Basic.

Girard, Philippe. 2017. "Philippe Girard." Interview by Andrew M. Davenport. *Full Stop*, February 8. https://www.full-stop.net/2017/02/08/interviews/andrew-mitchell-davenport/philippe-girard.

Girard, René. 1986. *The Scapegoat*. Translated by Yvonne Freccero. Baltimore: Johns Hopkins University Press.

Goetschel, Willi, and Ato Quayson. 2016. "Introduction: Jewish Studies and Postcolonialism." In *Cambridge Journal of Postcolonial Literary Inquiry* 3, no. 1: 1–9. https://doi.org/10.1017/pli.2015.32.

Goodman, Amy. 2023 "Kimberlé Crenshaw on Critical Race Theory, Intersectionality and the Right-Wing War on Public Education." *Democracy Now!*

February 6. https://www.democracynow.org/2023/2/6/kimberle_crenshaw
_black_studies_censorship.

Goodman, Amy. 2024a. "From Plagiarism to Gaza: Khalil Gibran Muham-
mad on How a GOP Campaign Ousted Harvard's Claudine Gay." *Democracy Now!* January 3. https://www.democracynow.org/2024/1/3/harvard
_president_claudine_gay_resigns.

Goodman, Amy. 2024b. "'No Other Land': Israeli Director Slams Claims of Antisemitism for Apartheid Comment at Berlinale." *Democracy Now!* April 5.
https://www.democracynow.org/2024/4/5/no_other_land.

Gordon, Lewis R. 1995. *Fanon and the Crisis of European Man: An Essay on Philosophy and the Human Sciences.* New York: Routledge.

Gordon, Lewis R. 2016. "Rarely Kosher: Studying Jews of Color in North America." *American Jewish History* 100, no. 1: 105–16.

Gramsci, Antonio. 2011a. *Prison Notebooks,* vol. 2. Edited and translated by
Joseph A. Buttigieg. New York: Columbia University Press.

Gramsci, Antonio. 2011b. *Prison Notebooks,* vol. 3. Edited and translated by
Joseph A. Buttigieg. New York: Columbia University Press.

Gramsci, Antonio. 2021. *Subaltern Social Groups: A Critical Edition of Prison Notebook 25,* edited by Joseph. A. Buttigieg and Marcus E. Green. New York:
Columbia University Press.

Grosfoguel, Ramón. 2007. "The Epistemic Decolonial Turn: Beyond Political-
Economy Paradigms." *Cultural Studies* 21, nos. 2–3: 211–23.

Grosfoguel, Ramón. 2011. "Decolonizing Post-colonial Studies and Paradigms
of Political-Economy: Transmodernity, Decolonial Thinking, and Global
Coloniality." *Transmodernity* 1, no. 1: 1–38.

Grundgesetz. 2024. "II. Der Bund und die Länder. Artikel 20." Deutscher
Bundestag. Accessed August 1, 2024. https://www.bundestag.de/parlament
/aufgaben/rechtsgrundlagen/grundgesetz.

Guha, Ranajit. 2010. "The Small Voice of History." In *Subaltern Studies 9: Writings on South Asian History and Society,* edited by Shahid Amin and Dipesh
Chakrabarty, 1–12. Delhi: Oxford University Press: 1996.

Gurley Flynn, Elizabeth. 1916. *Sabotage: The Conscious Withdrawal of the Workers'
Industrial Efficiency.* Cleveland: International Workers of the World Publishing Bureau.

Habermas, Jürgen. 1982. "The Entwinement of Myth and Enlightenment: Re-
reading Dialectic of Enlightenment." *New German Critique* 26: 13–30.

Habermas, Jürgen. 1983. *The Theory of Communicative Action,* vol. 1. Boston: Beacon.

Habermas, Jürgen. 1987. *The Philosophical Discourse of Modernity.* Cambridge,
MA: MIT Press.

Habermas, Jürgen. 1990. *The Philosophical Discourse of Modernity: Twelve Lectures.*
Cambridge, MA: MIT Press.

Habermas, Jürgen. 1992. *The Structural Transformation of the Public Sphere.* Cambridge: Polity.

Habermas, Jürgen. 1994. "The Gulf War: Catalyst for a New German Normalcy?" In *The Past as Future*, edited and translated by Max Pensky, 5–32. Lincoln: University of Nebraska Press.

Habermas, Jürgen. 1999. "Bestiality and Humanity: A War on the Border Between Legality and Morality." *Constellations* 6: 263–72.

Habermas, Jürgen. 2002. *Religion and Rationality: Essays on Reason, God and Modernity*. Cambridge: Polity.

Habermas, Jürgen. 2011. *Zur Verfassung Europas—Ein Essay*. Berlin: Suhrkamp.

Hall Stuart. 1991. "Ethnicity: Identity and Difference." *Radical America* 23: 9–20.

Hall, Stuart. 1996. "When Was 'the Post-colonial'? Thinking at the Limit." In *The Postcolonial Question: Common Skies, Divided Horizons*, edited by Ian Chambers and Lidia Curtis, 242–60. London: Routledge.

Hall, Stuart. 2000. "Professor Stuart Hall." BBC, February 18. https://www.bbc.co.uk/programmes/p0094b6r#p0094b6r.

Hall, Stuart. 2018. *Familiar Stranger: A Life Between Two Islands*. London: Penguin.

Hannah, Matthew G., Jan Simon Hutta, and Christoph Schemann. 2020. "Thinking Through COVID-19 Responses with Foucault: An Initial Overview." *Antipode Online*, May 5. https://antipodeonline.org/2020/05/05/thinking-through-covid-19-responses-with-foucault.

Hardiman, David. 2003. *Gandhi: In His Time and Ours*. Delhi: Permanent Black.

Harithaworn, Jin, and Jennifer Petzen. 2011. "Integration as a Sexual Problem: An Excavation of the German 'Muslim Homophobia' Panic." In *Karriere eines Konstruierten Gegensatzes: Zehn Jahre "Muslime versus Schwule" Sexualpolitiken seit dem 11. September 2011*, edited by Koray Yilmaz-Gunay, 115–34. Berlin: Schmohl.

Harvey, David A. 2012. *The French Enlightenment and Its Others: The Mandarin, the Savage, and the Invention of the Human Sciences*. New York: Palgrave Macmillan.

Hay, Colin. 2014. "If It Didn't Exist We'd Have to Invent It . . . Further Reflections on the Ontological Status of the State." *British Journal of Sociology* 65, no. 3: 487–91.

Hazareesingh, Sudhir. 2020. *Black Spartacus: The Epic Life of Toussaint Louverture*. New York: Farrar, Straus and Giroux.

Hecking, Claus, Michael Sauga, Thomas Schulz, and Gerald Traufetter. 2021. "Patent Suspensions Threaten Germany's Booming Biotech Industry." *Spiegel International*, May 11. https://www.spiegel.de/international/business/biontech-curevac-and-co-patent-suspensions-threaten-germany-s-booming-biotech-industry-a-2d4907f3-a03f-4a7c-8d2d-c5c455b45c8f.

Hegel, Georg W. F. 1968 [1802]. "Einleitung. Über das Wesen der philosophischen Kritik überhaupt und ihr Verhältnis zum gegenwärtigen Zustand der Philosophie insbesondere." In *Jenaer Schriften 1801-1807, Gesammelte Werke*, vol. 4, 117–28. Hamburg: Felix Meiner.

Hegel, Georg W. F. 1977 [1807]. *Phenomenology of Spirit*. Oxford: Clarendon.

Hegel, Georg W. F. 1988 [1837]. "Introduction to *The Philosophy of History*." In *Introduction to The Philosophy of History: With Selections from The Philosophy of Right*. Indianapolis: Hackett.

Hegel, Georg W. F. 1991 [1821]. *Elements of the Philosophy of Right*. Translated by Hugh B. Nisbet. Cambridge: Cambridge University Press.

Hersch, Charles. 2013. "'Every Time I Try to Play Black, It Comes Out Sounding Jewish': Jewish Jazz Musicians and Racial Identity." In *American Jewish History* 97, no. 3: 259–82.

Heuss, Herbert. 2017. "Nachruf auf Simone Veil." *Zentralrat Deutscher Sinti und Roma*, July 1. https://zentralrat.sintiundroma.de/nachruf-auf -simone-veil.

Hewitt, Andrew. 1992. "Feminine Dialectic of Enlightenment? Horkheimer and Adorno Revisited." *New German Critique* 56: 143–70.

Hewitt, Marsha. 1995. *Critical Theory of Religion: A Feminist Analysis*. Minneapolis: Augsberg Fortress.

Higgins, Michael. 2024. "The Voice of Reason on the International Court of Justice." *National Post*, January 26. https://nationalpost.com/opinion/the -voice-of-reason-on-the-international-court-of-justice.

Hill, Samantha. 2023. "Hannah Arendt Would Not Qualify for the Hannah Arendt Prize in Germany Today." *The Guardian*, December 18. https://www .theguardian.com/commentisfree/2023/dec/18/hannah-arendt-prize-masha -gessen-israel-gaza-essay.

The Hindu. 2021. "Kangana Ranaut Plays Defiant Card, Asks Which War Took Place in 1947." November 23. https://www.thehindu.com/news /national/kangana-plays-defiant-card-asks-which-war-took-place-in-1947 /article37469671.ece.

hooks, bell. 1990. *Yearning: Race, Gender, and Cultural Politics*. Boston: South End.

hooks, bell. 1994. *Teaching to Transgress: Education as the Practice of Freedom*. London: Routledge.

Hobbes, Thomas. 1998 [1651]. *Leviathan*. New York: Oxford University Press.

Hobsbawm, Eric. 1969. *Bandits*. London: Weidenfeld.

Hobsbawm, Eric. 1971 [1959]. *Primitive Rebels: Studies in Archaic Forms of Social Movement in the Nineteenth and Twentieth Centuries*. Manchester: Manchester University Press.

Hobsbawm, Eric. 1993. *The Jazz Scene*. New York: Pantheon.

Hohendahl, Peter U. 1985. "The Dialectic of Enlightenment Revisited: Habermas' Critique of the Frankfurt School." *New German Critique* 35: 3–26.

Hölderlin, Friedrich. 1968. *Poems and Fragments*. Translated by Michael Hamburger. Ann Arbor: University of Michigan Press.

Holub, Miroslav. 1977. "Brief Thoughts on Maps." Translated by Jarmila and Ian Milner. *Times Literary Supplement*, February 4.

Honneth, Axel. 2009. *Pathologies of Reason: On the Legacy of Critical Theory*. New York: Cambridge University Press.

Horkheimer, Max. 1985a [1936]. "Die Funktion der Rede in der Neuzeit." In *Gesammelte Schriften* 12, 23–38. Frankfurt am Main: Fischer.

Horkheimer, Max. 1985b [1946]. "Rettung der Aufklärung. Diskussionen über eine geplante Schrift zur Dialektik." In *Gesammelte Schriften* 12, 593–605. Frankfurt am Main: Fischer.

Horkheimer, Max. 1993 [1931]. "The Present Situation of Social Philosophy and the Tasks of an Institute for Social Research." In *Between Philosophy and Social Science: Selected Early Writings*, edited by Frederick Hunter, Matthew S. Kramer and John Torpey, 1–14. Cambridge, MA: MIT Press.

Horkheimer, Max. 1996. "Briefe 1947." In *Gesammelte Schriften*, vol. 17, 776–911. Frankfurt am Main: Fischer.

Horkheimer, Max. 2012 [1961]. "The German Jews." In *Critique of Instrumental Reason*, 101–118. London: Verso.

Horkheimer, Max, and Theodor W. Adorno. 2002 [1947]. *Dialectic of Enlightenment. Philosophical Fragments*. Stanford, CA: Stanford University Press.

Huggins, Katherine. 2024. "'Intersectional Civil War': Clash Between Pride Marchers, Palestine Supporters Quickly Becomes Right-Wing Meme." *Daily Dot*, June 3. https://www.dailydot.com/debug/philadelphia-pride-parade-palestine-protesters.

Hulme, Peter. 1990. "The Spontaneous Hand of Nature: Savagery, Colonialism and the Enlightenment." In *The Enlightenment and Its Shadows*, edited by Peter Hulme and Ludmilla Jordanova, 16–34. London: Routledge.

Human Rights Watch. 2020. "US Sanctions on the International Criminal Court." December 14. https://www.hrw.org/news/2020/12/14/us-sanctions-international-criminal-court.

Husserl, Edmund. 1970 [1935]. *The Crisis of the European Sciences and Transcendental Phenomenology*. Evanston, IL: Northwestern University Press.

International Court of Justice (ICJ). 2024a. "Dissenting Opinion of Judge Sebutinde." January 26. https://www.icj-cij.org/node/203449.

International Court of Justice (ICJ). 2024b. "Application of the Convention on the Prevention and Punishment of the Crime of Genocide in the Gaza Strip (*South Africa v. Israel*)." Press release, March 28. https://www.icj-cij.org/sites/default/files/case-related/192/192-20240524-pre-01-00-en.pdf.

International Court of Justice (ICJ). 2024c. "Legal Consequences Arising from the Policies and Practices of Israel in the Occupied Palestinian Territory, Including East Jerusalem." Advisory opinion, International Court of Justice, July 19. https://www.icj-cij.org/sites/default/files/case-related/186/186-20240719-adv-01-00-en.pdf.

Ingram, James D. 2018. "Critical Theory and Postcolonialism." In *The Routledge Companion to the Frankfurt School*, 500–513. London: Routledge.

Ivanova, Alena. 2021. "Vaccine Apartheid Is Prolonging COVID—Not Vaccine Hesitancy." *OpenDemocracy*, December 2. https://www.opendemocracy.net/en/vaccine-apartheid-is-prolonging-covid-not-vaccine-hesitancy.

James, Cyril L. R. 2001 [1938]. *The Black Jacobins: Toussaint L'Ouverture and the San Domingo Revolution.* New York: Vintage Books.

James, Daniel, and Franz Knappik. 2022. "Exploring the Metaphysics of Hegel's Racism: The Teleology of the 'Concept' and the Taxonomy of Races." *Hegel Bulletin* 44, no. 1: 99–126. https://doi.org/10.1017/hgl.2022.38.

Jay, Martin. 2016. *Reason After Its Eclipse: On Late Critical Theory.* Madison: University of Wisconsin Press.

Jessop, Bob. 2013. *State Theory: Putting the Capitalist State in Its Place.* Last modified December 5. https://bobjessop.wordpress.com/2013/12/05/state-theory -putting-the-capitalist-state-in-its-place.

Jessop, Bob. 2014. "Towards a Political Ontology of State Power: A Comment on Colin Hay's Article." *British Journal of Sociology* 65, no. 3: 481–86.

John, Tara. 2024. "'A Pack of Lies.' Israeli Prime Minister Denies He Is Starving Civilians in Gaza as a Method of War." *CNN World*, May 21. https://edition .cnn.com/2024/05/21/middleeast/israel-netanyahu-interview-icc-intl-latam /index.html.

Jones, Dave. 2006. "Angela Davis: Remaking the World." University of California, Davis, October 20. https://www.ucdavis.edu/news/angela-davis -remaking-world.

Kamdar, Mira. 1990. "Subjectification and Mimesis: Colonizing History." In *American Journal of Semiotics* 7, no. 3: 91–100.

Kane, Alex. 2022. "Deutsche Welle Firings Set Chilling Precedent for Free Speech in Germany." *Jewish Currents*, February 16. https://jewishcurrents.org /deutsche-welle-firings-set-chilling-precedent-for-free-speech-in-germany.

Kant, Immanuel. 1907 [1798]. "Anthropologie in pragmatischer Hinsicht." In *Akademie Ausgabe* 7, 119–333. Berlin: de Gruyter.

Kant, Immanuel. 1923 [1802]. "Immanuel Kants physische Geographie." In *Akademie Ausgabe* 9, 151–436. Berlin: de Gruyter.

Kant, Immanuel. 1913. "Reflexionen aus dem Nachlaß: Entwürfe zu dem Colleg über Anthropologie aus den 70er und 80er Jahren." In *Akademie Ausgabe* 15, 655–899. Berlin: de Gruyter.

Kant, Immanuel. 1970. *Philosophical Correspondence: 1759–99.* Chicago: University of Chicago Press.

Kant, Immanuel. 1991a [1784]. "An Answer to the Question: 'What Is Enlightenment?'" In *Kant: Political Writings*, edited by Hugh B. Nisbet and Hans S. Reiss, 54–60. Cambridge: Cambridge University Press.

Kant, Immanuel. 1991b [1795]. "Perpetual Peace." In *Kant: Political Writings*, edited by Hugh B. Nisbet and Hans S. Reiss, 93–130. Cambridge: Cambridge University Press.

Kant, Immanuel. 1991c [1797]. *The Metaphysics of Morals.* Edited and translated by Mary J. Gregor. Cambridge: Cambridge University Press.

Kant, Immanuel. 1997. "Vorlesungen über Anthropologie." In *Akademie Ausgabe* 25. Berlin: de Gruyter.

Kant, Immanuel. 1999 [1793]. "On the Common Saying: That May Be Correct in Theory, but It Is of No Use in Practice." In *Practical Philosophy*, edited and translated by Mary J. Gregor, 273–310. Cambridge: Cambridge University Press.

Kant, Immanuel. 2001a [1793]. "Religion Within the Boundaries of Mere Reason." In *Religion and Rational Theology*, edited by Allen W. Wood and George di Giovanni, 39–216. Cambridge: Cambridge University Press.

Kant, Immanuel. 2001b [1798]. "The Conflict of the Faculties." In *Religion and Rational Theology*, edited by Allen W. Wood and George di Giovanni, 233–328. Cambridge: Cambridge University Press.

Kant, Immanuel. 2002 [1790]. *Critique of Judgment*. Indianapolis: Hackett.

Kant, Immanuel. 2006 [1798]. *Anthropology from a Pragmatic Point of View*. Cambridge: Cambridge University Press.

Kant, Immanuel. 2007a [1775]. "Of the Different Human Races." In *Anthropology, History, and Education*, edited by Günter Zöller and Robert B. Louden, 82–97. Cambridge: Cambridge University Press.

Kant, Immanuel. 2007b [1785]. "Determination of the Concept of a Human Race." In *Anthropology, History, and Education*, edited by Günter Zöller and Robert B. Louden, 143–59. Cambridge: Cambridge University Press.

Kant, Immanuel. 2011 [1764]. *Observations on the Feeling of the Beautiful and Sublime and Other Writings*. Edited by Patrick Frierson and Paul Guyer. Cambridge: Cambridge University Press.

Kant, Immanuel. 2012. *Lectures on Anthropology*. Edited by Allen W. Wood and Robert B. Louden. Cambridge: Cambridge University Press.

Kant, Immanuel. 2020. "Vorlesungen über Physische Geographie." In *Akademie Ausgabe* 26.2. Berlin: De Gruyter.

Kellman, Steven G., and Jai Chakrabarti. 2021. "In the Warsaw Ghetto, Where an Indian Play Imagined the Worst That Was Yet to Come." *Forward*, October 27. https://forward.com/culture/477123/warsaw-ghetto-korczak-tagore-jai-chakrabarti-play-for-the-end-of-the-world.

Kester, Grant. 2012. "The Noisy Optimism of Immediate Action: Theory, Practice and Pedagogy in Contemporary Art." *Art Journal* 71, no. 2: 86–99.

Khan, Karim A. A. 2024. "Statement of ICC Prosecutor Karim A. A. Khan KC: Applications for Arrest Warrants in the Situation in the State of Palestine." International Criminal Court, May 20, 2024. https://www.icc-cpi.int/news/statement-icc-prosecutor-karim-aa-khan-kc-applications-arrest-warrants-situation-state.

Kimani, Mary. 2009. "Pursuit of Justice or Western Plot?" *Africa Renewal*, October. https://www.un.org/africarenewal/magazine/october-2009/pursuit-justice-or-western-plot.

King, Martin L., Jr. 1959. "Address at the Thirty-sixth Annual Dinner of the War Resisters League." Martin Luther King, Jr. Research and Education

Institute, February 2. https://kinginstitute.stanford.edu/king-papers
/documents/address-thirty-sixth-annual-dinner-war-resisters-league.

King, Martin L., Jr. 1968. "The Other America." March 14. Grosse Pointe Historical Society. Accessed August 1, 2024: http://www.gphistorical.org/mlk
/mlkspeech/index.htm.

King, Martin L., Jr. 1987 [1967]. "Beyond Vietnam (April 4)." In *Eyes on the Prize: A Reader and Guide*, edited by Clayborne Carson, 201–4. New York: Penguin.

King, Richard. 2000. *Indian Philosophy. An Introduction to Hindu and Buddhist Thought*. New Delhi: Māyā and Edinburgh University Press.

Kingsley, Patrick. 2013. "Eighty Sexual Assaults in One Day—The Other Story of Tahrir Square." *The Guardian*, July 5. https://www.theguardian.com
/world/2013/jul/05/egypt-women-rape-sexual-assault-tahrir-square.

Kipling, Rudyard. 1899. "The White Man's Burden." In *Internet Modern History Sourcebook*. Fordham University. Accessed August 1, 2024. https://origin-rh
.web.fordham.edu/Halsall/mod/kipling.asp.

Klasen, Isabelle. 2018. "Rather No Art than Socialist Realism: Adorno, Beckett, and Brecht." In *The SAGE Handbook of Frankfurt School Critical Theory Volume 2*, edited by Beverley Best, Werner Bonefeld and Chris O'Kane, 1024–37. London: Sage.

Kleingeld, Pauline. 2007. "Kant's Second Thoughts on Race." *Philosophical Quarterly* 57: 573–92.

Kleingeld, Pauline. 2011. *Kant and Cosmopolitanism: The Philosophical Ideal of World Citizenship*. Cambridge: Cambridge University Press.

Kleingeld, Pauline. 2014. "Kant's Second Thoughts on Colonialism." In *Kant and Colonialism: Historical and Critical Perspectives*, edited by Katrin Flikschuh and Lea Ypi, 43–67. Oxford: Oxford University Press.

Kleingeld, Pauline. 2019. "On Dealing with Kant's Sexism and Racism." *SGIR Review* 2, no. 2: 3–22.

Klor de Alva, Jorge. 1995. "The Postcolonization of the (Latin) American Experience: A Reconsideration of 'Colonialism,' 'Postcolonialism,' and 'Mestizaje.'" In *After Colonialism: Imperial Histories and Postcolonial Displacements*, edited by Gyan Prakash, 241–75. Princeton, NJ: Princeton University Press.

Koselleck, Reinhart. 1988. *Critique and Crisis. Enlightenment and the Pathogenesis of Modern Society*. Cambridge, MA: MIT Press.

Krishnan, Revathi. 2021. "Outlook's 'Missing Govt' Cover Page Goes Missing Online, Magazine Says Part of New Format." *The Print*, May 14. https://
theprint.in/india/outlooks-missing-govt-cover-page-goes-missing-online
-magazine-says-part-of-new-format/658444.

Krook, Mona L. 2021. "Misogyny in the Capitol: Among the Insurrectionists, a Lot of Angry Men Who Don't Like Women." *The Conversation*, January 13. https://theconversation.com/misogyny-in-the-capitol-among-the
-insurrectionists-a-lot-of-angry-men-who-dont-like-women-153068.

Kumar, Aishwary. 2015. *Radical Equality: Ambedkar, Gandhi, and the Risk of Democracy*. Stanford, CA: Stanford University Press.

Lal, Vinay. 2008. "The Gandhi Everyone Loves to Hate." *Economic and Political Weekly* 43, no. 40: 55–64.

Lal, Vinay. 2009. "Gandhi's West, the West's Gandhi." *New Literary History* 40, no. 2: 281–313.

Lapidot, Elad. 2020. *Jews Out of the Question. A Critique of Anti-Anti-Semitism.* New York: State University of New York Press.

Latour, Bruno. 2004. "Why Has Critique Run out of Steam? From Matters of Fact to Matters of Concern." *Critical Inquiry* 30, no. 2: 225–49.

Lenin, Vladimir I. 1987 [1929]. "What Is to Be Done?" In *Essential Works of Lenin: "What Is to Be Done?" and Other Writings*, edited by Henry M. Christian, 53–176. New York: Dover.

Limone, Noa. 2012. "Germany's Most Important Living Philosopher Issues an Urgent Call to Restore Democracy." *Haaretz*, August 16. https://www.haaretz.com/2012-08-16/ty-article/germanys-most-important-philosopher-issues-an-urgent-call-for-democracy/0000017f-e9d0-df5f-a17f-fbdeoee20000.

Liu, Lydia H. 1995. *Translingual Practice: Literature, National Culture, and Translated Modernity—China, 1900–1937*. Stanford, CA: Stanford University Press.

Locke, John. 2003a [1689]. "Two Treatises of Government." In *Two Treatises of Government and A Letter Concerning Toleration*, edited by Ian Shapiro, 1–210. New Haven, CT: Yale University Press.

Locke, John. 2003b [1689]. "A Letter Concerning Toleration." In *Two Treatises of Government and A Letter Concerning Toleration*, edited by Ian Shapiro, 211–56. New Haven, CT: Yale University Press.

Lorde, Audre. 1978. "A Litany for Survival." In *The Collected Poems of Audre Lorde*. New York: W. W. Norton.

Lorde, Audre. 1983. "There Is No Hierarchy of Oppressions." *Bulletin: Homophobia and Education* 14, nos. 3–4: 9.

Lorde, Audre. 2007. *Sister Outsider: Essays and Speeches*. New York: Quality Paperback Book Club.

Lorde, Audre. 2009. "A Burst of Light: Living with Cancer." In *I Am Your Sister. Collected and Unpublished Writings of Audre Lorde*, 81–152. Oxford: Oxford University Press.

Lorde, Audre, and James Baldwin. 2014 [1984]. "Revolutionary Hope: A Conversation Between James Baldwin and Audre Lorde." *The Culture*. Accessed August 1, 2024. http://theculture.forharriet.com/2014/03/revolutionary-hope-conversation-between.html.

Louden, Robert. 2000. *Kant's Impure Ethics*. Oxford: Oxford University Press.

Louverture, Toussaint. 2008 [1797]. "Address to Soldiers for the Universal Destruction of Slavery." In *The Haitian Revolution*, edited by Nick Nesbitt, 28–29. London: Verso.

Love, Nancy S. 1989. "Foucault and Habermas on Discourse and Democracy." *Polity* 22, no. 2: 269–93.

Lu-Adler, Huaping. 2023. *Kant, Race, and Racism: Views from Somewhere*. Oxford: Oxford University Press.

Macaulay, Thomas B. 1952 [1835]. "Indian Education: Minute of the 2nd of February 1835." In *Macaulay: Prose and Poetry*, edited by George M. Young, 719–30. London: Hart-Davis.

Mack, Michael. 2003. *German Idealism and the Jew*. Chicago: University of Chicago Press.

MacKinnon, Catharine. 1989. *Toward a Feminist Theory of the State*. Cambridge, MA: Havard University Press.

Magloire, Marina. 2024. "Moving Towards Life." *Los Angeles Review of Books*, August 7. https://lareviewofbooks.org/article/moving-towards-life/.

Mahbubani, Kishore. 2001. *Can Asians Think? Understanding the Divide Between East and West*. Hannover, NH: Steerforth.

Maldonado-Torres, Nelson. 2004. "The Topology of Being and the Geopolitics of Knowledge: Modernity, Empire, Coloniality." *City* 8, no. 1: 29–56.

Malik, Kenan. 2021. "Where Were the Protesters When the Rohingya Were Being Murdered?" *The Guardian*, February 21. https://www.theguardian.com/commentisfree/2021/feb/21/where-were-the-protesters-when-the-rohingya-were-being-murdered-myanmar.

Mamdani, Mahmood. 1996. *Citizen and Subject: Contemporary Africa and the Legacy of Late Colonialism*. Princeton, NJ: Princeton University Press.

Mamdani, Mahmood. 2001. *When Victims Become Killers: Colonialism, Nativism, and the Genocide in Rwanda*. Princeton, NJ: Princeton University Press.

Mantena, Karuna. 2012. "On Gandhi's Critique of the State: Sources, Contexts, Conjunctures." *Modern Intellectual History* 9: 535–63.

Marasco, Robyn. 2006. "'Already the Effect of the Whip': Critical Theory and the Feminine Ideal." In *Differences* 17, no. 1: 88–115.

Marasco, Robyn. 2015. *The Highway of Despair: Critical Theory After Hegel*. New York: Columbia University Press.

Marwecki, Daniel. 2020. *Germany and Israel: Whitewashing and Statebuilding*. London: Hurst.

Marwecki, Daniel. 2024. "Es ist ein Ersatznationalismus." Interview by Kersten Augustin and Daniel Bax. *Die Tageszeitung*, May 25. https://taz.de/Deutschland-Israel-und-der-Gaza-Krieg/!6010016.

Marx, Karl. 1975 [1842]. "The Philosophical Manifesto of the Historical School of Law." In *Marx/Engels, Collected Works* 1, 203–10. Moscow: Progress Publishers.

Marx, Karl. 1978a [1843]. "For a Ruthless Criticism of Everything Existing." In *The Marx-Engels Reader*, edited by Robert C. Tucker, 12–15. New York: W. W. Norton.

Marx, Karl. 1978b [1848]. "The Communist Manifesto." In *The Marx-Engels Reader*, edited by Robert C. Tucker, 469–500. New York: W. W. Norton.

Marx, Karl. 1978c [1853]. "The British Rule in India." In *The Marx-Engels Reader*, edited by Robert C. Tucker, 653–64. New York: W. W. Norton.

Marx, Karl. 1983 [1852]. "Marx to Joseph Weydemeyer. 5 March." In *Marx Engels Collected Works* 39, 58–59. London: Lawrence and Wishart.

Marx, Karl. 1990 [1867]. *Capital, Volume 1*. London: Penguin Classics.

Marx, Karl. 1992a [1843]. "Letters from the Franco-German Yearbooks." In *Early Writings*, translated by Rodney Livingstone and Gregor Benton, 199–209. London: Penguin Books.

Marx, Karl. 1992b [1843–44]. "A Contribution to the Critique of Hegel's Philosophy of Right. Introduction." In *Early Writings*, translated by Rodney Livingstone and Gregor Benton, 243–58. London: Penguin Books.

Marx, Karl. 1993 [1857–58]. *Grundrisse: Foundations of the Critique of Political Economy*. London: Penguin Books.

Marx, Karl, and Friedrich Engels. 1956 [1844–45]. *The Holy Family, or Critique of Critical Criticism*. Moscow: Foreign Languages.

Marx, Karl, and Friedrich Engels. 1998 [1845]. *The German Ideology*. Amherst, NY: Prometheus.

Massad, Joseph A. 2007. *Desiring Arabs*. Chicago: University of Chicago Press.

May Schott, Robin. 1996. "The Gender of Enlightenment." In *What Is Enlightenment? Eighteenth-Century Answers and Twentieth-Century Questions*, edited by James Schmidt, 471–87. Berkeley: University of California Press.

Mbeki, Thabo, and Mahmood Mamdani. 2014. "Courts Can't End Civil Wars." *New York Times*, February 5. http://www.nytimes.com/2014/02/06/opinion /courts-cant-end-civil-wars.html?_r=0.

Mbembe, Achille. 2008. "What Is Postcolonial Thinking? An Interview with Achille Mbembe." *Eurozine*, January 9. https://www.eurozine.com/what-is -postcolonial-thinking.

Mbembe, Achille. 2015. "The State of South African Political Life." *Africa Is a Country*, September 19. https://africasacountry.com/2015/09/achille -mbembe-on-the-state-of-south-african-politics.

Mbembe, Achille. 2017. *Critique of Black Reason*. Durham, NC: Duke University Press.

Mbembe, Achille. 2019a. *Necropolitics*. Durham, NC: Duke University Press.

Mbembe, Achille. 2019b. "Thoughts on the Planetary: An Interview with Achille Mbembe." Interview by Sindre Bangstad and Torbjørn T. Nilsen. *New Frame*, September 5. https://www.newframe.com/thoughts-on-the -planetary-an-interview-with-achille-mbembe.

Mbembe, Achille. 2021. *Out of the Dark Night: Essays on Decolonization*. New York: Columbia University Press.

McCabe, David. 2019. "Kant Was a Racist: Now What?" *APA Newsletter on Teaching Philosophy* 18: 2–9.

McCarthy, Thomas. 2009. *Race, Empire and the Idea of Human Development*. Cambridge: Cambridge University Press.

Medovoi, Leerom, Shankar Raman, and Benjamin Robinson. 1990. "Can the Subaltern Vote? Representation in the Nicaraguan Elections." *Socialist Review* 20, no. 3: 133–50.

Mehta, Uday S. 1999. *Liberalism and Empire: A Study in Nineteenth-Century British Liberal Thought.* Chicago: University of Chicago Press.

Memmi, Albert. 1992. *The Pillar of Salt.* Translated by Edouard Roditi. Boston: Beacon.

Mercer, Kobena. 1996. "Decolonisation and Disappointment: Reading Fanon's Sexual Politics." In *The Fact of Blackness: Frantz Fanon and Visual Representation,* edited by Alan Read, 114–31. London: Institute of Contemporary Arts and Institute of International Visual Arts.

Middle East Eye. 2024. "Jonathan Glazer Calls Out Israel's Weaponisation of the Holocaust." Video, March 11. https://www.youtube.com/watch?v=3ymiyNmr1WY.

Mignolo, Walter D. 1993. "Colonial and Postcolonial Discourse: Cultural Critique or Academic Colonialism?" *Latin American Research Review* 28: 120–34.

Mignolo, Walter D. 1995. *The Darker Side of the Renaissance: Literacy, Territoriality and Colonization.* Ann Arbor: University of Michigan Press.

Mignolo, Walter D. 2002. "The Geopolitics of Knowledge and the Colonial Difference." *South Atlantic Quarterly* 101, no. 1: 57–96.

Mignolo, Walter D. 2005. "On Subalterns and Other Agencies." *Postcolonial Studies* 8, no. 4: 381–407.

Mignolo, Walter D. 2007. "Coloniality of Power and De-colonial Thinking." *Cultural Studies* 21, no. 2: 155–67.

Mignolo, Walter D. 2009. "Epistemic Disobedience, Independent Thought and De-colonial Freedom." *Theory, Culture and Society* 26, nos. 7–8: 1–23.

Mignolo, Walter D. 2011. "Epistemic Disobedience and the Decolonial Option: A Manifesto." *Transmodernity: Journal of Peripheral Cultural Production of the Luso-Hispanic World* 1, no. 2: 44–66.

Mignolo, Walter D. 2013. "Geopolitics of Sensing and Knowing: On (De)coloniality, Border Thinking, and Epistemic Disobedience." *Confero* 1, no. 1: 129–50.

Mignolo, Walter D. 2014. "Decolonial Options and Artistic/AestheSic Entanglements: An Interview with Walter Mignolo." Interview by Rubén Gaztambide-Fernández. *Decolonization: Indigeneity, Education and Society* 3, no. 1: 196–212.

Mignolo, Walter, and Rolando Vazquez. 2013. "The Decolonial AestheSis Dossier." *Social Text Online,* July 15. https://socialtextjournal.org/periscope_article/the-decolonial-aesthesis-dossier/.

Mikkola, Mari. 2011. "Kant on Moral Agency and Women's Nature." *Kantian Review* 16: 89–111.

Mill, John S. 1977 [1835]. "M. de Toqueville on Democracy in America." In *The Collected Works of John Stuart Mill, Volume 18: Essays on Politics and Society* 1, edited by John M. Robson, 47–90. Toronto: University of Toronto Press.

Mill, John S. 1989 [1859]. *On Liberty and Other Writings*. Edited by Stefan Collini. Cambridge: Cambridge University Press.

Mills, Charles. 1997. *The Racial Contract*. Ithaca, NY: Cornell University Press.

Mills, Charles. 2017a. "Kant's *Untermenschen*." In *Black Rights/White Wrongs: The Critique of Racial Liberalism*, 91–112. Oxford: Oxford University Press.

Mills, Charles. 2017b. "Criticizing Critical Theory." In *Critical Theory in Critical Times: Transforming the Global Political and Economic Order*, edited by Penelope Deutscher and Cristina Lafont, 233–50. New York: Columbia University Press.

Mills, Charles. 2018. "Black Radical Kantianism." *Res Philosophica* 95, no. 1: 1–33.

Milmo, Dan. 2021. "Rohingya Sue Facebook for £150 [Billio]n over Myanmar Genocide." *The Guardian*, December 6. https://www.theguardian.com /technology/2021/dec/06/rohingya-sue-facebook-myanmar-genocide-us-uk -legal-action-social-media-violence.

Minnerup, Günter. 2003. "Introduction." *Debatte: Journal of Contemporary Central and Eastern Europe* 11, no. 2: 103–6.

Montefiore, Simon S. 2023. "The Decolonization Narrative Is Dangerous and False." *The Atlantic*, October 27. https://www.theatlantic.com/ideas/archive /2023/10/decolonization-narrative-dangerous-and-false/675799.

Moraña, Mabel, Enrique Dussel, and Carlos A. Jáuregui, eds. 2008. "Colonialism and Its Replicants." In *Coloniality at Large: Latin America and the Postcolonial Debate*, edited by Mabel Moraña, Enrique Dussel, and Carlos A. Jáuregui, 1–20. Durham, NC: Duke University Press.

Morris, Martin. 1996. "On the Logic of the Performative Contradiction: Habermas and the Radical Critique of Reason." *Review of Politics* 58, no. 4: 735–60.

Morrow, Raymond A. 2013. "Defending Habermas Against Eurocentrism: Latin America and Mignolo's Decolonial Challenge." In *Deprovincializing Habermas: Global Perspectives*, edited by Tom Bailey, 117–36. London: Routledge.

Morton, Stephen. 2003. *Gayatri Chakravorty Spivak*. London: Routledge.

Morton, Stephen. 2007. *Gayatri Spivak: Ethics, Subalternity and the Critique of Postcolonial Reason*. Cambridge: Polity.

Moses, A. Dirk 2021. "The German Catechism." *Geschichte der Gegenwart*, May 23. https://geschichtedergegenwart.ch/the-german-catechism.

Moses, A. Dirk 2022. "The Documenta, Indonesia, and the Problem of Closed Universes." *The New Fascism Syllabus* (blog), July 24. https://newfascismsyllabus .com/opinions/documenta/the-documenta-indonesia-and-the-problem-of -closed-universes.

Mufti, Aamir. 2007. *Enlightenment in the Colony: The Jewish Question and the Crisis of Postcolonial Culture*. Princeton, NJ: Princeton University Press.

Mukherjee, Dalia. 2015. "Tagore's Dakghar in Warsaw Ghetto." *Telegraph Online*, April 10. https://www.telegraphindia.com/west-bengal/tagore-39-s-dakghar -in-warsaw-ghetto/cid/1323716.

Muñoz, José E. 2009. *Cruising Utopia: The Then and There of Queer Futurity*. New York: New York University Press.

Murithi, Tim. 2024. "South Africa's ICJ Case Against Israel: A Judicial Stress Test for the Multilateral System." *Heinrich-Böll-Stiftung*, January 10. https://www.boell.de/en/2024/01/10/south-africas-icj-case-against-israel-judicial-stress-test-multilateral-system.

Muthu, Sankar. 2003. *Enlightenment Against Empire*. Princeton, NJ: Princeton University Press.

Muthu, Sankar. 2012. *Empire and Modern Political Thought*. Cambridge: Cambridge University Press.

Mutua, Makau. 2000. "What Is TWAIL?" *American Society of International Law Proceedings* 94: 31–40.

Mutua, Makau. 2002. *Human Rights. A Political and Cultural Critique*. Philadelphia: University of Pennsylvania Press.

Naas, Michael. 2008. *Derrida from Now On*. New York: Fordham University Press.

Nancy, Jean-Luc. 2014. "What Is to Be Done?" *Diacritics* 42, no. 2: 100–19.

Natali, Marcos. 2012. "Postcolonial Writing in Latin America, 1850–2000." In *Cambridge History of Postcolonial Literature*, edited by Ato Quayson, 309–28. Cambridge: Cambridge University Press.

Neiman, Susan. 2019. *Learning from the Germans: Race and the Memory of Evil*. New York: Farrar, Straus and Giroux.

Neiman, Susan. 2021. "Why Postcolonial Anti-Enlightenment Discourse Is not a Leftwing Position: Susan Neiman in Conversation with Oana Camelia Serban." *Institut Français*. Video, December 14. https://www.youtube.com/watch?v=gyDNKpoUYn4.

Neiman, Susan. 2023. "Historical Reckoning Gone Haywire." *New York Review*, October 19. https://www.nybooks.com/articles/2023/10/19/historical-reckoning-gone-haywire-germany-susan-neiman.

Nesbitt, Nick. 2008. *Universal Emancipation: The Haitian Revolution and the Radical Enlightenment*. Charlottesville: University of Virginia Press.

Neurath, Otto. 1983 [1935]. "Pseudorationalism of Falsification." In *Philosophical Papers 1913–1946*, edited and translated by Robert S. Cohen and Marie Neurath, 121–31. Dordrecht: Springer.

New Arab. 2024. "Palestinian and Israeli Winners at Berlinale Urge Germany to 'Stop Sending Weapons to Israel.'" Video, February 26. https://www.youtube.com/watch?v=nZBbOBPLSvA.

Newman, Saul. 2004. "Terror, Sovereignty and Law: On the Politics of Violence." *German Law Journal* 5, no. 5: 569–84. https://doi.org/10.1017/S2071832200012694.

Newton, Isaac. 1999 [1687]. *The Principia, Mathematical Principles of Natural Philosophy*. Translated by I. Bernard Cohen and Anne Whitman. Berkeley: University of California Press.

Nichols, Michelle. 2024. "US Blocks Ceasefire Call with Third UN Veto in Israel-Hamas War." Reuters, February 20. https://www.reuters.com/world /us-casts-third-veto-un-action-since-start-israel-hamas-war-2024-02-20.

Nicholson, Peter. 1976. "Kant on the Duty Never to Resist the Souvereign." *Ethics* 86: 214–30.

Niesen, Peter. 2007. "Colonialism and Hospitality." *Journal of International Political Theory* 3, no. 1: 90–108.

Nietzsche, Friedrich. 1968 [1901]. *The Will to Power.* New York: Vintage.

Nietzsche, Friedrich. 1998 [1889]. *Twilight of the Idols or How to Philosophize with a Hammer.* New York: Oxford University Press.

Nietzsche, Friedrich. 2006 [1883–85]. *Thus Spoke Zarathustra: A Book for All and None.* New York: Cambridge University Press.

Nietzsche, Friedrich. 2019. *Unpublished Fragments (Spring 1885–Spring 1886).* Stanford, CA: Stanford University Press.

Niranjana, Tejaswini. 1992. *Siting Translation: History, Post-structuralism, and the Colonial Context.* Berkeley: University of California Press.

Nussbaum, Martha. 2015. *Political Emotions: Why Love Matters for Justice.* Cambridge, MA: Harvard University Press.

Okiji, Fumi. 2018. *Jazz as Critique: Adorno and Black Expression Revisited.* Stanford, CA: Stanford University Press.

Oltermann, Philip. 2020. "Uğur Şahin and Özlem Türeci: German 'Dream Team' Behind Vaccine." *The Guardian,* November 10. https://www .theguardian.com/world/2020/nov/10/ugur-sahin-and-ozlem-tureci -german-dream-team-behind-vaccine.

Olusoga, David, and Casper Erichsen. 2010. *The Kaiser's Holocaust: Germany's Forgotten Genocide and the Colonial Roots of Nazism.* London: Faber and Faber.

Omvedt, Gail. 2005. *Ambedkar: Towards an Enlightened India.* New Delhi: Penguin.

Outram, Dorinda. 2019. *The Enlightenment.* Cambridge: Cambridge University Press.

Pagden, Anthony. 2014. "The Law of Continuity: Conquest and Settlement Within the Limits of Kant's International Right." In *Kant and Colonialism: Historical and Critical Perspectives,* edited by Katrin Flikschuh and Lea Ypi, 19–42. Oxford: Oxford University Press.

Pahuja, Sundhya. 2011. *Decolonising International Law: Development, Economic Growth and the Politics of Universality.* Cambridge: Cambridge University Press.

Panel of Experts in International Law. 2024. "Report of the Panel of Experts in International Law." May 20. https://www.icc-cpi.int/sites/default/files/2024 -05/240520-panel-report-eng.pdf.

Parents Circle–Families Forum (PCFF). 2024. "About PCFF." Accessed August 1, 2024. https://www.theparentscircle.org/en/about_eng-2.

Parker, Pat. 2000. "For the White Person Who Wants to Know How to Be My Friend." *Callaloo* 23, no. 1: 73.

PEN America. 2024. "PEN America Release on War in Israel and Gaza." PEN America, February 7, 2024. https://pen.org/press-release/pen-america-release-on-israel-hamas-war/.

Persson, Asha. 2004. "Incorporating Pharmakon: HIV, Medicine, and Body Shape Change." *Body and Society* 10, no. 4: 45–67.

Phillips, Adam. 2015a. "Against Self-Criticism." *London Review of Books* 37, no. 5 (March 5). https://www.lrb.co.uk/the-paper/v37/n05/adam-phillips/against-self-criticism.

Phillips, Adam. 2015b. "On Losing and Being Lost Again." Architectural Association School of Architecture, video, July 15. https://www.youtube.com/watch?v=rt70m-p2AkY.

Pitts, Jennifer. 2005. *A Turn to Empire: The Rise of Imperial Liberalism in Britain and France*. Princeton, NJ: Princeton University Press.

Plato. 2008. *Crito*. In *Defence of Socrates; Euthyphro; Crito*, edited by David Gallop. Oxford, New York: Oxford University Press.

Plato. 2012. *Republic*. New York: Penguin Books.

Pollock, Sheldon. 1993. "Deep Orientalism? Notes on Sanskrit and Power Beyond the Raj." In *Orientalism and the Postcolonial Predicament: Perspectives on South Asia*, edited by Carol A. Breckenridge and Peter van der Veer, 76–133. Philadelphia: University of Pennsylvania Press.

Poovey, Mary. 2010. "Financing Enlightenment, Part One: Money Matters." In *This Is Enlightenment*, edited by Clifford Siskin and William Warner, 323–35. Chicago: University of Chicago Press.

Popkin, Jeremy D. 2017. "Colonial Enlightenment and the French Revolution: Julien Raymond and Milscent Créole." In *Enlightened Colonialism*, edited by Damien Tricoire, 269–86. New York: Springer.

Prakash, Gyan. 1992. "Can the 'Subaltern' Ride? A Reply to O'Hanlon and Washbrook." *Comparative Studies in Society and History* 34, no. 1: 168–84.

Pratinav, Anil. 2023. "Gandhi Hasn't Aged Well: Anti-imperialists Need to Be Honest About Their Idols." *UnHerd*, January 31. https://unherd.com/2023/01/gandhi-hasnt-aged-well.

Pritchard, Elizabeth A. 2002. "Bilderverbot Meets Body in Theodor W. Adorno's Inverse Theology." *Harvard Theological Review* 95, no. 3: 291–318.

Psaledakis, Daphne, and David Brunnerstrom. 2024. "Russia, China Veto US-Led UN Resolution on Gaza Ceasefire." Reuters, March 23. https://www.reuters.com/world/middle-east/un-security-council-fails-pass-us-resolution-calling-immediate-ceasefire-gaza-2024-03-22.

Puar, Jasbir K. 2007. *Terrorist Assemblages: Homonationalism in Queer Times*. Durham, NC: Duke University Press.

Quijano, Aníbal. 2000. "Coloniality of Power, Eurocentrism, and Latin America." *Nepantla: Views from South* 1, no. 3: 533–80.

Quijano, Aníbal. 2007. "Coloniality and Modernity/Rationality." *Cultural Studies* 21, nos. 2–3: 168–78.

Ramgotra, Manjeet, and Simon Choat. 2023. *Rethinking Political Thinkers*. Oxford: Oxford University Press.

Randeria, Shalini. 2003. "Cunning States and Unaccountable International Institutions: Legal Plurality, Social Movements and Rights of Local Communities to Common Property Resources." *European Journal of Sociology* 44, no. 1: 27–60.

Rao, Rahul. 2020. *Out of Time: The Queer Politics of Postcoloniality*. Oxford: Oxford University Press.

Reclaimfeminism. 2016. "Unser Feminismus ist antirassistisch—Reclaim Feminism." Interventionistische Linke Koln, March. https://il-koeln.org/12-3 -demo-unser-feminismus-ist-antirassistisch-reclaim-feminism/.

Reemtsma, Jan P. 2024. "Sagt, hab ich recht?" *Frankfurter Allgemeine Zeitung*, June 24. https://www.faz.net/aktuell/feuilleton/thema/immanuel-kant.

Reiss, Hans. 1956. "Kant and the Right of Rebellion." *Journal of the History of Ideas* XVII: 179–92.

Revolution. 2024. "Malcolm X and by Any Means Necessary: Letter from a Reader." February 19. https://revcom.us/en/malcolm-x-and-any-means -necessary.

Richter, Gerhard. 2010. "Appendix: Who's Afraid of the Ivory Tower? A Conversation with Theodor W. Adorno." In *Language Without Soil*, edited by Gerhard Richter, 227–38. New York: Fordham University Press.

Robbins, Bruce. 2014. "Response to Vivek Chibber." *n+1*, January 9. https://www .nplusonemag.com/online-only/online-only/response-to-vivek-chibber.

Robinson, Cedric J. 1983. *Black Marxism: The Making of the Black Radical Tradition*. London: Zed.

Robinson, Joan. 1964. *Economic Philosophy*. Harmondsworth: Penguin.

Rocco, Christopher. 1994. "Between Modernity and Postmodernity: Reading *Dialectic of Enlightenment* Against the Grain." *Political Theory* 22, no. 1: 71–97.

Rocha, Leon. A. 2012. "'That Dazzling, Momentary Wake' of the Lettre de Cachet: The Problem of Experience in Foucault's Practice of History." In *Foucault, the Family and Politics*, edited by Robbie Duschinsky and Leon A. Rocha, 189–219. London: Palgrave Macmillan.

Ronell, Avital. 1994. *Finitude Score: Essays for the End of the Millennium*. Lincoln: University of Nebraska Press.

Rose, Gillian. 1976. "How is Critical Theory Possible? Theodor W. Adorno and Concept Formation in Sociology." *Political Studies* 24, no. 1: 69–85.

Rose, Jaqueline. 1998. "Negativity in the Work of Melanie Klein." In *Reading Melanie Klein*, edited by Lyndsey Stonebridge and John Philipps, 126–59. New York: Routledge.

Rose, Paul. 1992. *Revolutionary Antisemitism in Germany from Kant to Wagner*. Princeton, NJ: Princeton University Press.

Rose, Sven-Erik. 2014. *Jewish Philosophical Politics in Germany, 1789-1848*. Waltham, MA: Brandeis University Press.

Rosen, Steven J. 2019. "Bundestag's BDS Resolution." *European Leadership Network*, June 11. https://elnetwork.eu/country/germany/bundestags-bds -resolution.

Ross, Alison. 2004. "Historical Undecidability: The Kantian Background to Derrida's Politics." *International Journal of Philosophical Studies* 12, no. 4: 375–93.

Rothberg, Michael. 2009. *Multidirectional Memory: Remembering the Holocaust in the Age of Decolonization*. Stanford, CA: Stanford University Press.

Rothberg, Michael. 2020. "Debatte um Achille Mbembe. Das Gespenst des Vergleichs." *Zeitgeister*, May. https://www.goethe.de/prj/zei/de/art/21864662 .html.

Rothberg, Michael. 2022. "Michael Rothberg zur Documenta: 'Antisemitismus als Bumerangeffekt.'" *Berliner Zeitung*, July 5. https://www.berliner-zeitung .de/kultur-vergnuegen/antisemitismus-als-bumerang-was-die-documenta -debatte-verschleiert-li.243351.

Rousseau, Jean-Jacques. 2012 [1762]. *Of The Social Contract and Other Political Writings*. London: Penguin Classics.

Roy, Arundhati. 2017. *The Doctor and the Saint: Caste, Race, and Annihilation of Caste, the Debate Between B. R. Ambedkar and M. K. Gandhi*. Chicago: Haymarket.

Rucker, Philip, and Robert Costa. 2017. "Bannon Vows a Daily Fight for 'Deconstruction of the Administrative State.'" *Washington Post*, February 23. https://www.washingtonpost.com/politics/top-wh-strategist-vows-a-daily -fight-for-deconstruction-of-the-administrative-state/2017/02/23/03f6b8da -f9ea-11e6-bf01-d47f8cf9b643_story.html?noredirect=on.

Rufo, Christopher F. 2023. "Conservatives Need to Create a Strong Association Between Hamas, BLM, DSA, and 'Academic' Decolonization in the Public Mind." X, posted October 13, 2023. https://x.com/realchrisrufo/status /1712938775834185891?lang=en.

Rushdie, Salman. 2021. *Midnight's Children*. New York: Penguin.

Said, Edward. 1978. *Orientalism*. London: Pantheon.

Said, Edward. 1992. *The Question of Palestine*. New York: Vintage.

Said, Edward. 1993. *Culture and Imperialism*, London: Chatto and Windus.

Said, Edward. 1994. *Representations of the Intellectual*. New York: Vintage.

Said, Edward. 1996. *Peace and Its Discontents*. New York: Vintage.

Said, Edward. 2001. *The End of the Peace Process: Oslo and After*. New York: Vintage.

Sarna, Jonathan D. 2021. "A Scholar of American Anti-Semitism Explains the Hate Symbols Present During the US Capitol Riot." *The Conversation*, January 9. https://theconversation.com/a-scholar-of-american-anti-semitism -explains-the-hate-symbols-present-during-the-us-capitol-riot-152883.

Scheible, Hartmut. 1989. *Theodor W. Adorno*. Hamburg: Rohwolt.

Schiller, Friedrich. 2016a [1793]. "Letters to Prince Fredrick Christian von Augustenburg." In *On the Aesthetic Education of Man and Letters to Prince Fredrick*

Christian von Augustenburg, translated by Keith Tribe. London: Penguin Classics.

Schiller, Friedrich. 2016b [1795]. "On the Aesthetic Education of Man" In *On the Aesthetic Education of Man and Letters to Prince Fredrick Christian von Augustenburg*, translated by Keith Tribe. London: Penguin Classics.

Schlindwein, Simone. 2024. "Die Zionistische Fundamentalistin." *Die Tageszeitung*, January 31. https://taz.de/Proisraelische-Richterin-am-IGH/!5985718.

Schmidt, James, ed. 1996. *What Is Enlightenment? Eighteenth-Century Answers and Twentieth-Century Questions*. Berkeley: University of California Press.

Schmidt, James. 1998. "Language, Mythology, and Enlightenment: Historical Notes on Horkheimer and Adorno's 'Dialectic of Enlightenment.'" *Social Research* 65, no. 4: 807–38.

Schnädelbach, Herbert. 1995. "Remarks about Rationality and Language." In *The Communicative Ethics Controversy*, edited by Seyla Benhabib and Fred Dallmayr, 270–92. Cambridge, MA: MIT Press.

Schoolman, Morton. 2005. "Avoiding 'Embarrassment': Aesthetic Reason and Aporetic Critique in Dialectic of Enlightenment." *Polity* 37, no. 3: 335–64.

Schönecker, Dieter. 2021. "How White Is Kant's White Race, After All?" *Telos*, February 23. https://www.telospress.com/how-white-is-kants-white-race-after-all.

Scott, David. 1999. *Refashioning Futures: Criticism After Postcoloniality*. Princeton, NJ: Princeton University Press.

Scott, David. 2004. *Conscripts of Modernity: The Tragedy of Colonial Enlightenment*. Durham, NC: Duke University Press.

Scott, David. 2014. "The Theory of Haiti: The Black Jacobins and the Poetics of Universal History." *Small Axe* 18, no. 3: 35–51.

Scott, James C. 2010a. *The Art of Not Being Governed: An Anarchist History of Upland Southeast Asia*. New Haven, CT: Yale University Press.

Scott, James C. 2010b. "James Scott on Agriculture as Politics, the Dangers of Standardization and Not Being Governed." *Theory Talks*. Accessed July 1, 2025. https://www.files.ethz.ch/isn/155099/Theory%20Talk38_Scott.pdf.

Senate Department for Culture and Social Cohesion. 2024. "Weltoffenes Berlin." Accessed August 1, 2024. https://www.berlin.de/sen/kultur/en/funding/funding-programmes/weltoffenes-berlin.

Seneca. 2010. *Anger, Mercy, Revenge*. Translated by Robert Kaster and Martha Nussbaum. Chicago: University of Chicago Press.

Sharma, Jyotirmaya. 2021. *Elusive Nonviolence: The Making and Unmaking of Gandhi's Religion of Ahimsa*. Noida: Westland.

Sharp, Gene. 2013. *How Nonviolent Struggle Works*. Boston: Albert Einstein Institution.

Sharpe, Jenny. 2014. "What Use Is the Imagination?" PMLA 129, no. 3: 512–17.

Sharpe, Jenny, and Gayatri C. Spivak. 2003. "Politics and the Imagination." *Signs* 28, no. 2: 609–24.

Shatz, Adam. 2023. "Vengeful Pathologies: Adam Shatz on the War in Gaza." *London Review of Books* 45, no. 21, November 2. https://www.lrb.co.uk/the -paper/v45/n21/adam-shatz/vengeful-pathologies.

Shatz, Adam. 2024. *The Rebel's Clinic: The Revolutionary Lives of Frantz Fanon*. New York: Farrar, Straus and Giroux.

Shell, Susan M. 2009. *Kant and the Limits of Autonomy*. Cambridge, MA: Harvard University Press.

Shiva, Vandana. 1993. *The Monocultures of the Mind: Perspectives in Biodiversity*. London: Zed.

Shiva, Vandana. 2017. "Women's Economic Empowerment: Let's Act To-gether." Inauguration speech to the European Parliament for International Women's Day, March 8. Accessed August 1, 2024. https://www .europarl.europa.eu/cmsdata/115353/Speech%20Vandana%20Shiva_EN .docx.

Shohat, Ella. 1988. "Sephardim in Israel: Zionism from the Standpoint of Its Jewish Victims." *Social Text* 19–20: 1–35.

Sintiundroma.org. 2024 "'Racial Diagnosis: Gypsy': The Nazi Genocide of the Sinti and Roma and the Long Struggle for Recognition." Accessed August 1, 2024. https://www.sintiundroma.org/en/auschwitz-birkenau-2 /deportation-from-childrens-homes.

Smart, Carol. 1989. *Feminism and the Power of Law*. London: Routledge.

Smith, Justin E. H. 2013. "The Enlightenment's 'Race' Problem, and Ours." *New York Times*, February 10, 2013. https://archive.nytimes.com/opinionator .blogs.nytimes.com/2013/02/10/why-has-race-survived.

Snyder, Timothy. 2015a. *Black Earth: The Holocaust as History and Warning*. London: Bodley Head.

Snyder, Timothy. 2015b. "Understanding Hitler's Anti-Semitism." Interview by Edward Delman. *The Atlantic*, September 9. https://www.theatlantic.com /international/archive/2015/09/hitler-holocaust-antisemitism-timothy -snyder/404260.

Snyder, Timothy 2016. "Beware the Destruction of the State! An Interview with Timothy Snyder." Interview by Luka L. Gabrijelčič. *Eurozine*, September 9. https://www.eurozine.com/beware-the-destruction-of-the-state.

Sontag, Susan. 2004. *Regarding the Pain of Others*. New York: Picador.

Soyinka, Wole. 2007. "Interview: Nobel Laureate Wole Soyinka." *The Guardian*, May 28. https://www.theguardian.com/books/2007/may/28 /hayfestival2007.hayfestival.

Spivak, Gayatri C. 1985. "Three Women's Texts and a Critique of Imperialism." *Critical Inquiry* 12, no. 1: 243–61.

Spivak, Gayatri C. 1989. "A Response to 'The Difference Within: Feminism and Critical Theory.'" In *The Difference Within: Feminism and Critical Theory*, edited by Elizabeth Meese and Alice Parker, 207–20. Amsterdam: John Benjamins.

Spivak, Gayatri C. 1990. *The Post-colonial Critic: Interviews, Strategies, Dialogues*. London: Routledge.

Spivak, Gayatri C. 1991. "Theory in the Margin: Coetzee's Foe Reading Defoe's Crusoe/Roxana." In *Consequences of Theory: Selected Papers from the English Institute, 1987–88* 14, edited by Jonathan Arac and Barbara Johnson, 154–81. Baltimore: Johns Hopkins University Press.

Spivak, Gayatri C. 1993a. *Outside in the Teaching Machine*. New York: Routledge.

Spivak, Gayatri C. 1993b. "Echo." *New Literary History* 24, no. 1: 17–43.

Spivak, Gayatri C. 1994a. "Can the Subaltern Speak?" In *Colonial Discourse and Post-colonial Theory*, edited by Patrick Williams and Laura Chrisman, 66–111. Hemel Hempstead: Harvester Wheatsheaf.

Spivak, Gayatri C. 1994b. "Bonding in Difference." In *An Other Tongue: Nation and Ethnicity in the Linguistic Borderlands*, edited by Alfred Arteaga, 273–85. Durham, NC: Duke University Press.

Spivak, Gayatri C. 1994c. "Translators Preface." In *Imaginary Maps*, by Mahasweta Devi, xxiii–xxx. London: Routledge.

Spivak, Gayatri C. 1999. *A Critique of Postcolonial Reason: Towards a History of the Vanishing Present*. Calcutta: Seagull.

Spivak, Gayatri C. 2003a. "A Conversation with Gayatri Chakravorty Spivak: Politics and the Imagination." In *Signs* 28, no. 2: 609–24.

Spivak, Gayatri C. 2003b. *Death of a Discipline*. New York: Columbia University Press.

Spivak, Gayatri C. 2004. "Righting Wrongs." *South Atlantic Quarterly* 103, nos. 2–3: 523–81.

Spivak, Gayatri C. 2006. *In Other Worlds*. New York: Routledge.

Spivak, Gayatri C. 2007. "Feminism and Human Rights." In *The Present as History: Critical Perspectives on Global Power*, edited by Nermeen Shaikh, 172–201. New York: Columbia University Press.

Spivak, Gayatri C. 2008. *Other Asias*. Malden, MA: Blackwell.

Spivak, Gayatri C. 2009a. "They the People: Problems of Alter–globalization." *Radical Philosophy* 157: 31–36.

Spivak, Gayatri C. 2009b. "Nationalism and the Imagination." *Lectora* 15: 75–98.

Spivak, Gayatri C. 2012a. *An Aesthetic Education in the Era of Globalization*. Cambridge, MA: Harvard University Press.

Spivak, Gayatri C. 2012b. "Occupy Education: An Interview with Gayatri Chakravorty Spivak." Interview by Rahul K. Gairola. *Politics and Culture*. https://politicsandculture.org/2012/09/25/occupy-education-an-interview-with-gayatri-chakravorty-spivak.

Spivak, Gayatri C. 2013. "Many Voices." Inamori Foundation: Kyoto Prize and Inamori Grants, September 30. https://www.kyotoprize.org/wp-content/uploads/2019/07/2012_C.pdf.

Spivak, Gayatri C. 2014. "Postcolonial Theory and the Specter of Capital." *Cambridge Review of International Affairs* 27, no. 1: 184–98.

Spivak, Gayatri C. 2016. "Critical Intimacy: An Interview with Gayatri Chakravorty Spivak." Interview by Steve Paulson. *Los Angeles Review of Books*, July 29. https://lareviewofbooks.org/article/critical-intimacy -interview-gayatri-chakravorty-spivak.

Spivak, Gayatri C. 2018a. "Closing Keynote." Speech delivered at the Berlin Conference on Myanmar Genocide, Jewish Museum of Berlin, video, February 26. https://www.youtube.com/watch?v=jSQKojA_XRk.

Spivak, Gayatri C. 2018b. "A Borderless World?" *Shuddhashar Magazine*, vol. 10, October 3. https://shuddhashar.com/gayatri-chakravorty-spivak-a -borderless-world-3.

Spivak, Gayatri C. 2021. "In Conversation with Bulan Lahiri." *The Hindu*, December 4. https://www.thehindu.com/books/In-Conversation-Speaking-to -Spivak/article15130635.ece.

Steinmetz, George. 2016. "Social Fields and Subfields at the Scale of Empires: Colonial States and Colonial Sociology." *Sociological Review* 64, no. 2: 98–123.

Tahmasebi-Birgani, Victoria. 2014. *Emmanuel Levinas and the Politics of Nonviolence*. Toronto: University of Toronto Press.

Thomson, Alex J. P. 2005. "What's to Become of 'Democracy to Come'?" *Postmodern Culture* 15, no. 3. https://doi.org/10.1353/pmc.2005.0028.

Thoreau, Henry D. 1992 [1849]. "Resistance to Civil Government." In *Walden and Resistance to Civil Government: Authoritative Texts, Thoreau's Journal, Reviews, and Essays in Criticism*. New York: W. W. Norton.

Tiedemann, Rolf. 1994. "Gegen den Trug der Frage nach dem Sinn." In *Eine Dokumentation zu Adornos Beckett-Lektüre, Frankfurter Adorno Blätter*, vol. 3, 18–77. Munich: Text + Kritik.

Transnational Decolonial Institute. 2024. "Decolonial Aesthetics (I)." Accessed August 1, 2024. https://transnationaldecolonialinstitute.wordpress.com /decolonial-aesthetics.

Traverso, Enzo. 2016. *Left-Wing Melancholia: Marxism, History, and Memory*. New York: Columbia University Press.

Traverso, Enzo. 2022. "No, Post-Nazi Germany Isn't a Model of Atoning for the Past." *Jacobin*, June 6. https://jacobin.com/2022/06/post-nazi-germany -colonialism-holocaust-israel-atonement.

Traverso, Enzo. 2024. "The Gaza Massacre Is Undermining the Culture of Democracy." *Jacobin*, June 4. https://jacobin.com/2024/04/gaza-genocide -holocaust-memory-democracy.

Trouillot, Michel-Rolph. 1995. *Silencing the Past: Power and the Production of History*. Boston: Beacon.

TRT World. 2024. "Twelve US Republican Senators Threaten ICC with Sanctions if They Target Israeli Officials." Video, May 9. https://www.youtube .com/watch?v=Aq2aDR6MqoQ.

Trump, Donald. 2016. "Trump in Nevada: 'I Love the Poorly Educated.'" Associated Press, February 24, 2024. https://www.youtube.com/watch?v =Vpdt7omPoao.

Tuck, Eve, and K. Wayne Yang. 2012. "Decolonization Is Not a Metaphor." *Decolonization: Indigeneity, Education and Society* 1, no. 1: 1–40. http://resolver .scholarsportal.info/resolve/19298692/v01i0001/nfp_dinam.xml.

Tullock, Gordon. 2001. "A Comment on Daniel Klein's 'A Plea to Economists Who Favor Liberty.'" *Eastern Economic Journal* 27, no. 2: 203–7.

Valdez, Inés. 2017. "It's Not About Race: Good Wars, Bad Wars, and the Origins of Kant's Anti-colonialism." *American Political Science Review* 111, no. 4: 819–32.

Valdez, Inés. 2019. *Transnational Cosmopolitanism: Kant, Du Bois, and Justice as a Political Craft*. Cambridge: Cambridge University Press.

van der Heyden, Ulrich. 2001. *Rote Adler an Afrikas Küste. Die brandenburgisch-preussische Kolonie Grossfriedrichsburg in Westafrika*. Berlin: Selignow.

van der Veer, Peter. 1994. *Religious Nationalism: Hindus and Muslims in India*. Berkeley: University of California Press.

van der Veer, Peter. 2001. *Imperial Encounters: Religion and Modernity in India and Britain*. Princeton, NJ: Princeton University Press.

Varadharajan, Asha. 1995. *Exotic Parodies: Subjectivity in Adorno, Said, and Spivak*. Minneapolis: University of Minnesota Press.

Vázquez–Arroyo, Antonio y. 2008. "Universal History Disavowed: On Critical Theory and Postcolonialism." *Postcolonial Studies* 11, no. 4: 451–73.

Viswanathan, Gauri. 1989. *Masks of Conquest: Literary Study and British Rule in India*. New York: Columbia University Press.

von Mallinckrodt, Rebekka. 2016. "There Are No Slaves in Prussia?" In *Slavery Hinterland: Transatlantic Slavery and Continental Europe, 1680–1850*, edited by Felix Brahm and Eve Rosenhaft, 109–32. Woodbridge: Boydell and Brewer.

Weber, Max. 2004 [1919]. *The Vocation Lectures*. Indianapolis: Hackett.

Weizman, Eyal. 2022. "In Kassel." *London Review of Books* 44, no. 15 (August 4). https://www.lrb.co.uk/the-paper/v44/n15/eyal-weizman/in-kassel.

Wiener Holocaust Library. 2024. "Case Study: Warsaw Ghetto." Accessed August 1, 2024. https://www.theholocaustexplained.org/the-camps/the -warsaw-ghetto-a-case-study.

Wikipedia. 2024a. "Strange Fruit." Accessed August 1, 2024. https://en.wikipedia .org/wiki/Strange_Fruit.

Wikipedia. 2024b. "SlutWalk." Accessed August 1, 2024. https://en.wikipedia .org/wiki/SlutWalk.

Wikipedia. 2024c. "American Service-Members' Protection Act." Accessed August 1, 2024. https://en.wikipedia.org/wiki/American_Service -Members%27_Protection_Act.

Williams, Howard. 1983. *Kant's Political Philosophy*. New York: St. Martin's.

Wintour, Patrick. 2024. "ICJ's Gaza Decision Shores Up Rules-Based Order and Puts West to Test." *The Guardian*, January 26. https://www.theguardian

.com/law/2024/jan/26/icj-gaza-decision-shores-up-rules-based-order-and
-puts-west-to-test.

Wolff, Michael. 2020. "Kant war ein Anti-Rassist." *Frankfurter Allgemeine Zeitung*,
July 9.

Wood, Allen. 2008. *Kantian Ethics*. New York: Cambridge University Press.

X, Malcolm. 1965. "Interview with Malcom X." *Young Socialist* 8, no. 3: 3–5.
Marxists Internet Archive. Accessed August 1, 2024. https://www.marxists
.org/history/etol/newspape/youngsocialist/1964-1965/v08n03-w63-%5B2nd
-w63%5D-mar-apr-1965-young-socialist-ysa.pdf.

Yeung, Jessie, and Esha Mitra. 2021. "The World's Biggest Vaccine Producer Is
Running Out of COVID-19 Vaccines, as Second Wave Accelerates." *CNN
World*, April 18. https://edition.cnn.com/2021/04/17/india/covid-vaccine
-shortage-covishield-covaxin-intl-hnk-dst/index.html.

Youkee, Mat. 2023. "Indigenous Knowledge, Bravery, Vigilance: How Young
Siblings Survived in Colombia's Perilous Jungle." *The Guardian*, June 12.
https://www.theguardian.com/world/2023/jun/12/colombia-plane-crash
-how-four-siblings-survived-jungle.

Ypi, Lea. 2014. "Commerce and Colonialism in Kant's Philosophy of History."
In *Kant and Colonialism: Historical and Critical Perspectives*, edited by Katrin
Flikschuh and Lea Ypi, 99–126. Oxford: Oxford University Press.

Zantop, Susanne. 1997. *Colonial Fantasies: Conquest, Family and Nation in Precolonial Germany, 1770–1870*. Durham, NC: Duke University Press.

Zeuske, Michael. 2020. "Auch der Philosoph Immanuel Kant Steht zur Debatte." *Deutschlandfunk Kultur*, June 13. https://www.deutschlandfunkkultur
.de/antirassistischer-denkmalsturm-auch-der-philosoph-immanuel-100
.html.

Index

Brecht, Bertolt, 256, 275–76; *Lehrstücke* (learning-play), 276
BRICS (Brazil, Russia, India, China, South Africa, et al.), 113
Brock, Bazon, 2
Brumlik, Micha, 31, 313n2
Buck-Morss, Susan, 160
Burke, Edmund, 30–31, 158
Butler, Judith, 1, 2, 14, 17, 163–68, 170, 172, 176, 182, 199, 207–9, 213, 217, 244, 247; on nonviolence, 208–9; on normative violence, 236

"Can the Subaltern Speak?" (Spivak), 109–11
"Can the Subaltern Vote?" (Medovoi, Raman, and Robinson), 280
capitalism, 23, 28, 34, 52, 54–55, 60, 263, 275, 278–79, 283–85, 298; and colonialism, 23, 28, 34, 52, 54–55, 60, 129; electronic, 274; global, 279; varieties of, 124, 133
Carter, J. Kameron, 47, 49
Cascardi, Anthony, 14, 22, 24
caste system, 213, 217, 222–26. *See also* Ambedkar, B. R.; Gandhi, Mohandas K.
Castro Varela, Maria do Mar, 307
categorical imperative (Kant), 36; racialized critique of, 36
catharsis, 267. *See also katharsis*
Caygill, Howard, 150–51, 210, 212, 214
Césaire, Aimé, 49, 67, 85, 95, 128
Chakrabarty, Dipesh, 12–13, 87, 103; *Provincializing Europe*, 12, 116, 126, 130, 134
Chatterjee, Partha, 30, 60, 132
Chernyshevsky, Nikolay: *What Is to Be Done?*, 293
Chibber, Vivek, 128, 131–33
Chimni, Bhupinder S., 250
Chow, Rey, 111
Christianity, 37, 39, 95, 123, 317n4
citizenship, 288, 298
civil disobedience, 144, 146–50, 214, 223
civil society, 163, 168; as arena of hegemony, 164, 183, 185, 198; as extension of the state, 183, 199; as safety valve, 186; as site of nonviolent practice, 168
civilizing mission, 26, 29, 36
class consciousness, 150–51, 171
Clausewitz, Carl von, 212
clicktivism, 163
coalitions, 297, 306–7; across difference, 306–7
Coetzee, J. M.: *Foe*, 176–77
cogito ergo sum, 79, 121
Cohn-Bendit, Daniel, 153
collectivity, 296, 299, 307
Collins, Patricia Hill, 232
colonial difference, 125; rule of, 60
colonialism, 22–64, 85–86, 89–90, 93–94, 98, 104–5, 108, 207, 209, 210, 214, 217, 262, 264, 267, 274; and capitalism, 23, 28, 34, 52, 54–55, 60, 129; epistemic violence of, 264; internal, 186; and international law, 237, 250–51; legacies of, 288–90, 300; as "necessary evil," 26, 60; and Nazism/Holocaust, 67–70, 83, 233; as victim blaming, 237; violence of, 26, 28, 52–53, 208, 211, 234, 238, 244, 245, 290, 292, 299. *See also* imperialism; postcolonialism
colonial matrix of power (*patrón de poder colonial*), 120, 264. *See also* coloniality of power, 120, 123
colonization of the mind, 120, 135
compassion fatigue, 262
concentration camps, colonial precedents, 67
constitutionalism, 223–25, 236, 244, 255
Cook, Deborah, 73, 80, 86, 100, 106, 152, 154, 191, 193, 294
Cornell, Drucilla, 241
Coronil, Fernando, 125–26
cosmopolitanism, 118; Kantian, 33–34, 49, 51–57, 59
counterpublics, subaltern, 163, 178
counterviolence, 211, 218
COVID-19 pandemic, 247–48
Crenshaw, Kimberlé, 232
Creoles, 120

economic inequality, 288, 290
Edelman, Lee, 292
education, 297; colonial, 274; as slow cooking of the soul, 281. *See also* aesthetic education
ego conquistus, 121
Einstein, Albert, 206, 258
elites, postcolonial, 300
emancipation, 290, 294, 296, 1052
Engels, Friedrich, 193, 208, 227
Enlightenment, the, 8-18, 145-47, 155-57, 159-60, 202, 207, 213, 225, 232, 246, 262-64, 266, 268-70, 308-9; ab-use of, 299; ambivalent legacy of, 22-64, 69-112, 291, 299-300, 302; anticolonial impulses in, 26, 30-31, 33, 41-42, 48-49, 61; barbarous, 72, 74; coercive and enabling aspects, 291, 299, 302; and colonialism, 69-70, 93-94, 98, 237, 244; critique of, 70-112, 235, 238, 244, 290, 299-300, 302, 305; decolonizing, 9-16, 22-23, 41, 59, 62-64; defending, 32-35, 41-42, 45-47, 61, 70, 97-98, 101; double-bind with postcolonialism, 15; emancipatory norms, 9, 12-14; and empire, 22-64; and fascism, 71, 74-75, 83; financing of, 22, 52; and gender/sexism, 31-32, 35, 42-45, 48; ideals of, 290, 302, 305; legacies of, 288, 290-91, 299-300, 302, 308; nonperformativity of, 12, 14; post-colonial engagement with, 8-9, 11-14, 213, 233-34, 250, 257, 258; and race/racism, 24-25, 32, 42-50, 61, 91-101; and religious tolerance, 35-40; rescue of, 9, 12, 71, 80-81, 101-12; selective legacy of, 300; self-critique (European), 13-14; stadial view of history, 26, 29; using from below, 279; weaponization of, 299
enunciation, 120, 125, 127
epistemic: agency, 305, 306; change, 138-39; delinking, 114, 119; disobedience, 262; extractivism, 306; justice, 305; performance, 273, 283; servitude, 127; violence, 116, 264, 305

erotics of resistance, 163, 170
EU (European Union), 5
Eurocentrism, 114, 116, 119-21, 128-29, 134-37, 224, 239, 246, 251, 255, 260, 262, 264-65, 272, 305, 308
Europhobia, 116, 128
Europe, 115-17; as cultural capital, 117; self-critique of, 115-16
Eurovision, 6
Eze, Emmanuel Chukwudi, 27, 43-44, 91-93

Fanon, Frantz, 8, 14, 17, 49, 66, 67, 85, 95, 99, 103, 120-21, 124-25, 145, 190, 224, 234-35, 245; on anticolonial violence, 206, 207, 210-12, 217; on Hegel's master-slave dialectic, 210
fascism, 71, 75-76, 83, 85, 151, 170, 192, 200-201, 263, 267, 278
feminism, 31-32, 35, 42, 44, 62; intersectional, 298; postcolonial, 31, 35, 62, 64; postcolonial-queer-feminist perspectives, 294, 295, 299; white feminism, critique of, 297. *See also* postcolonial-queer-feminist perspective
feminist theory, 296-99
Fischer, Sybille, 161
Flikschuh, Katrin, 34, 42, 46-47, 55
Flynn, Elizabeth Gurley, 301
Forsdick, Charles, and Christian Høgsbjerg, 156-59
Foucault, Michel, 10, 14, 22, 25, 32, 63, 77, 79-80, 96-97, 105, 123, 125, 217; on biopolitics, 244, 245; on civil disobedience, 145; on critique, 154, 228-30, 249; on governmentality, 191, 193, 196-97, 201, 249; "history of the present," 7; on power, 154, 173-74, 176, 240, 247, 249; on state phobia, 191-93, 196, 201
Frankfurt School. *See* Critical Theory
Fraser, Nancy, 163
free speech, 3, 7, 9
Freud, Sigmund, 206-7, 209, 233; on death drive (*Todestrieb*), 207; *heimlich* vs. *unheimlich*, 118, 269

philosophy, 295; *Rettung der Aufklärung* (Rescuing the Enlightenment), 9

hospitality (Kantian concept), 54, 56–59; Derrida's critique of, 58–59; unconditional, 118

Hulme, Peter, 26–28

human rights, 4, 11–13, 18, 220, 233, 235, 236, 238, 241, 246, 251, 254, 255, 257, 290, 299, 305

Husserl, Edmund, 115–16

identity politics, 87–89, 306

identity thinking, 82–83

ideology critique, 176

IHRA (International Holocaust Remembrance Alliance), 7

imaginaries, 289, 292, 294

imagination, 268, 271–73, 280–81, 283–86; political, 292, 294, 306, 309; training of, 262, 268, 273, 281, 283

imperialism, 26, 30, 40–41, 54–55, 57–58, 61; enlightened, 29. *See also* colonialism; postcolonialism

India, 113–14, 121, 124, 129–32, 135, 137

Indigenous: epistemologies, 114, 119–20, 123, 127–28; knowledge, 120, 122; languages, 124–25

indignados, 179

instrumental philosemitism, 5

instrumental reason, 72–74, 78, 81–83, 92, 101, 270, 277, 283. *See also* pseudorationalism

intellectual labor, 293, 294, 305

intellectuals, 280–82, 287; subaltern, 281, 914

International Court of Justice (ICJ), 233, 251, 252, 253, 257, 258

International Criminal Court (ICC), 237, 251, 252, 253, 254

international law, 4, 51–52, 54, 56, 233; colonial origins of, 237, 250; and human rights, 241, 251; and sovereignty, 250, 251, 254–55, 257; TWAIL (Third World Approaches to International Law), 250–51

intersectionality, 122, 125, 189, 191, 298; of hate, 65–66, 70

Israel, 2–5

Israel-Hamas war, 3, 4, 6, 51, 108, 205, 233, 251, 253, 257, 306

James, C. L. R., 83, 85, 156, 159, 162; *The Black Jacobins*, 211–12

Jay, Martin, 107

jazz, 277–78; Adorno's view of, 84

Jessop, Bob, 195–96

Jewish studies, 4: and postcolonial studies, 10

Jews, 65–68; Mizrahi and Sephardi, 68. *See also* antisemitism

Jordan, June, 298

jouissance, 163, 170

Judaism and Jews: in Enlightenment thought (Kant), 36–39

justice, 207, 213, 250, 253, 258, 260, 288, 290, 302, 305; and law, 239, 241–43; and nonviolence, 240; normative violence of, 236

Justin, Eva, 284–85

Kant, Immanuel, 14, 16, 22–64, 70, 74, 82, 91, 99, 106, 146–49, 160, 168, 206, 220, 231, 234, 237, 260, 262, 266, 280–81, 304; and anti-Semitism, 36–39; Black radical appropriation of, 305; and cosmopolitanism, 33–34, 49, 51–57, 59; *The Critique of Judgment*, 269–70; on critique, 228, 231; defenses of, 32–35, 41–47; on Enlightenment, 292; *Observations on the Beautiful and the Sublime*, 264; on public use of reason, 270; questions of reason, 292, 293, 303; and race/racism, 24–25, 32, 42–50; revisionist readings of, 9–10; on right to revolution, 210; and sexism, 31–32, 42–45, 48; on sovereignty, 250, 256; tutelage, concept of, 18

katharsis, 202. *See also* catharsis

Khan, Karim, 251, 252, 253

Khap Panchayats, 121

King, Martin Luther, Jr., 8, 145, 205, 212, 221, 244
King, Richard, 135
Kipling, Rudyard, 117
Kleingeld, Pauline, 35, 42, 44–45, 47–50
Klor de Alva, Jorge, 126–27
Korczak, Janusz, 261–62
Koselleck, Reinhart, 228
Kumar, Aishwary, 223–25

labor, 130
Lal, Vinay, 213–16, 218
Lapidot, Elad, 48, 312
Latin American exceptionalism, 126
Latour, Bruno, 303–4
law, 207; and force/violence, 241, 244; and justice, 239, 241–43; rule of, 207, 236–37, 239, 244, 253, 257
Lenin, Vladimir, 150–51; on "What is to be done?," 294, 295
lettre de cachet, 197–98
Levinas, Emmanuel, 240
Locke, John, 27–28, 40
Lorde, Audre, 18, 232, 297–99, 309
Louverture, Toussaint, 61, 156–59, 162
Love, Nancy, 89
Lu-Adler, Huaping, 46, 49–50
Luxemburg, Rosa, 151, 212

Macaulay, Thomas Babington, 273
MacKinnon, Catharine, 195
Mahbubani, Kishore, 120
Malcolm X, 205, 206, 212
Maldonado-Torres, Nelson, 99
Mamdani, Mahmood, 195
Mandela, Nelson, 205, 231
Mao Zedong, 212
Marasco, Robyn, 102, 104, 212, 229, 277
Marcuse, Herbert, 153
Marwecki, Daniel, 255, 257
Marx, Karl, 128–30, 150, 171, 174, 180, 217, 222, 229, 234, 287, 304; on critique, 227, 231; on praxis, 294, 303; and "weapon of criticism," 231
Marxism, 76, 83–84, 89, 93, 100, 102, 150–51, 171, 174, 191, 193, 195; Black,

128; Eurocentrism in, 114, 128–29; and postcolonial theory, 114, 124, 128–33; universalism of, 130–33
Massad, Joseph, 188–89
master's tools, 302, 308; Lorde on, 18, 297; Spivak on, 103, 105, 280, 299
Mbembe, Achille, 14, 17, 71, 83, 91, 93–101, 106, 154, 164, 244, 289, 290; accusations of antisemitism, 2; critique of decolonial delinking, 266; on necropolitics, 217, 245–47
McCabe, David, 42
McCarthy, Thomas, 26
Medovoi, Leerom, 281
Memmi, Albert, 68
memory politics, 69–70
Mercer, Kobena, 190
Merkel doctrine (*Staatsräson*), 5, 255
metalepsis, 175, 187
metonymy, 284
Mignolo, Walter, 11, 16, 71, 89–91, 96, 113–14, 119–25, 137, 262, 264–66
Mills, Charles, 10, 36, 44–45, 62, 86–87
modernity, 79, 86–87, 103–4, 107–8, 213, 214, 215, 222, 225, 260, 290, 299, 300; and coloniality, 119–20; incomplete project of, 77, 97, 103, 116
modernity/coloniality, 266
monstre froid (state as), 164, 186, 201
Morrow, Raymond, 123
Morton, Stephen, 129–30, 178, 180
Moses, A. Dirk, 3
Mufti, Aamir, 49
Muñoz, José Esteban, 292–93
Muthu, Sankar, 34, 41, 44, 48, 61
Mutua, Makau, 250–51

Nakba, 68
Nancy, Jean-Luc, 303
Natali, Marcos, 119, 127
nationalism, postcolonial, 299
National Socialism (Nazism), 65, 72, 75–76, 206, 213, 220, 233, 245, 255; and colonialism, 67, 69–70, 85
nativism, 128
Nazi regime, 261, 263, 284–85

necropolitics, 164, 217, 245–47, 261

Négritude, 91–92, 94–95

Neiman, Susan, 1, 3–6; atonement gone haywire, 4, philosemitic McCarthyism, 4

neocolonialism, 232, 237, 238, 250, 251, 254

neoliberalism, 163, 165, 180, 191, 194, 196–97, 307

Nesbitt, Nick, 155–57, 160

Newton, Isaac, 72

Niesen, Peter, 53, 56

Nietzsche, Friedrich, 74, 77–78, 81, 164, 201, 229, 293

non-identity thinking, 83

nonviolence (*ahimsā*), 8, 17, 145, 147, 168, 182, 204, 205–8, 212, 214–21, 231, 240, 258, 260; as gendered, 217; skepticism of, 209, 231

non-Western knowledge systems, 299

normative nihilism, accusation of, 70–71, 77–78, 83, 87, 99

norms/normativity, 206, 213, 218, 232, 250, 258, 260–61, 305; violence of, 207, 234, 236, 258

Nussbaum, Martha, 132, 268, 274

objectivity, limits of, 303

Occupy Wall Street, 182

oppression, 291, 294, 297–98, 304

Orientalism, 131, 136

Orientalism (Said), 9, 67

Other, the/othering, 232, 236, 237, 284, 286; non-European, 118

pachamama, 138

Palestine, 204, 234, 254, 257, 298; occupation of, 2; queer solidarity with, 306–7. *See also* Israel-Hamas war

Pan-Africanism, 94, 95, 255

pariah, Arendt on, 222

Parker, Pat, 95

PEN America, 6

performative action, 166

performative contradiction, 291; accusation of, 78, 81, 107, 110

pharmakon: Derrida's concept, 187, 203; Greek concept, 202–3; state as, 144, 180, 185–86, 203–4

Phillips, Adam, 14

pinkwashing, 191, 194

pinkwatching, 194

planetarity, 137–39, 292, 306

planetary ethics, 134, 137–39, 306

Plato, 268; *Republic*, 268

poetics, 265

poiesis, 265

political friendships, 307

political imagination, 292, 294, 306, 309

Popkin, Jeremy, 159–60

positivism, 73–74

postcolonial condition, 300, 305

postcolonial critique, 137; of theory and practice, 293–96; of white feminism, 297

postcolonial scare, 6–7

postcolonial studies, 2–18, 22, 25, 32, 61–64, 65–66, 69–71, 83–91, 103–4, 108, 263, 272, 274, 280; accusations against, 2–4, 6–11, 34–35, 87–89; as anti-Enlightenment, accusation of, 8–9, 11; as critique and appropriation, 299–300, 305, 308; critique and impasse, 290; and Critical Theory, 10, 16; and decolonial studies, 89–91; defense of, 8–9; differences from decolonial option, 305; as Eurocentric, accusation of, 11; and Holocaust/Jewish studies, 10, 89; and Latin America, 125–27; and Marxism, 114, 124, 128–33; mistaken identity with decolonial studies, 10–11; origins of, 119, 124; use of post-, 122–23; utopias and nightmares, 290. *See also* colonialism; imperialism; decolonization

postcolonial-queer-feminist perspective, 12, 15, 31, 103–4, 116, 122, 134, 136–7, 217, 243; on praxis, 294, 295. *See also* feminism

postcolonialism. *See* postcolonial studies

postmodernism, 303

post-Occidentalism, 119

untouchability, 223–25. *See also* Ambedkar, B. R.

US Capitol, storming of, 65–66

utopia, 309; colonial uses of, 289–90; queer visions of, 292. *See also* hope; futurity

Valdez, Inés, 49

Vastey, Pompée Valentin, 158

Vazquez, Rolando, 264–65

Vergangenheitsaufarbeitung (coming to terms with the past), 1, 69, 289

Vertretung (speaking for) and *Darstellung* (speaking about), in Spivak, 125, 173

Villadsen, Kaspar, 196–99

violence, 7–8, 12–13, 85, 93, 99–100, 108, 145, 147–48, 151, 153, 164–65, 168, 182–83, 187, 195–96, 204–12, 217–18; anticolonial/resistant, 206–7, 210–12, 217; colonial, 26, 28, 52–53, 85, 105–6, 108; and critique, 207, 218, 226, 230–31; and decolonization, 205–6, 211, 258; epistemic, 305; gendered, 217, 238–39, 243; intra-community, 298; and law, 239, 241, 244; legitimate vs. illegitimate, 206–7, 210, 237, 239; normative, 13, 35–36, 207, 234, 236, 258;

of the state, 224, 239, 244–50; state and anti-state, 17; structural, 290

Viswanathan, Gauri, 274

Vitoria, Francisco de, 27, 237

Vocabulario de la lengua Aymara (Bertonio), 125

vulnerability, 132, 163, 165–66, 172, 174, 182–83

Wallerstein, Immanuel, 123

Warsaw Ghetto, 261–62

Washington, Booker T., 282

Weber, Max, 93; on *Entzauberung*, 314n5

welfare state, 169, 178, 191, 197

Weltbürgertum (world citizenship), 53

"What is to be done?," 293; Adorno's response, 293–95; Chernyshevsky on, 293; Derrida on, 295, 302–3; Lenin on, 294,

white feminism, 297

white genocide conspiracy theory, 66

white man's burden, 7

Wiredu, Kwesi, 124

world-systems theory, 123

Ypi, Lea, 34, 42, 46–48

Zionism, 68, 87–88: critiques of, 298

www.ingramcontent.com/pod-product-compliance
Lightning Source LLC
Chambersburg PA
CBHW020820270326
41928CB00006B/387